Beacons in the Landscape

The Hillforts of England and Wales

Ian Brown

WINDgather
PRESS

Windgather Press
is an imprint of
Oxbow Books, Oxford

ISBN 978-1-90511-922-6

A CIP record for this book is available from the British Library

This book is available direct from

Oxbow Books, Oxford, UK
(Phone: 01865-241249; Fax: 01865-794449)

and

The David Brown Book Company
PO Box 511, Oakville, CT 06779, USA
(Phone: 860-945-9329; Fax: 860-945-9468)

or from our website

www.oxbowbooks.com

Printed in Singapore by
KHL Printing Co Pte Ltd

Contents

List of Figures   v

Notes   ix

Acknowledgements   x

Preface   I

Part I The 'Elusive' Hillfort

    I   Definition and Distribution   2

    2   Great Surveys – Great Excavations   14

Part 2 Defining the Space

    3   Beginnings   24

    4   Enclosure   34

    5   Interiors   68

Part 3 Hillforts and Society

    6   People   81

    7   Economy   114

    8   Superstition, Belief and Ritual   134

    9   Coins, Tribes, Rome and Resistance   158

Part 4 Hillfort Location, Function and Social Significance

    10   Beacons in the Landscape: New Theories – New Questions   183

    11   Hillforts: A Synthesis of Ideas   224

Bibliography   239

Index   257

List of Figures

1. Bryngaer Dinas (Dinas hillfort), Llanfairfechan, Caernarfonshire xii

2a. Selected defended enclosures and small hillforts of less than 1.4ha in England and Wales 2

2b. Hillforts of over or equal to 1.4ha in England and Wales 3

3. Pen Dinas, Aberystwyth in its landscape 5

4. Old Oswestry, Shropshire 5

5. Wall Camp marsh fort, Kynnersley, Shropshire 6

6. The ramparts and ditches of Hambledon Hill, Dorset 8

7. Moel Fenlli, Clwydian Range, Denbighshire 9

8. Bredon Hill promontory fort, Gloucestershire 10

9. The Clawdd y Milwyr coastal promontory fort, St David's Head, Pembrokeshire 10

10. Maiden Castle, Dorchester, Dorset 17

11. Excavations at Cadbury Camp, Tickenham, Somerset, 1922 18

12. Excavations at Danebury, Hampshire, 1986 21

13. Rybury hillfort and causewayed enclosure, Wiltshire 26

14. Cissbury Ring, Sussex 28

15. Moel Drygarn (Trigarn), the 'Hill of the Three Cairns', Pembrokeshire 30

16. Trevelgue Head, Newquay, Cornwall 33

17. Ramparts and ditches, Maiden Castle, Dorchester, Dorset 34

18. The walls with walkway, Tre'r Ceiri, Llŷn peninsula, Caernarfonshire 36

19. Moel y Gaer, Llantysilio Mountains, Denbighshire 36

20. The snaking ramparts of Hod Hill, Dorset 36

21a. From the eye of the horse, below Uffington Castle on the chalk Berkshire Downs 39

21b. Outline of the Uffington White Horse 39

22.	Bindon Hill from Lulworth Cove, Dorset	39
23.	Internal quarry scoops, Hod Hill, Dorset	41
24.	Counterscarp bank, Penycloddiau, Clwydian Range, Flintshire	42
25.	Rampart constructions	43
26.	Remnants of box ramparts at Moel y Gaer (Rhosesmor), Flintshire	43
27.	Remnants of dump ramparts, Midsummer Hill, Herefordshire	46
28.	Damage to remnants of chalk dump ramparts, Liddington Castle, Wiltshire	47
29.	Intact stone facework, Caer Drewyn, Merioneth	50
30.	Stone-faced rampart, Bolt Tail, Devon	50
31.	Stone walls and deep ditches, Worlebury, Weston-super-Mare, Somerset	51
32.	Walls of small enclosure, Castell Caer Seion, Conwy, Caernarfonshire	52
33.	North-eastern gate and walls, Pen y corddyn Mawr, Denbighshire	52
34.	The entrance and ramparts of Crickley Hill, Gloucestershire from the interior	53
35.	The *chevaux-de-frise*, Castell Henllys, Pembrokeshire	54
36.	The annexe, Earl's Hill, Shropshire	57
37.	Walled enclosures downslope, Carn Ingli, Pembrokeshire	57
38.	The Period I South Gate, Midsummer Hill, Herefordshire	58
39.	Slight inturns to the entrance, Bodbury Ring, Shropshire	59
40.	The south-west inturned entrance, Hod Hill, Dorset	62
41.	The 'staggered' south-west entrance, Bury Ditches, Shropshire	62
42.	Out-turns at the western gate, Uffington Castle, Berkshire	63
43.	Entrance to the large enclosure, Castell Caer Seion, Conwy, Caernarfonshire	63
44.	Reconstructed lintel, Tre'r Ceiri, Llŷn peninsula, Caernarfonshire	66
45.	The ramparts, Gaer Fawr (Guilsfield), Montgomeryshire	69
46.	The grassy interior, Cadbury Hill, Congresbury, Somerset	70
47.	Walls of a stone hut, Tre'r Ceiri, Llŷn peninsula, Caernarfonshire	71
48.	Reconstructed roundhouses, Castell Henllys, Pembrokeshire	74
49.	Hut plans	75

50.   Stone-lined storage pit, Maiden Castle, Dorchester, Dorset   78

51.   Reconstructed 'four-poster' structure, Castell Henllys, Pembrokeshire   79

52.   Items from the house and the home   83

53.   Cauldron-hangers, Hunsbury, Northamptonshire   84

54.   Bronze cauldron, Spettisbury Rings, Dorset   84

55.   Spinning and weaving   94

56.   Pins and brooches   96

57.   Adornments and talismen   97

58.   Warrior equipment   104

59.   Hunsbury sword and scabbard   107

60.   Hypothetical reconstruction of Grimthorpe warrior burial   108

61.   Boar helmet figurine, Gaer Fawr (Guilsfield), Montgomeryshire   110

62.   Horse and chariot fittings   110

63.   Bull or terrier chariot figurines, Bulbury, Dorset   112

64.   The Moel Hiraddug shield-boss   113

65.   Anchor and chain, Bulbury, Dorset   116

66.   Wains Hill and anchorage, Clevedon, Somerset   118

67.   Iron Age barrel-shaped pottery jar, Salmonsbury, Bourton-on-the-Water, Gloucestershire   123

68.   Slave chains, Bigberry hillfort, Tunbridge Wells, Kent   126

69.   North Ronaldsay ram   131

70.   Farming and general tools   133

71.   Ritual objects   135

72.   Silver-washed figurine of three-horned bull, Maiden Castle, Dorchester, Dorset   141

73.   Bird figurine, Milber Down, Devon   143

74.   Horse and dog pit deposition, Danebury, Hampshire   143

75a–b.   Plans of hillfort shrines and temples   150–151

76a.   The tribes and coin users of Britain   161

76b.   Dobunnic coin, Salmonsbury, Bourton-on-the-Water, Gloucestershire   162

77.   Currency bars, Salmonsbury, Bourton-on-the-Water, Gloucestershire   165

78.   Port of Hengistbury Head, Hampshire   172

79.   Caer y Tŵr, Holyhead, Anglesey   175

80.   Sinodun Camp (Wittenham Clumps), Berkshire, above
       Dorchester-on-Thames   182

81.   The Wrekin, Shropshire, in July cloud   186

82.   The chalk cliffs of Belle Tout from Seaford Head, Sussex   187

83.   The erosion of Dinas Dinlle, Llandwrog, Caernarfonshire   187

84.   Pen y Dinas, Llandudno, Caernarfonshire   191

85.   Hillfort distribution on the River Wye   199

86.   'Intervisibility' between Moel Arthur and Penycloddiau,
       Clwydian Range, Flintshire   202

87.   Craig Rhiwarth, Tanat Valley, Montgomeryshire   206

88.   Helsby Hill, Cheshire   213

89.   Ingleborough, Yorkshire   216

90.   Fell Beck flowing into Gaping Gill, Ingleborough, Yorkshire   216

91.   Yeavering Bell, Cheviot Hills, Northumberland   217

92.   The inner ditch and surrounding bank, Figsbury Rings,
       Wiltshire   223

93.   Magnetometer survey, Cherbury Camp, Berkshire   230

94.   The medieval castle and hillfort, Castell Dinas Brân,
       Denbighshire   233

95.   Rodney's Column, Y Breiddin, Montgomeryshire   236

96.   Possible reconstruction of an idealised hillfort during its use   237

All photographs and illustrations are by the author unless stated.

Notes

As there continue to be substantial changes to local administrative boundaries, and as the county names prior to the 1974 local government reorganisation are embedded in the archaeological literature, these will be used throughout this book. For the sake of brevity, for the most part they are only mentioned at the first reference to each site.

Unless stated, 'Maiden Castle' refers to Maiden Castle hillfort near Dorchester in Dorset, as shown in Figure 10.

Acknowledgements

The idea for this book was conceived many years ago on the slopes opposite Moel Arthur hillfort in the Clwydian Range of north Wales, when embryonic questions passed through my mind – what was the purpose of such an earthwork, perched precariously as it is on an isolated summit, and what relationship did it have to the series of similar magnificent sites strung along the Range, from far inland almost to the coast? Who were the people involved and how did they live their everyday lives? In later years, being involved in the management of these and other hillforts with Clwyd County Council in a very practical way, as well as undertaking research on the hillforts of Wales and the Marches at the Institute of Archaeology at Oxford, these past thoughts once more came to the fore – and this book is the result.

Inevitably, a book of this sort relies on the work of past and present researchers, and they are referred to in detail in the text. Thus, very many people have contributed consciously and unconsciously to its final outcome. Grateful thanks are due to all. However, foremost must be Professor Sir Barry Cunliffe, my former supervisor at Oxford and to whom I am eternally grateful, whose sheer enthusiasm for Iron Age studies, especially hillforts, certainly rubbed off onto me. Without him this book would not have been written. But so many others at Oxford have helped. In particular, Philip de Jersey for his expertise on Celtic coins and Professors Chris Gosden, Gary Lock and the late Andrew Sherratt for invaluable support. My time working from the Department of Archaeology and Anthropology at the University of Wales, Lampeter was also especially fruitful, and I am indebted to Professor David Austin for discussions on hillforts and their functions.

I am also indebted to all my past colleagues at the Countryside, Archaeology and Museums Services of the former Clwyd County Council, notably John Manley, whose reference to hillforts being 'beacons' one day helped me with the title of this book, and Fiona Gale, Hazel Hawarden, Andre Berry, John Ablitt, Huw Rees and Howard Sutcliffe, and staff of the Clwyd Powys Archaeological Trust, all whom have made notable contributions to hillfort research, interpretation and management.

Similarly, I would like to thank those involved in supplying illustrations. Naturally, homing in on images that best fit the text among many thousands available has been a monumental task in itself. The valuable contributions made by Ian Cartwright and William Wintle of Oxford University and staff of English Heritage, the National Museums and Galleries of Wales, the Ashmolean Museum at Oxford, the British Wool Marketing Board, Cheltenham Museum and Art Gallery, Dorset County Museum, Maidstone Museum and Bentlif Art Gallery, Northampton Museum and Art Gallery, Powysland Museum, the Society of Antiquaries, South Downs Joint Committee/PPL Ltd and Torquay Museum are gratefully recognised. Thanks are also due to Toby Driver of the Royal Commission on the Ancient and Historical Monuments of Wales and David Allen of Hampshire County Council.

Special thanks, of course, to Harold Mytum for his most helpful comments on the very first draft, and staff of my publishers, notably Richard Purslow, David Brown, Val Lamb and Tara Evans of Windgather Press/Oxbow Books, and Sarah Harrison for editing the book.

Finally, I am especially indebted to Helen Manley Jones for her assistance in Pembrokeshire and John Shillam, Valerie Bate, Marcia Brown and Harold Davies for essential help with fieldwork and an unremitting pot of patience.

Ian Brown, Oxford and Wrexham, September 2008

For Barry Cunliffe and Marcia Brown who made it all possible.

Preface

....

Hillforts are one of the most common archaeological monuments but, despite more than a century of investigation, they are still one of the least understood. Were they recognised as something special by those who created them, or are they just an archaeologist's 'construct', defined to help us delve into the past? Their great variability poses many problems, but an inherent prominence in the landscape does suggest a deliberate act on the part of their creators, and something more than the many thousands of farmstead enclosures that probably housed the majority of the late Bronze Age and Iron Age populations. This book will look at these and many other questions in an accessible way and is particularly aimed at those who have little knowledge of the subject and who are keen to find out more about these much-neglected features of the present English and Welsh countryside and, in a few cases, the urban environment. It forms, therefore, an introduction, and will not only look at the location and significance of hillforts, but will attempt to put them in the context of prehistoric and later societies. The book relies on photographs augmented by line drawings to illustrate points, and thus, for those who wish to delve much deeper, a comprehensive bibliography, complemented by detailed citations in the text, is included.

FIGURE I. Bryngaer Dinas (Dinas hillfort), Llanfairfechan, Caernarfonshire, in its ancient landscape. The Dinas outcrop formed part of the Graig Lwyd stone axe factory group in the Neolithic and Graiglwyd itself can be seen in the distance beyond the hillfort. Here, at its western end, was the site of the destroyed Braich-y-Ddinas, one of the finest stone-built hillforts in Britain.

The subject of hillforts is immensely wide, encompassing not only the structure of these gigantic monuments but also their social, political and economic make-up, as well as the beliefs, customs and superstitions of the people involved in their construction and subsequent use. Overshadowed as they have been in the national psyche by the more recognisable prehistoric stone henges and medieval castles, hillforts are of equal importance to the heritage of both England and Wales (Figure I).

Land use in the modern era has not been kind to hillforts, with a significant number being either disfigured or lost, but abuse began in earlier times. The most important objective of this book, therefore, is to ensure that, by publicising them to a wider audience, they will be better appreciated and their future conservation and management improved and assured.

CHAPTER ONE

Definition and Distribution

....

The context

Hillforts occur in well-defined areas of both England and Wales, although how we define the borderline between an actual 'hillfort' and what we will call, for the sake of argument, 'small defended enclosures' has taxed archaeologists for years. They are distributed over most of the south and extend up the Welsh

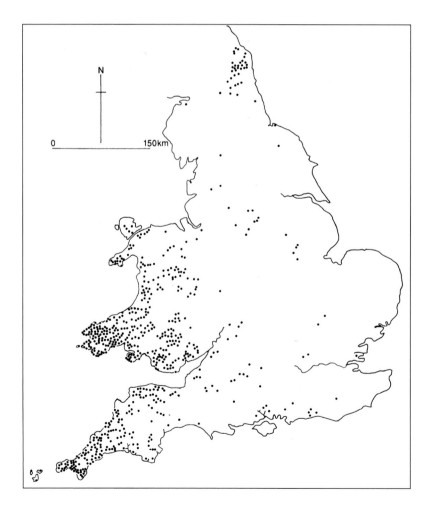

FIGURE 2a. Small hillforts and selected defended enclosures of less than 1.4ha (three acres) in England and Wales. The difference between a small hillfort and a small defended enclosure is much debated. The latter, prevalent in the west, and in particular south-west Wales and Cornwall, are clearly shown. Some of these can be called hillforts, but definition is unclear. As further small enclosures are continually coming to light, and because at this scale sites have had to be omitted, the map should be viewed as a representation only. Redrawn and adapted after: Ordnance Survey 1962; Avery 1976; Hogg 1979.

Marches and western Midlands into the Principality (Figures 2a and 2b). To the east, in Northamptonshire and Leicestershire, numbers decline, with a few on the edge of the Cambridgeshire Fens and in Norfolk and Suffolk. Numbers increase in Essex but drop again to the south in eastern Kent. To the north-west, Cheshire has significant numbers along the sandstone ridge, but there are fewer in Lancashire and beyond. To the north-east, however, Yorkshire and Northumberland have spectacular examples. In comparison, there are over twenty, mostly coastal, forts on the Isle of Man and many in southern Scotland, but only around fifty in Ireland. Hillforts continue to be found as our knowledge increases.

The debate as to whether there was continuity or change at the end of the Bronze Age and into the Iron Age, if we are to use these terms, has gone on for some time. Although the former theory has, in general, held sway, recent work has suggested the latter; perhaps they occurred to differing degrees in different areas. However, the use of 'Bronze Age' and 'Iron Age' implies that there was a

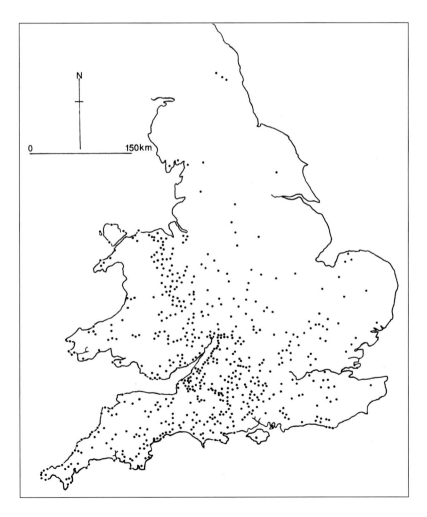

FIGURE 2b. Hillforts of over or equal to 1.4ha (three acres) in England and Wales. Because of the vagaries of definition this map should also be considered as a representation only of the situation 'on the ground'. Note the wider distribution of these larger sites in Wessex, up the Welsh Marches and towards the east. Redrawn and adapted after: Ordnance Survey 1962; Avery 1976; Hogg 1979.

rigid cut-off point in the use of bronze and a distinct start to the use of iron. This was not so; iron was used for some items before the traditional end of the Ewart Park phase of the Bronze Age and the cessation of bronze hoarding at the end of the ninth century BC. However, around 800 BC a change in society can be detected, and this was manifested by the storage of grain in pits, the finding of different ceramic forms, metalwork, land use and settlement patterns and an alteration in belief systems (Haselgrove *et al.* 2001, 26–7; Haselgrove and Pope 2007, 6). It has been suggested that this gradual move towards the use of iron appears not to have been spurred on by technological advance, but by a lack of metal ore from about 100 BC resulting in a reduced supply of bronze (Bradley 2007, 227).

Chronologies differ, but a subsequent transitional period (sometimes called the 'earliest Iron Age'), which may have lasted for several hundred years, is thought to have merged into an 'early Iron Age', ending in about 400 BC. Around this time further changes in pottery, settlement patterns, social organisation and land use, again differing from area to area, heralded another period of transition. The 'middle Iron Age' finally lasted to around 100 BC and a 'late Iron Age' extended into the first century AD.

FIGURE 3. A defining characteristic of hillforts is their dominance over the landscape; none more so than Pen Dinas at Aberystwyth on the west Wales coast, located where the Rivers Rheidol and Ystwyth meet the sea.

By the time of the Roman Conquest of AD 43 various types of enclosure were already a feature of non-Mediterranean continental Europe and Ireland, with an estimated 60,000 now surviving, 20,000–30,000 of which might be considered as hillforts (Ralston 1995, 60; 2006, 16). Some achieved massive proportions, as at Manching in Bavaria, whilst others were very small indeed.

Those seen dominating the landscape today (Figure 3) are characterised by enclosing 'defences', of bank or stone wall ('ramparts'), with or without a ditch, which can occur singly, the so-called 'univallate' sites, or in greater multiples, the 'multivallate' sites, double defences sometimes being called 'bivallate'. The simpler univallate type does not necessarily signify an earlier design; multivallation was a feature of some early hillforts, such as Danebury in Hampshire and Rainsborough in Northamptonshire. However, to categorise hillforts by these rampart sequences is to ignore their complexity, as both single and multiple sections can be found at the same location depending on topography and need and, of course, many sites went through periods of alteration as time progressed, some of which were very extensive indeed. But these terms have proved to be a useful and convenient, if not entirely accurate, means of description. Whatever is the case, boundaries define, surround and enclose an interior which is accessed by, usually, one, two or three entrances, but sometimes more. Often, but by no means exclusively, sites are located on a dominant hilltop or significant geomorphological feature in the landscape. Today, grassy humps and hollows, rocky outcrops and fallen stone tend to be the only visible remains, but some hillforts still form very impressive features indeed, with deep ditches and high banks – up to four in number at Maiden Castle near Dorchester in Dorset and five to seven at Old Oswestry in Shropshire (Figure 4).

By as early as the sixteenth century these enigmatic enclosures had become

FIGURE 4. The multiple banks and ditches of Old Oswestry in Shropshire. The impressive western entrance with its huge flanking hollows can be seen in the foreground.

CLWYD-POWYS ARCHAEOLOGICAL TRUST 95–C-1041.

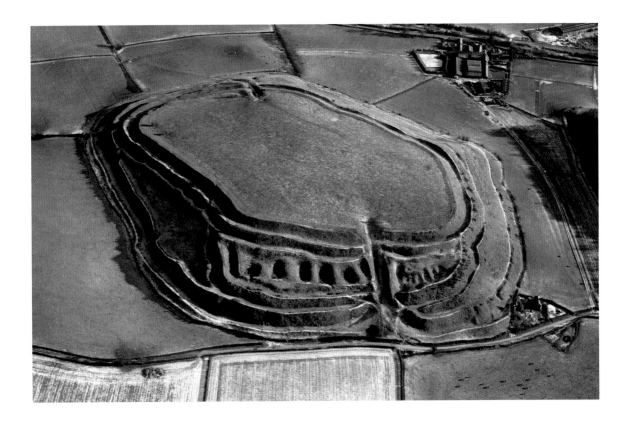

FIGURE 5. The low banks of Wall Camp at Kynnersley in Shropshire, a 'marsh-fort', formerly protected by marsh and fen and accessed by causeway.

mixed up with folklore and Arthurian legend, some being considered mystical 'druid's circles' or the realm of fairies. Later, into the seventeenth century, they gradually became seen as something more 'of this world' and certainly of 'great antiquity', and as the mid nineteenth century progressed, more scientific explanations emerged. The banks were now viewed as defensive mechanisms, and the word 'rampart' was coined to imply an element of fortification, refuge and defence to the enclosures, which became known as 'encampments', 'camps' or 'temporary camps'. Later the most influential investigators happened to be military men and it was only natural that they would use military terms. As a result, and reinforced by Christopher Hawkes's classic paper of 1931, 'hillfort' became the general descriptive term and is in use today.

However, 'hillfort' (or 'hill-fort', as often written), used as a general term, is not all that it appears at first sight. Firstly, some sites are not located on hills at all – Ebury Hill Camp in Shropshire, for example, sits on a low-lying outcrop of hard andesitic tuff at only 90m OD (Stanford 1985a, 9). Stonea Camp in Cambridgeshire, Warham Camp, east of the Wash in Norfolk on the 15m contour, Wall Camp (Kynnersley) and the Berth, both in Shropshire, are all located on still lower flat land, and were formerly protected by river, marsh, fen or mere and probably accessed by causeways; at the Berth a causeway may also have acted as a dam to create a lake (Morris and Gelling 1991, 58). Wall Camp is perched on a sandstone and boulder clay rise surrounded by peat (Figure 5). The term 'marsh-fort' has been coined for the multivallate Sutton Common in Yorkshire (Van de Noort *et al.* 2007), and would be apt generally for these low-lying forts. Moreover, as we shall see, the vast majority of sites do not appear to have served as defensive 'forts' as normally understood, and as epitomised by P.C. Wren's French Foreign Legion novel *Beau Geste*.

'Hillfort', therefore, does not describe the true situation well, but has nonetheless been used indiscriminately for a wide variety of sites surrounded and enclosed by banks, walls and ditches, some on hills, some not, some small, some large, with little regard to function or place in prehistoric or later society. Furthermore, a large number of enclosed 'forts' are located inland or on the coast and defined by cutting off the neck of promontories: the so-called 'promontory forts' (Muir 2004, 215). Clearly, Dennis Harding (2004) was correct when he wrote that: 'the association of sites, large and small, simple or complex, into a single category of hillforts has undoubtedly been an oversimplification of archaeological classification.'

It is indeed tempting to regard an enclosing obstacle, whether it be a crude wall or palisade or a more elaborate bank and ditch, as a simplistic defensive device, either to keep those with malevolent intent out, whether they be people or wild animals, or valuable stock in, and it is this interpretation that has been in the past the unquestioned basis of hillfort study. For example, A.H.A. Hogg (1975) proposed the following definition: 'a hillfort may be described as an enclosure, apparently fortified, and so placed as to gain some defensive advantage from its position; as being a type generally built during the native Iron Age; and normally not less than 0.2 ha in enclosed area.' Michael Avery (1976, 3) had a different interpretation, defining a 'fort' as: 'a site fortified so as to be defensible against human attack' and above a quarter of an acre in area; below that size, enclosures were to be called 'fortlets'. Not all 'forts' were also 'hillforts' and he defined the latter as: 'a fort which not only has artificial man-made defences raised to protect it, but also exploits the natural terrain so as to give defenders an advantage of height over those approaching the site.' He later proposed that: 'all hillforts are connected by the fact that each was in one way or another used for defence of the community which built it' (1993, 1).

We will return to these defensive theories later in this book but, whilst not belittling defence as a factor that must have been in the minds of the constructors of these sites, it is being increasingly felt by archaeologists that 'enclosure' was a complex process having multiple connotations and serving different purposes at different times and places in later prehistory and early history (Harding 2004, 298). Such purposes could have been social, economic, political or ritual in nature, or a combination of all of these; all would have been very significant for the people concerned. The basis of hillfort design, therefore, was that, *by enclosing a site*, a special place was defined, distinct from the outside world; the surrounding banks possibly themselves imbued with, or imbued an interior with, symbolic powers.

There have been various attempts, predominantly based on topographical location, at classifying types of hillfort. Some of these have been successful and are still in use, some not, and it could be argued that, because of the inherent variability of both hillfort types and siting, any classification will inevitably be spurious. However, purely as an example, James Dyer (1981, 6) suggested five main groups: contour forts; promontory forts; plateau forts; valley forts;

and multiple-enclosure or hill-slope forts. Thus, a contour fort will follow the contours almost exactly. There are many in both England and Wales, fine examples being Caesar's Camp at Easthampstead in Berkshire, Borough Hill in Northamptonshire, British Camp (Herefordshire Beacon) on the high ridge of the Malvern Hills in Herefordshire and Hambledon Hill in Dorset (Figure 6). However, this term can itself be misleading, for at some sites, such as Moel Fenlli (Figure 7) and Penycloddiau in the Clwydian Range of Denbighshire and Flintshire respectively, their apparent relationship with the contours masks a considerable deviation in altitudinal range from one end of the fort to the other. This phenomenon appears to tip the hillfort towards a particular aspect and, therefore, perhaps towards a defined territory: at Moel Fenlli towards the fertile grounds of the Vale of Clwyd, and at Penycloddiau towards neighbouring Moel Arthur hillfort in Flintshire and access through the Clwydian Range.

Promontory forts, as the name implies, are located where the land forms a defined promontory, either inland or on the coast. Notable examples inland, of which there are many, are Bredon Hill in Gloucestershire (Figure 8) and Bryn Alun near Wrexham in Denbighshire. Coastal promontory forts (called 'cliff

FIGURE 6. The ramparts and ditches of Hambledon Hill in Dorset use the natural topography to superb effect.

FIGURE 7. Some hillforts
are deliberately tilted
towards specific locations:
in the case of Moel Fenlli
in the Clwydian Range
of Denbighshire towards
the fertile land of the
Vale of Clwyd.

castles' in Cornwall) extend from around the Thames Estuary, south and west
to Pembrokeshire (Figure 9) and north to Anglesey.

Plateau forts are situated on flat ground with no natural physiographic
advantage, as at Rainsborough, and can cover a wide variety of different
topographical situations, as can lower-lying valley forts, such as Risbury
in Herefordshire. Multiple-enclosure or hill-slope forts, which are found
predominantly towards the south-west and south Wales (Scratchbury in
Wiltshire and sites on Harding's Down in the Gower of Glamorgan, for
example) may not occupy prominent topographical positions.

It follows that, with this great variability in location and type, not only is
classification difficult and invariably unsatisfactory, but, as we have seen, the
use of a single term is undoubtedly erroneous. As a result it is a salutary fact
that the old definitions of 'camp', 'British camp' or 'encampment', despite
their Baden-Powellish connotations and intimations of a short-lived nature, are
nearer the mark. However, for a variety of reasons, mostly non-academic, and
of which convenience is one, 'hillfort', 'rampart' and 'defences' will be used in
this book.

In later chapters choice of location will be considered, but several basic
points are pertinent here. Firstly, many hillforts are sited in significant and
'commanding' positions in the landscape, rather than being located at random

FIGURE 8. Inland promontory forts are located on defined promontories in the landscape cut off by bank and ditch, as at Bredon Hill overlooking the River Avon in Gloucestershire.

FIGURE 9. The Clawdd y Milwyr coastal promontory fort on St David's Head in Pembrokeshire. The promontory, jutting out into the Irish Sea, was cut off by a massive dry-stone rampart, now about 100m long, with two lesser stone walls outside and possibly shallow ditches between. Fine hut circles are still clearly visible.

HELEN MANLEY JONES.

(Brown 2002; 2004; Corney and Payne 2006a). As a result, severe exposure to the elements is common, as shown, for example, by Yeavering Bell in Northumberland, Mam Tor in Derbyshire and Titterstone Clee in Shropshire. Some sites are at a very high altitude indeed, as on the summit of Ingleborough in the Yorkshire Dales, where climatic conditions are extreme. All of this suggests that a great deal of strategic thinking went into their building in the first place. Secondly, there is considerable evidence that, at a large number of hillforts, there was a long-standing 'interest' in the location which pre-dated hillfort construction. Some sites saw activity as far back as the Mesolithic (see

Chapter 3). Thirdly, although we have to be careful in the interpretation of the exceptional or unusual as evidence of some form of 'ritual', and especially so if we wish to use the term 'religion' (Dark 2002, 148), a significant feature of the limited number of detailed excavations undertaken has been evidence of widespread symbolic observance. The finding of human remains does not necessarily mean ritual sacrifice, of course – the person might just have been murdered and disposed of – but the context of human and animal bone in pits, four-poster structures, rampart burials and, in some cases, shrines, all suggest that propitiation was an essential part of hillfort life – an important consideration indeed, about which more will be said.

Considering the above, it is inevitable that the question arises of which enclosures are actually hillforts and which are not. Certainly, the numbers are daunting. Hogg, in his 1979 index of hillfort sites (pp. 1–5), lists 3,840 in Britain as being: 'enclosures with substantial defences, usually on high ground and probably built between 1000 BC and 700 AD, but showing no significant Roman influence'. His invaluable inventory includes 'related structures' as well as 'hillforts', and it is implicit that an unspecified number 'merely acted as homesteads' or something similar. Let us, therefore, look very briefly at some of these smaller enclosures.

As sites get smaller so scope for confusion increases and, as Carver (1991, 4) pointed out for lowland Shropshire, the variety of enclosures 'does not divide easily into "hillfort" and "lowland farm"'. In Pembrokeshire there are many univallate sites under 1ha in area which are commonly called 'hillforts', but most are in fact the 'raths' (small 'defended' settlements or farmsteads) common to the area and located in lowland situations on better soils; these are similar to enclosures in south-west England and Armorica (Henderson 2007, 314). Although the best-known of these is the excavated Iron Age Walesland Rath near Haverfordwest (Wainwright 1969; 1971), there are literally many hundreds of small defended enclosures in south-west Wales, some rectangular in outline, some round, many of which are now just cropmarks. Most show few, if any, artefacts on excavation (Harold Mytum pers. comm.). Similarly, in north-west Wales, surveys by the Royal Commission on the Llŷn peninsula also suggest an emerging wide variety of smaller sites.

Looking to northern England, work by Oswald and Pearson (2005, 119–20) in the Cheviot Hills questions whether Yeavering Bell may be the only 'true' hillfort in Northumberland, as most 'hillforts' there enclose less – many much less – than 0.1ha. However, small defensive enclosures here, such as those at Dod Law and others surrounding the Milfield Plain, although not above 0.5ha in area, do show hillfort characteristics in terms of both location and prominence in the landscape, and pure size, therefore, should not be seen as a defining characteristic in its own right. To date, however, the complexity of these small sites nationally and the nature of the kinship or other groups that occupied them is poorly understood.

'Ring-forts' are another case in point, examples of which are found in the

Llawhaden group of enclosed settlements in Carmarthenshire (Williams and Mytum 1998). These are typified by a weak defensive position but a strong univallate defensive bank and ditch, the interior containing up to half a dozen roundhouses in less than half an hectare, as at Dan y Coed and Woodside. Similar sites are found from Glamorgan to the upper Severn (Davies and Lynch 2000, 146) and into northern England. Again, ring-forts have often been defined as hillforts in the past, but are now better looked upon as 'defended farmsteads'.

Inevitably, small enclosures are eminently variable, and those of the central Marches, which Wigley (2007a) calls 'non-hillfort' or 'small settlement' enclosures, are well explained – here some are on hilltops, some on slopes and others on the valley floor. High-status living has been suggested at Collfryn in Montgomeryshire (Britnell 1989), and, to the north-west of Wales at Bryn Eryr on Anglesey (Longley 1998) and Castell Odo on the Llŷn peninsula in Caernarfonshire (Alcock 1960). On the other hand, the small stone-walled enclosure of Bryn y Castell, Ffestiniog in Merioneth, with cobbled yard and circular hut, was a much more frugal affair (Crew 1984; 1986). A parallel situation occurs in north-west England, where the difference between enclosed farmsteads of generally under 1ha (the majority of sites) and small hillforts 'becomes an issue of semantics' (Harding 2004, 50). A wide variety of other examples are coming to light nationwide, such as in Cornwall, south and west Devon and increasingly in Somerset, where small banked and ditched homesteads of *c.*1ha – the 'rounds' – have been found in profusion. But to add to this expanding field is beyond the scope of this book.

Whatever their classification, these small farmstead and settlement enclosures would have formed the most numerous features of late Bronze Age and Iron Age landscapes, but most would have been very different from the dominating hillforts, which are certainly a 'step up' in character, and have been interpreted by Barry Cunliffe (1991, 312) as representing: 'a level of social organisation above that of the farmstead and hamlet [which] may legitimately be considered as a separate phenomenon'. Undoubtedly, when looking to classify, the very nature of some sites poses problems, and, although convenient, as we have hinted at above, size alone cannot be seen as an overriding factor when defining hillforts. It has been noted, however, that hillforts are often located in commanding, controlling and strategic positions in the landscape and exhibit substantial and often massive defences, but within this observation wide variations do exist.

Dating can also be problematical and, purely as an example, in East Anglia in particular there are questions over a number of sites, notably Tasburgh in Norfolk and Clare Camp in Suffolk. The former was occupied in the middle and late Saxon period and has parallels with enclosures of tenth-century date at Witham and Maldon in Essex; but whether the banks were new at this time or modified from an earlier design is open to question (Davies *et al.* 1991, 71–2). In Wales, Bryn Euryn at Rhos-on-Sea in Denbighshire could also be earlier than its Dark Age credentials suggest.

As a result of these issues the number of actual hillforts in England and

Wales will remain obscure until some form of worthwhile classification has been worked out, but the 1,400 suggested and explained by Forde-Johnston (1976a, 168; 1976b) is probably an underestimate. Beyond doubt is that hillforts involved massive feats of civil engineering on the part of late Bronze Age and Iron Age communities and that the parameters of structure, location and timescale – some 1,000-plus years of development – are wide. A large number of true hillforts have been examined to some degree, but only at a comparative few has investigation been adequate. For example, although Danebury (57 per cent), Crickley Hill in Gloucestershire and Castell Henllys in Pembrokeshire had over 50 per cent of their interiors excavated, at the 18.5ha Maiden Castle the excavations of Sir Mortimer Wheeler (Wheeler 1943) and Niall Sharples (Sharples 1991a and b) covered less than 2 per cent of the hillfort's area between them. Hard evidence is often lacking and much excavation, some of questionable value, has centred on the sectioning of ramparts, which has also contributed to the emphasis on the defensive nature of sites. Because of this, and as it is not possible to 'get into the mind' of prehistoric people, it is probable that the role of hillforts within society will never be truly understood.

It is inevitable that the very complexity and variety of hillforts has given rise to numerous models of function within specific regions (Collis 1981); one drawn up for one area may not be applicable to others. Indeed, it is most unlikely that all hillforts functioned in exactly the same way, either on a temporal or spatial basis, and evidence has to be considered extremely carefully.

As subsequent chapters will show, it is clear that hillforts were manifestly a social, economic and political phenomenon within which superstition and belief played an important part. Much work remains to be done on the definition of terms and, as further information on small settlements comes to light, the relationship between these and the larger sites may become clearer. It could be that there is no such thing as a 'hillfort' as such, but just a wide variety of different types of enclosure yet to be fully investigated and understood. The above problems will be returned to later, but first, to put things into further context, some potted history.

CHAPTER TWO

Great Surveys – Great Excavations

Although interest in hillforts has a long history it was not until the mid nineteenth to early twentieth centuries that tentative survey and excavation began. Since then a number of excavations, mostly in the *central southern zone* of Cunliffe (1991, 344), which extends from Wessex and the South Downs through the Cotswolds and Welsh Marches to north Wales, have shed light not only on structure and design but also on origin, function and societal significance. The majority of these investigations, however, only sectioned ramparts and opened trenches on a small scale. The large size of even the smallest hillfort has made adequate excavation either very difficult or impossible. Today research is focused more on their status in the landscape and the 'environs' in which they appear to have assumed such a dominant role, and less on invasive techniques.

Early recordings 1700–1875

Early interest in the 'ancient camps' was often mixed up with folklore. There are six hillforts with the name 'Cadbury', but Cadbury Castle (called South Cadbury throughout this book) near South Cadbury in Somerset is associated with Arthurian legend: in 1542 John Leland wrote: 'At South Cadbyri standith Camallate [Camelot], sumtyme a famous toun or castelle'. It was also reputed to be the site where 'the fairies stored grain grown on the surrounding plain' (Alexander 2002, 41–2). This reference to grain storage through folklore is interesting when the possible function of the many pits found within hillfort interiors is considered, as we shall see in later chapters.

Examples of eighteenth-century interest in hillforts abound. Edward Lhuyd first described the hillfort at Strumble Head in Pembrokeshire in his *Archaeologia Britannica* of 1707, while Poston Camp in Herefordshire was recorded on Isaac Taylor's map of 1754. The perimeter of Yeavering Bell was depicted on John Warburton's map of 1716 and on a plan and view drawn by William Hutchinson in 1776, the whole being 'of very remote antiquity' (Oswald and Pearson 2005, 100–1). In 1791 the first account of Worlebury, above Weston-super-Mare, was published in Collinson's *History of Somerset* and in 1805 a plan was produced by the artist George Cumberland.

The first three-quarters of the nineteenth century saw casual finds amassed into private collections and museums with little attention paid to provenance, function or origin; this was the fate of the hoard of metalwork from Moel Hiraddug in Flintshire, found in 1872. Such beginnings, however, gave way to an expansion of interest on more substantive lines.

The first volume of *Archaeologia Cambrensis* in 1846 described 'British forts' on the Caernarfonshire coast, and as early as 1849 hillforts in the Clwydian Range and Dinorben, to the west, received attention from local antiquarians. In the Marches, Old Oswestry, Wapley Camp and Y Breiddin were investigated (Lines 1889). However, a more critical approach was adopted by George Tate at Yeavering Bell, where, in 1861, sponsored by the Duke of Northumberland, he surveyed the site, dug into the ramparts and identified gateways and hut platforms.

Survey, description and excavation 1875–1914

The mid nineteenth century saw the foundation of many learned societies: for example, in Herefordshire the Woolhope Naturalists Field Club was formed in 1851, and in Montgomeryshire the Powysland Club began a few years later, in 1867. It was this impetus, perhaps more than any other, that encouraged a greater 'scientific' approach to hillforts as distinct from the earlier 'artistic' study, and this began to appear in the later years of the century.

During this time the nature of Iron Age settlement began to be considered more fully, and the period 1880–1914 saw notable surveys and excavations. For example, Grimthorpe, on the edge of the Yorkshire Wolds, the site of a warrior burial with rich grave goods which was 'excavated' in 1868, was later carefully investigated by J.R. Mortimer, who presented his results between 1895 and 1911 (Stead 1968). Similarly, one of the first excavation reports of a hillfort was published for Worlebury by C.W. Dymond in 1886; it described the ninety-three pits and eighteen skeletons of previous diggings.

Nevertheless, most hillforts became known only gradually. It was not until 1861 that Bigberry (or Bigbury) Camp, just west of Canterbury in Kent, was mentioned by the local antiquary John Brent, who described the first of a series of ironwork and pottery finds up to 1895. Subsequently Sir William Boyd Dawkins gave an account of the site and 'sundry relics', including La Tène metalwork.

There was much small-scale work in Dorset. In 1894 Edward Cunnington investigated Hambledon Hill, and in 1897 Boyd-Dawkins examined enclosures and pits at nearby Hod Hill. Piper and Hilton Price excavated part of British Camp (Herefordshire Beacon) and Midsummer Hill in the Malvern Hills in 1879, Pitt Rivers visiting the excavations and drawing a plan of the former. At South Cadbury Dymond (1882) made a detailed description and plan, but it was not until 1913 that St George Gray opened five trenches and suggested Neolithic as well as 'Late Celtic' use (Freeman 2000, 7–8).

The work of Major General Pitt Rivers (Augustus Henry Lane Fox) on Cranborne Chase, (Pitt Rivers 1887; 1888), was notable in emphasising the significance of regional studies and the importance of occupation debris as a means by which the lives of people could be reconstructed. He had earlier worked in Kent at the medieval Caesar's Camp near Folkestone and then in Sussex at Cissbury, Highdown and Mount Caburn near Lewes in 1887–8, and concluded that, although hillforts were occupied in the Iron Age, they could have had earlier origins.

Meanwhile, this approach was developed by the Rev. S. Baring-Gould in Pembrokeshire. His excavation at Clawdd y Milwyr fort on St David's Head in 1898 (Baring-Gould *et al.* 1899) was a model of its time, but he also 'explored' Moel Drygarn (Trigarn), one of the stone-built forts that dominate the Preseli Range (Baring-Gould *et al.* 1900).

In north Wales, forays on large sites produced little evidence of structure or chronology, but the huts at Tre'r Ceiri on the Llŷn peninsula were examined by Baring-Gould and Burnard (1904), with some excavation by Hughes in 1906 (Hughes 1907), and the first excavations of Castell Caer Seion, which overlooks the Conwy Estuary, took place (Picton 1909; Bezant Lowe 1909). But by far the most significant work of the time was the excavation at Pen y corddyn Mawr, near Abergele, by Willoughby Gardner in 1905 (Gardner 1910), invaluable for its gateway plans and structural details. Meanwhile, the inventories of the Royal Commission on Ancient and Historical Monuments in Wales and Monmouthshire (beginning with Montgomeryshire in 1911) gave valuable insight into hillfort form and location and continue today.

Major developments 1914–1945

After the First World War hillfort investigation in both England and Wales continued and the publication of the British Museum's *Guide to the Antiquities of the Early Iron Age* (Smith 1925) resulted in the Iron Age really 'coming of age'.

Although this renewed interest in the Iron Age encouraged excavation, theory was lacking, but this was to change and Hawkes's paper on hillforts of 1931 reflected the then-current (although now considered unlikely) hypothesis of waves of folk movement affecting Iron Age culture in southern England, and proposed the divisions of Iron Age A, B and C.

Despite the work of others at the now destroyed Braich-y-Ddinas on Penmaenmawr and on the Llŷn, Willoughby Gardner was the most influencial researcher in north Wales and the Marches until the 1940s, and he has rightly been called the 'father' of hillfort study in the area. Along with Pen y corddyn Mawr, his later work at Dinorben and Ffridd Faldwyn was significant and his presidential address to the Cambrian Archaeological Association (Gardner 1926) on the 'Native Hill-forts of N. Wales and their Defences' summarised the state of knowledge at the time.

Meanwhile, Hawkes concluded that the earliest phase of Dinorben must be pre-Roman, as was thought to be the case with the La Tène metalwork from Moel Hiraddug (Hemp 1928). Likewise, the rectangular guard chambers at Pen y corddyn Mawr, initially considered to be Roman, seemed more like those at

FIGURE 10. Maiden Castle, Dorchester, Dorset, showing, in particular, the complex western entrance in the foreground. Wheeler's 1930s excavations included a Romano-British shrine in the interior and the eastern gateway.

ENGLISH HERITAGE NMR 15834/30, 29/10/1997.

the Iron Age St Catharine's Hill at Winchester, and at Leckhampton in the Cotswolds (Savory 1976). Attitudes to the complexity and 'richness' of society during the Iron Age were, therefore, gradually changing. But ultimately progress towards a greater understanding of Welsh hillfort chronology was due to work in south Wales by, among others, Sir Mortimer Wheeler at Lydney (Wheeler and Wheeler 1932), Nash-Williams at Llanmelin and Sudbrook (Nash-Williams 1933a; 1939) and Audrey Williams on the Gower (Williams 1939; 1940; 1941).

In the Marches, although Jack and Haytor (1925) had excavated Caplar Camp near Hereford, hillforts were studied only spasmodically until the first specialised map was produced by Nash-Williams in 1933 (b). This distinguished contour from promontory forts, highlighting the contrast between farmed land of the eastern river valleys and the Welsh seaboard, and the interior, where hillforts are few. In 1932 O'Neil excavated Titterstone Clee (O'Neil 1934) and, across the border in Montgomeryshire, Y Breiddin between 1933 and 1939 and Ffridd Faldwyn from 1937 to 1939 (O'Neil 1937; 1942). The Shropshire sites of the Wrekin and Old Oswestry were excavated by Kenyon in 1939 (Kenyon 1942) and Varley respectively (Hughes 1994), the latter also digging Maiden Castle at Bickerton in Cheshire (Varley 1935; 1936). With the discovery of pottery at Old Oswestry comparable with Iron Age examples from Wessex, Varley pushed back the dates of univallate Marcher forts to the third century BC and bivallate ones to a century later (Varley 1948). Meanwhile, Lily Chitty (1937) proposed a route by which the builders of inturned hillfort entrances had reached the central Marches – showing a reliance again on hillfort form to interpret social

FIGURE 11. Excavations by H. St. George Gray at Cadbury Camp, Tickenham, Somerset in 1922.

H. ST. GEORGE GRAY 1922.

structures. Further north there were fewer investigations, but Varley's work at Castle Hill (Almondbury) in Yorkshire was notable (Varley 1939; 1976).

However, it was the excavation of Leckhampton Hill in Gloucestershire by Burrow in 1925 that was the first project to thoroughly record everything uncovered (Champion 1976). Here, the previous norm of sectioning ramparts in places, as with Gardner's later excavations at Y Gardden at Ruabon near Wrexham, sometimes coupled with a description of the gate, was replaced by the study of ramparts and ditch, excavation at the entrance and recording of levels and finds in detail. This more diligent approach developed throughout the 1930s, particularly in Sussex, Hamphire and Dorset, with, for example, the excavation of St Catharine's Hill by Hawkes, Myres and Stevens in 1930.

In southern England there was a flurry of activity, as at Poundbury and Chalbury in Dorset in 1939, but the most famous and influential investigations were Wheeler's excavations at Maiden Castle near Dorchester between 1934 and 1938 (Wheeler 1935; 1943)(Figure 10). Being nothing short of brilliant, he adopted a grid-like form of horizontal trenching to expose the complex archaeology, and proved Neolithic origins. His monograph is an outstanding display of archaeological eloquence which, despite some questioning as a result of later excavations in 1985–6 (Sharples 1991a and b), has stood the test of time.

In Somerset, Cadbury Camp (Tickenham) was investigated by H. St George Gray in 1922; the results of this work suggesting late Iron Age and Roman activity (Figure 11). However, his excavation of Ham Hill was a major project of the 1920s (Gray 1924; 1925; 1926). Meanwhile, research at Hembury Castle by Dorothy Liddell between 1930 and 1935, followed by Cotrill's work on Milber Down Camp in 1937–8 (Fox *et al.* 1949–50), formed part of a programme of study prompted by the Devon Archaeological and Exploration Society. The outbreak of war curtailed planned excavations at Blackbury Castle (Young and Richardson

1955). In Cornwall there was less work, and Leeds's investigations at Chûn Castle (1927; 1931) were perhaps typical of the time. The excavation at Trevelgue Head, undertaken as long ago as 1939, was notable, although never published, and has been the only really large-scale excavation in Cornwall so far.

These projects were led, with notable exceptions such as Hawkes and Wheeler, by enthusiastic but knowledgeable amateurs and in this respect Cecil Curwen and Maud Cunnington were exceptional. Both carried out high-quality excavations and published equally good studies on a wide variety of hillforts: for example Curwen at The Trundle (1929 and 1931), Hollingbury, Cissbury and Mount Caburn in Sussex, and Cunnington at Lidbury (1917), Oldbury, Oliver's Castle, Yarnbury Castle, Casterley Camp and Figsbury Rings in Wiltshire.

Wealden sites, such as the unfinished High Rocks at Tunbridge Wells (Money 1941; 1960; 1962; 1968), were also of interest. Trenches cut at Saxonbury Camp (Winbolt 1930) suggested construction in the early Iron Age, while in 1938 Ward Perkins (1939) excavated part of Oldbury Hill, which commands the Medway Gap, the natural routeway into Wealden Kent, and considered the possibility of a specific 'Wealden culture'.

In the Midlands, however, it was the excavation of Bredon Hill, overlooking the River Avon, that proved to be the most 'infamous' of all in its findings (Hencken 1938), as here was evidence of the cult of the severed head personified (see pages 103, 156).

Expansion, survey and rescue 1945–1975

Difficult post-war conditions discouraged large-scale excavation and efforts concentrated on fieldwork, but, as time progressed, a number of important studies increased the understanding of social structure and economy, and research on regional groupings and settlement sites became widespread. Developmental pressure and, in particular, quarrying, resulted in rescue excavation becoming a pressing need; Sutton Walls in Herefordshire, Ham Hill, Y Breiddin, Dinorben, Breedon-on-the-Hill in Leicestershire and Moel Hiraddug among others. Both Balksbury and Winklebury in Hampshire became sites for road construction and/or building. At Sutton Walls valuable information was gleaned on function and occupation and comparison made with other hillforts in the area, while the Society of Antiquaries funded subsequent investigations at Dinedor, Aconbury and Credenhill in Herefordshire (Kenyon 1954) – one of the first 'environs' projects. Although some excavations before the war contained reports of fauna and flora, no real attempt was made to synthesise this data and adequate analysis of animal bones was lacking; but this was to change.

The 1960s and early 1970s saw research in England and Wales spurred on by increasing interest in Iron Age society and political structure together with the continual necessity for rescue. A major advance in this period was the publication of the *Map of Southern Britain in the Iron Age* by the Ordnance Survey in 1962. Developments in theory since the war had been considerable, with modifications made to Hawkes's ABC system and the idea of folk movements becoming increasingly questioned. Archaeologists also began taking into account trade and exchange, cultural and political organisation, and landscape.

In both England and Wales larger-scale excavations eventually began again, encouraged by a dissatisfaction nationally with small-scale work producing minimal results and, as with the study of hillforts in their landscapes, the pressures of development. In 1958 Hope-Taylor (1977) excavated at Yeavering Bell, and later at Dinorben Savory picked up Willoughby Gardner's work and excavated the site in advance of complete destruction by quarrying (Gardner and Savory 1964; Savory 1971). The important excavation report is substantial and includes a consideration of the hillfort in its socio-economic and environmental setting. Again in advance of destruction, the rescue excavation at the promontory fort Coygan Camp (Wainwright 1967) was the most extensive excavation in Carmarthenshire undertaken up until that time. Quarrying has also taken all but the southern part of Moel Hiraddug, which was the subject of rescue excavations in 1954–5 under Christopher Houlder (1961), who examined the north-west gateway, and during the 1960s under M. Bevan-Evans. J.L. Davies continued alone from 1970 to 1972 and the Clwyd Powys Archaeological Trust, under Ken Brassil, finally completed the task (Brassil *et al.* 1982). Another rescue excavation, at Moel y Gaer above Rhosesmor in Flintshire, was conducted in advance of a water-storage scheme between 1972 and 1974 (Guilbert 1975, 1976a), the comprehensive excavations covering a fifth of the interior and sections of the defences. However, apart from excavations on the Roman structure at Caer y Tŵr on Holyhead Mountain, there has been little work on Anglesey hillforts since around 1970.

Further south in the Marches four notable hillforts were excavated by Stanford: Croft Ambrey, Midsummer Hill and Credenhill in Herefordshire and the Wrekin in Shropshire (Stanford 1967; 1971; 1974; 1981; 1985b). All produced important information and finds and the reports are comprehensive in their description of environmental conditions. The discovery of regularly spaced structures (as also found at Moel y Gaer (Rhosesmor)) led Stanford to speculate about a function as densely populated hilltop settlements. Between 1969 and 1975 important excavations took place at Y Breiddin near Welshpool in three areas all now quarried away, proving Neolithic/early Bronze Age occupation (Musson 1970; 1972; 1976; Musson *et al.* 1991).

Work elsewhere was widespread. Mam Tor in Derbyshire (Coombs and Thompson 1979), Wandlebury in Cambridgeshire (Hartley 1957) and Hollingbury in Sussex (Holmes 1984) were excavated in the 1950s and 60s. In Cornwall, Carn Brea (Mercer 1981a), The Rumps cliff castle (Brooks 1974) and Killibury (Miles 1977) all saw activity, and there was a small-scale excavation at the impressive Castle-an-Dinas at St Columb Major (Wailes 1963), but when compared with the attention placed on hillforts in Wessex and parts of Wales, there has been much less invasive investigation generally in the far south-west over the years. However, in advance of a housing scheme, about one half of

FIGURE 12. Excavations at Danebury 1986. The many pits can be clearly seen.

INSTITUTE OF ARCHAEOLOGY, OXFORD UNIVERSITY.

the small fort at St Mawgan-in-Pyder was mostly trenched in 1948, uncovering significant information and finds (Threipland 1956).

More significant were the excavations of Peter Dixon at Crickley Hill in Gloucestershire (Dixon 1972a and others – see Bibliography), Leslie Alcock at South Cadbury in Somerset (Alcock 1971; Barrett *et al.* 2000) and Barry Cunliffe at Hengistbury Head in Hampshire (Cunliffe 1987). At Conderton Camp, next to the Bredon Hill fort, excavations and geophysical surveys enabled socio-economic factors to be addressed and the hillfort's place in the landscape to be determined (Thomas 2005). These important studies will be referred to throughout this book, as will the most detailed and influential excavation so far undertaken at a British hillfort, that of Danebury in Hampshire by Barry Cunliffe, which began in 1969 and, with the succeeding 'Danebury Environs Programme', has lasted for over thirty years (Figure 12).

Changing perspectives: landscape, environment and public interpretation 1975–present

The formation of the archaeological trusts in Wales and the dedicated archaeological units in England allowed rescue archaeology to respond to political and developmental pressure and many investigations have subsequently taken place. The programme at Hunsbury by Northampton Archaeology, designed to both conserve and investigate remaining features and allow improved public access and interpretation of this important, but much neglected, site, is a case in point. Hillfort research and management over the past thirty years has followed seven broad themes:

- Selected excavations
- Concentration on investigation by non-invasive methods
- Changing perspectives on enclosure and the place of hillforts in prehistoric society
- Consideration of the relationship between hillforts and smaller defended settlements
- Expansion of hillfort environs study
- Management of sites as an integrated resource, taking into account their landscape context, wildlife and environmental significance
- Site interpretation

Apart from continued work at Danebury and Hengistbury Head, most excavations, although relatively numerous, have been on a small scale, for example Ditchling Beacon in Sussex (Rudling 1985), Dod Law West in Northumberland (Smith 1989), and more recently (2008) the sectioning of ramparts at Credenhill. Excavations in 2000 at Lodge Hill Camp above Caerleon in Glamorgan (Pollard *et al.* 2006) also produced interesting results. However, there have been a few larger-scale projects, as recently at Sutton Common (Van de Noort 2007) and the excavations of the Taplow hillfort in Buckinghamshire running between 1999 and 2005 (Allen *et al.* in press). Projects at Balksbury (Wainwright and Davies 1995; Ellis and Rawlings 2001) and Uffington Castle, Segsbury Camp and Alfred's Castle in Berkshire (Miles *et al.* 2003a; Lock *et al.* 2005; Gosden and Lock 2007), as part of the 'Hillforts of the Ridgeway Project' of Oxford University, are also notable. However, in both England and Wales there has been a move away from pure excavation towards investigation by non-intrusive methods using new technology, as the RCHME field survey of Yeavering Bell (Pearson 1998) and the 'Wessex Hillforts Survey Project' (Payne *et al.* 2006) of English Heritage show. This has had advantages in terms of time and cost, if lacking the detail of excavation, and has been given impetus by changing perspectives on the place of hillforts within prehistoric society.

In similar fashion, there has been much work nationally on small defended settlements concerning the way they interacted with the larger hillforts and the context of hillforts within their wider environs. The 'Montgomeryshire Small

Enclosures Project' of the Clwyd Powys Archaeological Trust, for example, examined relationships between hillfort location and surrounding settlement, and showed that small enclosures were a major settlement pattern of the upper Severn Valley (Britnell 1989). Similarly, there is ongoing research into the origin and development of smaller Iron Age and Romano-British enclosures in south-west Wales, in this case involving excavation (Harold Mytum pers. comm.).

These studies have considered enclosure as part of the wider environment and, together with impetus from the Danebury excavations and the Danebury Environs Programme (Cunliffe and Poole 2000a; 2000b), have made the investigation of hillfort environs (placing them in a landscape and area context) an important part of recent hillfort study, as the 'South Cadbury Environs Project' shows (Tabor 2008).

Rural developmental pressure has continued apace, and changes in land-use patterns and the intensification of farming and forestry during the 1970s to 1980s resulted in hillforts becoming especially vulnerable. However, as the 1980s and 1990s progressed the importance of archaeological monuments in the landscape and their place within natural systems became recognised and a series of initiatives designed to integrate the archaeological and environmental disciplines resulted (Berry and Brown 1994; 1995; Brown 1994; 1995). Caer Drewyn in Merioneth, for example, was taken into public ownership to alleviate the damaging effects of ploughing.

The interpretation and opening-up of hillforts to the public has received considerable attention over the past twenty-five years. The Danebury programme stands out, but at Tre'r Ceiri a ten-year project of consolidation and conservation, completed in 1999 prior to sensitive public interpretation, provided a wealth of information on social conditions and building construction techniques (Hopewell undated). In Cambridgeshire a programme of excavation, interpretation and reinstatement of the ramparts at Stonea Camp showed what can be achieved with a little imagination (Jackson and Potter 1996). Here, the ramparts were well protected during the 1950s when under pasture, but Government grants subsequently encouraged ploughing and by the 1990s little was visible on the ground. By 1992 most of the banks had been remodelled, grazing reintroduced and interpretation boards erected.

Hillforts have also received National Lottery grants, including funds for the 'Discovering Our Hillfort Heritage Project' of the Northumberland National Park (Oswald *et al*. 2006), 'Heather and Hillforts' of Denbighshire County Council and 'Habitats and Hillforts of Cheshire's Sandstone Ridge' of Cheshire County Council, but it has been the work at Castell Henllys (Mytum 1999; 2004) that has proved to have been among the most influential in the interpretion of a hillfort to the public. A long and detailed excavation allowed reconstructions of roundhouses and structures to be built on the original post-holes, and an adjoining visitor centre was opened by the Pembrokeshire Coast National Park Authority. This relationship between research, public involvement and environmental management is now a firm part of hillfort study.

CHAPTER THREE

Beginnings

It is easy to fall into a number of traps when looking at the origin of hillforts. What, for example, is meant by origin? Is it the time when the first ramparts were raised or the first palisade erected? Is earlier activity on the site relevant? Should sites be considered as a continuum of interest culminating in a specific structural and cultural manifestation – the hillfort – or not? Or did it all happen purely by chance? This chapter will look at some of these factors, beginning with the beginning.

Glimpses of the Neolithic and before

Hillforts are intimately associated with the Iron Age, but as long ago as the 1880s Pitt Rivers was suggesting earlier origins in Sussex, as mentioned above. This perceptive observation has been proved correct at an increasing number of sites, with Hill (1996) proposing that: 'we need to see them [hillforts] in terms of the specific manifestation of a long tradition of marking special places by enclosure with origins in the Neolithic.'

It has long been noticed that there is a relationship between early activity and sites where hillforts were later constructed. Long attachment to places does not in itself, of course, mean origin of anything, but there are tantalising glimpses nationwide of Mesolithic and even Palaeolithic interest in hills later occupied by hillforts. At Ham Hill later Mesolithic microlith(s?) and a (possible) Palaeolithic waste flake were found in the 1980s and Mesolithic flint comes from Moel Arthur, Hengistbury Head and Trevelgue Head. Middle Palaeolithic rock shelters lie below the edge of the precipitous eastern face of the Greensand plateau of Oldbury Hill in the Kentish Weald on which the present hillfort stands.

Chapter 1 looked at the general context of enclosure: it was not just a matter of defence but rather the manifestation of a series of complementary factors – as we shall see these could have been community aspiration, control of landscape and resources, status, superstition and symbolism among others. But how significant was the juxtaposition of hillforts to earlier ritual monuments, what evidence is there for pre-Iron Age enclosure and can this evidence, where it exists, be seen as a precursor to hillfort development?

Mercer (1989) and Ralston (1995) both suggest that enclosure and fortification developed in Europe from the Neolithic period onwards. In Britain the most recognisable manifestation of these phenomena in this period are the 'causewayed enclosures', a feature of England south of a line from the Humber to the Severn Estuary, with around seventy examples identified (Oswald *et al.* 2001). Despite nearly a third of these having been excavated, they still remain an enigma, a situation which has not been helped by their structural differences locally and regionally. However, all normally exhibit at least two, not necessarily complete, concentric circles of ditch interspaced with earth 'causeways' (possibly a common enclosure construction technique) and banks made up of spoil from each ditch, possibly crowned by a palisade and revetted with timber or turf. At Crickley Hill, Hambledon Hill and Hembury Castle (Payhembury) post-holes have been interpreted as the location of wooden gates (Dyer 1990, 33).

Causewayed enclosures varied according to local conditions and were re-cut, altered and added to over time; some possibly remodelled as continuous earthworks (Bradley 2007, 73). Human and animal skeletal remains, along with domestic rubbish, are features of the ditches, and seem usually to have been placed as part of specific rites. This is particularly so in Wessex and Sussex, where regularly placed human skulls often have the lower jaw removed, as on Hambledon Hill. It could be that the discontinuous nature of the ditches signified deposition by specific individuals or groups in each section, although joining potsherds have been found in different circuits at Windmill Hill, Wiltshire (Oswald *et al.* 2001, quoting Smith 1965, 14). Evidence of buildings is slight, although Dixon (1988a, 82) argues for three rectangular structures in the later phase of the causewayed enclosure at Crickley Hill.

The function of causewayed enclosures is as problematic as that of the later hillforts and probably just as variable. Settlement sites and arenas for gatherings, exchange, manufacture of goods and feasting have all been proposed, as has defence. Favourite among the theories is that of causewayed enclosures as places of assembly and ceremonial, where the dead would be venerated and life and fertility celebrated – chalk phalluses and possible representations of the female form have been found in the ditches at Windmill Hill and a carefully carved bone phallus comes from The Trundle hillfort as shown in Figure 57a. Phalluses have a long tradition as emblems to ward off the 'evil eye' into Roman times. As Hutton (1991, 48) points out: 'All this suggests that mid-Neolithic religion was bound up with the continuous dialogue with the dead, or with death itself.' Thus, a space would have been defined (in this case by ditches and banks) with a specific meaning, the ditches themselves performing a symbolic role.

Some of these characteristics resonate with some aspects of the later hillforts, as we shall see later, but there has been much debate as to whether causewayed enclosures (or henges for that matter, as could be the case at Castell Bryn-gwyn in Montgomeryshire) were actual precursors to hillforts and the theory has been generally rejected, there being only around eight on-site instances of some form of juxtaposition (Oswald *et al.* 2001, 139–42). However, there might have been some socially conditioned attachment to a site (Cunliffe 1974; Bradley 1981), or the same position might have been chosen later merely because it was good physiographically. The hillforts of Maiden Castle, Crickley Hill and Hembury

FIGURE 13. The hillfort of Rybury in Wiltshire partially overlies a causewayed enclosure (showing on the left of the site), the interiors of both being clearly visible from the higher ground to the north, from where this photograph was taken.

Castle (Payhembury) were all built directly on top of causewayed enclosures, and at Maiden Castle the fort followed the line of the existing ditch rather than the bank. It also appears that Hembury Castle and the unusual polygonal circuit of The Trundle followed the plan of earlier monuments, but in other instances, as at Rybury in Wiltshire (Figure 13) and Maiden Bower in Bedfordshire, the later hillforts were placed only partly over the earlier enclosure. There has also been speculation that concentrations of Neolithic artefacts in the vicinity of Ham Hill and South Cadbury, and in a ditch of Blewburton Hill in Berkshire, could have been from possible causewayed sites. There could be one at Beacon Hill at Burghclere in Hampshire and there is a slight possibility of such an enclosure within Scratchbury Camp in Wiltshire. A magnetometer survey has also suggested a probable plough-levelled enclosure within Salmonsbury in Gloucestershire, but all of these sites require further investigation.

Whatever is the case, there does seem to have been a considerable time-lag before hillforts were constructed on abandoned causewayed enclosures. At Hembury Castle (Payhembury) the latter was abandoned before 2500 BC (Darvill *et al.* 2002, 437), but the first box rampart of the hillfort was not in place until around the mid first millennium BC. But, considering the range of Neolithic influences at a wide variety of locations, it is tempting to suggest that certain sites did hold a long attraction and a special significance and veneration for those seeking a commanding location for a specific purpose. This could be the case on Hambledon Hill, where the later hillfort is positioned directly adjacent to two causewayed enclosures, two long barrows and over nine outworks and cross dykes, not to mention further earlier sites below the hillfort on the northern spur (Mercer and Healy 2004, 10); another causewayed enclosure beneath the hillfort is possible but unlikely (Oswald *et al.* 2001, 151). Here the principal Neolithic enclosure could have been a place of excarnation, where bodies were exposed after death for the elements and birds and mammals to consume.

In the south-west of England enclosed hilltop Neolithic 'tor enclosures' are a well-known feature of the landscape; these may be just settlements, or may be more significant. In Cornwall a massive stone and boulder wall initially surrounded the eastern of the three summits of Carn Brea, enclosing less than 1ha, but later multi-phase developments added nearly 19ha. It is probable that all of these were initially of Neolithic date (with radiocarbon dates of 3190–2687 BC), but there is evidence of an Iron Age hut circle and it is possible the walls were partly remodelled then.

Likewise, in Pembrokeshire, the rocky hilltop of Clegr Boia near St David's (Williams 1952) has rectangular and round huts dated to the Neolithic. One is sited under later earthen ramparts with an inner and outer stone revetment, inturned entrance, double timber gates and 'guardroom' (Rees 1992, 71–2), the latter somewhat debatable. The date of these defences is uncertain, and may be Iron or even Dark Age, but a whole Neolithic complex is quite possible.

This does not mean, of course, that enclosure was the norm in the Neolithic – far from it – and at South Cadbury there was an unenclosed farmstead (Barrett 2000b, 46). Neolithic activity can take other forms at later hillfort sites. On the White Horse Hill at Uffington in Berkshire, for example, worked flint assemblages and the white chalk 'long mound' (although no definite Neolithic evidence for it has been found), indicate at least possible sporadic Neolithic activity and, with the constituent long barrows 'remained visible for many centuries' (Barclay *et al.* 2003, 253). At Bratton Castle, above Pewsey Vale in Wiltshire, a fine long barrow is located within the enclosure and at Walbury Camp, also in Wiltshire, another is located some 500m west of the western entrance. Cissbury, a site of about 400 BC (Donachie and Field 1994), partially overlies Neolithic flint mine shafts, dating to around 3600 BC, which were excavated by Lane Fox (Pitt Rivers), among others, in the nineteenth century and by John Pull between 1952–56 (Russell 2001) (Figure 14).

Evidence of Neolithic activity on hillfort sites can also be less definite, but suggested instead by finds, although their stratified context is often unclear or disturbed. At Danebury (Cunliffe 1993a, 24) there was sufficient evidence in polished stone axes and chipped flint axes to suggest that the hill was 'frequented, if not settled' during that time. On the Marcher hillforts Neolithic material has been found; Ffridd Faldwyn and Moel y Gaer (Rhosesmor) for example, the first occupation at the latter dated to way before the hillfort was constructed. Flint and chert knives, scrapers, arrowheads, blades and pottery fragments were found in shallow pits and a foundation trench for a short length of fence (possibly a windbreak), together with post-holes, indicated some form of settlement, albeit temporary (CPAT n.d.). A possible Neolithic rectangular house was suggested in excavations, but appears to have been isolated and undefended.

Theories abound, and, of the Marches, Trevor Rowley writes that at the summit of Titterstone Clee St John O'Neil excavated a 'wall of local dolerite (dhu stone) set in clay' some 0.9m high and 20.9m in diameter (the 'Earth Circle'). This was of Neolithic origin, and traces of such circles have been found elsewhere in the borders, usually at a high altitude, suggesting that: 'it seems

FIGURE 14. Cissbury
Ring in Sussex, the site
of Neolithic flint mines,
seen in the foreground
and south-east section of
the hillfort.

WEST SUSSEX COUNTY COUNCIL/
PPL LTD.

possible that some of these sites represent the predecessors of Iron Age hillforts'
(Rowley 2001, 27).

Similarly, in Pembrokeshire the possibility of Neolithic associations with later
enclosures is being increasingly debated (Vyner 2001; Driver 2007a). One idea
is that Carn Ingli, above Newport, could have been enclosed in the Neolithic
and later adapted for use in the Iron Age, whilst another theory proposed
development in the Iron Age and life extending into the medieval period (Rees
1992, 63–4). This area of Preseli has strong associations with the Neolithic
– the blue dolerite 'bluestones' used in the inner circle at Stonehenge came
from nearby Carn Meini. Along these ridges a series of stone-walled enclosures
comparable to confirmed Neolithic enclosures sited elsewhere in south-western
Britain have been recognised – Garn Fawr, Dinas Mawr, Garn Fechan, Mynydd
Dinas, Carn Ingli, Carn Alw and Moel Drygarn (Darvill and Wainwright 2002;
2003a and b; Wainwright 2005).

These tentative associations will be debated and perhaps only excavation will
tell, but in the Bronze Age more definitive connections with Iron Age hillforts
become evident.

Bronze Age beginnings

In the period 1300–1150 BC, Cunliffe (1997, 43–5) suggests that hillforts appeared
in the Alpine and Transalpine regions of the 'Urnfield culture' of continental
Europe during a period of 'economic and social stability'. Upland spurs
were often cut off by a massive timber-lined rampart, and in Britain hilltops
continued to exert the same magnetic pull for enclosure during the Bronze
Age as they had in the Neolithic. In southern England, in particular, a series

of 'hilltop enclosures' and lengths of earthwork defined large areas of upland, possibly for communal gatherings with or without ritual intent. Harrow Hill in Sussex (the site of extensive Neolithic flint mines (Curwen and Curwen 1926)) showed much animal bone when excavated and could have served as a central facility for the scattered farms around the base of the hill, perhaps for ritual slaughtering. Rams Hill in Berkshire, Highdown Hill in Sussex and Norton Fitzwarren in Somerset could all have performed similar communal functions (Cunliffe 1991, 37).

Other lengths of earthwork enclosed substantial areas of flat upland by cutting off spurs; these features are sometimes called 'plateau enclosures'. With the banks outside the ditches they could also have served as sites for communal gatherings, as at Cold Kitchen Hill in Wiltshire and Butser Hill in Hampshire. Castle Ring (Stitt Hill) and Ratlinghope Hill, outlying from the Long Mynd in Shropshire, have been classified as hillforts in the past. Associated with extensive cross-dyke systems of the central Marches, these sites were probably similar pastoral enclosures used for gatherings, shearing, culling and general tending of stock, possibly using portable hurdles, and date to the late Bronze Age/early Iron Age (Guilbert 1976b).

Many hillforts show signs of Bronze Age activity in various forms. At the Berth analysis of sediments has shown woodland clearance from the late Bronze Age through to the middle to late Iron Age (Watson 2002, 19). Likewise, on the slopes of Worlebury hill, Bronze Age burial urns, bronze spearheads, a palstave and a socketed axe, together with barbed and tanged flint arrowheads, all indicate continued interest from the Neolithic.

More significant is that many sites have Bronze Age barrows nearby: Maiden Castle and Badbury Rings in Dorset, and Cley Hill (Corsley), which dominates and controls the Frome Gap in Wiltshire and Sidbury Camp on Sidbury Hill, flanking the Nine Mile river in the same county, are only a few of many examples of this phenomenon. At other hillforts Bronze Age barrows or cairns (single or multiple) are present within the enclosure itself, suggesting a regard for the site or hill or use of a commanding position, possibly to define territory. There are many and widespread examples throughout England and Wales too numerous to mention, but some of the most spectacular are those at Moel Drygarn in Pembrokeshire – the 'Hill of the Three Cairns' – which possibly commemorate persons of standing within the community (Bradley 2007, 168) (Figure 15), and the one which dominates the huts of Tre'r Ceiri. Driver (2007a, 136) points out that the fact that these cairns were not plundered for stone during the prehistoric period indicates that they must have been held in some veneration at the time.

Of course, evidence of a Neolithic or Bronze Age presence does *not* necessarily mean a later hillfort developed *out* of this earlier interest; they may have been quite separate events, as reported by Barclay *et al.* (2003, 116, 249) for Uffington Castle. Here, according to the excavators, the origins of the hillfort, which could have existed at the same time as the White Horse, although the latter might

have been constructed earlier: 'must be sought through parallels and contacts with other local sites, including hillforts, and its setting within the landscape context'.

On the other hand, some hillforts show direct evidence of prior unenclosed Bronze Age occupation. At South Cadbury a small farming settlement, part of the 'Early Cadbury' sequence of 1000–300 BC, was located on the protected plateau crest of the hill, with a possible roundhouse, post-built structures, pits and fenced yard approached by a series of well-defined paths. Ploughing created lynchets and erosion scars, and field banks and fence lines defined the area. Occupation debris included late Bronze Age metalwork. At the end of Early Cadbury enclosure began with a timber-revetted stone bank, but the question to be asked is whether this was a construction sequence or not. The authors of the excavation report suggest that: 'to describe that occupation as a single sequence is … a simplification of the complex and varied histories of building and other activities which are represented by the archaeology' (Barrett 2000a, xiv, 319). Here the situation is difficult to unravel, as it is at the rocky hillfort of Carn Alw in Preseli, which is surrounded by fields, enclosures and evidence of cleared rocks and boulders. Although possibly preceded by a late Bronze Age unenclosed farming settlement nearby to the south (Rees 1992, 61), connections are obscure. Later still, on the northern approach to Battlesbury, pits, post-holes and ditch suggest an open settlement dated to 700–500 BC (McOmish *et al.* 2002, 68 after Chadwick and Thompson 1956), the hillfort itself dating from the mid to late Iron Age.

In France and Germany Neolithic farming villages were surrounded by defensive palisades, but in Britain it was only in the south-west that there was anything comparable (Dixon 1988b; Lynch 2000, 53). Nevertheless, at the beginning of the first millennium BC the use of palisades for small enclosures,

FIGURE 15. The three Bronze Age cairns at Moel Drygarn (Trigarn), the 'Hill of the Three Cairns', in Pembrokeshire. More than one hundred hut platforms can be seen at this outstanding site.

HELEN MANLEY JONES.

possibly containing only a single structure, became evident. The earliest occupation of Castell Odo shows late Bronze Age pottery from the occupation layer of roundhouses beneath later banks and the use of palisades with a small ditch outside (Alcock 1960; Lynch 1995, 79).

There is substantial evidence, therefore, that the very earliest 'hillforts' employed this type of 'defensive barrier' – possibly only a rough wattle or closely knitted timber palisade – rather than a bank and ditch, to form an initial enclosing circuit. Ralston (2006, 45) has also outlined the possible use of planted or laid thorn hedges. Whether succeeding bank and ditch exactly followed the line of these early circuits is open to question, but at Hembury Castle (Payhembury) Cunliffe (1991, 313–14) points out that the later defences did follow a line of palisade 'more or less exactly on at least two sides of the circuit', and that the later earthworks rose quickly after the palisade was abandoned. This could have been a conscious abandonment of one method of enclosure for something more sophisticated and effective on the same or a similar line. Palisades were widespread and many examples can be quoted, but Varley (1950) found a palisade preceded rampart construction at Castle Ditch (Eddisbury) in Cheshire, and to the north they have been found at Skelmore Heads in Lancashire and Eston Nab in Yorkshire (Vyner 1988; Harding 2004). To the south, Madmarston Camp in the Cotswolds had an unditched timber palisade (Fowler 1960, 26) and in the excavations of Hollingbury Camp at Brighton Cecil Curwen found a trench thought to support a palisade and experimented with reconstructing the line of its timber posts (Curwen 1932). Some examples of other direct evidence of Bronze Age origins are considered by region below.

In Sussex Hamilton and Manley (1997, 95–7) observed that the majority of later prehistoric enclosures belonged to the late Bronze Age: among others, these included Chanctonbury Ring, Harting Beacon and Ditchling Beacon, but the pre-rampart enclosure of Thundersbarrow Hill was radiocarbon dated to the middle Bronze Age. Some of these earlier enclosures continued into the early and middle Iron Age – at Harting Beacon a human skull from a rubbish scoop had a date of cal. BC 400–500 (HAR-2411); Castle Hill (Newhaven) also lasted until the middle Iron Age.

On the Berkshire Downs early hillfort development has been proven. Lock *et al.* (2003, 116) indicate that the first single timber-framed box rampart with outer ditch and two entrances of Uffington Castle was constructed during the transitionary period of the late Bronze Age/early Iron Age of the eighth century BC. Elsewhere on these chalk downs linear ditches can pre-date hillforts and be 'an influencing factor in their location' (Bradley and Ellison 1975). Lock and Gosden (1997; 1998) suggest that at Segsbury Camp, another hillfort on the Ridgeway, a late Bronze Age ditched enclosure at the end of a linear ditch preceded the first phase of the ramparts and that Bronze Age sherds from within the hillfort could indicate activity before the ramparts were constructed. Rams Hill (Bradley and Ellison 1975) is a complex site between Uffington Castle and Segsbury, and its inner enclosure had a single timber-framed wall-and-fill rampart in its first phase, which was dated to the twelfth century BC (Needham and Ambers 1994), and at Liddington Castle, to the west of Uffington, the early rampart, dated to the Bronze Age/Iron Age transition, was seemingly revetted in timber (Hirst and Rahtz 1996) and associated with pottery of the sixth century BC. Sometimes evidence is more diffuse and Moore (2007, 262) cautions against too much dating interpretation of Cotswold sites – an example being Bathampton's (Somerset) possible late Bronze Age/early Iron Age credentials. Similarly, the limited excavation by Margaret Whiteley (1943) of Chalbury in Dorset showed some later Bronze Age activity at the predominantly early Iron Age fort, but nothing more.

In the Welsh Marches early developmental sequences have also been found. At Old Oswestry the excavations by Varley showed a simple late Bronze Age palisade and ditch surrounding the 'hilltop', which was followed from about 600 BC by the succession of banks and ditches which form the present site. At Dinorben several pre-rampart palisades were dated to before the middle of the first millennium BC (Guilbert 1980), and an approximate tenth-century BC date for Period 1 has been suggested (Gardner and Savory 1964). Moel y Gaer (Rhosesmor) shows an early sequence well. Initially there were at least two Bronze Age barrows on the site, one of which was destroyed by the Iron Age rampart. In the late Bronze Age a 'stockaded camp' containing roundhouses was built and around all of this a wooden fence was embedded into a slot in the ground, possibly enclosing a similar area to that encircled by the later rampart, which was built during the fourth century BC. Elsewhere in the northern Marches, whilst there was no evidence for palisades at Moel Hiraddug, with an early fifth- to sixth-century BC radiocarbon date (Brassil *et al.* 1982, 84), an earlier sequence has been proven for the imposing Llwyn Bryn-dinas hillfort above the Tanat Valley in Montgomeryshire. Here a rampart of the tenth to ninth centuries BC was later enlarged in the fourth or third centuries BC (CPAT 1994, 14–15).

It was the excavation at Y Breiddin, however, that set the seal on Bronze Age origins for a variety of Marcher hillforts, with an early date for the initiation of bank and ditch defences. The excavations in the 1970s unearthed later Neolithic and early Bronze Age evidence and a hard-standing area around a pond dated to around 1200 BC, suggesting sporadic use of the site well before the Iron Age enclosure (Musson *et al.* 1992; Burnham 1995, 67). A line of parallel post-holes from the fire-damaged timber framework of a rampart of the tenth or ninth centuries BC was found beneath the Iron Age defences and there were indications that the Bronze Age fort enclosed a similar area to that of the later Iron Age defences. A late Bronze Age socketed axe, rare in settlement sites but also found at Mam Tor, Beacon Hill in Leicestershire and Portfield in Lancashire, together with pottery, add weight to these Bronze Age beginnings.

Looking to the north, at Castle Hill (Almondbury) in Yorkshire a radiocarbon date of 2100 ± 130 BC was found underlying the earliest defences (Varley 1976) and at Mam Tor pottery, shale bracelet fragments and a bronze axe fragment varied in date from the late Bronze Age to the early Iron Age. There might have been a palisade, and charcoal from the rock-cut platforms was radiocarbon-dated to 1180 and 1130 BC. On the North Yorkshire Moors a number of monuments date from the Bronze Age to the Roman period. Eston Nab has already been mentioned, but at Boltby Scar gold basket-shaped earrings of Beaker to late Bronze Age date from beneath the rampart, together with the hillfort being an integral part of the Cleave Dyke system, suggest an early first millennium BC date.

To date, fifty-four coastal promontory forts have been identified in Pembrokeshire (Driver 2007a, 101) and some are beginning to show early origins. At Dale Point timber palisades and bank and stone revetment of the Bronze Age/Iron Age transition (radiocarbon date of 790 BC), were followed by an Iron Age bank with a deep ditch, stone revetment and massive gate (Benson and Williams 1987; Rees 1992, 79). An early date has also been proven for the formidable defences of Porth y Rhaw, near St David's. Elsewhere, Cornish cliff castles, such as Treryn Dinas and Trevelgue Head, could well have Bronze Age origins (Figure 16). Coastal promontory forts might, therefore, be much earlier than previously thought.

It appears that in Britain enclosure by bank, wall and ditch has origins well within the Neolithic, although, apart from possibly at a very limited number of sites, such as Maiden Castle, it is impossible to say at present whether hillfort developmental sequences can be observed from then on. However, some hillforts do have definite beginnings in the middle to late Bronze Age/early Iron Age, from about 1200 to 600 BC, an increasing number being found with just a simple palisade first of all, with or without a ditch, prior to rampart construction proper. Hillforts are therefore not purely a creature of the Iron Age, but in that period things became much more complicated, as we shall see in the next chapter.

FIGURE 16. One of the finest cliff castles, and one which certainly has 'landmark' status, Trevelgue Head at Newquay in Cornwall is split off from the mainland by a chasm, with access via a bridge, and was formerly defended by six principal ramparts. A large roundhouse was positioned in the centre of the site. The fort has origins which may go back to the Bronze Age.

CHAPTER FOUR

Enclosure

The construction of a hillfort was a monumental task and the builders were superb engineers, considering how much evidence has survived after over 2,000 years of mostly neglect. The sheer size of ditch and bank can be seen at Maiden Castle where, after several millennia of erosion and infilling, the depth still reaches 25m-plus (Figure 17). Although the, now destroyed, Dinorben was a multivallate site of only 2.4ha, the main southern rampart reached over 13m in height and thousands of tonnes of earth had to be removed and modelled. This does not mean, of course, that all was excavated at the same time and, most likely, the

FIGURE 17. The high *glacis* ramparts and deep ditches of Maiden Castle, Dorchester, Dorset, would have provided a formidable obstacle. Note the 'berm' in the middle distance between the high interior rampart and its ditch and second rampart.

whole of the active community would have been involved, including woman and children, but *in toto* the task was massive. Finney (2006, 10) estimates that the excavated material from a hillfort ditch per linear metre would have been four times greater than that required for an enclosed settlement, while Darvill *et al.* (2002, 429) estimate that the walls of the first Neolithic enclosure of 0.8ha at Carn Brea took 30,000 hours of work to build. At Breedon-on-the-Hill in Leicestershire Wacher (1964, 142) calculated that the quantity of rock quarried from the ditch in an 8ft sample width would have been 1760 cu ft.

Locations for hillforts would have been very carefully chosen and the integration of the existing topography and underlying geology into the design extremely skilful. Whilst, at a macro-level, it would appear that rampart lines, entrances and the like often slavishly followed natural conditions, recent detailed investigation by Toby Driver (2007b) of hillfort form and location in the landscape of mid Wales has suggested that, at least in the area of Cardiganshire that he studied, this was not always so, and, although construction was made more difficult as a result, a better 'monumental' effect to the site was subsequently achieved. This will be returned to later, but it is suggested that detailed study at a micro-level on similar lines at hillforts in other areas might achieve surprising results. Nevertheless, the use of topography in general is shown well at Yeavering Bell (see Figure 91), where a massive stone wall bounded the two summits of the hill, and similarly the defences of Moel Hiraddug followed the contours in accordance with the 'inherent defensibility of the perimeter of the hill' (Brassil *et al.* 1982, 15). Where required at Moel Hiraddug a single rampart was built, as on the western scarp, but on the east, where access was easiest, the ridge was enclosed by three or four ramparts, the inner of rubble and outer of earth, conforming to the natural lines of the hill.

Where rock outcrops existed on the defensive line these were exploited and artificial ramparts were unnecessary. There are many examples nationwide of this construction technique, particularly in Wales and the Marches, and shown to particular effect at Tre'r Ceiri (Figure 18). In similar fashion, high above the Sychnant Pass near Conwy, Allt Wen is perched on an inaccessible rocky summit, taking full advantage of all-round visibility, whilst Craig yr Aderyn, above the Dyfi Valley in Merioneth, has an L-shaped bank which ends on the south and east, where slopes are precipitous, a massive stone wall on the site giving added strength. Moel y Gaer (Llantysilio) in Denbighshire, sits on an isolated, if overlooked, ridge deep in the Llantysilio Mountains (Figure 19) and, among others, Penycloddiau in the Clwydians and Nordy Bank and Chesterton Walls in Shropshire, have ditches cut in places into solid rock.

The clever placing of banks and walls using the topography to best effect allowed a degree of shelter at most sites, as the snaking ramparts of Hod Hill show (Figure 20), but none more so than at Craig Adwy Wynt near Ruthin in Denbighshire, where the stepped nature of the limestone provided a separate annexe some way below the main enclosure. However, Hambledon Hill shows the exploitation of the natural slope particularly well (see Figure 6).

FIGURE 18. The wide south-eastern walls, with surmounting walkway, of Tre'r Ceiri on the Llŷn peninsula, Caernarfonshire, perhaps the greatest of the surviving stone-walled hillforts.

FIGURE 19. Moel y Gaer, isolated high in the Llantysilio Mountains of Denbighshire, from just below the Bronze Age cairn on Moel y Gamelin. The hillfort might have guarded a natural north–south route across the ridge.

FIGURE 20. The snaking ramparts of Hod Hill in Dorset partly follow the contours and would have provided considerable shelter from the elements.

Construction techniques

The oft-cited unfinished 2.8ha Ladle Hill in Hampshire gives some idea of simple construction techniques (Piggott 1931), which became more complicated as time progressed. Here the line of the ditch was marked out first of all and there is evidence of a shallow setting-out trench which could have been defined by a plough line. Then came the enlargement of the ditch, its discontinuous nature possibly suggesting separate gangs, or indeed family or kinship groups, involved in the work, as also seems a possibility at Y Breiddin and Moel y Gaer (Rhosesmor) and maybe Mam Tor. The integration of these separate sections into a whole ditch line, with the grading of the banks into a smooth profile, without any movement back of material, never took place. Ladle Hill is on the chalk, where slumping would have been a problem, and to mitigate against this large blocks were positioned at the edge of the ditch to give a firm core and loose material then banked up against them. This chalk core can now be seen as an irregular bank, behind which are small dumps ready to be added to the rampart by the various gangs; a similar process to that found at Quarley Hill, also in Hampshire (Hawkes 1939; Clark 1940, 83).

The abandonment of hillforts with work still to be done seems to have been more common than first thought, and Ranscombe Camp, near to the Caburn in Sussex, where there is a gateway but no post-holes for the gate (Burstow and Holleyman 1964, 65–6), is often referred to. However, there are others and not all of the seemingly fully constructed sites are so – the ramparts on the south side of Maiden Castle are only half-built; at Castercliff in Lancashire the outer rampart remains unfinished (Coombs 1982), and the southern outer ditch of Ivinghoe Beacon in the Chiltern Hills of Buckinghamshire is incomplete (Cotton and Frere 1968, 192). Eggardon in Dorset, Casterley Camp in Wiltshire and Five Barrows, Gatcombe, on the Isle of Wight all remain with work to be done. Of course, there could be many reasons why hillforts were sometimes left unfinished, but one reason might be related to why hillforts were constructed in the first place, and this will be returned to in Chapter 10.

Unless labour was plentiful it is unlikely that the task of construction would have been achieved in one season, especially on the high, bleak and exposed sites. Miles *et al.* (2003a, 119) suggest that individual stretches of bank and ditch would have been finished by the end of each summer season rather than just left to the winter elements. Thus, some stretches would be completed before others had begun; Ladle Hill being a case in point. Construction techniques would have been adapted and improved according to the requirements of the topography and geology at any specific location, the workforce availability and probably the skill and efficiency of those involved – an 'evolution of ideas'. Thus, in Wessex Corney and Payne (2006a, 136) noticed that, at some sites, banks and ditches were constructed in short straight lengths, with peaks and troughs along the length of the rampart tops seemingly correlating with similar features along the base of the ditch. Naturally, this was most obvious at univallate sites, multivallate construction tending to blur the image somewhat, but it is nevertheless still hinted at even at complicated Hambledon Hill and Maiden Castle. This may have resulted from the organisation of labour at the sites, construction in straight lengths being the most efficient method available for gang or family/kinship group labour, and is an interesting finding; apart from work at some of the larger-scale excavations, there has been little published on hillfort construction techniques in a social context.

A wide variety of wood and iron implements would have been used in construction – picks, scrapers and so on, according to availability – but from Dinorben and near Bwrdd Arthur on Anglesey come socketed antler tools, formerly fitted with wooden handles, and these seemingly primitive instruments would have been extremely effective in skilled hands.

Hillforts were not static entities – they were continually reconstructed, modelled and remodelled over many hundreds of years. This dynamism was not all about maintenance, which must have been an immense task in itself, but could have involved an element of ritual. The re-cutting of ditches might have been a regular event, as much to do with celebration or affirmation of seasons, events or territory than anything else (after Pollard *et al.* 2006, 48). As Miles *et al.* (2003a, 10) indicate, many of the features of the Berkshire Downs, such as the linear ditches, and enclosures, of which Uffington Castle, located just above the White Horse (Figure 21), Liddington Castle and Barbury Castle are examples, were not just dug and then left, but continually 'kept in an active state over many centuries'. This fastidiousness is also a feature of Danebury, where Cunliffe (1995a, 23) found that the ditches had been cleaned between twelve and seventeen times. But who the architects of such engineering feats were will never be known. They probably came mostly from within individual communities, but the very nature of what is, in effect, a favoured architectural style over vast areas of England and Wales, could suggest that some individuals were blessed with the required skills more than others, just as today not everyone is capable of designing a building. Perhaps the possibility of itinerent hillfort 'architects' travelling the country in search of 'commissions' cannot be discounted.

Whatever and whoever were involved, the actual design would be changed according to circumstances (see also pages 49, 64–5). Eggardon provides a good example of alteration. Initially a univallate site with simple gap entrances, additional ramparts and ditches were added, the entrances offset to lengthen the approach and inturns at the eastern entrance possibly added later (Wells 1978, 54). At other sites sometimes things did not go according to plan, and at the huge Bindon Hill fort (Figure 22), which extends from Lulworth Cove in Dorset eastwards along the coastline for some 2.5km in circuit, Gale (2003, 116) suggests that the surviving bank appears to be the 'remnants of one which had been piled on the inside of the rear revetment'. Thus, the original design had probably not been followed, perhaps either because of the enormity of the task or just changing circumstances. No one can be sure.

FIGURE 21. a) Looking down the dry valley of 'the Manger' and the sacred landscape beneath Uffington Castle hillfort, from the eye of the fastidiously cleaned from antiquity White Horse on the chalk Berkshire Downs. Note how it's beak appears deliberately positioned to point down this valley; b) outline of the Uffington White Horse.

FIGURE 22. Bindon Hill, the largest hillfort in England and Wales, from Lulworth Cove in Dorset. It is tempting to consider a relationship between the two features in terms of stock management.

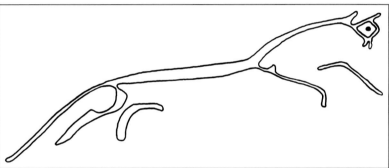

Ramparts and ditches

Much attention has been paid to descriptions of ramparts and ditches and it is not intended to reiterate past work in any detail here. However, in general, there was an increase in complexity as time progressed, depending on area, the builders' response to specific physical, socio-political and symbolic criteria and, of course, additions to the circuit.

Construction materials of earth, timber and stone would depend upon availability of supply on-site or nearby, and it seems that very few hillforts had them brought in from afar. Oak and local stone would have been plentiful in most hillfort areas, the ramparts of Alfred's Castle, for example, being constructed of the local sarsen stone, found lying about the downs in quantity, and augmented by chalk. Along the Ridgeway the dump rampart of Phase 2 of Uffington Castle was contained both to the front and rear by a chalk and sarsen kerb to prevent spreading into the ditch or interior. Similarly the massive southern dump rampart of Segsbury also had a rear revetment of sarsen (Lock *et al.* 2003, 119; Gosden and Lock 2007, 287). At Yeavering Bell the local pink coloured andesite used in construction, which must have given the site a remarkable appearance when unweathered, was quarried from a hollow just behind the rampart (Oswald and Pearson 2005, 110–11). Countrywide, these materials would have been used to construct the palisades (fences of stakes and/or wattle) and ramparts (banks or walls), and categorised by Hawkes (1971 quoted by Ralston 1995, 61) as 'fence, wall and dump'. An outside sloping ditch, for the most part, would have been dry. Internal quarry scoops, as at Penycloddiau or Hod Hill (Figure 23), or a longer quarry ditch, as found at Castell Cawr near Abergele in Denbighshire and Midsummer Hill (see Figure 27), could also provide much stone/earth for the bank, but these materials might also have been scraped into position, Hambledon Hill showing this technique well. Internal terracing at Bury Walls in Shropshire, and possibly Caer Drewyn, could be the vestiges of excavation of stone for the ramparts and the Wrekin and Earl's Hill in Shropshire show terracing in front of the ramparts on the very steep slopes giving the impression of a ditch (Wigley 2007a, 180). At Moel y Gaer (Llantysilio) the material from a possible inner quarry ditch seems to have been thrown forward to form the single rampart set at the top of a very steep natural slope, but whether there is a discontinuous outer ditch or whether one is absent, similar to an arrangement at Haresfield Beacon in Gloucestershire, will have to wait for a detailed survey. On top of the ramparts there might have been a vertical timber or stone palisade to give greater height and strength to the structure; Wheeler (1943) found evidence for this at Maiden Castle. Sometimes there is a 'counterscarp bank' (Figure 24), the result of continual ditch cleaning and maintenance, and which can form a substantial feature itself, as Figure 28 of Liddington Castle shows, whilst between the bank and ditch can be a flat area or 'berm' and this can be seen at Maiden Castle in Figure 17. There is great variability from site to site.

FIGURE 23. Internal quarry scoops at Hod Hill, Dorset, shown in the upper left of the photograph.

The description of rampart construction by Barry Cunliffe (1991, 313–29) is still the most succinct. For England and Wales he came up with two simple categories: 'earth and timber structures' and 'stone and timber defences', and, although there is considerable overlap between the two, it is convenient in general terms to use them here. Figure 25 shows the main types encountered.

Earth and timber structures

Initially, earth and timber ramparts were characterised by a 'box' of timber, usually secured by two rows of substantial posts rammed into the ground, mostly strengthened with internal timbers, and infilled with earth and rubble – the so-called 'timber-faced' or 'box ramparts'. At Maiden Castle and South Cadbury the box had stone infilling. In southern England they are of early Iron Age date and in Wales may also be early; at Moel y Gaer (Rhosesmor) at least of the sixth century BC where upright timbers 0.6–0.9m apart had the gaps between infilled with dry-stone walling with large orthostats (Figure 26). There are a variety of different types which show, among other features, variations in the width between the vertical timbers and use or not of sloping rampart additions and, apart from the Poundbury type, where they are absent, the nature

FIGURE 24 (opposite). Counterscarp bank at Penycloddiau in the Clwydian Range, Flintshire. The summit of Moel Famau, the highest point in the Clwydian Range of hills, can be seen in the distance.

FIGURE 25. Rampart constructions: a) timber palisade; b) dump rampart with retaining kerbs (Phase 2a Uffington Castle); c) *glacis* defence (Maiden Castle – western defences); d) timber faced ('box') rampart (reconstruction); e) *Fécamp* type (Oldbury, Kent); f) stone rampart with timber-lacing (reconstruction); g) stone-faced rampart (Dinorben); h) stone-faced rampart (Worlebury). Redrawn and adapted after: a) author; b) Lock *et al.* 2003; c) Wheeler 1943; d) and f) Avery 1976; e) Ward Perkins 1939; g) Savory 1976; h) Dymond 1902.

FIGURE 26. Remnants of the box ramparts at Moel y Gaer (Rhosesmor), Flintshire.

of internal timbers. Cunliffe (1991, 316–20) categorises them, after the style of timber-strengthening at the type-hillfort, into:

- The Ivinghoe Beacon style
- The Hollingbury Camp style
- The Moel y Gaer style
- The Hod Hill type
- The Poundbury type

He describes them in detail, but suffice to say the object was to construct a 'vertical wall of timber confronting the outside world', possibly faced with stone or turf, usually with a ditch in front and, apart from the Ivinghoe Beacon type, variations on this sloping rampart at the back. There are many examples, but purely as an illustration in one area, Northamptonshire, Kidd (2004, 49, after various authors) describes how, of the eleven known hillforts or other defended sites in the county, such box-like 'timber-strengthening' has been found at Hunsbury, Rainsborough, Guilsborough, Castle Yard at Farthingstone and perhaps Crow Hill at Irthlingborough; the earliest ramparts at Hunsbury and Rainsborough definitely dated to the early Iron Age.

The 'dump rampart' was also an old technique emanating from at least Bronze Age times and possibly as early as the Neolithic. In its simplest form, a 'dump' of earth/spoil forms a barrier, with the inevitable ditch left where the earth has been extracted. This form of construction appears to have been reintroduced in Britain as early as the eighth century BC, either replacing or covering box structures, Uffington Castle, Segsbury and Liddington Castle showing this especially well (Lock *et al.* 2003) (see Figure 28), or built from stage one, as at Croft Ambrey and Midsummer Hill (Figure 27), both of around the fifth century BC. A kerb of stone blocks might be used to keep the dumped material from spilling into the ditch or interior of the fort as at Uffington. Construction was relatively simple and did not require as much engineering skill as the box rampart, as well as not having the problems of fire associated with timber revetting (see page 67). Sometimes, a low dump rampart can resemble a counterscarp bank, making interpretation difficult. In Wales Davies and Lynch (2000, 156) indicate that it is likely that multivallate dump ramparts were constructed from the middle Iron Age onwards.

However, it was a development of the dump rampart, the *'glacis* defence', which provided a more sophisticated and effective barrier from the fourth to second centuries BC. Used to great effect in the design of the later fortresses of the military orders of Knights Templar and Hospital of St John (such as Krak des Chevaliers in Syria), this involved the formation of a single and steep slope from the bottom of the ditch to the very top of the rampart in one go, to as much as 45°. Especially if surmounted by an additional timber or stone palisade/wall, as at Ravensburgh in Hertfordshire, this would have formed a most formidable obstacle indeed. If on chalk such a slope would have been extremely slippery and at some sites would have been immense – at Maiden Castle 25m-plus, as we have seen in Figure 17; Danebury 16.1m and Hod Hill 17.4m. There is substantial evidence that dump and *glacis* defences replaced former box ramparts, and this is shown to effect in the Marches, the huge outer ramparts of Old Oswestry being especially fine. It appears that this technique would have been considered the ultimate construction method, one which would impart a great deal of power, prestige and ability to intimidate to its owner. *Glacis* are not as common in Wales as they are in England, but both Llanmelin and Lodge Hill, which began as univallate enclosures with a 'structured' bank, eventually became multivallate with *glacis*-style defences (Pollard *et al.* 2006, 54). The massive earthen banks and ditches of the remodelled Dinas Dinorwic in Caernarfonshire, some 12m thick and 9m in total height, are also fine examples (Lynch 1995, 73–4). Later, a variation on this theme, probably imported from Gaul, the '*fécamp*' type, provided a further degree of sophistication. Here a massive dump rampart was fronted by a wide flat-bottomed ditch (implying Roman influence), much quoted examples being Quarry Wood (Loose) and Oldbury in Kent.

Maintenance of defences would be required on a continual basis, not only on the banks themselves but also in the ditches. Erosion of exposed soil surfaces by only one continuous downpour can be very rapid and the mechanics of erosion at exposed hillfort sites are poorly understood and little researched. At Eggardon, landslips on the chalk seem to have been a problem leading to remodelling of the defences, and the internal bank of the middle southern rampart can be seen collapsed into the ditch below. One of the outworks on the site may have strengthened the structure at this point (Gale 2003, 151). A similar situation occurred at the south-east entrance of Pilsdon Pen, also in Dorset. Access to past flint digging in the interior was probably the cause of slumping at Liddington Castle (Figure 28), but shows how fragile chalk strata can be. Clearly slippage and infilling was a substantial problem that must have been addressed and Danebury's eleven different episodes of ditch clearance identified on the counterscarp bank proves the point (Cunliffe 1991, 320). Such maintenance might have been an annual occurrence involving ceremonial and ritual – a symbolic cleansing of both site and people.

Stone and timber defences

In areas with an adequate stone supply, dry-stone construction, with or without a rubble core, or dumped rubble would have formed the principal building techniques. Rubble ramparts, with dry-stone walling at front and rear, was a common technique, found in single form at Chalbury in Dorset and Carn Goch in Carmarthenshire (Hogg 1972) and in multiple form at Moel Hiraddug, among other sites. These walls may also have been surmounted by timber palisades. To provide additional strengthening to the walls timber would be used. Such 'timber-lacing' is evident in the Cotswolds, Crickley Hill and Leckhampton Hill in Gloucestershire and Corley Camp in Warwickshire being good examples. However, among many other sites, its use extends into south Wales to Lodge Hill

Camp at Caerleon, up the Welsh Marches to Ffridd Faldwyn, into Cheshire at Castle Ditch (Eddisbury) and Maiden Castle (Bickerton) and into north Wales to Dinorben and Moel y Gaer (Rhosesmor). In Yorkshire, timber-lacing was used in the first and second construction phases of Castle Hill (Almondbury).

Other combinations of stone with timber or earth show the great variability of construction techniques used. A partially circling palisade of large upright stones was (possibly) interspaced with strengthening timbers at Castell Henllys, and Pen y Gaer (Llanbedr y Cenin), above the Conwy Valley in Caernarfonshire, shows, of its three ramparts, the outermost ones to be of earth with a stone facing, the middle ones of stone on the west and earth on the south, and the innermost entirely of stone. The eastern ramparts of Caer Drewyn are built entirely of stone, but downslope the western half appears earthen with either stone frontage or breastwork, possibly suggesting different phases of development (Engineering Archaeological Services 2006, 4, 5) (Figure 29). Such stone-faced earthen banks are rare in Wales, but Caer Bach (Rowen) in Caernarfonshire is another, more definite, example.

Stone defences can come singly, in multiples or both and can be simple or complex depending on topography, sometimes reaching massive proportions. At the coastal promontory fort of Bolt Tail in Devon (Figure 30), despite erosion, the well-preserved simple stone-faced rampart is still some 275m long, so defining the site and cutting off the headland (Berresford Ellis 1991, 77). The single stone rampart of Yeavering Bell reaches 4m in width, enclosing 5.2ha above the confluence of the Rivers Glen and Till. At some sites walls could be

over 3m in height, as at Carn Ingli and Worlebury, reaching 11m in width at the latter (Figure 31).

Two north Wales hillforts with single walls are particularly worthy of note – Tre'r Ceiri and Castell Caer Seion. To the west, Tre'r Ceiri is perched on the eastern peak of Yr Eifl, which runs as a spine down the Llŷn peninsula (Garn Boduan and Carn Fadryn are other fine sites on the ridge), and is one of the greatest stone-built hillforts. The main 2.5ha enclosure is bounded by a single massive dry-stone wall 2.3–3m thick, with intact parts still surviving to an original height of 3.5m; remnants of a surmounting single wall-walk are clearly visible, and this can be seen in Figure 18. Wall-walks are likely to have been an essential feature of stone-built ramparts and double versions have been recognised at both Caer y Tŵr and Caer Drewyn (Lynch 1991, 264). Castell Caer Seion, which commands the Conwy Estuary in Caernarfonshire (Griffiths and Hogg 1956), has an enclosing single stone wall which has parallels in both construction and choice of site with Worlebury in Somerset, although the latter has multiple walls in places and possible *murus duplex* (additional internal stone facings within dry-stone walls). The southern wall of a small 'citadel' at the western end of the enclosure is massively constructed of laid masonry about 3.7–4.9m wide (Figure 32), whilst the outer face of the south wall of the main enclosure has large roughly-coursed blocks with on-edge slabs, the inner face mostly being constructed of laid masonry/slabs. These strongly defended points are a feature of some Welsh hillforts, as at Garn Boduan, but their date and context is problematical – they could be prehistoric, they could be medieval. At Caerau (Ely) in the Vale of Glamorgan, for example, the 'citadel' at the north-eastern corner is definitely medieval.

Into mid Wales stone-walled forts become less numerous, with only three in Montgomeryshire, and at Pen y Gaer above the Clywedog reservoir a single wall 3.7m in width without a ditch encircles the hilltop; but nationally there are many nuances in both design and construction.

When we look at some examples of multiple-walled stone hillforts throughout England and Wales, as with the single-walled sites, their inherent variability comes to light, and the west, in particular, has some outstanding examples. In Cornwall, Chûn Castle dominates much of Land's End. Two extremely strong dry-stone walls standing 3.7m high, each with an internal ditch, are faced with large granite blocks, whilst, travelling north into Pembrokeshire, Gaer Fawr (Llanwnda), on Strumble Head, has formidable, and complicated, dry-stone defences. Here a surviving inner rampart without a ditch makes use of four natural rock outcrops. There are two outer walls on the gentler eastern side, ending in crags, and an outer wall on the west provides an annexe, with short stretches of walling on the precipitous north and south. An outer wall on the east is strengthened by a bank 4m high with external stone revetment, ditch and counterscarp (Rees 1992, 67).

Moving to the north Wales coast, Braich-y-Ddinas was formerly the finest of all the multiple-walled sites, and its complete destruction is a great loss to the nation's heritage. There, three rubble walls once faced the east, whilst two on the west and one on the south protected the site (Williams and Davidson 2002, 4). Hillforts such as these were often enlarged and added to over time, but at Moel Drygarn in Pembrokeshire the seemingly multiple defences mask what is in fact a series of three single walled enclosures built successively over a period of time. Additions to hillforts are many and varied and will be returned to below.

At many stone hillforts a facing ditch is barely present or absent, but they do occur. Both Dinorben, with up to four ramparts, and Pen y corddyn Mawr, with two stone-revetted ramparts around 12m apart (Figure 33), had outside ditches, and at Moel Hiraddug, as well as Mam Tor, there is evidence of ditches with counterscarp bank, but, because of scree from collapsed ramparts at the former, they are not easy to identify. The ditches (in part) of Castell Caer Seion, outside the north-west wall of the large enclosure, must have made a formidable obstacle.

Undoubtedly cappings, parapets and towers would have crowned stone ramparts, but inevitably the ravages of time have taken their toll. However, at Crickley Hill Dixon (1976) found evidence of stone capping on top of one of the stone ramparts and Tre'r Ceiri had high bastions at the main entrance, possible parapets and the wall-walk, as we have seen.

In common with the replacement of box ramparts, a feature of some hillforts is the replacement of stone ramparts also by dump and *glacis* styles of defence. This appears to have been a widespread phenomenon from north Wales and the Marches and the northern Midlands southwards – from Dinas Dinorwic and Dinorben to the Wrekin, Croft Ambrey and Rainsborough and to Llanmelin. At Caer Caradoc (Chapel Lawn), in Shropshire, for example, an initial dry-stone faced rampart of flat siltstone flags was later heightened and widened by one of dump construction (Watson 2002, 24); yet another example of the great variability of hillfort construction depending on local need and preference.

Throughout the above sections the immense development and change in rampart design (and ultimately in site area) over time has been stressed, and the construction sequences of Mam Tor, Crickley Hill and Caynham Camp near Ludlow in Shropshire are just three examples of many and show this well. The Mam Tor excavators found complex evidence of a possible earlier timber palisade, a later rampart, with a core of stone mixed with clay and rubble, being constructed on an artificial platform cut into the slope. It appears that an earlier and smaller rampart had been cut away in the construction of the final bank, the front of which had stepped revetting and a single line of stones at the back. A vertically sided flat-bottomed ditch around 2m wide completed the project. At Crickley Hill a timber-laced rampart destroyed by fire was replaced by massively reconstructed stone defences using the initial burnt rampart as its core. This new rampart was itself burnt and the site subsequently abandoned (Figure 34) (Dixon 1976, 161–2). Caynham's earliest defences, consisting of a timber-laced rampart dating to *c*.390 BC, were later replaced by a smaller stone-revetted bank and later still by the substantial rampart visible today (Watson 2002, 26).

FIGURE 29. Intact stone facework behind extensive collapsed loose stone extending downslope at Caer Drewyn, above Corwen and the River Dee, in Merioneth. The hillfort appears deliberately sited to be seen from the Dee Valley below.

FIGURE 30. The present stone-faced rampart, some 275m long, at the coastal promontory fort of Bolt Tail, overlooking Bigbury Bay in Devon.

FIGURE 31 *(opposite)*. The high stone walls and deep ditches of Worlebury, above Weston-super-Mare in Somerset.

FIGURE 32. Remnants of the massively constructed laid masonry wall of the small enclosure at the western end of Castell Caer Seion, Conwy, Caernarfonshire.

FIGURE 33. The multiple walls and deep inturned north-eastern gate of Pen y corddyn Mawr, Denbighshire set at the head of a natural gully.

FIGURE 34. The entrance and ramparts of Crickley Hill, Gloucestershire (surmounted by a modern observation platform) from the considerable flat interior of the fort. The entrance in Phase 3b would have been a massive and ornate stone structure, with walkway over and barbican with separate gate.

Chevaux-de-frise

The possibility of status enhancement and ability to intimidate and control others, as expressed in hillfort architecture, cannot be ignored (see page 193). One feature of this may be the '*chevaux-de-frise*', which involved the siting of offset rows of stones or, more rarely, timber stakes rammed into the ground, to form, at first sight, a 'minefield' or defensive obstacle seemingly to hamper an attacker's progress. There has been considerable speculation about their purpose and origin, and an Iberian beginning or a common central or eastern European wooden prototype have been proposed (Harbison 1971, 195).

The excavations of Castell Henllys unearthed a fine example (Figure 35) and, at Craig Gwrtheyrn (Llandyssul), in the Teifi catchment of Carmarthenshire, there are remnants of a *chevaux-de-frise* up to 0.6m high outside the outer rampart on the south-western side. But Pen y Gaer (Llanbedr y Cenin) is the most quoted. Here groups of stones up to 1m in height have been placed outside the western and southern outermost rampart and between the two outer ramparts, whilst to the south the feature has a bounding ditch with causeways. That the *chevaux-de-frise* was long-standing at this site is proven by remains below one of the ramparts. The possibility of natural outcrops also serving the same purpose is suggested at Skelmore Heads in Cumbria (Powell 1963, 6), and Gardner (1922, 114) proposed that a 'natural' version exposed across the causeway to the main entrance of Caer Drewyn would have made access difficult for any 'attacker'; but whether one actually existed, or indeed whether any attacker existed, has yet to be ascertained.

However, the *chevaux-de-frise* at Carn Alw in Pembrokeshire is another fine example worth looking at (Mytum and Webster 1989, 263–6; Driver 2007a). The site, located on a rhyolite crag on the northern slopes of Preseli, has defences only on the vulnerable western side, where a dry-stone wall encloses a natural triangular shelf. The stones extend below this wall in an arc, and consist of large boulders *in situ* some 1.5m-plus across and smaller positioned uprights up to 1m in height. Through-access was via a track 1.5m wide lined with boulders, which led to a gap entrance, and the stones are for the most part to one side of the entrance; Castell Henllys has them all to one side. In addition, the overall plan of the entrance track is similar to a variety of small banked enclosures south of the Preselis (possibly all with wooden *chevaux-de-frise*) and to 'banjo' enclosures of southern England. Perhaps local preferences might have applied in this case.

Although evidence for *chevaux-de-frise* in England and Wales is relatively scarce, examples are probably waiting to be found with excavation. Driver (2007a, 138–39), for example, mentions one recently exposed by coastal erosion at the Black Scar Camp coastal promontory fort at Broadhaven in Pembrokeshire and possibly another at the Clawdd y Milwyr fort on St David's Head. However, even a candidate as likely as Castell Caer Seion has proved negative so far, despite investigation. In fact wooden *chevaux-de-frise* might have been the answer in most cases, and there is evidence of five rows of posts being located outside the rampart of the South Barrule fort on the Isle of Man (Gelling 1963). Generally, however, post-hole evidence is lacking, but this might be purely because excavation is so rare outside of existing ramparts and wooden posts would, of course, have been subject to rot, even if made of oak. Wainwright (1970) has calculated a life of around fifteen years for each inch of oak heartwood radius and Harbison (1971, 212) stated that a 15cm post of the same wood would last about forty-five years. Stone, if available, would probably have been favoured.

Additions, annexes and satellites

Annexes are found at many hillforts, but their functions are obscure, much debated and no doubt differed from place to place. Corrals for livestock and extensions of 'living space' have been suggested, whilst the ritual element cannot be ignored. They can be large or small, simple or complex. That of 6ha at Salmonsbury is open to the east where it meets the marsh towards the River Dikler (Dunning 1976, 76), while the sloping annexe of Pen y corddyn Mawr extends for 5.3ha from the 10ha main enclosure. On the other hand, the two additions to Caynham Camp are less than 1ha each, the original western side of the main site being extended to create a new rectangular enclosure and western end, and an additional annexe, perhaps a corral, defined further to the west by a single bank.

The superb annexe to the south-west of the 1.2ha main enclosure at Earl's Hill (Pontesbury) is similar in character to those at Caynham in being more of an 'extension' (Figure 36). Access to it's 1.6ha of elongated hill is via a gap in the southern rampart with a steep slope and causeway across a ditch. A high bank

FIGURE 35. The *chevaux-de-frise* on one side of the entrance at Castell Henllys, Pembrokeshire.

and intermittent counterscarp with outer ditch defines the southern boundary and to the east the precipitous slope is definition enough (Watson 2002, 28). In similar fashion, in south Wales the narrow high-altitude summit enclosure of Allt-y-Esgair, Llangasty near Brecon, with its single, albeit quite strong, rampart, has an annexe to the south of similar construction. As time went by a series of annexes or compounds, possibly for some farming purpose, could be added far downslope of the main enclosure, as at Carn Ingli hillfort (Hogg 1973a) (Figure 37), which lies within a finely preserved area of prehistoric farming and settlement remains.

Although more evidence of annexes or additions to hillforts is coming to light, by the Royal Commission's surveys of Gaer Fawr (Guilsfield) in Montgomeryshire for example, care must be taken in definition. At Caer Drewyn what was initially thought to be an annexe on the northern side is, in fact, part of an earlier enclosure bisected by the wall of the later fort. Similarly, an annexe located outside the main gate of Castell Henllys appears to have been the site of a later Romano-British settlement created after abandonment of the main site, but the exact relationship between the two and the reasons why habitation moved have yet to be decided (Harold Mytum pers. comm.).

Additional features to a site were sometimes provided by outworks of bank and ditch outside the main enclosure, as found at Earl's Hill downslope of the northern entrance. Among others, Tre'r Ceiri, Ffridd Faldwyn and Gaer Fawr (Guilsfield) all have examples, but whether they are incomplete additions to the main enclosure or constructed for some other purpose is unclear. Llanymynech Hill is on the border between Montgomeryshire and Shropshire and an additional section of rampart to the north defines a long narrow strip, perhaps an extra embellishment on the more vulnerable eastern side. The strange 'Outpost' earthwork 250m to the north-east of the Llanmelin fort in south Wales, which has a complex annexe tied to the south-east of the enclosure, seems to have been an early feature and part of the first phase of the site (Pollard *et al.* 2006, 52), but its use is unknown.

The possibility of some hillforts being intimately associated with other 'satellite' sites has also been observed, particularly in the Welsh Marches. Small outlying enclosures at the Lawley, the Roveries and the strongly defended Pontesford, below Earl's Hill, could all be associated with the larger enclosure upslope. But how the two sites interacted, if at all, and what their function was, has been much debated. Did the satellites form an additional defensive mechanism? Was there some social reason similar to that proposed for the pairing of sites (see pages 225–26), or was there no connection at all other than location on the same hill at the same or different times? It has even been suggested that the strange horseshoe shape of Radnor Wood, below Bury Ditches in Shropshire, could indicate an unfinished satellite of the latter, assuming that they were contemporaneous (Hird 2000, 8). There is no answer to these questions as yet.

Entrances and gates

Hillforts often had more than one entrance, and these were sometimes furnished with elaborate gateways. Maiden Castle has entrances to the east and the west, a common feature at Wessex sites to which we will return. The later fort of Burrow Hill Camp in Shropshire has three entrances and Hod Hill five of varying dates, whilst additions to Carn Ingli show twelve entrances through the various, now shattered, walls. The basic form, however, is a simple gap

FIGURE 36. The less-exposed annexe at Earl's Hill, Shropshire, more than doubled the size of the original enclosure, which is located on the crest of the hill.

FIGURE 37. Walled enclosures downslope of and outside the main enclosure of Carn Ingli, above Newport in Pembrokeshire.

FIGURE 38. The dual-portal Period I South Gate at Midsummer Hill, Herefordshire, viewed from the interior of the hillfort. The two flanking guard chambers can be clearly seen. Redrawn after Stanford 1981.

and passageway through the defences, as found at Caer Cadwgan and Caer Pencarreg in Cardiganshire and Chalbury in Dorset.

At most hillforts, stout timber gates would have been located at the end of, or along, the passageway. The eastern gate of Hollingbury was hung simply on two vertical timbers 3.7m apart at the ends of the box rampart (Cunliffe 1991, 330). It is probable that this simple 'single-portal' design would have been followed at many hillforts, especially, but not always, in the early phases of development. Danebury's first gate probably dates from the sixth century BC and that at Ffridd Faldwyn from the late Bronze Age/early Iron Age. Ralston (2006, 72), however, poses the intriguing possibility that at some sites there might have been no permanent gates as such; rather, temporary arrangements brought into service only as need arose.

As time progressed gates and entrances could become more complicated, often in response to alterations and/or additions to a site, with, at some, a 'dual-portal' arrangement. Such gates are seen in a later phase of Ffridd Faldwyn, around the sixth to four centuries BC, and at Croft Ambrey, of similar date. Pen Dinas (Aberystwyth) had four posts in a square holding the gates and at Caer Cadwgan even more posts were involved. But at Midsummer Hill a dual-portal gate preceded the final single-portal arrangement at the south gate (see pages 64–5) (Figure 38).

More sophisticated were entrances involving a lengthy passageway overlooked by ramparts, such as the magnificent western entrance of Old Oswestry, which can be seen in the foreground of Figure 4, and corridors were often formed by 'inturning' the ramparts towards the interior of the fort. Sometimes only a hint of an inturn remains, with a short gap through the ramparts, as Bodbury Ring, above the Cardingmill Valley in Shropshire shows (Figure 39). There can be many slight variations: Pen y Crug near Brecon, for example, shows a single

FIGURE 39. The short gap entrance at Bodbury Ring in Shropshire. With no visible causeway across the ditch, possibly dated later than the bank.

relatively simple and slightly inturned entrance well, but the passageway narrows towards the high innermost rampart, where there was possibly a gate. Sometimes one inturn is much longer than the other, as at Castell Cawr, here probably to accommodate a single guard chamber, features to which we will return below.

However, inturns could also be imposing, the south-western Iron Age gate of Hod Hill being a fine example (Figure 40), and the massive 5m-high ramparts of Caynham Camp are cut through by a deeply inturned passageway at the original south-east entrance. Stone-built hillforts exhibit these features particularly well, the ramparts at Caer Drewyn being deeply inturned on both sides of the stone entrance passage, as are the north-eastern and north-western gates of Pen y corddyn Mawr, which, like their simpler southern counterpart, are set at the head of natural gullies (see Figure 33). Work is needed on any regional variations that might exist, but Davies and Lynch (2000, 156, after Probert 1976) suggest that deeply inturned entrances are associated with multivallate dump ramparts in Wales, those at Twyn y Gaer in Monmouthshire formed by additions to the ends of the inturned ramparts.

The corridors formed by inturning the banks could be very long, and the north-eastern entrance of Bury Ditches in Shropshire is formed by the inner rampart and the second on the northern side turning inwards on either side, producing a passageway 40m long (Figure 41) (Watson 2002, 22). Although a small site, Moel y Gaer (Llantysilio), as already shown in Figure 18, has a 20m inturned entrance to the east through the single 3m-high bank.

Sometimes corridors were formed by 'out-turning' the banks away from the interior; those of Uffington Castle connected with the counterscarp (Gary Lock pers. comm.) (Figure 42). An unusual variant at Earl's Hill has, at the north-eastern gate, a simple inturn to the eastern bank and an out-turn to the western, possibly the result of restrictions in construction imposed by the precipitous terrain of the eastern flanks.

Simple entrances in both north-east and north-west Wales tended to be just passageways through the rampart wall (Davies and Lynch 2000, 153), but even this required the use of considerable building techniques. Looking again at Castell Caer Seion and Tre'r Ceiri gives an idea of the skill and effort required in construction. The entrances to both enclosures at Castell Caer Seion had *c.*5m long corridors with a possible wooden bridge over; the ends of the ramparts forming the passages comprised of large orthostats (Figure 43). Bridge access over such passageway entrances would have had obvious strategic advantages and has been found at Midsummer Hill, Croft Ambrey and possibly at Uffington Castle (Lock *et al.* 2003, 93), but could have been a much more common feature.

At Tre'r Ceiri Hogg (1962) found that there were two narrow main entrances through the inner dry-stone rampart to the south-west and north-west, with additional, also narrow, openings to the north, west and south. The principal north-west entrance had a 15m-long passage with outer flanking walls extending below the rampart for 8m. This led to a terraced path with another gate through an outer defensive wall. The northern narrow postern or 'sally port' entrance through the inner rampart is today bridged by a massive (reconstructed) stone lintel (Figure 44), suggesting that the wall had been carried over the entrance.

Entrances could be embellished with protecting outworks, hornworks and barbican, all inserted to either confuse, intimidate or impress the visitor, benign or not. These could become extremely complicated, and none more so than at the two entrances of Maiden Castle shown in Figure 10.

Paradoxically, although quite large forts, such as Caer y Tŵr on Anglesey, might only have one entrance – here a concealed and overlooked narrow gully (Lynch 1991, 264), as shown in Figure 79 – small forts could have complex entrances, Pen y Clun, overlooking the Clywedog reservoir in Montgomeryshire, with its crooked entry passage being one (Haslam 1979, 145). Complex multiple defences at the entrance are characteristic of these western and mid Wales sites, as found by Toby Driver (2007b) in Cardiganshire at Pen y Bannau (Strata Florida), Castell near Tregaron and Pen'r Allt (Llandiloes) which has triple defences, and we will look at some reasons for this in Chapter 10.

Guard chambers

The excavations at the early entrance of Castell Henllys showed an elaborate arrangement. A long passageway, revetted in stone, ended in a timber tower on which the gates were hung and behind which were four semi-circular 'guard chambers' in pairs. Much space has been devoted in the literature to the construction and use of these stone or timber structures found at many sites behind the gate, and which appeared around the fifth century BC or earlier (their radiocarbon date at Croft Ambrey and Rainsborough). Although they are mostly found along the Welsh Marches, into south Wales, as at Lodge Hill Camp (Pollard *et al.* 2006, 48), and the east Midlands to Northamptonshire, there are some possible examples in Wessex. One interpretation of the gate at Uffington Castle has guard chambers linked to the possible walkway over as mentioned above (Lock *et al.* 2003, 93).

There appear to be two general types of guard chamber in terms of their location: those set behind the rampart ends, for example, Caer Caradoc (Church Stretton), Dinorben and Moel Hiraddug, and those located at the end of long corridors, as at Pen y corddyn Mawr, the Wrekin, Titterstone Clee and Caer Drewyn. Although they usually occur in multiples, both Castell Cawr and Penycloddiau appear to have only one. At Croft Ambrey, where a sandstone pivot-stone supposedly for a simple door of an earlier guard chamber was found (Stanford 1974, 185), there were changes in layout over time, and other sites show this as well. For example, there was no made road through the south-western gate of South Cadbury during the Iron Age and this resulted in the track becoming so heavily rutted by cart-wheels, feet and hooves that the underlying rock became worn down to a depth of nearly 2m. It was necessary, therefore, to construct successive guard chambers to somehow accommodate these changes in levels in a very complicated sequence (Woodward and James 2000, 84).

FIGURE 40. The imposing Iron Age south-west inturned entrance, reused in the Roman period, at Hod Hill in Dorset.

FIGURE 41. The complicated and intimidating 'staggered' south-west entrance (in the foreground) of Bury Ditches in Shropshire, formed by the northern ramparts overlapping those coming from the south and resulting in an overlooked passageway 90m long. Opposite, the north-east gate is formed by deep inturns creating 40m of exposed passage into the hillfort interior.

FIGURE 42. Out-turns connecting with the counterscarp at the main and western gate of Uffington Castle, Berkshire.

FIGURE 43. The entrances to both enclosures at Castell Caer Seion, Conwy, Caernarfonshire showed a passageway between large orthostats which formed the ends of the rampart. Traces of paving have been found.

Guard chambers tend to be either rectangular or semi-circular in form; the former seem to dominate in the Welsh Marches (see Figure 38 of Midsummer Hill), while the latter are shown to effect in the Midlands; Rainsborough for example, which also has a hearth and evidence of floor repair, as at Pen y corddyn Mawr and Moel Hiraddug.

The information base on which to consider guard chambers is extremely poor and finds within them very scarce, making interpretation difficult if not impossible, but perhaps the excavation of their wider setting would help. 'Guard chamber', of course, implies fortification and military use and, undoubtedly, this idea has been overplayed. However, among other possibilities, a ritual use for these structures has been proposed – Mark Bowden (2006, 433) suggesting 'spirit houses' akin to those of the Amba people of the Ruwenzori Mountains of present-day Uganda, whose enclosure entrances are guarded by spirits inhabiting a pair of huts immediately inside. A form of gatehouse designed to shelter those manning the gate is the obvious possibility, but why two or four? And why mainly at only one of often multiple entrances? Another major question is why these structures are not seen in any quantity in other areas of northern and southern England and, other than pure fashion, for which we have no real answers as yet.

Change over time

Entrances, gates and adjacent guard chambers were often blocked, added to and altered over time. The north-eastern entrance of Garn Boduan was blocked by a well-built wall whilst the gateway was in good working order (Hogg 1962, 26), and at the Wrekin alterations to the ramparts around 400 BC resulted in the inner south-west entrance being extended inwards and timber-roofed guard chambers added (Watson 2002, 34). The blocking of entrances is returned to in Chapter 8.

The south gate of Midsummer Hill, investigated by Stanford (1981), is one of the two entrances to the fort and here he recognised seventeen phases of development. It is worth looking at in more detail and has been shown in Figure 38. The first inturned entrance through the defences was initially revetted in timber and stone and had a 6.1m-wide corridor constructed against the foot of Hollybush Hill and terraced into the valley side to keep it clear of adjacent springs and marsh. The revetted timber posts would have been flush with the stonework (as at Maiden Castle: Wheeler 1943, 34), and are similar to a timber-laced rampart at Moel y Gaer (Rhosesmor) (Guilbert 1973, 22). Initially there were two rectangular timber guard chambers, east and west, the latter measuring 3 × 2.1m. The wide entrance required a two-portal arrangement, but the trackway appears to have been surfaced only on one side, which was seemingly sufficient for access most of the time. Metal hinges are absent in the British Iron Age and, as a result, a lintel was probably used. Around 404 BC the timber guard chambers were replaced by stone versions which were in turn demolished *c.*337 BC, and the gateway redesigned with the first of a series of simple, narrower, stone-walled corridors leading to a gate between two posts (single portal) at the end. A bridge, sited obliquely behind the gate, was added later; such an arrangement allowing for the different heights of the ramparts, a feature also found at Croft Ambrey.

Gates would have had to be constructed of stout and durable materials and oak was the obvious choice for structural work, being also easily cleaved. Stanford averaged the useful life of an oak gatepost at Midsummer Hill at thirty-three years, and at Croft Ambrey thirty-eight years (Stanford 1974, 243).

There was also change at Maiden Castle and the complex entrances seen today are the result of alteration from the time of the extended earlier enclosure of around 450–300 BC. The eastern entrance is a redesign of the earlier 600 BC model and seems to have been associated with a box rampart with double gate and an outer hornwork. Similarly, the more elaborate western entrance, of about the same date, has multiple outworks, giving an imposing and frightening introduction to any visitor, and is shown in Figure 10.

Was it all about access?

Entrances and gateways appear to have performed functions apart from simple access or its prevention although, no matter how we try to ignore the point, at a wide variety of hillforts the design and complexity of entrances seem well adapted for defensive purposes. However, status, display and intimidation must also be considered, Mytum (1996) suggesting that the size and complexity of the gates and defences of the larger hillforts invested them with 'monumental and symbolic functions'. There is nothing unusual in this. The social status of the owners of the great medieval castles and stately houses has long been manifested in an imposing entrance, the first 'port of call' of the visitor. Thus, the subsequently blocked entrance to the small enclosure of Castell Caer Seion was impressive, with a passage 5.8m wide and 7m long and 'megalithic' orthostats facing the overlapping ends of the ramparts (Griffiths and Hogg 1956, 72). At Ring Chesters in Northumberland the nature of the commanding entrance, with architectural elaboration and massive stone flanking ramparts, suggests that it was to be seen and approached from a specific direction, a feature also of Yeavering Bell and other small sites in the area (Oswald and Pearson 2005, 122).

This might also have been the case at Old Oswestry. Whilst the eastern entrance passageway is flanked and overlooked by a bank on its south side, it is a meagre affair compared with the western entrance, which must have been nothing short of spectacular. To gain entry a deep uphill 20m-wide passageway, flanked and overlooked on either side by ramparts, would have had to be negotiated. Between the third and fourth ramparts on either side of the trackway are eleven deep pits or hollows. The exact purpose of these unique features is unknown and theories abound – from quarry scoops (they do have some similarity to those at Hod Hill) to water storage tanks and livestock corralls – but to enhance the formidable and

imposing nature of the entrance and site as a whole, with its serried ranks of five to seven high ramparts, they have no equal in British hillforts. Figure 4 shows them well. As Watson (2002, 31) succinctly puts it: 'prehistoric psychological warfare or an ostentatious statement of self-esteem? Perhaps both.'

Other sites suggest an element of ostentation and display – Rainsborough and Crickley Hill for example. The former had an elaborate entrance, with a causewayed approach between massive defensive ditches flanked by bastions and palisades to a gateway overlooked by a bridge with two flanking guard chambers (Avery *et al.* 1967). At Crickley Hill there was a complex stone-built structure of barbican and projecting gate, resulting in a courtyard before the main gate itself, with bastions and over-walkway (Dixon 1972a). However, as in all hillfort architecture, the ritual element cannot be ignored. The entrance or doorway has held an element of superstition from prehistory to modern times; this will be returned to in Chapter 8. Moreover, as with annexes, care must always be taken when looking at hillfort entrances without adequate investigation. A gap in the rampart seen today, such as the south-west entrance of Chalbury, the southern entrance of Moel Fenlli and those at Warham Camp, may not be original.

FIGURE 44. The reconstructed northern postern entrance lintel, over which would have run the wall-walk, at Tre'r Ceiri, on the Llŷn peninsula in Caernarfonshire.

The problem of fire

As well as the susceptibility to rot and collapse a major problem with the use of timber in hillfort construction was the danger of fire and, as a result, it seems that by the fourth century BC timber-lacing had stopped being used. Accidental or deliberate firing would have taken their toll, but to fire a gate from outside the fort, perhaps at the end of a long inturned passage, whilst being assailed by those positioned on ramparts above, would not be easy, although possible ritual firing has been proposed (Hill 1996). The bronze finds from the burnt defences at Moel Hiraddug have also been suggested by Bowden and McOmish (1987, 78) as indicating fire with a ritual dimension rather than being just the vestige of some military intervention. However, the frequency of lightning strike on exposed hilltops must not be discounted and could have been one of the most common causes of fire damage.

There are many examples of fire from north to south, too numerous to mention, but a few will give some idea of the problem. At Dinorben rafts of timber staged on a timber-revetted clay bank of circa tenth-century BC date were subsequently destroyed by fire, and the destruction of the ramparts and gateway of Rainsborough possibly followed an attack, as a charred skeleton was found beneath the burnt timbers of the southern guard chamber roof (Kidd 2004, 50). Similarly, the timber-laced rampart of the first fort of Ffridd Faldwyn suffered the same fate, as did the gates and part of the timber-laced rampart at Castell Henllys.

However, whilst the destruction by fire of the north-east gate of Bury Wood Camp in Wiltshire (possibly Roman work: King 1962, 192–3) is thought to have reached some 500–600°C, the process of 'vitrification', whereby stone is heated to 1,000°C-plus and fuses together to form a solid mass (experiments undertaken by Childe and Thorneycroft (1938) at Scottish hillforts), is rarely found in England and Wales. Whether a construction technique or aggressive act, it has been suggested at Moel y Gaer (Llanbedr) (Fiona Gale pers. comm.) and at Caer Euni, near Bala in Merioneth, where evidence for this process from the north-west corner ditch had probably fallen from the rampart above (Lynch 1995, 84). Likewise, at Castercliff the inner timber-laced rampart appears partly vitrified (Haselgrove 1996, 67; Harding 2004, 47). Anecdotal evidence for vitrification of Haughmond Hill's rampart, near Shrewsbury in Shropshire, has not been substantiated.

All of these examples testify to the danger hillfort inhabitants faced, made even more terrifying on hilltops exposed to the prevailing wind. Although work is required on whether the design of hillfort interiors shows any sign of taking the problem of fire into consideration, the inhabitants may have considered fire to be, not only revered, but also to have been just another aspect of life 'in the lap of the gods'. In the next chapter we will look inside these defensive circuits and see how things were organised.

CHAPTER FIVE

Hillfort Interiors

....

Having looked at the predominantly exterior features of hillforts from an 'architectural' viewpoint, what can be said about the area enclosed within these banks, walls and ditches?

First of all, size differs greatly from place to place. In the past Stanwick in Yorkshire, at 340ha, has often been referred to as the largest in area, but, although the original Tofts hillfort of 5.3ha was within its borders, this huge enclosure really served similar functions to the southern oppida, more of which will be said later. Having said that, the largest 'hillfort' in Britain (if indeed it can be called one) is probably Bindon Hill, the result of an earthwork of over 2300m in length following the cliffs overlooking the English Channel from near Worbarrow Bay westwards to meet the north-western cliffs of Lulworth Cove, as shown in Figure 22. Other large enclosures which may more properly be called hillforts include the 85ha Ham Hill, the 56ha Llanymynech Hill (the largest site in Wales) and the 54ha Borough Hill in Northamptonshire. These put into perspective the 22ha Hod Hill and 18.5ha Maiden Castle. Most, however, are much smaller – Croft Ambrey of 4ha, Pilsdon Pen of 3.2ha and Conderton Camp of around 1.95ha are typical.

Site layouts

The shape of hillforts is extremely variable: they may be virtually round (Badbury Rings); more or less square (Hod Hill); triangular (Abbotsbury Castle overlooking Chesil Beach in Dorset) or hourglass-shaped (Beacon Hill in Hampshire). Within, what is often seen today, if not covered by trees as at Gaer Fawr (Guilsfield) (Figure 45), are grassy areas grazed by a few sheep or cattle, as Figure 46 of Cadbury Hill (Congresbury) in Somerset shows. Interior layouts can be as variable as their architecture: they can be very simple or very complex, random or zoned, and only a few rudimentary words can be attempted here. Some show no sign of order, with structures scattered about Tre'r Ceiri (Figure 47) and the sheltered Castell Henllys, or huddled out of the wind next to the ramparts in hollows or in quarry scoops, as found at Sutton Walls. The imposing Dinedor Camp, above Hereford, had its heaviest occupation 3.7–11m behind the ramparts, with nothing on the crest of the hill (Kenyon 1954), and the protection afforded by a high bank or wall should not be underestimated. However, some hillforts exhibit a very definite order in the way the layout of

FIGURE 45. The ramparts of Gaer Fawr at Guilsfield in Montgomeryshire, managed as an amenity and conservation woodland now being lost to trees and scrub.

the interior was arranged. Norsebury Ring in Berkshire is zoned, with a high concentration of features (pits, quarries, huts) in only two areas, the rest being left emptier, whilst the structures of Yeavering Bell were clustered around the two summits of the exposed hill. Both Segsbury and St Catharine's Hill, Winchester, have a concentration of activity in the centre dominating the rest of the enclosure.

Some sites exhibit more order still and examples are widespread about the country. Castle Ditches (Tisbury), a large multivallate hillfort in Wiltshire, exhibits a rudimentary street plan with hut emplacements (Corney and Payne 2006b, 107), and the excavation of Woolbury, in Hampshire, as part of the Danebury Environs Programme, revealed that the interior settlement area had been divided by small ditches into a number of enclosures or paddocks (Cunliffe and Poole 2000a; Corney and Payne 2006b, 80). Further north in the Marches, despite the 1:3 and 1:4 gradients, Stanford (1981) found that Midsummer Hill's four-post structures were set out in lines on small terraces cut into the hillside along the contours, of which some 483 have been recorded on both constituent hills of the site, but especially on the eastern slopes of Midsummer Hill itself (Bowden 2005a, 22). These showed a permanence and stability, akin to those of Credenhill and Croft Ambrey, which lasted for over 500 years of occupation, with between four and six phases of post replacement. Graeme Guilbert also found indications of a street plan at Moel y Gaer (Rhosesmor) and, although interpretation is hampered by destruction, there are indications of a zoning of different types of structure about Moel Hiraddug. As there is no evidence so

far for roundhouses in the western part of Lodge Hill Camp, this is inferred by the excavators as possibly the result of an 'industrial' or 'specialised', rather than 'domestic', use (Pollard *et al.* 2006, 47).

It is possible that a stable orderly layout could have been far more widespread than is indicated by the limited excavations which have taken place so far. At Danebury this appears to be the case and the detailed excavation and reports have thrown substantial light on how a Wessex hillfort developed over some 500 years. A main road crossed the interior from gate to gate, and was kept open virtually for the whole life of the fort, with other roads servicing the various structures. Granary-type buildings ran along these roads, with huts sited in the lee of the rampart for shelter.

However, at other sites things could change over time and, whilst the initial dense clustering of huts and associated features of the 600 BC enclosure of Maiden Castle did not suggest any internal planning, after a period of abandonment a major developmental phase of post-450 BC showed a more regular plan, with a line of huts behind the rampart in seemingly ordered plots and associated areas for metalworking or other uses. The hillfort was split up

FIGURE 46. The grassy interior of Cadbury Hill at Congresbury in Somerset, kept reasonably clear of scrub by grazing stock.

FIGURE 47. The remnants of the walls of one of the many stone huts at Tre'r Ceiri on the Llŷn peninsula in Caernarfonshire; the site has been the subject of extensive reconstruction and conservation of stonework.

into specific compartments by tracks, but whether these delineated discrete social units or were for some other purpose is not known. Later, around 100 BC, the chaotic layout of earlier times seems to have returned (Gale 2003, 121).

Interior structures

The archetypal image of the Iron Age is the 'roundhouse', typically thatched with reed or straw and sitting conveniently in the middle of a hillfort or small farmstead enclosure. But whether this model, of which the 'Pimperne' build of Peter Reynolds' at Butser has provided the basis for many later reconstructions, was really like those of the Iron Age has been questioned (Townend 2007). Although in some areas with readily available hard stone vestiges of actual buildings still remain, despite post-hole evidence, it will never be known what habitation was really like – but we can make an informed guess. Buildings were probably very variable in design and would have employed a wide variety of construction materials according to geographical location and availability; the resources of the chalk downs of Wessex very different from those coming from the rocky areas of Cornwall, Wales or the north. It has also been suggested by Townend (2007) that these many materials would not have been thought of as being purely 'raw materials to be exploited', but as having a 'meaningful' entity in themselves in coming from highly charged symbolic places – reed from water; clay from the earth etc. and, as such, would have imbued the structure itself with a sacred identity which was not seen merely as a place just to live in. With this in mind let us look at a little archaeological evidence from hillforts and construct some models of what things may have been like.

Structural convention dictates that a thatched roof of reed or straw requires a 45° slope to be watertight, and modern reconstructions of the typical conical-shaped roundhouse have relied on this fact of life. Thus, poles extend from a circular wall built of wattle, wattle and daub, stone or planks up to a central apex with or without interior supporting poles, the roof thatched accordingly. Fine dry-stone hut walls have been found at both Conderton Camp and Chalbury, one at the latter estimated to have reached 0.75m in height. Materials could vary about an individual site as well – there was a mix of stone and timber-framed walls at Maiden Castle, although the latter predominated (Thomas 2005, 84). Daub (a mixture of clay, straw and animal dung) would be applied to wattle walls, and impressions of this process have been found at Eggardon (Wells 1978, 61), or just used for the walls alone. Burnt daub comes from Salmonsbury (Dunning 1976, 85). This does not mean, however, that all roundhouses were thatched with reed or straw. Heather and turf could perform perfectly well and indeed the walls could also be made of the latter. Thatch might have been kept in place by the use of weights, with limestone and sandstone examples from both Croft Ambrey (one of 21.4kg) and The Rumps cliff castle. Porches were also a widespread feature, found, for example, from Moel y Gaer (Rhosesmor) to Castell Henllys to Danebury. Reconstructed roundhouses have proved popular attractions: Butser in Hampshire, St Fagans in south Wales and Castell Henllys, where roundhouses and associated structures have been reconstructed on the exact position of excavated post-holes, all give an idea of what these structures might have looked like (Figure 48).

Thus, the roundhouse is probably only one of many types of building using different materials depending upon time, location, availability, need and perhaps even fashion. For example, beginning about 700 BC at Crickley Hill a village accommodating about 100 people and defended by a strong timber-reinforced stone wall with ditch, had long timber houses and granaries aligned along a street running east to west on the flat top of the hill. A bridge crossed the single gate in the defences. Later, around 500 BC, a new settlement was established on the same site with small roundhouses, four-posters and a larger building 15m in diameter, with no roof-supports, and situated just inside the entrance.

Large structures such as this have been found near the gate of other hillforts – notably two large roundhouses at both Hambledon Hill and Yeavering Bell – and there has been speculation as to whether they were either the abode of important individuals or embodied some ritual meaning. A magnetometer survey in 1996 of Liddington Castle revealed a roundhouse 18m in diameter standing in the centre of the site, and one of 14.5m in diameter was similarly positioned at Trevelgue Head. The investigations of Hod Hill and Dinorben revealed large buildings described as the 'chief's quarters', but there is scant evidence for this, and places for meetings, ceremonial or maybe spirit houses, cannot be discounted as possibilities.

We will never really know what these buildings were like as no whole prehistoric roofed examples survive in England and Wales, but where building stone was aplenty it is possible that huts were constructed entirely of stone, and certainly the larger 'brochs' of Scotland point to this direction. What type of roof these structures had is a matter of guesswork, but there is a great deal of evidence of stone-built structures in north Wales for example, and those at Tre'r Ceiri come in a wide variety of shapes and sizes, seemingly jumbled together, criss-crossing the hillfort, as we have seen in Figure 47. Some are round (Gurnard's Head cliff castle, near St Ives in Cornwall), or almost round (Garn Boduan on the Llŷn), some D-shaped, some rectangular. Good outlines of round stone structures can also be seen at St David's Head, Carn Ingli and Castell Caer Seion. Climatic factors, contours, site characteristics and pure function would no doubt have dictated outline and roof design. The building of stone huts on the less steep and more sheltered eastern side of Gurnard's Head was helped by natural platforms in the rock (Gordon 1940, 97), but, even so, some foundations had to be hewn into solid rock, so dictating the final outcome. Mant 'huts' at Croft Ambrey resemble 'four-posters' (Figure 49).

On sloping and irregular sites, therefore, it was common to excavate terraces into the hillside to form a flat base for construction, particularly on the hard rock sites of the north, Wales and the Marches and the south-west. This arrangement is visible, among other sites, at Mam Tor, the Wrekin, Midsummer Hill and Pen Dinas, with the shape and size of buildings depending on conditions. Pen Dinas has one hut 'semi-eliptical' in shape with a straight front dicated by the physical nature of the site (Forde *et al.* 1963, 145). However, many other hillforts, such as Maiden Castle, Old Oswestry and Cadbury Hill (Congresbury), as we have seen in Figure 46, have a flat interior which would not have required much preparation.

The term 'roundhouse' implies habitation, but not all such structures would have served as houses and, as in the medieval period, a single building could have housed both people and animals together. No doubt separate byres and barns for stock would have been required, at least at certain times of the year, and tools and equipment would have needed some form of storage. In addition, the existence of post-holes does not necessarily mean that a structure would have had a roof, and simple corrals may also have existed.

Excavation reports are littered with measurements of buildings and it is not intended to analyse any of these in detail. Nevertheless, Thomas (2005, table 4), in looking at the internal diameter of eighty Iron Age roundhouses, mostly from hillforts, found that just over two-thirds measured between 6m and 11m.

FIGURE 48. The reconstructed roundhouses and structures at Castell Henllys, Pembrokeshire, have stood for some twenty years.

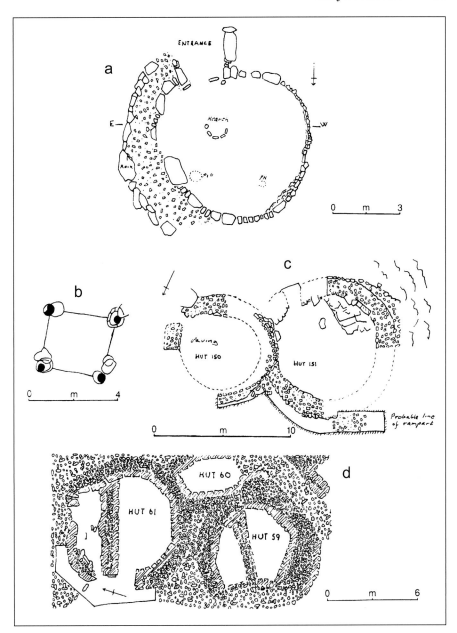

FIGURE 49. Hut plans:
a) Gurnard's Head,
Cornwall; b) Croft
Ambrey, Herefordshire;
c) Garn Boduan,
Caernarfonshire; d) Tre'r
Ceiri, Caernarfonshire.
Redrawn after: a)
Gordon 1940; b)
Stanford 1974;
c) and d) Hogg 1962.

At Danebury the principal house-type was a circular structure some 6–9m in diameter, the seventy examples excavated falling into two distinct types: those whose walls were made up of upright planks (the most common) and those whose walls were made of wattle. Whilst a conical roof may have been taken down to the ground, there was also evidence of a 'shallow porch-like structure' with the doorframe kept rigid by lintels. No doors survived but a removable planked or wattle barrier may have been used. Inside were rammed chalk floors. In some examples there was no evidence that wall-timbers had been embedded in the ground, suggesting that they could have been removable, a common feature of many primitive societies today. It is also possible that there were conical wattlework buildings, thatched and easy to move (Cunliffe 1993a, 57–63).

An example of a hut built in the sheltered lee of a rampart comes from Bredon Hill. Here, 2.4m away from the tail of the bank, a circular hut 3.7m in diameter was defined by six large post-holes set in pairs nearly 0.6m across and 0.3m in depth. The walls appeared to be of wattle and daub. An additional pair of post-holes on the western side indicated a projecting porch, and three shallow post-holes on the south side may have formed a lean-to, seen also at Sutton Walls. Drainage was also important and there was evidence of one of two pits serving as a drainage sump with a shallow water catchment and small drain or gully; a drainage ditch encircled the structure with paving up to the rampart (Hencken 1938, 28–9). The posts were positioned by first digging a pit 1.5m across with one face vertical and the other sloping. The posts were then set against the vertical side and small stones packed into the hole and around the post from the sloping side until secure; the hole was finally filled in with earth and rubble.

The floor of such a building would probably have been of puddled clay or chalk, which forms a surprisingly durable surface especially if it contains a modicum of animal dung, hay or straw and/or ashes from the fire, and perhaps with small stones added for strength, as found at Castell Caer Seion. In early Ireland a flock of sheep would be left in a new building for some time to puddle the floor, whilst a ceremony or gathering within the building would have had a similar effect. Paving of part of the floor, especially of the periphery, was also likely earlier on in the Iron Age; complete paving or cobbling of hut interiors was a later practice (Pope 2007, 219). But the excavations of Salmonsbury unearthed evidence that irregular rough-stone paving provided an occupation surface (Dunning 1976).

Pits and 'four-posters'

The sunken pit and the so-called 'four-post' (or more) structure also characterise Iron Age enclosures and hillforts. Their distribution varies about the country and both had ritual connotations (see Chapter 8), but from a strictly utilitarian point of view, they filled a specific niche in the domestic and community calendar.

Well into the last century, and indeed up to around the 1950s, a favourite theory was that pits served as 'dwellings'. This interpretation appears strange and amusing today but was taken quite seriously at the time. Thus, it was considered that (at Maiden Castle): 'a respectable pit, which presumably housed at least the members of the family and the dogs, was often no more than five or six feet across on the floor with the sides overhanging to form a smaller entrance' (Benfield 1947, 31). However, more scientific interpretations had emerged earlier. The German archaeologist Gerhard Bersu excavated the Iron Age farmstead of Little Woodbury in Wiltshire in 1939 (Bersu 1940) and, dismissing pit-dwellings, suggested water storage, general rubbish collection or storage of grain over the winter; the latter hypothesis emanating from the excavations of Pitt-Rivers (1888) on Cranborne Chase. Here grain was found in post-holes, and there have been odd occurrences of this in settlement and hillfort contexts ever since.

The finding of carbonised cereal grains within pits does not necessarily mean storage, of course, and other uses have been considered (Ellison and Drewett 1971, 183–5), such as water storage, as at Staple Howe in Yorkshire, clay-puddling pits for pot-making or just general use. However, the predominant feeling is that they were primarily for grain storage. This has been backed up by historical and ethnographic evidence, Bersu himself referring to corn pit storage in Middle Age Hungary, later pit use among the Omahas North American Indians (where dried meat and furs as well as corn were stored) and 'present day' use in Romania (Bersu 1940). The Shimshal of northern Pakistan continue to bury yak butter underground before it is consumed.

Whilst it has been suggested that some shallower pits might have contained baskets or pottery jars to act as more portable means of storage (Bersu 1940; Cunliffe and Phillipson 1968), many excavated pits contain human and animal bone, and Richard Bradley (2005, 170) has considered pit function in relation to ritual and domestic life in prehistory. Pits used for human burial provided 'an ideal symbol of death and regeneration'. Quoting Williams (2003), he proposed that grain, in being buried after the harvest, comes to life again the following year and eventually, after this utilitarian use, pits perform a ritualistic function.

However, it was the work of Barry Cunliffe at Danebury, coupled with experiments at Butser (Reynolds 1979), which set the seal on grain storage for a considerable number of pits at least. It was found that grain keeps well under such conditions for long periods providing conditions are air-tight. Thus, in prehistory when a pit was closed the remaining oxygen around the grains would be taken up by fungal growth and the resultant carbon dioxide would assist the preservation process. This system was best employed for dormant grain to be sown the following season, whilst this year's harvest for consumption would be stored above ground in granaries. However, as Cunliffe (1993b, 18) pointed out, not all pits fit in with this theory on design grounds – a vertical-sided pit would be more difficult to seal than a narrow-mouthed version and, therefore, the former might have been used for other purposes.

The sheer density of pits from southern English hillforts is astonishing. The various excavations at the Caburn produced 140 chalk-cut pits (Hamilton 1998, 24; Drewett and Hamilton 1999); at Worlebury ninety-three pits were exposed and undoubtedly many more remain; and at Barbury Castle, magnetometer survey has determined the existence of many thousands of pits, although relatively few hut sites (Corney and Payne 2006a, 147). The greatest density so far actually discovered was the 2,399 at Danebury, 1,707 of which were examined. As over half of the site was excavated this sample was more than enough to allow analysis. It follows that there could have been around 5,000 pits in total, with storage capacity greatly in excess of the needs of those living

FIGURE 50. Stone-lined storage pit from Sir Mortimer Wheeler's excavations at Maiden Castle. Now considered to be predominantly for the storage of grain, these pits were formerly thought to be 'dwellings'.

SOCIETY OF ANTIQUARIES OF LONDON.

there (Cunliffe 1993a, 80). The Maiden Castle pits would also have run to many thousands (Figure 50).

Many hillforts show a great deal of post-hole evidence for small square or rectangular structures with sides around 2.5m to 3.5m in length (Figure 51). Often called 'four-posters', they can come in 'six-post' or, less commonly, up to 'nine-post' variations – Harting Beacon, for example, had both four-post and six-post variants (Bedwin 1978, 230–1). For years archaeologists have agonised over their use. Were they granaries (two at Crickley Hill were full of barley when

FIGURE 51. Reconstructed 'four-poster' structure at Castell Henllys in Pembrokeshire. Although this example has been thatched, this would not always have been the case and a variety of other durable roofing materials would have been used – if, that is, there was a roof at all, the post holes signifying a corral or some other structure.

they caught fire: Dyer 1981, 19), some other type of roofed building or, perhaps, entirely unroofed? Excarnation platforms and watch towers have been mooted at Staple Howe (Brewster 1963, 47–55), for example, and a four-post structure near the 'Central Entrance', overlooking the dead ground towards the spring water-supply of Conderton Camp, could have served as some sort of tower as a response to 'uneasy times within the region' (Thomas 2005, 82–3). There may be more here, therefore, than a pure storage function and the possibility of social display intimately associated with ritual is considered on page 153.

The actual location of four-posters on a site may be significant. At Grimthorpe and Wandlebury in Cambridgeshire four-posters were found on the edge of the hillforts, seemingly arranged in groups and possibly family-orientated. Sharples (2007, 180), in discussing the social and symbolic importance of food storage capacity of Wessex sites, suggests that four-posters, so positioned, would have enhanced the visibility of stored foodstuffs to those outside of the fort, with obvious implications for perceived status. In contrast, at Staple Howe a four-post structure was located for some reason in the centre of the hillfort (Stead 1968, 158), suggesting a degree of importance. It does seem probable, therefore, that the position of four-posters within a site could have had symbolic meaning.

Whereas four-posters are found throughout England and Wales pits are predominantly confined to southern areas and the Midlands. In Wales and the Marches deep pits are noticeably absent, with only a few shallow examples. Even in southern England their distribution is variable. The Ivinghoe Beacon excavations produced no pits nor evidence for corn growing as such, with only five quern fragments being unearthed (Cotton and Frere 1968, 202), and none came to light at Pilsdon Pen, suggesting either that the excavator was digging in the wrong place or that the fort was outside grain-producing areas and was purely pastoral in nature (Gelling 1970; 1971; 1972; 1977). Was there any connection between the use of pits and four-posters? Although Cunliffe (1993a, 79) indicates that the use of both as granaries is 'totally unproven', connections have been made. Initially it was thought that corn for consumption was stored in the pits and seed corn kept in the above-ground granaries, but after experimentation this hypothesis was reversed. Nevertheless, many questions still remain to be answered.

Variability again

From the small number of large-scale excavations that have taken place it can be said that hillfort interiors were extremely variable in character. The sheer magnitude of occupation debris suggests that some were densely occupied over hundreds of years, with continual replacement of structures over time, whilst others were not.

South Cadbury can be cited as a good example of what was probably a fairly typical developed hillfort containing the many different types of features found. Here, although the site was not fully occupied in all periods, were: 'lynchets, ramparts constructed of stone, soil and timber, ditches, gullies, fences, circular structures of post, gully and stakehole construction, 2-, 4-, and 6-post structures, rectangular gully structures, pits, hearths, ovens, middens, yards, paths and tracks, hollow-ways, animal burials and deposits of human remains' (Woodward 2000, 21). Change over time indeed. The next chapter will look at the people who occupied and used hillforts.

CHAPTER SIX

People

....

There are three basic requirements for life:

• Shelter
• Food
• Water

This chapter will see to what extent all three were satisfied at hillforts and look at what the people who used and inhabited these sites *may* have been like.

Shelter: the hearth and the home

The hearth and the fire have always been associated with superstition, custom and tradition, and form the focus of the home – the Latin *focus* means 'fireplace'. The lighting of a fire had special significance in the Welsh Laws, and the symbolism associated with the Welsh word *aelwyd*, which has a meaning wider than 'hearth', to include 'home/family' and even 'kin' and 'dwelling', is strong even today (Owen 1991, 24). The plethora of beliefs and portents surrounding the life-giving hearth and its fire must have played an important role within the hillfort abode.

In a wide variety of prehistoric and early historic buildings the hearth occupied a central or off-set position (Gurnard's Head: see Figure 49a), with smoke from an open fire disappearing through the roof. The image of cooking pots hanging 'Cinderella-like' from ceiling timbers or special supports, as in early Ireland, clearly set out by Estyn Evans (1957), is probably as near to the truth as we shall get, but hearths could also be located towards the side of the hillfort hut, as found at Castell Caer Seion. The fire not only gave warmth and life to family and animals, but the smoke kept the thatch and/or roof timbers dry and free from rot and insects – one reason for the persistence of house interiors open to the roof well into the sixteenth century. The less efficient house-warming chimney flue is a relative newcomer.

Surviving archaeological evidence from the Iron Age suggests a fire of peat, wood or animal dung glowing on a set-stone slab or cobbles lying directly on a mud floor. This type of fuel burns quickly if the draught is too strong, but this could be prevented by using upright slabs, as seen again at Castell Caer Seion. Seven (possible) hearthstones come from South Cadbury, one with a blackened flat surface which could have functioned as a type of griddle (Roe 2000, 267).

Bakestones and griddles are mentioned in the Welsh Laws (Owen 1991, 26).

Archaeological reconstructions have given a valuable insight into how a central hearth would have operated, and when fires are lit inside the reconstructed roundhouses of Castell Henllys the buildings remain remarkably smoke-free. Contrary to popular belief, the smoke does not exit through a hole at the apex of the roof, but seeps through the thatch itself, giving the element of protection mentioned above.

Some items relevant to the hearth and the home and mentioned in this section are shown in Figures 52–54. The firedog, for example, has become an integral part of Celtic tradition, but whether it served as a status-enhancing accoutrement or involved a form of ritual, rather than having a utilitarian purpose, has not been answered. The elaborate first-century AD example from Capel Garmon in Denbighshire has hooks at each end of the uprights which could have supported a spit (Stead 1996, 52), and those from Welwyn in Hertfordshire and Lord's Bridge, Barton, in Cambridgeshire, are also of high status. A possible iron firedog was found in 1881 in what could have been a blacksmith's scrap hoard of bronze and iron metalwork at Bulbury hillfort in Dorset (Cunliffe 1972, 304). A much-corroded zoomorphic dog of wrought iron from Bigberry Camp in Kent has two ears and a muzzle. This is of much lower status than those mentioned above, and might have taken the fire irons rather than a burning log (Jessup 1933, 111). To complete the ensemble an iron poker, formerly with a wooden handle held by a ferrule, comes from Sutton Walls, with another possible version included in the Madmarston Camp hoard.

Cooking pots would have been suspended over the fire, either from ceiling timbers, special supports and hooks or from a crook-stick (in the later black-houses of the Hebrides made of holly); with iron cauldron-hangers coming from Bigberry, Danebury and Hunsbury. A small length of chain from Bwrdd Arthur, possibly used for hanging such pots, has the oval links pinched together in the centre to prevent it from twisting, a technique used in the slave-gang chains of Llyn Cerrig Bach (Lynch 1991, 262). At Stanfordbury in Bedfordshire an iron tripod for suspending a cauldron was found in a grave, but a wooden or iron cradle with adjustable pivoting arm might also have been used. In early Ireland cranes were always on the left-hand side of the fire – convenient for the right-handed, but with overtones of superstition: important actions involving life-giving food – for example, taking the cooking pot off the fire – always following the direction of the sun across the sky (Ross 1998).

The cauldron or hanging pot is itself a feature of Celtic folklore with mystical connotations. A good small example was found at Spettisbury in Dorset, but fragments are more common and sometimes there is evidence of deliberate breakage, suggesting either some ritual involvement or perhaps the residue of metalworking.

Many other types of metal pots and pans would have been used, some embellished with decorative escutcheons and handles. The bronze ram's head handle from a pan found at Hod Hill and the Romano-British bronze

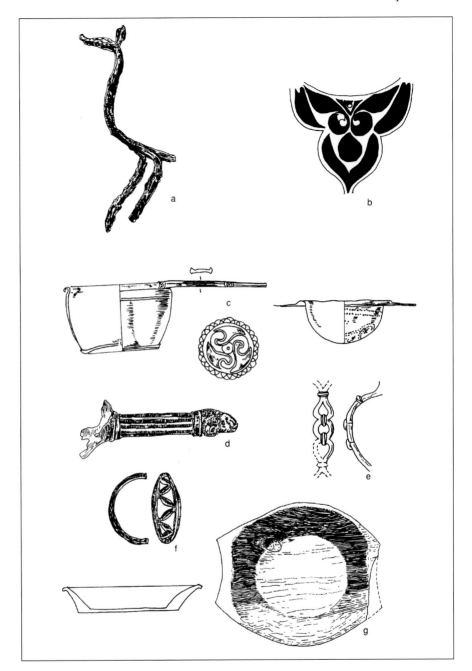

FIGURE 52. Items
from the house and
the home: a) firedog,
approx. height 300cms
(Bigberry); b) cooking
pot ornamentation
(Hunsbury); c) patera,
length 285mm (Coygan
Camp); d) ram's head
handle, length 16cm
(Hod Hill); e) tankard
handle, length 32mm
(Bulbury); f) tankard
handle (Bredon Hill);
g) wooden dish, length
45.5cm (Stanwick).
Redrawn and adapted
after: a) Jessop 1933;
b) and d–g) Jope 2000;
c) Wainwright 1967.

'Kyngadle' patera, comprising saucepan, base-plate and strainer, from Coygan
Camp are particularly fine. Fragments of at least two bronze bowls of around
20cm in diameter come from the Bulbury hoard (Cunliffe 1972, 298), and a
decorated bowl fragment from Spettisbury is similar to that of a Glastonbury
Lake Village bronze bowl. Hollows in the floor of some huts could be 'pot
holes', where a heavy iron pot was placed and food or animal feed pounded,

FIGURE 53 (*left*).
Cauldron-hangers,
such as these examples
from Hunsbury at
Northampton, would
have been essential in
cooking.

NORTHAMPTON MUSEUM AND
ART GALLERY.

FIGURE 54 (*right*).
Bronze cauldron from
Spettisbury Rings,
Dorset. Found in a
ditch, this first century
AD example, at 26cm
diameter, is only half
the normal size, but
nevertheless would
have been a valuable
possession.

or more mundanely they could have been where the chickens scratched and rested.

There is Maiden Castle evidence of turned shale pots, and pottery is found in plenty at hillforts, particularly in the south and this is returned to later in Chapter 7. With exceptions, its general absence from northern England and north and west Wales hillforts could mean that, for day-to-day activities, wooden bowls and leather vessels were used instead. These rarely survive in the record, but Y Breiddin produced examples of the former preserved in a cistern dated to around 300 BC. Whether these were for utilitarian purposes has been questioned, however; there have been suggestions of ritual substitution of wood for metal. A Stanwick waterlogged deposit produced another shallow hollowed-out wooden dish, which probably had a cloth covering attached by five nails.

Pits or holes sunk into the floor of huts existed into historic times. Evans

(1958, 62) describes holes sunk in the clay floor of a northern Irish Dark Age 'earth-house', possibly for storing milk products, but stone-lined holes from Skara Brae in the Orkneys could have stored limpets (Childe 1931). Simple holes some 50cm in diameter were found at Danebury, which might have been covered with wicker or board for storage (Cunliffe 1993a, 60), and this might also explain the use to which the few pits found in Wales and the Marches were put.

There is plenty of evidence for fires lit in the middle of buildings, so forming the principal focus of the living area, but there is little information regarding more intimate details of domestic arrangements, although the classical and early Irish literary sources give some clues. It is possible that low wooden partitions subdivided the space around the edge of interiors to form separate chambers or cubicles for man or beast, some possibly raised from the floor – a peripheral area away from the more active centre of the hut – and these outer areas might have assumed a greater importance than the centre. Double and triple-ring roundhouses, when compared with the smaller single-ring, were twice as likely to house stock as well as people (Pope 2007, 219), even if this extended only to overnight accommodation for young and pregnant animals. Lynch (1991, 278) specifies a raised 'sleeping area' found against the back wall of an Anglesey hilltop enclosure hut, and at another site a rectangular 'box' could have been filled with heather or straw to act as a bed. However, the Roman historian Diodorus Siculus observed that: 'their custom is to sleep on the ground upon skins of wild animals and to wallow among bed-fellows on either side', and there is plenty of present ethnographic evidence for such a practice. As for furniture, if any, nothing survives, but it has been suggested that the sheet-bronze plaque in the shape of a Romano-Celtic face from South Cadbury could have been a decorative mount from such an object.

Although cattle, sheep and pigs would probably have been kept on site when the young were born (there is evidence for this from South Cadbury: Hamilton-Dyer and Maltby 2000, 290), others must have been corralled or styed or put out into the fields during daylight hours. Domestic fowl (*Gallus gallus*), which first regularly appear in the record around the early Iron Age, would have roamed free, and at night might have roosted within domestic huts or four-posters. A few dogs (evidenced from a wide variety of hillforts) and the odd cat or two, kept as pets or for pest control, as found at Danebury (Cunliffe 1993a), Balksbury Camp (Wainwright and Davies 1995, 18) and Kingsdown Camp, Somerset (Jackson 1930, 95) complete the picture. Iron Age cats are the earliest recorded in Britain.

Food and drink

The classical and Irish texts given indications of what might have formed the staple diet, as outlined by Ross (1998). Posidonius (quoted by Athenaeus) says that: 'their food consists of a number of loaves of bread, together with a large amount of meat, either boiled or roasted on charcoal or on spits', and nearer the sea they would eat baked fish with added salt, vinegar and cummin. Archaeologically there is less to go on, but Cunliffe suggests that for Danebury all the food consumed was produced locally, with barley and wheat being the staples, supplemented by milk, cheese and pork and, when possible, beef, horse and mutton. Eggs and honey would be readily available and the all-important salt, both as a preservative and a dietary necessity, would have come from the south coast or, by bleeding cattle, from within the community (Cunliffe 1993a, 74). From the evidence of excavated bone from hillforts generally the main dietary animals were indeed cattle, sheep and pigs in variable amounts depending on the site (see pages 128–9). Pork appears to have been a favourite dish and figures prominently in the heroic classical and literary accounts. The importance of the boar will be returned to.

There is some evidence from hillforts scattered about England and Wales that wine was consumed and no doubt it became an important import. Amphorae fragments have been found as far afield as The Rumps, Hengistbury Head, Sudbrook and Caynham Camp, although it must be added their contents may not all have been wine. British beer was prized and under the price edict of the late third century of Diocletian its price was fixed (Green and Howell 2000, 72).

It has passed into folklore that the feast was an important part of Celtic life. Its significance in the development of the human species has been outlined by Jones (2007) and its great symbolic importance by Sharples (2007, 180). The latter author argues that, as enclosures were the dominant settlement type in Wessex during the early to middle Iron Age, then the very act of mobilising resources for construction would have been the dominant catalyst for social and political competition. Large quantities of food would have been required for construction festivals and gatherings, and the manipulation of elaborate exchange mechanisms between one community and another could have defined relationships. This possibly resulted in the rise in dominance of one hillfort over another and the erratic development of others. Certainly, some Wessex hillforts have massive storage capacities with a clear surplus, which would have enabled such events to take place.

Tankards seem to have appeared in the late Iron Age (Gwilt 2007, 313) and attachments from possible wooden examples have been found in a variety of hillfort contexts, including Castell Henllys, Braich-y-Ddinas, Hod Hill, Bulbury and Bredon Hill. The wood used (as on buckets) was probably yew, which is resistant to decay in damp conditions (Bevan-Jones 2002, 168). Posidonius comments that (no doubt referring to the Gauls): 'the drink of the wealthy classes is wine', whilst the 'lower classes drink wheaten beer prepared with honey, but most people drink it plain'.

Wild animals do not appear to have constituted a major part of the diet in comparison with pig, cattle and sheep, although, rather unusually, bone found in the midden deposits at Trevelgue Head showed that deer, as well as sheep, goats and cattle, formed an important part of the diet. In such a coastal location it might also be assumed that fish would be consumed in quantity. However, in general hillfort contexts it does not seem at first sight that fish were eaten much, despite their abundance. Fish bone is noticeably absent from most of the Iron Age record, although relatively plentiful in some Roman contexts. This is a substantial archaeological problem. Care must be taken when excavating and interpreting finds of bone, as those of smaller animals and fish tend to be degraded and are easily overlooked; fish bone is also both small and delicate and, therefore, not easy to identify (Green 1992, 38). Finds vary from site to site and whilst there is no evidence of fish bone from either Breedon-on-the-Hill or Croft Ambrey, the latter located directly above the River Lugg, there is some indication of bone at Maiden Castle and Balksbury. Why this is so is unclear. Of course, lack of fresh or saltwater fish in the record could mean a taboo surrounding the consumption of creatures coming from what may have been 'sacred' waters, and we will come back to this latter point in Chapter 10. Alternatively, wild animals, fish included, might have been deemed as having symbolic value themselves in prehistory, although being a desirable food source today. However, limited investigation suggests that marine resources might have been exploited differently on the continent at least, but even here things are not clear-cut. In the Netherlands there is evidence of Iron Age fishing of both marine and freshwater species, but less so in Belgium (Dobney and Ervynck 2007, 408–9), possibly due to inadequate archaeological recovery techniques and preservation and environmental conditions as much as anything else.

Water

The question of water supply within hillfort interiors, which is seldom evident, is an important one and is rarely addressed. If defence was the primary *raison d'être* for hillfort construction how was water provided in times of stress to large numbers of people? About 2 litres of water per day is required for the average human to keep going. For one hundred people that would mean 44 gallons simply for drinking, plus unknown quantities required for cooking and manufacturing. If animals were also kept on site amounts would rise substantially.

Here it is worthwhile considering the climate. The Bronze Age had long hot summers and until around 1000 BC the tree line in Scotland, Wales and northern England was at about 800m (Lamb 1981). For another 100–200 years a further warm and dry period ensued, but across Europe around 900 BC colder and/or wetter conditions set in and the Alpine glaciers began to expand and this deterioration is a common feature of many north-western European bog profiles (Briffa and Atkinson 1997, 101). This Sub-Boreal to Sub-Atlantic transition seems to have been abrupt (a timescale of between a decade to a century), possibly reflecting colder sea surface temperatures in the North Atlantic (Burroughs 2005, 257). To about 750 BC Lamb estimates that temperatures fell by about 2°C, shortening the growing season by up to five weeks. At Tregaron Bog in the south-west of mid Wales, the first climax of cold climate lasted between 750 and 400 BC, when peat formed at a rate of 1cm every four years, suggesting a very wet period indeed. In Somerset there is similar evidence in the establishment of the Glastonbury and Meare lake villages. Likewise, on Dartmoor tillage that had appeared up to the 400m mark during the Bronze Age was abandoned. After about 150 BC, however, the climate became milder again and by AD 43 it was probably similar to that experienced today. Apart from brief warm periods in AD 250–400 and AD 1100–1300 the temperatures of 1000 BC might not have been reached since. It is likely, therefore, that, in the early Iron Age at least, water tables would have been higher than today (Young and Richardson 1955, 45) and valley bottoms considerably wetter. It is also possible that, at some sites, springs might have been flowing within what are today dry enclosures.

Theories have been put forward regarding the catching of rainwater in tanks on site, but, apart from the hollows in front of the western ramparts of Old Oswestry, some of which hold water today and which could have so acted in prehistory, evidence is lacking. But why was this rather obvious means of water collection not used elsewhere? An alternative would have been clay-lined dew ponds. Another possible collection arrangement at the Castle-an-Dinas hillfort in Cornwall, built *c*.300–200 BC, is interesting. Here a large pit, 1.5 m × 1.2 m × 1.5 m deep, lay directly in the line of a slight channel (possibly lined with leather) and leading from a spring hollow (Wailes 1963, 54). Further downslope, springs would have been another source of supply: Conderton Camp, Little Solsbury Hill Camp near Bath in Somerset (Dowden 1957; 1962) and below Blackbury Castle in Devon at the junction of the Greensand with the underlying Gault Clay. Pen y corddyn Mawr had a postern gate through the eastern ramparts allowing access to a spring below. But water supply at coastal promontory sites appears even more problematical, and Bolt Tail and the narrow headland of Twyn y Parc on Anglesey, with on-site springs, appear to be the exception rather than the rule.

A nearby river would naturally have been ideal as a water source and over three-quarters of hillforts in the Severn, Wye and Usk catchments are located within just over 2km of a modern river course (Brown 2002). However, the most obvious sources of supply would have been the streams flowing at the base of slope of most hillforts.

Nevertheless, even today some hillforts *do* have water on site, the rocky eminence of Caer Caradoc (Church Stretton) being a well-known example, and a spring rising within the north-western rampart of Mam Tor flows across the line of the defences (Coombs 1976, 147). The Buckbean pond, a natural fissure in the dolerite in use in the late Bronze Age and followed by a later Iron Age cistern, was Y Breiddin's only water source, but was probably insufficient to provide for large numbers of people and animals (Buckland *et al*. 2001, 72).

The example of Midsummer Hill in the Malverns shows how a large site might have been serviced. Excavations by Stanford (1981, 71–2) concluded that issues from several springs in the Malvernian rock at the foot of the hillfort by the south gate were trapped by the inturned arm of the rampart to form the pond shown in Lines's plan of 1870; after the 1930s this area degraded to marsh. This may have served as a general water-source, potable supplies coming from other nearby springs. However, even so, Stanford questioned whether these would have been enough for his projected 1,500–2,000 occupants, despite greater rainfall than today. At Credenhill, also excavated by Stanford (1971), there are springs behind the east and west ramparts, but overall it was concluded that: 'an internal source of water is a rare amenity on English hillforts, which normally had to rely on supplies carried in daily from external springs'.

The possibility of wells within hillforts cannot be discounted: at Wapley Camp in the Marches of Herefordshire there is evidence of a shallow example of unknown age and the north-east corner of South Cadbury has a possible source, later known as 'King Arthur's well'. Certainly, medieval castles built on hillfort sites would have relied on an internal water supply - Castell Dinas Brân above Llangollen in Denbighshire, Llanstephan and Dryslwyn in Carmarthenshire and Bamburgh Castle in Northumberland all have one.

Thus, without the interruption of conflict, an adequate water supply would have been freely available at most hillforts downslope of, and outside, the perimeter. Although the siege does not seem to have been a feature of British prehistory, requiring as it did a considerable commitment and organisation of manpower and resources, and temporary raids were more likely, water supplies could still have been cut off by poisoning or diversion.

Iron Age society

It would be unwise to consider hillforts and Iron Age society in modern-day terms and one enters into this discussion with utmost trepidation. But whether economy, ritual, prestige and power were thought of during these times as *we would see them* is extremely unlikely, when the very act of living would be the all-embracing feature of a way of life dependent on farming. However, there is substantial evidence from a wide variety of sources that each of these factors *did* influence both hillfort location and society's need for their construction, and this will be returned to in Chapter 10.

It is not intended to look at Iron Age society in any detail, nor, in particular, at the debate over whether the 'Celts', as a term for the people who populated continental Europe from the Danube westwards to Britain and south to the Mediterranean, is correct or not (and certainly this has been much questioned, notably by James 1999 and Collis 1996a; 2003), but a few points are of relevance here to our consideration of hillforts.

As we have seen, changes in society, land use and belief were occurring from the end of the ninth century BC onwards, but their impact would probably have differed about the country. In the Marches at Y Breiddin, for example, woodland clearance began in the latter half of the Bronze Age and continued into the early Iron Age, the area surrounding the hillfort being considered a partially open landscape of 'cultivation plots, hill pasture, managed woodland, and floodplain grazing' (Wigley 2007a, 179). Similar clearance has also been noticed at other sites in north-west and south Wales and by 1000 BC forest cover on Dartmoor had all but gone (Harris *et al.* 2003, 14). Although in some parts of southern England tree cover increased in the Iron Age, probably as a result of local decline in farming as well as a wetter climate, renewed clearance towards the Roman period possibly indicated a greater demand for pasture (Dark 2000, 67–8) as well as greater exploitation of mineral wealth. Between 300 and 100 BC it has been estimated that iron production alone destroyed some 180–500 square miles of forest (Harris *et al.* 2003, 14), and this continued. An ensuing timber shortage resulted in the re-use of oak from abandoned forts (Meiggs 1982). Thus, by 300 BC in some areas a 'densely occupied and exploited landscape' could be seen (Hingley 1997, 14). The amount of timber (particularly of oak) required for hillfort construction and use in all its forms would have been immense and undoubtedly contributed to significant change in the landscape.

Against this physical backdrop it appears that, at a social level, the Iron Age was an insecure time in which to live, but the degree to which this was experienced would have depended on the location and status of those concerned. Whilst some hillforts show signs of conflict, others seem to have been stable over hundreds of years. Early theories of Iron Age societal development, as suggested by Hawkes and which much influenced hillfort study before the 1960s, emphasised an influx of invaders or migrants as we have seen. However, it is now thought that Iron Age society evolved in Britain from Bronze Age origins, and this change of interpretation has had a profound effect on the way the function and development of hillforts are now seen. Nevertheless, it should be remembered that Britain must have been as subject to seaborne contact then as it is today, and it is possible that concepts of 'invasion' in prehistory have been too hastily jettisoned (Dark 2002, 192). Maybe, as Harding (2006, 79) suggests, the effects of complex and subtle external relationships and movements of 'influential individuals and kin groups' have been underrated. This debate is likely to continue.

One theory of later prehistoric society is that, once established in Britain from about 600 BC, 'Celtic' society continued to flourish for nearly a century and more after Julius Caesar's forays of 55 and 54 BC, when increasing influence from Rome became felt; thereafter it evolved as a hybrid 'Romano-Celtic' or 'Romano-British' culture. Much depended on location: the Romans had greater influence in south-east England, as Chapter 9 will tell. From the first century BC classical writers such as Strabo, Tacitus, Posidonius, Lucan and Caesar began to write about Britain, and the names of tribes and client kings of Rome became known. These texts, and others described below, despite their often biased and embellished nature, are a great boon to the student of the Iron Age, and a source not available to scholars of earlier prehistoric periods. Nevertheless, the worth of these written sources must not be overemphasised, and the classical accounts mostly relate to the continental Celts rather than the people of Britain.

However, one view of Iron Age society is that, in general terms, there were similarities in social structure on both sides of the channel.

What we can be sure about is that Iron Age society was entirely oral in tradition, and it was not until the eighth century AD, at the earliest, that matters were written down in the Irish and, to a lesser extent, the Welsh vernacular texts. These writings, which centre on myth and legend, reflect a supposed archaic society, one that has been used as a model for pre-Roman Britain as a whole, as in the writings of Ross (1998). The Irish texts show much pagan belief, differing in this respect from the Welsh literary tradition, where the clerics responsible for putting the stories down in writing tended to 'Christianise' events. What is important is to see these sources for what they are: the past set down in myth and legend as an example to the present.

The Irish (Brehon) and Welsh Law tracts, which go back to about the seventh century AD in their written form, likewise give a valuable insight into how Celtic society was organised. Welsh Law was heavily influenced by Roman legal norms, whereas the Irish had a more ancient tradition; both were probably handed down in verse. The Irish Law tracts, in particular, dealt with a time which has resonances with that described by the classical authors.

What emerges from the Irish legends is an 'heroic' society of Iron Age warriors, head-hunting, cattle raiding and chariots in battle. Metal 'parade gear', in the form of sword pieces and the shield-boss from Moel Hiraddug hillfort, the Hunsbury swords, and other examples from South Cadbury, together with slingstones found at a wide variety of hillforts and the use of chariots from some, all indicate possible 'martial' activity at some stage.

These ideas are attractive, but whether they reflect the truth in its entirety must be questioned. A much simpler pattern also has its adherents in which at the end of the Bronze Age and into the early Iron Age society was farming-based, with hillforts, earthworks, rounded buildings and associated material culture. In this model local kinship groups formed the main social entity within a loose tribal structure. That is not to say that people were completely isolated and salt containers from Droitwich in the English Midlands are found in Marcher and Welsh hillforts. There was also continental and Irish contact and it was this that enabled new thoughts and ideas – for example new metalwork design – to be taken up throughout Britain. As Jope (2000, 3) observed: 'it seems now clear that there is little biologically heritable basis for the notion "Celtic".'

From the third century BC, however, new patterns emerged. Farming became more intensive and field systems and settlements developed. Many examples of farming tools and saddle (and later rotary) querns for grinding flour come from English and Welsh hillforts. In some areas, hillforts declined. From the fourth century BC fine examples of La Tène art appear, similar to those found on the continent: torcs, weapons, horse and chariot trappings and equipment for the feast, all of which have been found in hillfort contexts. Some burials show a move towards the individual, with growing social identification. However, the differences with continental examples are so great as to imply contact in an *insular* fashion, bringing ideas rather than people. After the middle Iron Age, the appearance of La Tène finery indicates a superior class developing, with possible warrior or heroic beliefs, and greater ceremonial. In the later Iron Age and the Roman period more definite 'tribal' groupings emerged from the mist of uncertainty surrounding earlier periods.

Which of the various current theories to believe is a matter of personal choice, but, within the basic framework of society, artefacts found within hillforts show a little of the personal detail of those who lived and worked in these austere surroundings.

Adornment and display

It is impossible to say exactly what the people who populated the hillforts of England and Wales were like, but excavated material and the literary sources give some clues. Both the classical and Irish texts suggest that the Celts were a distinctive people worthy of note, and Diodorus Siculus and Strabo write of their custom of washing their hair with lime-wash and drawing it back to the nape of the neck: 'for the hair is so thickened by this treatment that it differs in no way from a horses [sic] mane'. Celtic coins depict a warrior on his chariot with two prancing horses, his long stiff locks streaming behind, whilst the drooping moustache, with hair flowing to the neck, is a feature of Celtic iconography, so there must be some truth in this observation.

Naturally, in terms of physical appearance there would have been a mixture of types and hues and it would be wrong to generalise, but to the classical authors the blond strong-of-frame Celt appears to have been the ideal – and the women likewise. Dio Cassius, the Roman author, with probable bias, refers to Boudica, Queen of the Iceni of East Anglia, as 'huge of frame and terrifying of aspect', and it has been suggested that the wearer of the late Bronze Age 'gold cape', which was found in a round barrow beside the River Alun in north-east Wales, was a woman. The small dark Celt is of popular tradition and may be more applicable to the inhabitants of western Britain. Stead (1996, 36) shows from skeletal evidence in Yorkshire that the average height of a man at the time was about 1.69m and that of a woman was around 1.57m; the average lifespan was some thirty years, with only 8 per cent of the population above forty-five at the time of death.

Caesar writes that the Britons applied '*vitrium*' to their bodies – possibly woad (*Isatis tinctoria*), a member of the cabbage family, although other pigments were probably also used – to produce a characteristic blue colour, giving them a 'more terrifying appearance in battle'. This is a reasonable assumption, as woad has healing properties and its use in body decoration could have had a practical as well as psychological effect, fighting infection from wounds suffered in the heat of conflict. The leaves were dried, powdered and fermented to produce a very strong dye, only a little being needed to cover a large area of the body. A layer of fat, egg or semen would be applied first as a base and the dye then applied to give a luminescent effect, seemingly invisible in some light and in front of certain backgrounds. It is this characteristic of woad that gave it a 'magical' power – making the wearer 'invisible' to enemies – and the use of semen as a base would 'impart' strength and fertility. An element of, if not always complete, nakedness, together with tattoos, would have been an essential ingredient of the overall effect, giving credence to the theory that warfare, nudity and ritual were symbolically connected.

There have been few finds in any prehistoric context of clothing in either leather or cloth, but fragments of the latter have survived in a non-hillfort context at Burton Fleming in East Yorkshire, where a complex stripe and diamond twill pattern was attached to an iron brooch (Stead 1996, 37). However, many of the tools used for clothing manufacture come from hillforts and the classical texts also refer to the practice (Figure 55). Leather working must have been particularly important, and from Bredon Hill a bone hammer-head and iron 'dogs' for gripping thin sheets indicate the craft. In dress the native tribes appeared distinctive. Finds at many hillforts of fired clay, bone or stone spindlewhorls for spinning wool, loomweights and threaders for weaving, and bone or antler weaving-combs for both preparation and stages of weaving prove that the production of cloth and garment manufacture were important and widespread activities. Bone needles and bone or copper alloy toggles, buttons and dress fasteners complete the picture. A spindlewhorl from Bredon Hill was fashioned from a sea urchin (*Pygaster semisulcatus*) preserved in the Inferior Oolite of the Cotswolds.

Ross (1998, 46) details the type of dress that might have been worn. Trousers (*bracae*) appear to have been the everyday wear for men, their use originating from continental contact with horse-riding peoples, notably the warlike Iranians and Scythians. A knee-length tunic of elaborate woven design would have been caught at the waist by a belt (iron buckles come from Dinorben and belt-links/hook from Hunsbury and Bredon Hill), or girdle, with a cloak fastened by a pin or brooch. The Irish texts say that women wore tunics to the ground, with cloaks, resplendent brooches and other adornments. We shall be looking at Roman influences later, but a finely decorated Roman bronze end-buckle found by accident at Pen y corddyn Mawr, dating to around AD 370–400, does imply a military presence (Figure 57u). Originally fitting on the end of a belt, engravings of fish and peacocks facing a 'tree of life' adorn the plate, whilst a stylised dolphin's head surmounted by reversed horse heads make up the buckle itself (Sanderson 1992, 2).

The Celtic cloak was famous and heavily taxed in the Roman period and in its colourful and exotic form displayed the power and status of its wearer. Those of the Irish kings are well described and details of weaving and dyeing can be found in the Irish Law tracts. Ross (1998, 48) quotes Strabo's famous comment about the Celts of Gaul, which may or may not be appropriate to those in Britain: 'To the frankness and high-spiritedness of their temperament

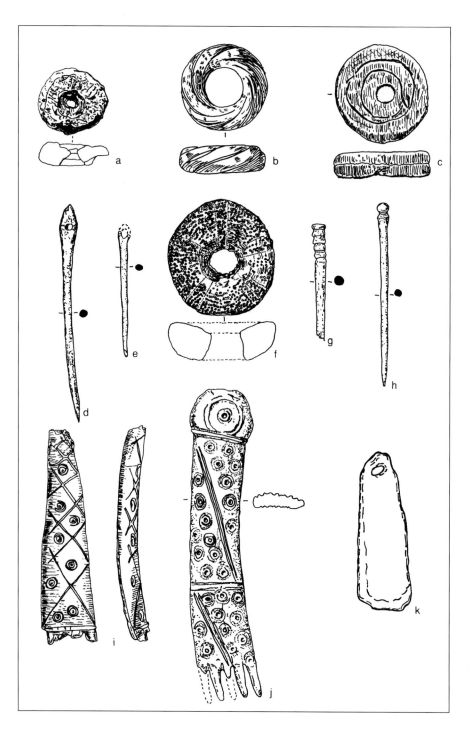

FIGURE 55. Spinning and weaving:
a) spindlewhorl, diameter 61mm (The Trundle);
b) spindlewhorl, diameter 36mm (Coygan Camp);
c) spindlewhorl, diameter 40mm (Hod Hill);
d) bone bodkin, length 87.5mm (Conderton Camp); e) bone bodkin, length 50.5mm (Conderton Camp);
f) sea urchin spindlewhorl, max. diameter approx. 96mm (Bredon Hill); g) bone pin, length 47mm, broken (Conderton Camp); h) bone pin, length 74mm (Conderton Camp);
i) weaving-comb, length 115mm (Spettisbury Rings); j) weaving-comb, length 126.5mm (Conderton Camp);
k) loomweight, length 65mm (Maen Castle).
Redrawn and adapted after: a) Curwen 1929;
b) Wainwright 1967;
c) Jope 2000;
d–e), g–h) and j) Thomas 2005; f) Hencken 1938;
i) Gresham 1939;
k) Herring 1994.

must be added the traits of childish boastfulness and love of decoration. They wear ornaments of gold, torques on their necks, and bracelets on their arms and wrists, while people of high rank wear dyed garments bespinkled with gold'. The finds of middle to late Bronze Age gold torcs, bracelets and other finery, including the gold cape, in a relatively small area surrounding the Clwydian Range (Brown 2004), and the probably late Iron Age gold torcs from Snettisham in Norfolk, indicate that Strabo was, in part, correct.

There is plenty of evidence from hillforts of the love of personal ornament and decoration, and a fastidiousness in appearance is suggested by widespread finds of pins and brooches, razors, tweezers and mirror fragments and other personal adornments and talismen in both England and Wales. A selection, mentioned below, are shown in Figures 56 and 57.

Pins designed to fasten a cloak, dress or cloth around the shoulders or secure hats or hair can be very beautiful items indeed. Generally, but not exclusively, of earlier design than the La Tène brooch, they fill many pages of text in the literature. Simple iron ring-headed examples, from as early as the third century BC, are common in southern English hillforts (for example, Maiden Castle) and have been found elsewhere, including Dinorben. Pins were made of bronze as well as iron and are more common in the Midlands and east, but the head of a 'shepherd's crook' pin of fine bronze wire was found, again, at Dinorben. The finest examples show a characteristic 'swan's neck' bend to the shaft and may be inlaid with coral, as an example excavated at South Cadbury, dated to around 300–250 BC and similar to those found at Dane's Graves in Yorkshire, shows (O'Connor and Foster 2000, 194). Pins could be large: a ring-headed version from Little Solsbury is 12.3cm long, whilst another swan's neck pin from Ham Hill is 12.7cm in length.

Many and varied brooches have been found at hillforts and their nature and context have been much researched (a subject outside the scope of this book), but from the Iron Age through to Roman times there were two general forms – 'pennanular' and 'bow'. The ingenious design of the former was ideal for use on a cloak and they are represented at a great number of excavated hillforts. A huge deposit of 150 bronze brooches of both types was found by Alcock in his excavations at the site of the conflict at the south-west gate of South Cadbury (Alcock 1971, 4), and these are well described in the excavation report (Barrett *et al.* 2000c). Brooches could be utilitarian or very elaborate and decorated with coral, tufa or enamel. From about 400 BC La Tène bow brooches seem to have become fashionable and there are many from hillforts. Produced in one piece, they can be of forged iron or more usually cast bronze and, although some may have been imported, most were of native manufacture. There is evidence that early La Tène brooches were also used as votive deposits and the example from Lodge Hill Camp of the first half of the fourth century BC found in a ditch terminal fits this pattern (Pollard *et al.* 2006, 47).

The 'trumpet' brooch is a variation of the bow having elaborate decoration, and is a particular feature of the Romano-Celtic period. A variety of examples

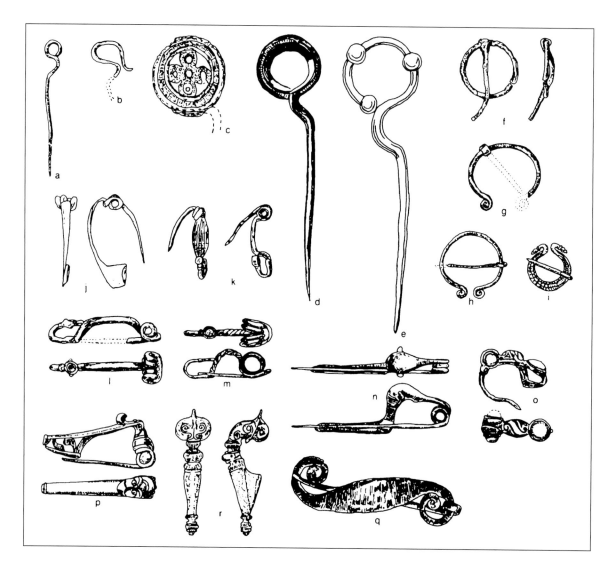

FIGURE 56. Pins and brooches: a) bronze ring-headed pin, length 86mm (Bredon Hill); b) 'shepherd's crook' bronze wire pin, max. thickness of wire 2mm (Dinorben); c) copper alloy ring-headed pin roundel, max. diameter 36mm (South Cadbury); d) large bronze ring-headed pin, length 12.4cm (Little Solsbury Camp); e) large bronze 'swan's neck' pin, length 12.7cm (Ham Hill); f) pennanular brooch, diameter 51mm (Dinorben); g) pennanular brooch, diameter 33mm (Salmonsbury); h) pennanular brooch, diameter 28mm (Salmonsbury); i) Romano-British silver pennanular brooch, diameter 21mm (Ham Hill); j) copper alloy bow brooch, length 41mm (South Cadbury); k) copper alloy bow brooch, length 32mm (Balksbury); l) low-arched bronze bow brooch, length 50mm (Maiden Castle); m) bronze leaf bow brooch, length 35mm (Maiden Castle); n) bronze bow brooch of Italic type, length 70mm (Hod Hill); o) bronze compact brooch with red enamel decoration, length 32mm (Maiden Castle); p) bronze bow brooch with zoomorphic design, length 68mm (Ham Hill); q) wrought iron bow brooch, length 7.5cm (Maiden Castle); r) Romano-British cast bronze trumpet brooch, length 56mm (Dinorben). Redrawn and adapted after: a) Hencken 1938; b), f) and r) Savory 1971; c) Barrett *et al.* 2000; d–e), l–m, o) and q) Jope 2000; g–h) Dunning 1976; k) Wainwright and Davies 1995; p) St George Gray 1923.

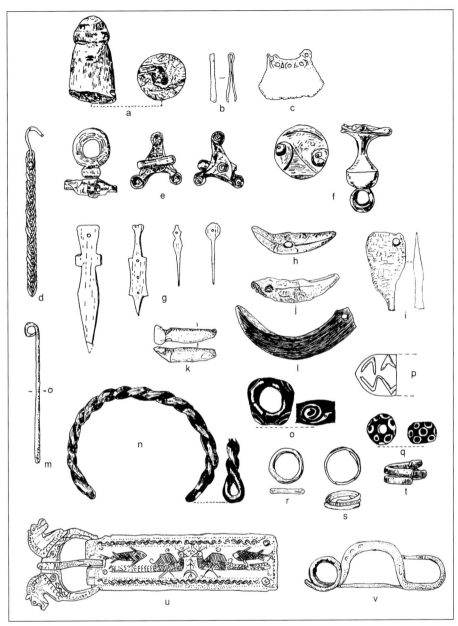

FIGURE 57. Adornments and talismens: a) bone phallus, length 20mm (The Trundle); b) tweezers, length 44mm (South Cadbury); c) razor, width 60mm (South Cadbury); d) gold chain, length 75mm (Croft Ambrey); e) bronze triskele pendant, length 30mm (Croft Ambrey); f) bronze triskele pendant, length 39mm (Croft Ambrey); g) bone objects, length 3–7.8cm (Spettisbury Rings); h) dog-tooth pendant, length 38mm (Conderton Camp); i) human bone pendant, length 35mm (Lidbury Camp); j) animal-tooth pendant, length 40mm (Lidbury Camp); k) cow-tooth pendant or toggle, length 28mm (Conderton Camp); l) boar's tusk pendant, length 77mm (Bredon Hill); m) bronze crook pendant, length 62mm (Croft Ambrey); n) iron torc, diameter 20.3cm, weight 400g (Spettisbury Rings); o) glass bead (Danebury); p) glass bead (Hunsbury); q) glass bead (Conderton Camp); r) ring (South Cadbury); s) ring (Dinorben); t) ring (Bredon Hill); u) bronze buckle, length 82mm, *c*. AD 370–400 (Pen y corddyn Mawr); v) bow brooch, length 64mm (Moel Hiraddug). Redrawn and adapted after: a) Curwen 1929; b–c) and r) Barrett *et al.* 2000; d–f) and m) Stanford 1974; n) Hawkes 1940; g) Gresham 1939; h), k) and q) Thomas 2005; l) Hencken 1938; v) Brassil *et al.* 1982.

come from hillforts, notably Hod Hill. A Dinorben example, which was excavated close to a hut circle and dated to around the early or middle second century AD, has a scroll pattern worked in niello (silver) on the trumpet head; the classical elements of the piece worked in a Celtic manner (Gardner and Savory 1964, 134). Part of the design is linked to a plaque found with the Moel Hiraddug shield-boss (see pages 112–13) and other examples from the west Midlands and Welsh Marches also suggest local manufacture.

Although in south-east Wales it was the iron brooch that was most favoured from the middle Iron Age to the Conquest (Gwilt 2007, 303), as time went by from the first century BC continental influence in British native design increased. From inside a hut at Tre'r Ceiri came a cast gilt-bronze brooch of the later first century AD which, like the example from Great Chesters (*Aesica*) in Northumberland, is a native copy of a Roman fan-tailed design developed in the period AD 60–100. Its description by Ruth and Vincent Megaw (1990, 226) is worth repeating: 'Its berried eyes are a late feature in British metalwork; its angled eyebrows sweep down to form comma-shaped moustaches'; this perhaps gives us some idea of the hirsute facial style of the native man.

Late third/early fourth-century AD bronze bracelets were found at Dinorben, but an earlier pair of complete and identical bronze bracelets on a copper core from Coygan Camp were decorated with incised ribbed lines; these were possibly for a child or woman. They have affinities with central European examples, and are thought to have been unearthed from a contracted inhumation in a rock-cut grave in 1842 (Wainwright 1967, 83). Such La Tène bracelets are rare in Britain outside of the Arras burials, but at Llanmelin fort in Monmouthshire two smaller ribbed bracelets of uncertain date, but in the past attributed to Hallstatt/La Tène, come from the inner ditch (Green and Howell 2000, 26), suggesting trade or gift exchange. High-status objects such as these and, for example, the deep ultramarine translucent glass arm-ring (part) unearthed at Castle Dore in Cornwall, were, no doubt, part of the accoutrements of the time. When complete, the bronze bracelet from Bredon Hill, a section of chain of twenty-five links of hammered roughly circular gold wire from Croft Ambrey, and an earlier late Bronze Age fragment of a gold bracelet from South Cadbury, would all have been very precious to the wearer.

Mirrors made of bronze or iron are some of the most beautiful examples of Celtic art and finely decorated examples have been found in non-hillfort contexts, in particular from the Birdlip burial in Gloucestershire (near Crickley Hill) and at the Stamford Hill cemetery near Mount Batten, overlooking Plymouth Sound (Cunliffe 1988a, 87–90). However, the Bulbury hoard included two fragments of a bronze mirror, of mainly south-western design (Cunliffe 1972, 296–7), and it is possible that bronze/copper alloy parts from South Cadbury could have come from a mirror with cut-out edging (Foster 2000, 197).

Stanford's Croft Ambrey excavations produced bronze triskele pendants cast in one piece and with parallels to those from the Roman fort at Abergavenny and Tre'r Ceiri (Gwilt 2007, 311), indicating that some sort of talisman or charm would have been as important to the wearer then as today. Necklaces, charms or pendants of fashioned bone, particularly dog tooth, boar's tusk or cow were also favourite adornments and are found at a variety of sites. The unusual ten bone pins from Spettisbury, all but one with single or multiple perforation, could have been pendants, although other uses can be surmised. Human bone was also used, and at Lidbury a piece of the temporal bone from a skull, perforated at one corner, may have been suspended and worn, possibly as an amulet (Cunnington 1917, 34). Formerly strung beads are also common hillfort finds – some of bone or stone, others of glass or amber. Many glass beads are plain, such as dark blue opaque examples from Bredon Hill and Hunsbury, while others are exquisitely decorated. Glassworking at the Meare Lake Village in Somerset in the early to middle Iron Age was well developed and beads from there found their way into hillforts such as Conderton Camp; sought-after goods, for sure. Amber beads are less common, but good examples come from Danebury, South Cadbury and Bredon Hill, again proving the existence of sophisticated trade and exchange mechanisms.

South Cadbury has produced fragments of at least twenty-eight knife-cut or lathe-turned armlets or ankle-rings of Kimmeridge shale and, with another Hod Hill piece, show that this material was popular, but glass was also used. Finger and toe rings come in a wide variety of shapes and sizes and generally, apart from Roman signet rings (several South Cadbury versions being of hand-wrought brass), are notoriously difficult to date. The plain hoop is the most common, as South Cadbury examples show, but bronze or iron spiral rings are well represented at many sites. Particularly good examples are a 'viper' finger ring from Casterley Camp in Wiltshire and a gold twisted-strand ring-ended wrist-ring from Hengistbury Head.

But it was the 'torc' (from the latin *torquis* – a twisted necklace, wreath or collar) which shows Celtic art at its best, and the image of the naked warrior wearing his torc is displayed in the Hellenistic statue of the 'Dying Gaul' of around 240–230 BC, originally erected by Attalos I of Pergamon in celebration of his victory over the Gauls. The torc would have indicated wealth and status and imbued the wearer with mystical properties and divine protection.

Although the gold torcs of north-east Wales and those of Pembrokeshire (Aldhouse-Green and Northover 1996) came from hillfort areas, examples from actual hillforts are rare. Whilst the epitomy of Celtic art are those made of gold (a ring-terminal of a possible gilt torc dating to around 75 BC is from Hengistbury Head), iron might have been considered just as valuable, and this was suggested by Herodian (at the time of Septimius Severus) of the northern Britons who adorned themselves so. A Ham Hill plain neck-ring, an iron torc from the 'war cemetary' at Spettisbury Rings in Dorset and another possible twisted iron fragment from Croft Ambrey testify to their place in hillfort society. The Spettisbury torc is made from a single hoop of wrought iron around 1cm in diameter, doubled upon itself and twisted to form the stem and two loop ends, and was possibly fixed by a leather thong at the back of the neck (Hawkes 1940b, 113). Weighing nearly one pound (400g), it would have been a massive item to wear. Perhaps this was of local manufacture, but the Tre'r Ceiri 'bead' from a torc of Lochar Moss type is definitely so and dates, as does the Spettisbury torc, to the first century AD (Savory 1971, 66).

The brooch and pin excavated at Moel Hiraddug give a fleeting glimpse of hillfort life and of the fine craftsmanship that existed away from the south-eastern 'core'. The brooch, as shown in Figure 57v, with a straight-profile bow-top and spring coils, was made from a single piece of bronze 65mm in length and probably held an inlay of coral or similar decoration. Such 'Marzabotto' types, found as far away as Switzerland, date to the fifth century BC (Brassil *et al.* 1982, 41) and would have adorned a cloak or cloth around the shoulders of the wearer. The bronze pin, probably used for a similar purpose, would have been of considerable length and was possibly decorated with tufa found locally at Prestatyn, a material used in Iron Age Britain as a substitute for imported Mediterranean coral, and would have been a much prized possession. The evident pride in, and concern for, their appearance of these hillfort people strongly contrasts, to modern eyes, with the crudity of their surroundings.

A status-conscious 'warrior', but agrarian, society

There has been much debate as to the nature and amount of Iron Age conflict. Although Strabo concludes that the Celts were 'madly fond of war, high-spirited and quick to battle', how far this was true of Britain is not clear and as a theory this is now generally out of favour. However, aggression and violence do appear to have formed an integral part of the native way of life, as James (2007) and Armit (2007) have recently outlined. In such 'underdeveloped' times the deliberate organisation of ceremony and ritual, in terms of real or contrived conflict, rites of passage and minimal systems of government, would have been important for the cohesion of society. In many tribes cattle-raiding has long been a way of enhancing status: for example, among the Karimojong of Kenya and the Suri of Ethiopia, where cattle remain important status symbols, acting as the dowry for young women. According to the written texts cattle played a pivotal role in the Celtic way of life, a role perhaps underplayed in past hillfort analyses.

Certainly, it was farming that was the main occupation for the vast majority of the populace, and, as J.D. Hill (2007, 21) succinctly proposed, perhaps the designation 'warrior farmers' would be a more appropriate description of those involved.

Conflict resolution, combat and display

Conflict and aggression are endemic traits and their place and scale in prehistory have been the subject of a wide variety of interpretations (Keeley 1996; Osgood and Monks 2000; Parker Pearson and Thorpe 2005; and James 2007, among others). 'Primitive' peoples have long traditions of ritualised combat and flamboyant display, preferably without the shedding of blood, with weapons carried as status symbols, as evidenced by, for example, the Moche of Peru; and literary sources suggest the same for Celtic tribes. In the modern era these events can last for days and involve onlookers encouraging the participants on as though the rituals were enacted on a stage. Such an exercise is important as an aggressive outlet at the end of which, if things do not get out of hand, all parties return home satisfied, and provides the bonds which hold the tribe together. It would not be to the advantage of anyone to lose the young men on whom the ultimate success of the group would depend, but such instincts have to be fulfilled. Ethnographic analogies of such conflict can be made. Herdsman of the Dinka of Sudan, for example, would 'fight' over the best pasturelands, but eventually mediation would be sought from the 'masters of the fishing spear' (Mair 1964, 48, 68), while Armit (2007, 33) cites the ritualised battles of the Dani of New Guinea.

The Suri of the lower Omo river valley of south-west Ethiopia, essentially a warrior people, are another case in point. The young men engage in ritualistic combat at stick fighting festivals or *sagenai* (Parry 2007, 87). Substantial posturing and controlled, but dangerous, aggression full of sexual potency prepare the naked combatants for real-world self-defence against the threat of neighbouring tribes. Ritual purging takes place before the *sagenai*. Whilst serious injury and even death do occur, the use of sticks as weapons and individual rather than communal fights keep this to a minimum and decisions on the champions can sometimes be made after only a few bouts. These conflict resolution mechanisms also act as a 'theatre' for the attraction of women, as well as being a way by which the young men learn how to fight outsiders. Body-cutting and the insertion of lip plates enable the pain threshold to be enhanced, as well as being thought of great beauty. Thus, whilst conflict in prehistory is often stated as being the result of population pressure, the above suggests that this might not always have been the case and raises the possibility of 'gatherings' taking place at hillfort arenas involving similar ritual combat and display and the emergence of 'champions'; important for the preparation of young men for manhood and possible combat.

Whether actual aggression was any more inherent in prehistory than it is now is a moot point, but, in general terms, 'weapons, battle tactics and elaborate codes of honour' (Ross 1998, 55) would undoubtedly have been important, and show up in the archaeological record. Certainly, tribes such as the Silures of south-east Wales appear to have been extremely warlike. Native battles, real or ritualised, could be noisy affairs, with much shouting, bravado, taunts and displays, and there is archaeological evidence that the ear-splitting blasts from the carnyx, the Celtic trumpet, would have added to the clamour. This instrument is well represented on the Thracian Gundestrup cauldron, and four late second- or first-century Gaulish examples, with tusked boar and snake head mouthpieces, come from the shrine complex of Arènes near Tintignac in France. That the carnyx was used in Britain is proven by a tube from Tattershall Ferry in Lincolnshire and a mouthpiece found at Deskford in Grampian, which is embellished with the eyebrows of a boar's head, a stylistic device shown on the Moel Hiraddug broken-back triskel plaque; the animal head gave a special musical quality to the sound (Megaw and Megaw 1990, 232; Hunter 2001, 100).

Evidence of earlier Neolithic conflict suggests insecurity, although Mercer and Healy (2004, 11) comment that, at the essentially 'frontier' site of Hambledon Hill, this was episodic and perhaps prompted by gatherings on the hill. Here, the finding of an intact male skeleton near a gateway in the Stepleton enclosure with a leaf-shaped arrowhead embedded in his thoracic cavity, and another young male felled also by an arrow, are timely reminders of dangerous times. This, together with evidence of fire damage to the timber-laced outwork on the Shroton spur and the burning down of the more substantial Stepleton outwork, could indicate localised trouble, the earliest example of its kind in Dorset (Gale 2003, 32). Subsequently it is thought that changing beliefs and practices rendered the site redundant. Similarly, some 800 Neolithic leaf-shaped arrowheads found among rampart debris at Carn Brea point to raiding and Crickley Hill's 400 arrowheads and burning suggest further conflict (Dyer 1990, 37; Dixon 1994).

However, with notable exceptions, direct archaeological evidence of inter-tribal trouble in Iron Age England and Wales is sparse and information has predominantly come from the trappings of warfare, although much depends on how 'warfare' is defined and certainly it should not be seen in modern terms. Evidence of fire damage does not necessarily mean conflict and could be the result of lightning strike or demolition, although which of these events caused the damage usually remains unclear, as at the north-eastern gate of Caer Cadwgan. This lack of substantial evidence from the several hundred hillforts investigated suggests that conflict was by no means common, but it must have occurred and could have been predominantly ritualised, as outlined above. But that is quite different to the role played by hillforts in the attempts to repel the Roman advance, as we shall see.

As a result of these unknowns we can only make guesses as to what really happened in any given case. Worlebury on the coast, for example, lay close to the southern territorial limits of the Dobunni tribe, who controlled the west from Somerset to Hereford and beyond, and to the south were the Durotriges of Dorset and south Somerset. The two tribes appear to have been in conflict over territory in the nearby Mendip Hills and Dobunnic inland sites such as Cadbury Hill (Congresbury), nearby Cadbury Castle (Tickenham), Dolebury, Banwell Camp, and Wains Hill and Worlebury, fronting the Bristol Channel, could all have provided a substantial controlling presence in an unstable border country. In fact the string of hillforts from Dolebury in the south northwards along the scarp overlooking the Severn Estuary to the Cotswold ridge, and to Meon Hill in the north above the Avon in Warwickshire, could all have served similar strategic purposes.

However, around 100 BC there is evidence from the number of hillforts abandoned that the socio-economic systems long underpinning society in southern Britain were in trouble. In Wessex the decline of Hengistbury Head as a port-of-trade suggests that the Atlantic seaway economy had been much affected by Caesar's conquest of Gaul in 58–51 BC, and Cunliffe (1993a, 115) considers that the new focus was eastern Britain. If the Roman slave trade was indeed important in southern Britain, then this would have had a major effect on tribal communities in both England and Wales.

At both Danebury and Worlebury there was furious and possibly tribal conflict, with the great gate at the former burnt down and the site effectively abandoned around 100 BC. At Worlebury nineteenth-century finds imply that the walls were breached, gates burnt and flanking towers razed (Evans 1980, 14). The bodies of at least eighteen individuals, ten with severe wounds, indicate fighting, although care must be taken when interpreting this elderly 'excavation'. But whether the hacked skull of a four-year-old child found in a ditch at Stonea Camp was the result of outside trouble, domestic violence or ritual is impossible to guess.

However, the most notorious event unearthed was that at Bredon Hill, where the mutilated remains of over sixty, mostly young, adult males were found immediately outside the inner gate, indicating a fierce struggle. The excavator, Mrs T.H. Hencken (1938), discounted Roman intervention and proposed native conflict, although this theory has since been questioned. The positions of the heavily mutilated bodies indicated that they lay where they fell and that the site must have been abandoned shortly afterwards, most probably in the early first century AD. Skulls found with burnt material (probably from the gate fired during the battle) may have been set up on the gate before the event, suggesting prior native conflict. Unlike at Sutton Walls, the site of a similar massacre, the lack of skulls at Bredon Hill does suggest trophy hunting, but nothing is conclusive. Although slingstones appear to have been used initially as a long-distance weapon from the inner rampart, spear and javelin heads, an iron sword scabbard, bronze dagger chapes and small iron hammers at the gate testify to heavy hand-to-hand fighting. There is compelling evidence to suggest, however, that this was Roman work after all: Manning (1985), having looked at spearheads associated with the fight, proposed that they were of Roman origin. If that is the case then here we have, along with Midsummer Hill, Croft Ambrey and Sutton Walls, another Midland's/ Marches example of a hillfort being taken in the Roman advance (Thomas 2005, 257), and to which we will return.

Warrior equipment

With the above in mind let us now look at the kind of weapons an Iron Age warrior-farmer would have used (Figure 58); outstanding pre-Conquest metalwork has been found in the few existing 'warrior burials', and particularly from hillforts.

Apart from a pair of attachments found *in situ* on iron chain-mail from

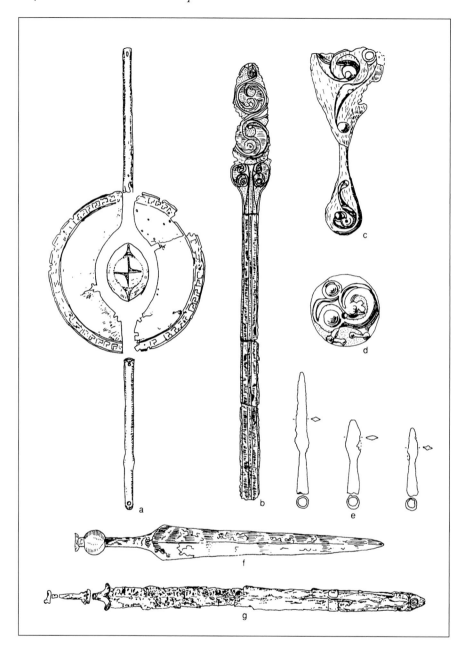

FIGURE 58. Warrior equipment: a) shield ornamentation (Grimthorpe); b) shield ornamentation, length 31cm (St Mawgan-in-Pyder); c) copper alloy shield-boss mount, length 81mm (South Cadbury); d) horse plaque, probably from a shield, diameter 33mm (South Cadbury); e) iron spear heads, lengths 76mm, 102mm, 93mm (Bredon Hill); f) dagger, length 29.5cm, *c.*late third-century AD (Coygan Camp); g) iron sword, *c.*79cm (Grimthorpe). Redrawn and adapted after: a) Jope 2000; b) Threipland 1956; c–d) Barrett *et al.* 2000; e) Hencken 1938; f) Wainwright 1967; g) Stead 1968.

Stanwick and items from the Arras sites, for example, there is little evidence that body armour was worn by Celtic tribes to any great extent, although, being equivocal, perhaps the statue of the naked 'Dying Gaul' has become an overdone prototype; it is echoed by the Roman memorial stones at Wroxeter and commemorative slabs from the Antonine Wall in Scotland showing defeated naked Celtic warriors with sword, spear and shield.

At a more mundane level the predominant weapons appear to have been the spear and the sling, both recently researched by Jon Bryant Finney (2006). Where projectile points are found it is often difficult to distinguish between those of javelins (which are thrown) and lances (which are thrusted), but most are of forged iron with only occasional decoration – practical weapons indeed. Iron spearheads have been excavated at a number of hillforts (including South Cadbury, Casterley Camp and Ham Hill), but a rare 'flambouyant-headed' (wavy) spear from Bredon Hill does show continental contact.

The occurrence of warrior equipment varies from site to site of course and, whereas Bury Hill in Hampshire produced a fine assemblage of horse and chariot trappings, the Dinorben excavations unearthed relatively few pieces. Those recovered were mostly of Roman origin: three projectile heads included a light spear or javelin, similar to those from early Roman deposits at Maiden Castle, and a type of ballista bolt was of the form found at Ham Hill and Hod Hill.

The other utilitarian weapon was the sling, which has very ancient origins. Slingstones are common at hillforts throughout England and Wales and are mostly glacial or water-worn pebbles, those made of baked or raw clay and carved stone (usually chalk) occurring in lesser numbers. Together with (possibly) some hand-throwing stones, a cache of over 22,000 was found in a pit at the eastern gateway of Maiden Castle; 11,000 came from one Danebury pit and 612 from one Castell Caer Seion hut. The sling was a most effective weapon. Unlike an arrow, the maximum range of a slingstone is also its effective range and the final impact speed is close to the initial velocity. At the end of its flight an arrow can cause little damage, but this is not true of the slingstone. However, whilst some suggest a range of 200–350m (Connolly 1981; Griffiths 1989), accuracy tails off in excess of 50m and the greater the elevation the greater the difference in range (Finney 2006, 6, 71, 74–5).

At some hillforts the source of stones can be determined. The roughly round water-worn pebbles scattered about Oldbury in Kent came from Eocene pebbles at Knockmill Wood, some 4.8km to the north, suggesting a route across the Weald to the North Downs (Ward Perkins 1939, 181). In Devon 1,271 slingstones came mostly from the entrance of Blackbury Castle, but twenty-five were located in a stone-lined pit near a possible hut or windbreak; these weighed between 2–2.5oz each and probably came from Branscombe Beach, 4.4km to the south (Young and Richardson 1955, 53).

The use of arrows in prehistory is well known, classical writers referring to their use in Gaul, but there is only spasmodic evidence of bows from British Iron Age sites. Whilst it might be expected that arrowheads would have been fashioned in bronze from the Bronze Age onwards both in the British Isles and continental Europe, this has proved not to have been the case and it was the (mostly flint) barbed and tanged arrowhead, which appeared from the early part of that period, that seems to have been used (Barber 2003, 147). There is evidence that flints were also worked in the Iron Age on a localised basis

(Young and Humphrey 1999; Humphrey 2007); a barbed and tanged arrowhead reported from the Wrekin (Stanford 1985b). Later, a socketed iron arrowhead found at South Cadbury has been dated to Late Cadbury (Romano-British) and arrowheads generally are a feature of the massacre at the south-west gate (Alcock 1971, 4). Why the bow is absent from the record virtually from the late Bronze Age to the late Iron Age is debated, but Finney (2006) suggests it could be to do with its status as an elite weapon within society in comparison with that of the sling.

However, swords and daggers were undoubtedly prestigious weapons, as much for status and display as for warfare, the sword in particular being imbued with special mystical qualities (Wells 2007, 470). The long sword was the one favoured in Britain, but corrosion has rendered relatively few intact – a 50cm sword from Croft Ambrey had been deposited in two pieces (possibly suggesting some ritual involvement), but the tip had completely rusted whilst the remainder was badly corroded. The swords from the so-called 'tinkers hoard' of Moel Hiraddug fell to pieces on discovery. Some remain, however, as we shall see below.

Scabbards in bronze and iron are also hard to come by. Some are highly decorated but, whilst sixteen La Tène iron scabbard remnants were excavated at South Cadbury, it was probably the leather or wooden version, bound with bronze, iron or leather, with a protecting chape at the end, that served the most utilitarian purpose, those of bronze being for more ceremonial activities. A strap-loop would attach the scabbard to a belt, as a possible iron example from Bury Hill in Hampshire shows.

It is the sword or dagger chape, sometimes with accompanying binding and hilt-guard, that often survives, rather than the weapon itself. Thus, ten iron chape fragments of La Tène I type (a rare find in Britain) were excavated at South Cadbury, but only a few (possibly) bits of the sword itself were recovered (O'Connor *et al.* 2000, 238). No doubt iron swords, such as that from Twyn y Gaer with a bone pommel (Howell 2006, 60), and the decorated daggers discovered at Coygan Camp and Ham Hill, were highly prized and not to be discarded lightly.

British and continental swords of early to middle La Tène can reach a considerable length, perhaps cavalry weapons (Harding 2007), one from Spettisbury Rings being 79cm in length, including a tang of 12.5cm. The following examples show the considerable quality of manufacture. The Hunsbury pits produced two iron swords. One had a blade of 67cm with tang and heart-shaped chape and fragments of bronze scabbard-binding, giving a total length of 85.9cm. The other sword, with a blade of 85cm but without a tang, was contained in a finely engraved middle Iron Age bronze scabbard with bronze plates front and back; the total length was 90cm. The solid bronze chape was all in one piece (Figure 59).

The Grimthorpe iron sword, in a scabbard with bronze plates to the front and iron at the back, came from a very different context: a rare crouched warrior burial with shield, sword and spear and other grave goods dated to around the first century BC (Figures 58a, g and 60). Hillforts are not a feature of the Yorkshire Wolds, but the site may have had its origins in the early first millennium BC (Harding 2004, 31). The sword, originally some 79cm long, was laid on the left side of the skeleton underneath the shield (described below), and had a bronze hilt-guard, but only part of the scabbard's bronze plate survived. The heavy bronze chape was seemingly decorated with six small red Mediterranean coral beads attached by a bronze pin.

With swords come shields, which also had great symbolic importance; examples come from both English and Welsh hillforts. Unlike the usual manufacture on the continent, in which perishable materials were used for most shields, those surviving in Britain are frequently decorated and completely or partly covered in bronze (Stead 1968, 173–6). But, even so, it is likely that those for day-to-day use would have been made of wood, perhaps painted or covered with leather to give added protection. There is one from Littleton Bog in Co. Tipperary. Ornate shields would have been more to do with status and display than battle, as the fine late Bronze Age example located just below the south-west entrance of South Cadbury shows.

The wooden Moel Hiraddug shield, described below, would have been a more practical weapon of war and remnants of metalwork from South Cadbury wooden Iron Age shields are described by O'Connor *et al.* (2000, 239–42). These included fragmented copper alloy shield-boss mounts, iron bosses and binding clamps to hold the copper alloy binding which finished off the wooden or leather edges. These clamps were scattered about the site, perhaps indicating that they often came loose and that the use of shields

FIGURE 59. The iron sword and bronze scabbard, from the pits on the site at Hunsbury, Northampton, would have been prized possessions.

NORTHAMPTON MUSEUM AND ART GALLERY.

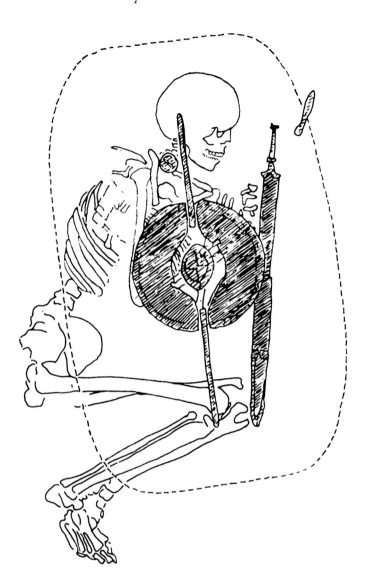

FIGURE 60. Hypothetical reconstruction of the Grimthorpe warrior burial. The shield covered the body and sword, with spearhead to the figure's left side and bronze disc and studs about the chest and shoulders. Sixteen bone pegs were also distributed about the remains. Redrawn after Stead 1968.

was common. No doubt, therefore, some shields would have been decorated, as the late Iron Age/Romano-British decorative bronze strip from St Mawgan-in-Pyder in Cornwall (see Figure 58b) and the sheet bronze plaque of a stylised horse from South Cadbury show. In the Grimthorpe warrior burial the remains of the La Tène shield covered the breast and arms of the crouched body, and included a bronze cap, which would have ornamented the centre of the shield-boss, and two crescentric flat bronze plates from either side of this central cap, which would formerly have been nailed to the shield itself. Sheet bronze covered the spine and rivets and pins secured the elements of the shield in position (Stead 1968).

Fine helmets or crowns come from the continent, but evidence of their use in Iron Age Britain is rare; a few examples are known from the middle Iron Age to the Roman period. There are representations of helmets on the Aylesford bucket and on some coins, the two complete existing helmets being the 'Waterloo' horned version from the Thames and one of 'jockey-cap' design of unknown provenance. The long-lost bronze 'Ogmore' helmets decorated with gold and silver wire from the Vale of Glamorgan and those from Cerrig-y-Drudion in Denbighshire and Lydney in Gloucestershire (Gwilt 2007, 312) indicate possible widespread use by a proud warrior elite. Fragments of possible 'Celtic' helmet iron cheek-pieces came to light at Croft Ambrey, one embossed with an apparent animal motif, but perhaps it was caps or helmets of leather that proved the most utilitarian wear, the fine bronze examples being either for ceremonial use or ritual deposition. However, Diodorus Siculus refers to the wearing of horned or animal-crested helmets by Gaulish tribes (Green 1992, 87), the elaborate decoration enhancing the stature of, and making more fearsome, the wearer.

Helmets from the continent can carry bizarre crests, sometimes in the form of an animated flapping bird, as that from Ciumeşti in Romania shows, but the wild boar was a favourite emblem on both helmets and armour. Boar effigies were found at the martial deposit at Arènes and boar and bird-crested helmets are depicted on the Gundestrup cauldron. Such protection would not only ward off blows, but was perhaps considered to act as a supernatural force; the animal was a powerful symbol and the depiction was often of a charging boar with raised hair along its back. A possible helmet-crest in the form of a boar from Gaer Fawr hillfort at Guilsfield in Montgomeryshire could be of native manufacture, although, as the boar was also the symbol of the XX Legion based at Chester just to the north, it could be Roman (Figure 61).

Horses and horse-gear

The horse was essential to Celtic tribes and its importance and sacred nature has been outlined by Creighton (2000) and Yeates (2008). Horse-gear (Figure 62) began to appear in late Bronze Age and early Iron Age hoards in both England and Wales, and at Parc-y-meirch, at the foot of the crags beneath the former Dinorben hillfort, the discovery of bronze harness and fittings in a hoard proved to be early evidence (around 900 BC) of the horse as a prestigious symbol in Wales.

The domestic horse came into Britain from origins in the Near East, Russia and Central Asia. In symbolism, the Celtic warrior mother-goddess Epona, identified by the horse, is associated with fertility and protection, and was a widespread deity in both Gaul and Britain. Venerated and relied upon, the horse was a high-status animal admired for its speed, courage, fertility and intelligence (Green 1992, 204, 210), and had particular feminine links. It was often represented in Celtic art.

The best of the Roman cavalry was recruited from the Celtic tribes of Gaul, and their prowess is well described in the texts. The picture of the chariot pulled

FIGURE 61. The boar helmet figurine from Gaer Fawr hillfort, Guilsfield, in Montgomeryshire, might be native or Roman.

NATIONAL MUSEUMS AND GALLERIES OF WALES.

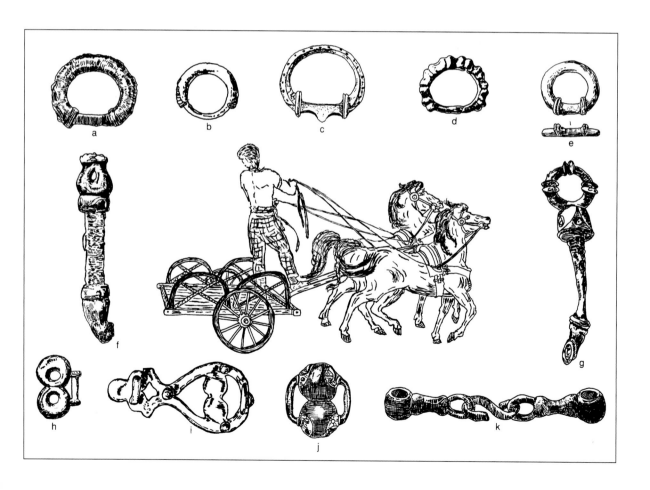

by two draught-ponies is a feature of many a school textbook and is often depicted on Celtic coins. A typical Iron Age pony would have been around 11–13 hands in height, one of the *Equus agilis* type from Kingsdown Camp estimated at 11.2–12.2 hands (Jackson 1930, 96). Bitting damage derived from samples of horse teeth from Danebury and Bury Hill (Hants) has been recently recorded (Bendrey 2007, 7).

There have been a number of reconstructions of Iron Age chariots and there is plenty of classical evidence for their use (Figure 62 centre after Cunliffe undated). A yoke would have been attached, Caesar noting that: 'they (the Britons) can run along the chariot pole, stand on the yoke, and get back into the chariot as quick as lightning' (Cunliffe 1993a, 50). Although the Arras graves have given us valuable insight into chariot design, trappings and gear are widespread in hillfort contexts. However, it is difficult to determine whether more mundane fittings were from a chariot or from a more humble cart, no doubt the most common form of vehicular transport in prehistory. Some items would probably have been used for both: Barbury Castle, Spettisbury and South Cadbury produced iron nave bands which bound the hubs of the wooden wheels.

Perhaps the finest collections of gear come from the Melsonby (Stanwick) hoard and Bury Hill (Hants) (Hawkes 1940a). Both linchpins, which secured the wheels from flying off in motion and often having an iron shaft surmounted by a bronze terminal and head, and terrets, which guided the reins along the yoke, are found in large and small, ornate or plain forms. Likewise, strap-unions or strap-junctions, which attached leather harness straps together, can be beautifully decorated.

At South Cadbury moulds for casting side-links of a bridle bit and terrets suggest on-site manufacture (Foster and Saunders 2000, 233–5). The most common Iron Age bit had three links (the double-jointed snaffle); the single-jointed snaffle, of which two come from South Cadbury, was the most common continental form and was used in Britain after the Conquest. Bits were often of iron, as the Bredon Hill example in Figure 62k shows, but fragments of an Iron Age bridle bit rein-ring from South Cadbury were in bronze and the Hengistbury excavations produced some made of sheet bronze over an iron core; all may be indicative of high-status use.

Such quality gear was finely cast, very decorative and colourful – both Hunsbury and Danebury having good examples – but perhaps the most enigmatic finds of this type are the two figures from Bulbury in the form of bulls or terrier dogs (Figure 63). Their actual use can only be surmised, but elaborate rein-guides are a possibility.

The famous White Horse beneath Uffington Castle hillfort deserves special mention. This was the subject of a geophysical survey and trenches in 1990 and 1994 (Miles *et al.* 2003b, 61–78). The majority of the Horse was made up of successive layers of puddled chalk and hillwash and has changed little in shape since it was dug. OSL (Optically Stimulated Luminescence) dating suggests the figure to be at least 2,500 years old, possibly going back to the late Bronze Age,

FIGURE 62. Horse and chariot fittings. a) terret, max. diameter 40mm (Hod Hill); b) terret, max. diameter 28mm (Bury Hill); c) terret, max. diameter 58mm (Stanwick); d) ribbed terret, max. diameter 32mm (Bury Hill); e) terret, max. diameter 21mm (Thetford Castle); f) linchpin, length *c.*42cm (Bury Hill); g) linchpin, length *c.*22cm (Stanwick); h) strap union, length *c.*30mm (Bury Hill); i) harness fitting, length 65mm (Rainsborough); j) strap union, length 33mm (Bury Hill); k) horse bit, length 15cm (Bredon Hill). Redrawn and adapted after: a), c) and i) Jope 2000; b), d), f), h) and j) Hawkes 1940a; e) Davies *et al.* 1991; k) Hencken 1938. Chariot, Cunliffe n.d., courtesy of the Museum of the Iron Age, Hampshire County Council.

FIGURE 63. The bull or terrier chariot figurines from Bulbury, near Poole, Dorset, might have been elaborate rein-guides.

DORSET NATURAL HISTORY AND ARCHAEOLOGICAL SOCIETY AT DORSET COUNTY MUSEUM.

but at least to the early Iron Age. This is about the time of the construction of the hillfort and the investigators suggested that the two might be linked, although which was constructed first has been open to debate. If the rampart of the hillfort had been faced with split timber, or indeed lime-washed, this would not only have enhanced the visibility of the enclosure but also that of the Horse (Barclay *et al.* 2000, 249). Clearly the Horse at Uffington formed a potent image and was of much significance to its builders, located, as is the hillfort, in a landscape of great symbolic importance as we have seen in Figure 21.

Moel Hiraddug

As a case study, Moel Hiraddug gives us a glimpse of the martial side of hillforts and the symbolism involved. In 1872 miners making a roadway outside the eastern innermost rampart found a hoard of corroded sword fragments, bronze plaques and ironwork from a shield. Of significance was a bright yellow bronze, formerly tin-plated, square plaque (now lost) with triskele decoration and possibly from a shield, box or chariot (Brown 2004, figure 35). The copper ore from which it was made had a distinctive zinc enrichment and came from the hillfort mines at Llanymynech Hill (see page 204). Four or five additional tinned three-cornered plaques, with concave sides and possible additional stud in the centre, were also found, but have also been lost. Whatever significance was assigned to these symbols, the number three was the common denominator.

The triskel, characterised by three swirling motifs from a central core, is an important design in Welsh Celtic art, although it is also recurrent throughout Europe. The number three, embodied in the triplism of deities (the *Deae Matres*

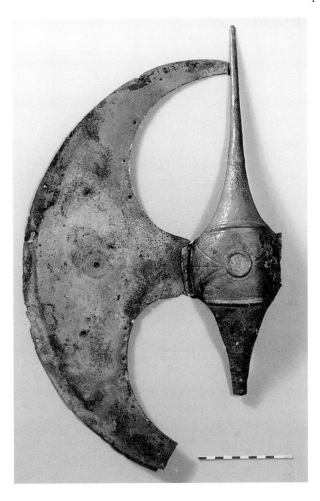

FIGURE 64. The Moel Hiraddug shield-boss adorned the centre of a shield.

THE POWYSLAND MUSEUM, POWYS COUNTY COUNCIL.

of Cirencester, for example), or objects such as the triple-vase from Chester, had powerful meaning in the Celtic world, a fact supported by the Irish and Welsh literary sources (Green 1986, 209). This tripartism could be linked to birth–life–death, or seed–growth–harvest.

Apart from the two sword fragments of just over 30cm in length, the remaining object from Moel Hiraddug was the sheath and crescent plate from the centre of a painted wooden shield, also made of Llanymynech ore (Figure 64). The curved sheath covered the grip and the wooden central ribs, and the crescent-shaped plates attached it to the shield itself. In describing a Celtic warrior with such a shield, Strabo stated that: 'their arms correspond in size with their physique; a long sword fastened on the right side and a long shield, and spears of like dimension'. In the epic Irish tale, *Táin Bó Cúalnge*, a youth ceremonially comes of age by receiving a shield and spear from his lord, and shields were undoubtedly prized objects. Whether there were shield-making centres will be returned to later, but economic factors played an important part in hillfort life, and it is to these that we will now turn.

CHAPTER SEVEN

Economy

Although farming, being the sustainer of life, would have been the main preoccupation of those involved with hillforts there is ample evidence that manufacturing was also important and that goods produced at sites such as Hengistbury Head were not confined to 'in-house' consumption but were also 'traded', bartered and exchanged and were, as a result, transported long distances, involving hazardous passages along recognised sea routes. This chapter will look first at how these networks operated, and then consider factors of importance to the hillfort 'economy'.

The nature of prehistoric trade and exchange

Wells (1995, 230) defines prehistoric 'trade' as the peaceful transmission of goods for other goods and 'exchange' as the transmission of goods primarily for social or political purposes, as in gift exchange or payment of tribute, and no doubt the two were linked. Archaeological evidence suggests regular contact between the peoples of Europe from the Neolithic period onwards, and by the Iron Age complex and extensive systems were in place. However, before the Roman Conquest 'buying and selling' would not have been as we would know it and even the advent of Celtic coinage did not result in the use of currency as such (see Chapter 9). Goods would have primarily formed part of elaborate mechanisms of gift exchange, tribute, clientage and the distribution of largesse according to the political and social structures operating at the time.

River systems as routeways in prehistory

In England and Wales before the advent of the canals from the sixteenth century onwards and the coming of the railways in the nineteenth, bulk goods were transported either by river or cart/pack animal, and short portages across narrow necks of land (the trans-isthmian routes) were a feature of early maritime trade. Thus: 'the articulation of lines of contact and communication was important for the flow of goods, usually in a series of exchange-relays "down the line", involving many changes of ownership along the way' (Sherratt 1996, 211–12). Such lines of flow resulted in the creation of nodal points and areas of importance in prehistoric times, and one theory is that these were marked by rich burials, river finds, monuments and fortifications.

Cunliffe (1995b) considered that Britain could be regarded for the purposes of mobility and information exchange in the prehistoric period not as an entity, but as three zones of contact, defined in terms of their relationship to the continent. The first, the 'Channel Zone', linked by the Straits of Dover, enabled the peoples of the south-east of Britain to maintain contact with the coast of France from Calais to Le Havre and hence the interior (and Mediterranean) by means of the Rivers Seine and Somme. The second zone of contact, the southern extremity of the North Sea, gave the river systems of eastern England, from the Yare to the Thames, access to the Low Countries. The third zone of contact, formed by the western-facing peninsulas of the Llŷn and Anglesey in the north to St David's Head and south to Land's End, gave access to Finistère in France, and Ireland. This ancient system of routes created broad corridors of movement reflected in the cultural similarity between these western British communities and Brittany today, matters that are well explained by Cunliffe (2001).

In putting flesh on these zones of interaction, two major British rivers stand out: first, the Thames, linked externally to the Rhine and Seine, and, second, the Severn, whose estuary faces away from continental Europe and is linked to Brittany and Normandy. However, as Sherratt (1996) points out, the nature of the coast from the Severn Estuary to the continent would have meant a hazardous voyage rounding Land's End in the face of the prevailing westerlies. A trans-isthmian route across the south-west peninsula of England would, therefore, have been an attractive proposition, with access from the Severn Estuary via the Bristol and Hampshire Avons to ports such as Hengistbury Head and Poole on the south coast and thence by ship to Gaul and south to the Mediterranean. The importance of the lowland areas of Wessex and the lower Thames to the flow of goods from north-west to south-east was therefore substantial. Likewise, the coastal trading networks of the Irish Sea, particularly from north Wales, could be linked in the same way southwards via the Dee, Clwyd and Conwy rivers with short portages overland to the Vyrnwy and thence to the Severn, the south coast and the continent. The rich Bronze Age gold and metalwork hoards of north-east Wales show Irish workmanship and/or raw material and testify to a substantial trading connection with Ireland (Brown 2002; 2004).

At the end of the first century BC Strabo wrote of the short sea journey from Gaul to Britain, stating that: 'people who set sail on the ebb-tide in the evening, land on the island at about the eighth hour on the following day', and describing the goods coming from Britain in the very late Iron Age as including: 'grain, cattle, gold, silver, iron, hides, slaves and hunting dogs'. There is archaeological evidence that, at this time, luxury items such as wine, amber, ivory necklaces and glass vessels were popular imports; Diodorus Siculus considered that: 'they [the Gauls] are exceedingly fond of wine and sate themselves with the unmixed wine imported by merchants'. There is evidence for possible widespread long-distance wine transportation in discoveries of amphorae at the hillforts mentioned on page 86.

The legacy of a voyage to north Wales may be found in the discovery off

FIGURE 65. Anchor and chain of Roman western European context from Bulbury, near Poole, Dorset. Length of anchor 1.44m; length of chain 6.5m.

DORSET NATURAL HISTORY AND ARCHAEOLOGICAL SOCIETY AT DORSET COUNTY MUSEUM.

Porth Felen, Llŷn peninsula, of a late second- or early first-century BC lead anchor stock (Boon 1977). Another anchor of a type 'found sporadically in Roman contexts in Western Europe' (Cunliffe 1972) comes from Bulbury hillfort, which overlooks the River Sherford flowing into Poole Harbour, some 3.2km distant (Figure 65).

Sea and river craft in prehistory

Celtic tribes were renowned for their seafaring skills and Celtic seamen had 'solved' the problem of deep-sea voyages by the fifth century BC or earlier (McGrail 1995, 274–6). Strabo noted that the Massiliotes 'have a natural ability in seafaring', while the Veneti of Armorica were considered amongst the best (Ross 1998, 82). It was the boat constructed of a wicker frame covered with a hide skin that probably provided the 'work-horse' of the period, and craft of this type are mentioned by both Caesar and Pliny. They are also referred to in the sixth-century BC *Massaliote Periplus* used by Avienus in his *Ora Maritima* of the fourth century AD. McGrail (1995 after Hawkes 1977; Murphy 1977) considers that, although there are difficulties in the interpretation of place-names, it seems likely that the *Periplus* describes hide boat voyages between Brittany, Britain and Ireland. Their use was widespread (McGrail 1981, 20; Cunliffe 2001), akin to that of the present-day seaworthy currach of western Ireland. A boat from the mouth of the River Ancholme in Lincolnshire, containing a skeleton of possible Roman date, was noted as being a coracle-type vessel (Sheppard 1926) and coracles were once numerous on the rivers of Wales, such as the Dee, Teifi, Towy and Wye, and can be seen on occasion today. Sewn plank boats were also widespread in Europe and may have been used in the Severn Estuary and Bristol Channel (Howell 2006, 56), while the Barlands Farm boat from the Gwent Levels, with its mast and sail, was perhaps what a Romano-British craft might have looked like (Nayling *et al.* 1994). Rafts and log boats akin to those excavated near Brownsea Island in Poole Harbour and at Fiskerton in Lincolnshire were certainly common on the rivers and estuaries of England and Wales in prehistory, and, with hide craft, enabled access far up their courses.

Landing methods and overland transport in prehistory

Most landing places for sea-going vessels in prehistory would have been fairly crude affairs with few facilities, and natural coastal protection would have been relied upon. However, the existence of more elaborate arrangements at Poole Harbour suggests that this was not always the case. Here, the scale of facilities between Cleavel Point and Green Island, where a mole with paved surface has been found, suggests a substantial cross-channel Iron Age port (Markey *et al.* 2002, 10). Elsewhere, where artificial structures were needed, a gravelled hard, as at Hengistbury Head, or pegged timbers and hurdles, found at Ferriby in Lincolnshire (Wright 1990), might have been provided. Boats would have been beached on an ebb-tide – small schooners were beached along the rural coasts of England and Wales well into the twentieth century – or anchored in the shallows below low-water mark off beaches and goods unloaded into smaller craft, possibly log or hide boats. Local drying tidal inlets on exposed coasts, such as the present Clevedon Pill directly below the Wains Hill promontory fort on the Bristol Channel, would have given much-needed shelter with direct access to estuary and sea (Figure 66). Lulworth Cove would have acted in a similar manner, as Wheeler suggests. The sheltered harbour of Solva, on the northern shore of St Bride's Bay in Pembrokeshire, guarded by a small hillfort on Solva Head, and beaches below Trevelgue Head (Figure 16) and Treryn Dinas in Cornwall would have served the same purpose. A similar situation may have existed at Dinas Gynfor, at Cemaes Bay on Anglesey, whose harbour, Porth Llanlleiana, to the north-west, was used in the nineteenth century for china stone and may well have had a well-used path to it from the fort (Lynch 1991, 272). Horse- or oxen-drawn carts and wagons, as well as manpower, would then have taken goods inland. Diodorus Siculus writes that tin was taken by wagon to an island he called 'Ictis', possibly St Michael's Mount in Cornwall or, more probably, Mount Batten at Plymouth (Cunliffe 1983; 1988a), finds there dating from the fourth to the first century BC.

Whilst the preferred means of transport to and from international landing places would have been the rivers, where the flow became too great or the depth too shallow, or where the river bed became encumbered with obstacles, riverside or valley tracks are certain to have been used, keeping to the lower ground if possible. In wet seasons these could become impassable and, no doubt, alternative routes on higher ground would be turned to. There is evidence from the continent that, in places, these lowland paths were connected to the higher 'ridgeways' by sunken roads (McGrail 1995, 277).

The long-established ridgeways of the late Neolithic and early Bronze Age

provided important communication links, but increasing density of settlement, coupled with a deteriorating climate, must have resulted in far-reaching changes in Iron Age communication patterns. Although there must have been a dense network of overland tracks, the archaeological evidence for their existence is poor. The deeply worn and sometimes embanked tracks associated with the Dan y coed enclosure in Pembrokeshire and Varchoel Lane in Montgomery (Davies and Lynch 2000), and the fourth-century BC multiple trackways at Goldcliff near the second Severn crossing (Bell and Neumann 1997, 98, 102–3) are exceptions, although these Severn routeways could also have been associated with fishing. Nevertheless, the construction of trackways across difficult ground has a long tradition and dendrochronology has determined a date of 3806 BC for the Sweet Track causeway across the boggy Somerset Levels.

There is also literary evidence for road construction in the Celtic period. Diodorus Siculus, for example, states that: 'they transport the wine by boat on the navigable rivers and by wagon through the plains'. The transport of such bulky items suggests that the hardest, driest land would be chosen and, where necessary, artificial surfaces constructed. Ross (1998, 79) suggests that the Romans must have 'utilised old trackways and existent routes and systematised

FIGURE 66. Wains Hill fort in the foreground and anchorage at Clevedon on the Bristol Channel, Somerset. Landing places such as this would have been much used in the Iron Age.

them' and, according to the Irish texts, wooden roads of some kind were laid, the Brehon Laws stipulating regulations governing their making and repair. Rivers were no doubt crossed by timber-built bridges, ferries and fords.

Water transport, or routeways associated with passable river valleys, would have provided the most efficient communication and access networks during the Iron Age and their relationship to hillfort location will be considered in Chapter 10. With this background let us now look at the hillfort economy in a little more detail, beginning with the most widely practised activity, metalworking.

Metalworking

The origins of metalworking in Britain go back to the third millennium BC, when the working of bronze began. Bronze in prehistory was composed of an alloy of copper (90 per cent) and tin (10 per cent). The relationship between bronze and iron at the Bronze Age/Iron Age transition has already been referred to in Chapter 1 but, although by the later Iron Age prestige metal goods from the continent had found their way into the graves of the wealthy in southern England, in Wales, despite pockets of wealth, more mundane tools predominated. Hingley (1997) has suggested that ironworking in Iron Age Britain had symbolic meaning related to regeneration and agricultural production, and that metalworking in general seems to have been imbued with the supernatural. According to the Irish and Welsh literary sources the smith was ranked highly in society (Harding 2007, 15). Many hillforts show some evidence of iron tools, weapons and domestic items, some of which, as we have seen, are exquisite examples of Celtic craftsmanship. Currency bars (see page 164) and other forms of bulk iron from southern Britain (see Chapter 9) suggest that trade and exchange was extensive (Crew and Salter 1993; Crew 1994).

The excavations of Peter Crew (1991; 1998) at the later prehistoric west Merioneth settlement of Crawcwellt and the hillfort of Bryn y Castell have shed much light on the role of ironworking generally. Crawcwellt was a primary ironworking site with an estimated production of either a tonne of smithed blooms or about half a tonne of refined bars (equivalent to about 1,000 currency bars), either for local or outside consumption or both. Experimental work concluded that each kilogram of bar iron would have required around one tonne of wood and twenty-five man-days of work. With this resource input iron was a very valuable commodity and worthy of ritual deposition. Finds from north-west Wales point to the relative wealth of the late prehistoric community there (or at least its leaders), which was based on iron. The Trawsfynydd yew stave tankard with bronze covering, found mid-way between Bryn y Castell and Crawcwellt, the 300kg of iron and steel objects from Llyn Cerrig Bach on Anglesey, included among which were swords, tyres, tongs and currency bars and, to the east, the Capel Garmon firedog could all be evidence of local production and wealth.

It is possible that there were relationships between production centres such as Crawcwellt and Bryn y Castell, but the existence of ironworking of the same late prehistoric period from at least three sites in the same valley make it pertinent to: 'ponder on the role of the cluster of hillforts in the Dolgellau area' and especially the hillfort of Moel Offrwm, which dominates the skyline and is of unusually large size for that part of Wales (Crew 1998). Dating evidence from Crawcwellt and Bryn y Castell suggests intense activity just before the Roman Conquest, which may represent the last flourish of the local industry before large quantities of Roman iron contributed to its demise. Although most excavated settlements and hillforts show some evidence of small-scale secondary iron production, there are relatively few known primary production sites in Britain. The quantity of slag from Crawcwellt and Bryn y Castell is unusually large, but lack of comparable knowledge precludes comparisons. As Crew (1998, 35) concludes, the two sites may be examples of centres that existed in Britain in their hundreds

During the Romano-British period one of the greatest concentrations of ironworking was in the Weald of Kent and Sussex. This industry used the easily workable sideritic ores of the Wadhurst Clay, which were naturally exposed in deep stream or valley bottoms or were dug from pits. It has been suggested that to the north of the Weald some of the later Iron Age hillforts were associated with the industry, Detsicas (1983, 172) citing the 2.7ha Garden Hill, Hartfield, with finds of bloomery cinder and slag from local working.

Similarly, the great mineral wealth of Cornwall is clearly reflected in its hillforts and it is possible that former Neolithic enclosures such as Carn Brea became centres of mineral exploitation during the Iron Age. Here caches of tin and copper ore have been found in storage pits in a way similar to that found at sites in Brittany. However, the lack of major published work on metal production in the Weald and the south-west in general is an impediment to its discussion here. Other hillforts and areas also demand more attention: the ironstone of the east Midlands and east Cotswolds, for example.

Although variable in quantity, evidence of metalworking in the form of slag, crucibles and other necessities is found at hillforts, but production tools are more common, from the very mundane hammer from Bredon Hill to the more exotic, such as the iron anvil of 75 × 58cm from a pit at Sutton Walls, which would have been an extremely valuable possession. The Pen Dinas (Aberystwyth) excavations unearthed only one lump of iron slag, but widespread slag and smithy-type work next to the rampart indicated large-scale iron forging at Danebury. Here, fragments of bronze-working crucibles suggest that scrap was melted down for recasting, and an alloy with high cobalt and nickel content, possibly from the south-west, was used for sheet bronze work (Cunliffe 1993a, 94–5). These local production centres, and the mines that provided the raw materials, would have had substantial effects on the surrounding environment in terms of both woodland clearance and pollution, and small statistical peaks of copper have been recorded corresponding to known early Bronze Age mining in mid Wales (Phillips and Mighall 2000, 59).

This does not mean that iron was traded and exchanged from every site, and production was probably mostly for internal consumption. At Blackbury Castle in Devon the iron slag scattered about the hillfort could have been detritus from essential work relating to farming (Young and Richardson 1955, 57). Simple metalworking and repair would have been the day-to-day ingredient of a stock-keeper's lot, akin to the making of pots or parching of corn – a part of everyday life. At Caer Cadwgan metalworking residue also seems to have been related to domestic farming concerns, and from Croft Ambrey to Maiden Castle the presence of iron 'dogs' used to grip metal, wood and leather suggests that the repair of utensils and general leatherworking and woodworking were widespread activities. Ironworking, of course, required its own tools and a long spatulate-ended hearth implement or 'poker' from Conderton Camp was used to rake the fuel and remove slag; dated to as early as the fourth century BC, these implements were used at least to Roman times (MacDonald 2005, 156).

Although local supplies of ore would be used if available, as at Blackbury and Hengistbury Head, the raw materials of iron, copper, tin and stone could be brought long distances. Thus, iron ore came in quantity from the Weald, the Forest of Dean and the Midlands ironstone belt, copper from north Wales and the northern Marches, and tin and copper from the south-west peninsula.

The significance of the mining and working of lead, silver and gold in England and Wales in prehistory is tantalisingly difficult to pin down, although Yeates (2008, 98 after Gough 1930, 19) states that lead was mined in later prehistory in the Mendips. But during the Roman period these minerals assumed great importance, and the lead and silver of areas such as north-east Wales and the Mendips (whose silver was of some quality) contributed significant sums to the imperial coffers (Brown 2004, 86–7). The source of the gold for the fine silver-gilt trumpet brooch of the first century AD from Carmarthen, which is believed to be of local manufacture, could have been the mines at Dolaucothi, which were certainly in use in the Roman period but probably of much earlier origin (Burnham and Burnham 2004). Finds of gold in general are few and far between, and whether the gold sources around the Mawddach Estuary/ Dolgellau area were exploited in prehistory can only be a source of speculation, but the late Bronze Age bracelets from the Graig-yr-Wolf hoard from Eryrys in Flintshire were from a Welsh source (Brown 2004, figure 27). As indicated, Bronze Age trade in luxury items such as Irish gold bracelets and lock-rings, as well as amber beads and bronze harness decoration, as found spasmodically in Anglesey and along the north Wales coast, gives an indication of sophisticated communications networks from Ireland to eastern England and the continent via Wales (Davies and Lynch 2000, 203).

There is abundant evidence of bronze production at a wide variety of hillforts throughout England and Wales and this, together with the relationship between hillforts and mining and metalworking in general, will be returned to in Chapter 10.

Salt

The importance of salt in prehistory cannot be overemphasised. It was not only a necessary component of the human diet, but was essential as a preservative and part of the leather-making process. Although salt could be obtained from cattle blood on-site, it appears to have come great distances to many hillforts: the four main sources being the brine springs of Droitwich in Worcestershire, which were in operation by the sixth century BC and lasted until the turn of the millenium (Riehm 1961; Morris 1985), those of the Middlewich area of mid-Cheshire, the sea, and specific local sources, such as the salterns of the Fens and fen-edge (Morris 2007) and coastal marshes (Lane and Morris 2001). Salt for Danebury came mostly from the evaporation of sea-water from Dorset and Hampshire (Cunliffe 1993a, 97), and the sea was possibly the source for most hillforts within easy reach of the coast and for the coastal forts themselves.

The paraphernalia of salt production – fired-clay containers for drying and transportation, supports and ovens – is called 'salt briquetage'. This is referred to in Wales and the Marches as VCP (very coarse pottery): an oxidised, orange to reddish-coloured roughware found at a number of Iron Age sites (Gelling and Stanford 1967; Morris 1985). Droitwich VCP comes in two general types: one sandy and the other with a more organic fabric, both of which are found at Midsummer Hill. VCP probably originating in Cheshire is very similar, but is a stony-tempered ware. VCP clay was also fired for common domestic items and especially for small stoves for baking, as found at Sutton Walls and Croft Ambrey, where, at the latter site, small sherds of this reddish baked clay with a grey core showed heavy thumb prints (Stanford 1974, 210).

The distribution of these wares gives some idea of the vast distances that might be travelled in this period and the nature of an active supply network. From the centres in Worcestershire and Cheshire (particularly from the latter) salt reached Sudbrook on the Severn Estuary and arrived at the valley of the Usk and Anglesey by the second century BC. Apart from the Llyn Cerrig Bach votive deposits, VCP comprises a significant proportion of the few artefacts of Iron Age date from Anglesey (Lynch 1991, 35–6). To the east, although imported articles are rare from middle Iron Age Northamptonshire, salt briquetage with origins in Cheshire has been found at Hunsbury. On the other hand, salt from the Fens appears not to have been transported in briquetage (Kidd 2004, 61), but rather in sacks or in bulk.

As well as at Midsummer Hill, Droitwich VCP comes from a variety of hillforts, from the Wrekin in the north to Twyn y Gaer, Sudbrook and Lodge Hill Camp in the south, sometimes in association with Cheshire stony-tempered ware, which is found on its own in many hillforts in north and mid Wales and the Marches. Certainly the major rivers, the Severn, Wye and Usk, would have served as essential corridors along which the commodity would have been transhipped. However, the absence of salt containers from south-west Wales could indicate the extraction of salt from the sea, also a feature of the Thames

FIGURE 67. Iron Age barrel-shaped pottery jar from Salmonsbury, Bourton-on-the-Water, Gloucestershire.

CHELTENHAM ART GALLERY AND MUSEUM.

and Medway marshes of Kent, which were perhaps one source supplying the Kentish hillforts. Here shallow oval hearths or wood-burning fires fired evaporation vessels which enabled the salt crystals to form, and briquetage made from local clay (sometimes with straw) litters many sites. Salt panning was also undertaken on the Sussex coast at Eastbourne and at the many tidal creeks of Romney Marsh, and continued well into the Roman period (Detsicas 1983, 170–1).

Over time, salt production must have formed a substantial industry, the investigations of Morris in the Fens (2007, 438–40) indicating a rapid intensification of use from the middle Iron Age into Roman times, after little change in production in the preceding 1,000 years. During the later Iron Age organic temper (such as wheat chaff) in the clay enabled higher oven temperatures to be reached, and the repair and reuse of containers made production more efficient. Demand was evidently increasing and the makers responded to this.

Pottery

To attempt a critique of the distribution and character of pottery within hillfort contexts is outside the scope of this book, and the discussion below can only be, at best, cursory, but pottery is a key component of any hillfort excavation and ubiquitous at most (Figure 67). The monumental task of analysis of the vast quantity of sherds often involved – at Danebury, nearly 160,000 (Cunliffe 1993a, 87) – is daunting.

Pottery assemblages can be extremely complicated, but, just to give a flavour of what is involved, one or two salient points can be made. Barry Cunliffe (1991) described three broad regional and chronological groupings in parts of Iron Age England as a number of ceramic style-zones constituted by the type of pottery used. These could have resulted from a pattern emanating from a particular production centre or, at best, just a zone of contact, and are as follows: Earliest Iron Age from *c.*800 to 600 BC; Early Iron Age from *c.*600 to 400/300 BC and Middle Iron Age from *c.*400/300 to 100 BC. For example, the Ivinghoe-Sandy group (as found at Ivinghoe Beacon) of the Earliest grouping, which spread from Somerset, Sussex and Kent to Norfolk and Yorkshire, is generally composed of traditionally made coarse pottery of various types and is found in association with bronze implements. The Early Iron Age grouping extends from the south-west to Somerset and Sussex, the east Midlands and the Yorkshire Wolds to the north. The Middle Iron Age grouping lies in a line from the far south-west north-east to the Humber, taking in parts of south-eastern Wales and the southern Marches, each of which areas have their own distinctive styles.

Purely as examples, are wares from the south-west and from the Midlands. From the former come notable highly decorated necked bowls and jars, termed 'South-Western Decorated Wares', which possibly originated in Brittany in the fifth century BC and continued throughout the middle Iron Age. There are six types according to the composition of the various rock types, which suggest different production centres (in Cornwall, Devon and Somerset, with the latter area seeming to have lasted in production the longest and until the Conquest). Also distinctive is pottery focused on the lake villages of Glastonbury and Meare in Somerset, of which the 'saucepan pot' type was dated at Danebury and Hengistbury Head to the late fourth century to *c.*100 BC (Harding 2007, 157).

The situation in the Midlands is somewhat different, with a quantity of generally poorly fired large plain vessels of bucket and barrel shape, as found at Mam Tor and the Markland Grips promontory fort. These poor-quality and rarely decorated wares are of a buff and red to black colour, with a few sherds showing decoration in the form of crude raised arcs or circles, as an example from Castle Pit Hill at Melbourne, also in Derbyshire shows. There is also evidence of a paucity of production in comparison with sites further south: of the eighteen hillforts at the southern end of the Pennines, Portfield and Markland Grips have produced some sherds, but, apart from Mam Tor and Ball Cross in Derbyshire, few have shown pottery in any quantity. The nearest hillfort to these with major pottery finds is Breedon-on-the-Hill in Leicestershire, but this pottery has no relationship with that from Mam Tor (Coombs 1976). Occasionally, however, a local product shows a greater degree of artistic endeavour and the Hunsbury globular bowls from around the third to the first centuries BC have a variant of the interlocking yin-yang design 'highlighted by rosettes in a running S-scroll design' (Harding 2007, 155).

The intricacies of manufacture and distribution of the various pottery types are too complex to be detailed here but, suffice to say, the centres of production of the 'duck-pattern' wares of the Malvern Hills and their widespread, if local, distribution must testify to a sophisticated, professional and commercial enterprise. Duck-stamped pottery has been found not only in Marches hillforts, but farther afield at Sutton Walls, Conderton Camp and Bredon Hill (from about 100–50 BC) and on the Cotswold scarp at Cleeve Hill and Leckhampton Hill. Cornish cliff castles, such as Gurnard's Head, have examples and sherds of duck-ornamented pottery have been found close to the coastal promontory fort of Giant's Castle, on St Mary's in the Scilly Isles (Ashbee 1974, 212). At Twyn y Gaer a vessel of stamped Malvernian ware was found in a fourth- to early third-century BC context and, although not in large quantities, pottery is a persistent feature of sites in south-east Wales, where much work has still to be done on portable material culture generally (Gwilt 2007, 303–4). Certainly the investigation of pottery distribution can tell us a lot about the socio-economic connections of the time. The pottery assemblage from Lodge Hill Camp, for example, is dominated by vessels from the Malvern region, but calcite-tempered wares from the Severn Estuary-Bristol Channel area are absent, Pollard *et al.* (2006, 51) inferring that their absence might well be 'indicative of regional political affiliation' and contact with communities to the north-east via the valley of the Usk rather than the Severn Estuary.

In contrast, noticeable in the generalised distribution of pottery nationally is the seemingly aceramic status of northern England and north and west Wales. In these areas vessels of leather, hide or wood could well have been favoured at the expense of pottery, as the wooden bowls from Y Breiddin and Stanwick referred to in Chapter 6 show.

Slaves

It is difficult to ascertain whether slavery was endemic in prehistory, but if it was widespread it would have had significant ramifications throughout society (Taylor 2005). Strabo and Tacitus referred in the first century AD to one of the 'attractive' features of Britain being the large number of slaves available, and there is a little evidence of a flourishing trade. Two slave-gang chains come from Llyn Cerrig Bach (Fox 1946, 84–5) and another, with six hinged collars, was found at Lord's Bridge in Cambridgeshire. Boyd Dawkins described two pairs of iron fetters from Bigberry Camp in Kent which could have acted as leg-irons or been used for hobbling an animal. Each was made of two trefoil links connected together with movable bars which hooked or locked together. Also from the hillfort were slave chain neck-rings of ingenious design which ensured that, apart from the first so fettered, no man in a gang could release himself without his neighbour being released first (Jessup 1933, 109). The hillfort was abandoned some time after 54 BC (Ashbee 2005, 160), but whether these chains were deposited as votive items before or after this date is open to question (Figure 68).

FIGURE 68. Slave chains
from Bigberry hillfort,
Tunbridge Wells, Kent.
MAIDSTONE MUSEUM AND
BENTLIF ART GALLERY.

Certainly, slavery was a fact of life in Rome and slaves from the peripheral parts of Britain were sold in the markets of the south and possibly at Hengistbury Head (Hawes and Holloway 1994, 7). A wooden tablet of a deed of sale of a slave girl from Gaul, who was sold for 600 *dinarii*, was found at the No. 1 Poultry site in London in 1994 (Miles 2005, 145). Of course gang chains and fetters could have been for prisoners and not slaves, but as Cunliffe (1991, 543) observed: 'While slavery no doubt existed in Iron Age Britain the production of slaves for export cannot have failed to have had a dramatic effect on social systems and may have been as disruptive in Britain in the first century BC as it was in west Africa in the sixteenth and seventeenth centuries AD'. Much evidence is lacking on this most important of subjects to the hillfort economy and the Iron Age social fabric in general.

Farming

There can be little doubt that farming was the mainstay of the Iron Age economy, and, surprisingly, at this time was probably above subsistence level. Surpluses are evident from as early as the Neolithic and the very existence of granaries and storage pits at hillforts, the importance of activities such as metalworking, and the vast amount of time required to construct such a labour-intensive structure as a hillfort all testify to considerable time available outside food production (Dark 2002, 118). In England, with regional variations, cereal production was important in clement areas from north to south, but especially in the south-east. In Wales, although Fox (1932) suggested that the dictates of topography, soils and climate would have resulted in a dominance of pastoralism over cereal production, a mixed farming regime was probably the norm except in mountainous areas. In most areas the interdependence of arable and livestock would have been felt.

Before around the turn of the second millennium, emmer wheat (*Triticum dicoccum*) and naked barley (*Hordeum tetrasticum*) provided the staple grains, to be replaced later by spelt wheat (*Triticum spelta*) and the hulled variety of barley (*Hordeum hexasticum*). Whilst emmer was best grown on the lighter, more easily worked soils, spelt was also suitable for heavier tilth, and therefore much larger areas of both England and Wales could be cultivated. As a result clay soils, which form vast areas of the country, began to be settled and rye (*Secale cereale*), oats (*Avena spp.*), and bread wheat (*Triticum aestivocompactum*) entered the scene in the later Iron Age.

Cereal finds at excavated enclosures have been few, despite increasing evidence of grain production at remarkably high altitudes, as at the Iron Age Erw Wen enclosure near Harlech (Kelly 1988, 141). However, querns for grinding grain for flour are common at hillforts and cereals formed a basic ingredient of the everyday diet. Around the fourth/third century BC the simple saddle quern was replaced by the rotary version (Cunliffe 1995b, 114), a major technological advance, although the former continued in use, at Salmonsbury for example, into the first century AD. It follows, then, that ovens and accoutrements used for crop processing have been found at hillforts, and from Uffington Castle a small Romano-British oven had an elongated flue and circular stoke-hole (Lock *et al.* 2003, 113–14). A late Roman corn dryer at Balksbury used the hypocaust principle to circulate heated air beneath the grain (Wainwright and Davies 1995, 26), and in the later occupation layers of Sutton Walls a typical Roman T-shape corn-drying oven was made of slabs of sandstone (Kenyon 1954).

It is outside the scope of this book to consider in any detail the whole question of ancient field patterns and their relationship to hillforts, which was considerable, and research on the subject has only scratched the surface. Evidence of the so-called 'Celtic fields', a much used but erroneous term, can be seen throughout England and Wales; typically small and roughly rectangular in shape and bounded by 'lynchets' or banks, which had accumulated as a result of ploughing, or walls of stone cleared from the fields. The size and shape of these fields has been attributed to the use of the primitive 'ard' plough which, without mouldboard to turn over the sod, was used in a criss-cross fashion. From Cornwall to the Berkshire and Wiltshire Downs, to south-west Wales and north to the Pennines fine examples of these fields can still be seen in close proximity to hillforts, such as Clawdd y Milwyr on St David's Head, and in parts of Wessex field systems were cut through by what were, in effect, ranch boundaries, suggesting a wholesale reorganisation of the Iron Age landscape (Muir 2004, 28). We have touched on the question of linear demarcation and hillfort siting in a previous chapter and this, together with the significance of a hillslope position for farming, will be returned to again in Chapter 10.

There is plenty of evidence of the types of animal kept in both farming and ritual contexts at hillforts. Within some sites the number of bones found is enormous, while at others adverse environmental conditions, especially high soil acidity, have rendered identification impossible. This was the case at the heavily calcined assemblage from Dod Law West in Northumberland (Smith 1989, 38), where only a little tooth enamel of cattle and horse was left. Pig bone does not survive as well as that of other species, which poses its own problems.

Cattle and sheep not only provided hides and wool, but fertilised the land. In general terms there was a gradual increase in sheep numbers over cattle nationally as the first millennium BC progressed, with a corresponding decrease in sheep over cattle and pigs in the Romano-British period (King 1991; Albarella 2007, 391). One theory is that this increase in sheep in Wessex reflected the specialist manufacture of woollen cloth for exchange. However, at Uffington Castle, Balksbury Camp and Maiden Castle there seems to have been little change in stock kept over time, apart from the appearance of domestic fowl (Ingrem 2003, 284), and no doubt there would have been considerable variations from region to region and site to site.

The age of animals at death is critical in the determination of the use to which they were put. Analysis of sheep bone from Conderton Camp suggests slaughter at between one and three years, implying production of meat over wool; also 40 per cent of cattle were between fifteen months and three years at slaughter. Young calves were also numerous at Danebury. Most Iron Age sites show sheep being killed off young in the autumn, Albarella (2007, 394–7) suggesting that this was more to do with the problem of keeping stock over the winter months rather than anything else, autumn also being a time of major festivals requiring quantities of meat. The Madmarston Camp excavations proved that both cattle and sheep were slaughtered for food (Fowler 1960, 30). However, despite local variations, overall, there was a consistency in animal husbandry over the first millennium, major change only coming with the Romans, with greater consumption of beef, mainly by the military, compared with that in the Iron Age.

It is difficult to compare hillforts statistically as animal populations differ and, apart from horn-cores, sheep and goat remains are notoriously difficult to differentiate and are usually included together in analyses. It is also probable that sheep, as a flock animal, would be more represented in the record: Table 1 gives some idea of proportions of sheep/goat, cattle and pig at a number of excavated hillforts. What is immediately noticeable is that, at nearly two-thirds of the sites analysed, there is a preponderence of sheep/goat in the record. It is natural, of course, that downland sites, such as Uffington Castle and Segsbury on the Ridgeway and Balksbury Camp and Maiden Castle to the south, would have had a preponderance of sheep (Ingrem 2003, 284); at Segsbury this is higher than at any other site excavated so far in the Upper Thames Valley (Mulville and Powell 2005, 117). The chalk downlands of Wessex are still famous for their sheep breeds, the dry nature and lower-growing and less nutritious sward of chalk grassland being much more suited to sheep than cattle.

Hillfort	Sheep/goat	Cattle	Pig
Balksbury Camp	53.8	30.8	15.4
Conderton Camp	61.2	20.5	18.3
Coygan Camp	17.7	63.6	18.8
Croft Ambrey	37.5	29.0	33.5
Danebury	62.7	21.5	15.8
Grimthorpe	28.6	62.6	8.8
Ivinghoe Beacon	31.4	59.4	6.7
Maiden Castle	67.4	23.5	9.1
Pitstone Hill	49.7	31.7	5.8
Rainsborough	47.5	37.0	15.5
Segsbury	67.5	18.6	14.1
South Cadbury	59.5	19.5	21.0
Stanwick	29.1	50.6	20.3
Sutton Walls	32.1	52.7	15.2
Uffington Castle	59.9	26.6	13.5

TABLE 1. Proportions of sheep/goat, cattle and pig bones at selected hillforts.

Nevertheless, to rely solely on geographical trends can be misleading and bone assemblages are complex; they can differ both within and between areas and may be very local in their significance. In Ivinghoe Beacon hillfort on the high Chilterns cattle predominated at 59.4 per cent, compared with 31.4 per cent of sheep and 6.7 per cent of pig, whilst 3.2km away, at Pitstone Hill in the drier part of the Vale of Aylesbury, the situation was reversed, with sheep at 49.7 per cent, cattle at 31.7 per cent and pig at 5.8 per cent, no doubt reflecting the different, less wooded environmental conditions at the latter (Cotton and Frere 1968, 202).

The low incidence of animal remains at Welsh hillforts, especially in the west, makes it very difficult to assess the role played by each type of animal. This is even the case at smaller farmstead enclosures such as Woodside in Pembrokeshire where, although cereals were found, the keeping of animals was probably the main activity. However, there are exceptions, and of the total animal bone from Coygan Camp cattle accounted for 63.6 per cent. In the Welsh Marches cattle also outnumbered sheep/goat at Sutton Walls, but Croft Ambrey showed the opposite, perhaps because of local conditions. This is reflected in pig numbers, the Welsh and Marches sites showing a clear difference from hillforts in south Wales. At Croft Ambrey (Herefordshire) they reached one-third of total animals but Coygan Camp (Carmarthenshire) showed only about one-fifth.

The extent to which valuable animals would have been kept within the confines of hillfort enclosures is unknown. Whilst the layout of some suggest a pastoral use, as we shall see, in others their steep banks and deep ditches, internal pits and *chevaux-de-frise* would have made stock management not only very difficult but dangerous; these features appear to have been more to do with keeping animals out than with safeguarding them within. But outside there would also have been plenty of dangers. The attraction of raiding the livestock of neighbouring communities has been mentioned, whilst the danger from wild animals must not be underestimated; wolves still roamed Snowdonia at the end of the thirteenth century AD. Opinions vary on when they were exterminated in Britain – from another 200 to 400 years later – but extra shepherding and herding would have been required, animals sometimes returning to the farms overnight. This practice would have been widespread in prehistory and possible wolf bones/teeth are reported by Wainwright (1970, 153) from Budbury fort in Wiltshire and Balksbury Camp (Harcourt 1970, 54).

A stocking density of two sheep per acre could have been appropriate for stock kept on Iron Age settlements (Mercer 1981b), or at least in a secure corral nearby, but this seems a little high for the more inclement upland areas and a maximum of 1.5 sheep per acre would be more realistic, taking into account present high-altitude open mountain densities in Snowdonia. Also in Wales, Hughes (1993, 360) calculated a mean stocking density of 1.3 bovine units per acre for the Penllyn townships between Bala Lake and the Arenig Mountains in 1318, whilst Moore-Colyer (1976) produced a figure of 1.6 units for sheep and cattle in the managed grasslands of Merioneth for the years 1875–1900. These figures are interesting for a model of Iron Age husbandry and the relationship of hillforts to the farming of the time. Perhaps densities of one unit of cattle and 1.5 of sheep would be appropriate maxima for most upland hillforts/environs.

If the danger of animal loss from predators left out overnight was as substantial as is likely, stock would have had to be driven back to a secure base until the next morning or rigorously shepherded. If that base was a hilltop enclosure the animals would have been driven uphill and down each day, leading to perhaps obvious problems with erosion unless there was some intermediate corral. There is some evidence for such an arrangement below the hillforts on the slopes of the Clwydian Range above the Vale of Clwyd, where a suitable enclosure of possible Iron Age date has been found (Brown 2004, 68–9).

Sheep and goats were domesticated some 10,000 years ago where modern Turkey borders on Iran and Iraq, the Asiatic Mouflon (*Ovis orientalis*) being the ancestor of all modern sheep (Butler 2006, 8). Ryder (1991) indicates that the original wild sheep of Europe, of which the Mouflon was the principal strain, did not have wool but rather hair, similar to that of a deer, and the coat would have moulted in the spring. The development of animals for their wool need not concern us here, but the Mouflon was the type of sheep kept in Neolithic Britain, about 6,000 years ago. At the end of this period and into the succeeding early Bronze Age sheep began to get smaller and evolve a fleece, probably through unconscious selection for breeding on the part of humans.

The Soay, surviving wild today on the island of Hirta, part of the St Kilda archipelago, is a development from the Mouflon. Both have primitive characteristics in common, such as a short tail, a predominant brown colour with a white belly, and a moult each spring. Each autumn the males fight for supremacy. The Soay has both hairy and woolly fleece types (found in Bronze Age textiles) and is a survivor of not only the first sheep but those of the Bronze Age.

The Soay would probably have been plucked and not sheared in Bronze Age times (and indeed other primitive breeds of today also have a tendency to moult), but the finding of hand-shears at Iron Age hillforts suggests that this inefficient method of gathering wool had begun to be replaced by shearing, with subsequent selective breeding for optimum wool growth. In addition, as the climate deteriorated at the end of the Bronze Age, natural selection would have favoured larger animals and we therefore have to look for a type of animal other than the Soay as an example of what an Iron Age sheep might have looked like.

Thus, the sheep of the Iron Age was probably not akin to the Soay, as is often thought, but was more like the small native sheep of Orkney (and formerly Shetland), seen today in those surviving on North Ronaldsay and Linga Holm, which have DNA related to sheep from the Neolithic Skara Brae on the Orkney mainland (Figure 69). Grey animals are likely to have predominated, as with other surviving Iron Age-type sheep breeds on the continent (Ryder 1991).

As we have seen, necessary 'tools' for the production of cloth at hillforts prove that this was an important activity; an example of a spindlewhorl from Hod Hill engraved with a serpent is shown in Figure 55c. The snake was associated with the underworld and death on the one hand and renewal and fertility on the other (both linked in the native mind), and in iconography is usually associated

FIGURE 69. A North Ronaldsay ram. The present sheep of North Ronaldsay in Orkney may be similar to typical Iron Age sheep.

BRITISH WOOL MARKETING BOARD.

with a goddess of fecundity, abundance and healing. It is therefore possible that this spindlewhorl may have been used to spin cloth for a sick person.

Iron Age cattle would have been much smaller in stature than those of today and the Celtic Shorthorn (*Bos longifrons*), a breed similar to the Dexter, would have been a familiar animal on both hillforts and hillslope fields. There is plenty of historical evidence to suggest that valuable stock in the Iron Age would have lived in juxtaposition with people, both within the same enclosure and the same hut, but care must be taken in assigning all of the animal bone found in enclosures to beasts actually reared and kept on site. Raiding and trading no doubt took place and a sophisticated farming regime was probably in place to deal with the basic requirements of stock-rearing and manuring. Cattle/oxen would also have been the animal of the cart and the plough, and were intrinsically involved in the social make-up; to own cattle would have enhanced status.

Farming tools come from many hillforts and tillage on the farms on the lower ground was essentially simple (Figure 70). To prepare a seed bed the ground would first have been broken up by an ox-drawn wooden ard (possibly from two directions, as an ard does not turn over the sod as does a plough as we have seen). The tool would possibly have been strengthened at the end with an iron tip, as found at Danebury. The seed would then have been broadcast-sown by hand and at harvest the corn reaped by hand sickle. Woodworking tools for the construction of buildings, fences, hurdles and so on are also a part of many hillfort assemblages: among many other examples, from Danebury come a saw, a hammer, a chisel, an adze and a gouge; while saws and awls come from Maiden Castle, Battlesbury and Hunsbury.

A hoard of predominantly farming tools was found in the nineteenth century in unknown circumstances at Barbury Castle in Wiltshire. Although formerly dated to 200–50 BC and indicative of a society more concerned with everyday living than with warfare (MacGregor and Simpson 1963), it is now considered to have been a late Roman votive deposit (Bowden 2005b, 159 after Corney pers. comm.). Here were sickles, awls, an earth anvil and simple single-edged knives, similar to examples from Winklebury. Elsewhere, among other sites a billhook came from Bredon Hill. Most intriguing of all finds, however, was the Wrekin iron cow bell, almost identical to the one found beside the 'sanctuary' of the Croft Ambrey annexe and similar to the one inside the Maiden Castle Romano-British temple. Anvils have long been items of ritual, even to the present day, but the finding of these cow bells in ritual contexts in prehistory suggests that superstition and belief played an important part in the farming year. The relationship of hillforts with the unknown will therefore be considered next.

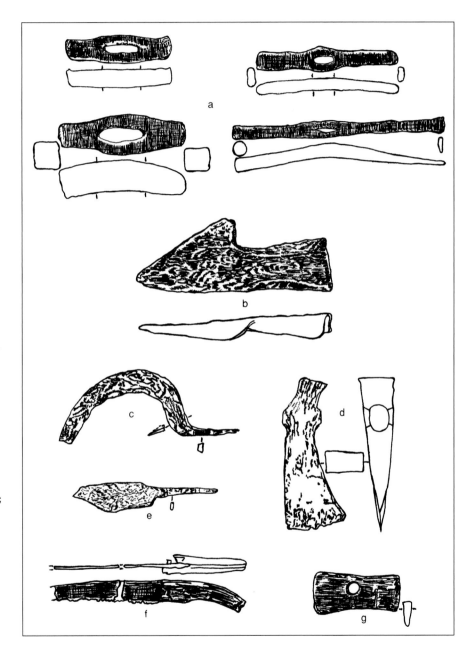

FIGURE 70. Farming and general tools:
a) iron hammer heads, lengths 66mm, 81mm, 91mm, 135mm (Bredon Hill); b) left-winged plough share, length *c.*30cm (Dinorben); c) iron sickle, length *c.*25cm (Dinorben); d) iron shaft-hole axe head *c.*20cm (Dinorben); e) iron knife, length *c.*18cm (Dinorben); f) iron saw, length of blade 17cm (Bredon Hill); g) bone hammer head, length *c.*6cm (Bredon Hill). Redrawn and adapted after: a), f–g) Hencken 1938; b–e) Savory 1971.

CHAPTER EIGHT

Superstition, Belief and Ritual

Superstition, belief and fear of the unknown permeated prehistoric society, as they do in even the most sophisticated of societies today. In contrast to earlier periods, in the late Bronze Age and the Iron Age direct evidence of ceremonial enclosures and ritual activity is scarce and has had to be teased out from excavations and artefact and landscape analyses.

Prehistoric people made no distinction between the supernatural and everyday life, whether in the domestic situation, farming or conflict. There is plenty of evidence for this, particularly addressed in the writings of Barry Cunliffe, Miranda Aldhouse-Green and Ronald Hutton, and encapsulated by Richard Bradley (2005), ritual being: 'the way in which different features of the domestic world were played out'.

Superstition is an irrational learnt behaviour, false links being made between the environment and certain outcomes. Thus, various acts are performed to prevent misfortune occurring or conversely to enhance the probability of good fortune (de Silva and Rachman 2004, 12) and undoubtedly would have been played out within the arena afforded by hillfort interiors. In prehistory, everyday objects, landscapes and natural features, the sun, the moon and the seasons, all exerted powerful influences on the way people conducted their lives and were deemed to decide whether good or evil might occur. The deities would have been manifest in the coming and going of the seasons, the ever-changing weather, good harvests and bad, success or failure, famine or plenty, death and rebirth and all important fertility – of the land and of the people. They would be present in the earth, the sky, water and fire, to be appeased, placated and feared. Although finds attributed to ceremonial are few and far between, and a variety, mentioned in this chapter, are shown in Figure 71, the construction of such an important feature as a hillfort would, in itself, be congenitally imbued with belief, custom and ritual, beginning right at the start of the project.

Deposits, entrances and orientation

Whilst we always have to be careful when considering prehistoric ritual, foundation deposits seem to be a key feature at a number of hillforts, whereby an offering was made to the gods to commemorate or bring good fortune to the new enterprise – a type of ceremonial found even today. This could take a variety of forms, but was often sacrificial in nature and remains of both men

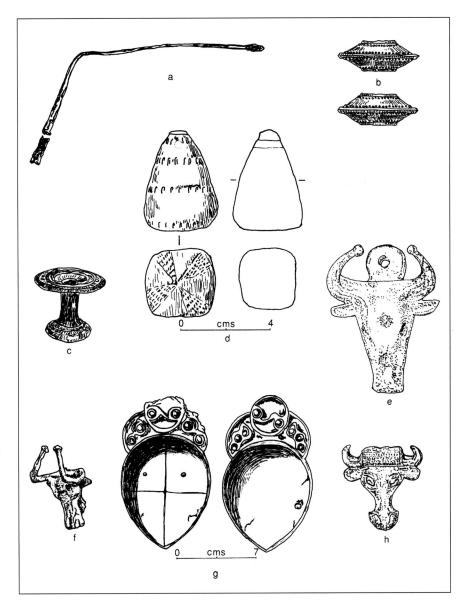

FIGURE 71. Possible ritual objects: a) wand or sceptre, length 24cm (Dinorben); b) gold objects, diameter 37mm (Harting Beacon); c) bronze finial, length 61mm (Ham Hill); d) stone 'pyramid', length 45mm (Salmonsbury); e) ox-head escutcheon, length 64mm (Dinorben, 1956); f) ox-head foot from bowl (Lydney Park); g) ritual spoons, length 104mm (Castell Nadolig); h) ox-head escutcheon, length 35mm (Dinorben, 1912). Redrawn and adapted after: a), e) and h) Savory 1971; b) Keef 1953; c) and f) Jope 2000; d) Dunning 1976; g) Way 1870.

and women have been found buried beneath ramparts, at Castell Henllys, for example (Harold Mytum pers. comm.). Other instances include a Bredon Hill woman covered by flint blocks; another trussed and bound female placed in a pit which was then covered with stones before the rampart was erected at Hod Hill; and, possibly, the crouched burial in a quarry section at Sutton Walls. Maiden Castle has examples in various stages of rampart construction (Taylor 2001, 66). Evidence also comes from bone placed in post-holes, as found at the Maiden Castle shrine and Bredon Hill, where the bone was from an infant. Considering the small number of excavations compared with the total number of sites, coupled with, in most cases, the very small areas actually investigated, rampart burial and the deposition of bone in post-holes are likely to have been common practices.

However, not all foundation offerings involved human sacrifice and the surrender of precious objects would have proved good intent to the gods. The Harting Beacon excavations in Sussex produced two gold penannular 'ornaments' placed 'against the side of the chalk causeway carrying the terraced entrance through the [unfinished] West gate' (Keef 1953). They could have decorated a bowl or vessel, and some connection with Ireland or northern France is possible. Clearly valuable items indeed and, being very fragile, their deposition had been carefully undertaken, suggesting a treasured possession 'sacrificed' when the hillfort was renewed. Likewise, of around 600 BC a Danebury hoard of scrap bronze (including Breton axes, Armorican metal ingots, local socketed axes, spear fragments, a sword hilt and razors) was buried in a small pit in the shadow of the defences, Cunliffe (1993a, 29) speculating that this might have been a dedication on the commencement of the building of the hillfort.

Entrances and doorways have always been imbued with superstition and belief, as has the hearth as we have seen earlier. Throughout the north and west of early Ireland the presence of two opposing doors in the kitchen, although helping to regulate the draught for the open fire, was also associated with luck and portents. Thus, a stranger must enter and leave by the front door lest he take the luck of the house with him. In the Aran Islands a corpse was always carried out of the back door (Estyn Evans 1957, 44–5). Folk customs of entry were also found in parts of Wales up to modern times.

Thus, Hamilton and Manley (2001, 11–12) found that the 'unifying characteristic' of the hillforts of south-eastern England was the western and eastern orientation of their entrances, as also indicated by Bowden (2005a, 19) for southern Britain as a whole, suggesting a possible connection with the rising and setting of the sun. Interestingly, in the Malvern Hills Bowden also found that at British Camp (Herefordshire Beacon), although two of the four entrances were sited at the northern and southern extremities, they had been deliberately orientated so as to face east and west.

A characteristic of some univallate enclosures in Wessex is the blocking of either one of the two east and west entrances. Liddington Castle and Uffington Castle, among others, all show this feature, whereas multivallate sites on the Ridgeway retain their two opposing entrances – Barbury, for example (Corney and Payne 2006a, 136). It was the eastern entrance of Uffington Castle that was blocked, probably within the early Iron Age but no later than 400 BC. Blocking would have severely hampered access to the interior, of course, and the finding of large amount of burnt All Cannings Cross fineware (used in the eighth and seventh centuries BC) in the dump rampart at the blocking point does suggest a deliberate symbolic act – an ancestral connection with those who first constructed the box rampart and eastern gate centuries before. If the Ridgeway had indeed bisected the site via the two gateways, as has been suggested, then this remodelling would have allowed better access to the White Horse and outside connections via a new route to the north of the hillfort (Gosden and Lock 2007, 284). The hillfort would then have been a much more enclosed space with greater definition and symbolic status in the landscape, and it is this aspect that could have also been important at other Wessex sites such as Liddington Castle, where the clearly seen white chalk ramparts would have been a stark reminder of both the importance of the enclosure within and those who built it. On the other hand Pollard *et al* (2006, 49) speculate that the episodes of the blocking of the western entrances at sites such as Lodge Hill and Llanmelin in south Wales, Danebury and Yarnbury (Wiltshire) in Wessex and Moel y Gaer (Rhosesmor) in north-east Wales might have been the result of the west being considered more 'inauspicious' than the east. To this list can be added Liddington, but it was the east entrance that was blocked at Uffington, so things may not have been so straightforward and perhaps more mundane.

It is quite clear, however, that entrances were places of superstition at hillforts and, as a result, were favoured areas for deposition. As boundaries or vulnerable thresholds they were mystical places – in archaeological theory a physical boundary as symbolic of a conceptual boundary (Bowden and McOmish 1987; Dark 2002, 149). Thus, the placement of coin at entrances, particularly if minted in gold, as the Dobunnic stater of Anted from the south-west entrance at South Cadbury shows (see page 163), may have been a very significant event. The possibility of deliberate firing of gates and spirit involvement in guard chambers reinforces the possibility of magico-religious intent, and it is interesting to note that a major find of some 4,000 coins was buried at the entrance of a previously unknown palisaded sanctuary of the Corieltauvi tribe in east Leicestershire (Miles 2005, 118).

It was suggested in the last chapter that the very act of smelting and smithing of iron had a regenerative symbolic meaning – of fertility, birth and death – to those involved in its production, and an association with both cosmology (the rising of the sun in the east) and hillfort entrances (Hingley 1997). At Maiden Castle iron was worked in the middle of the eastern entrance and at Bryn y Castell there is a connection with ironworking and the north-east entrance. As well as cosmological orientation, perhaps the very act of giving birth to metal at places of 'passage' was also significant. Thus, not only 'power' was put into the hands of those blessed with the skills required, but the very act of smelting and fashioning something as important and symbolic as a sword blade or plough share would have been both impressive and 'of another world'.

There are indications of superstition and belief at the entrances of Conderton Camp: an old (at the time) bone weaving-comb found beneath one arm of the inturned rampart terminal at the north entrance should be regarded as an act of dedication. But the presence of two pits in alignment along the line of the central entrance and a circular earthwork outside of the southern entrance and along the line of approach to the spring serving the fort are more enigmatic, and their placement could have had ritualistic overtones (Thomas 2005, 256). Further evidence of possible entrance deposition comes from Blewburton Hill where remains of horse, cow, deer and child were buried at the western passageway beneath earth and collapsed rampart stone. In similar fashion, at Crickley Hill entrance-gate post-holes contained both boar and goat bone: those of boar were especially significant and may have been deposited to impart strength to the new enterprise (Collins 1953; Dixon 1994; Ralston 2006, 138–9).

All of the above examples give strong credence to the great importance placed on the entrance in prehistory, not only to the enclosure itself as we have seen but to the structures within. Estyn Evans describes later myths associated with the orientation of the Irish dwelling house, whereby the west was associated with the setting sun and death. In the 'west-room', or *gaeltacht*, the body was placed for the wake. This fits in with the blocking of western entrances to enclosures as mentioned above, perhaps undertaken in times of stress to ward off potential evil happenings. Graeme Guilbert (1975), looking at the orientation of roundhouse entrances at Moel y Gaer (Rhosesmor), found that a preponderance faced east and south-east, while J.D. Hill (1996) found the same in southern England. There were, no doubt, practical reasons for this, as these aspects maximise light and heat and restrict the prevailing westerly winds from blowing into the building, but these are also the directions of sunrise at the equinoxes and at midwinter, and sun-worship must be considered a possibility. Further north, Oswald and Pearson (2005, 115) discussed doorway orientation at the fifty or so roundhouse platforms of Yeavering Bell; here, the majority were also pointed towards the south-east and due east (also referred to by Parker Pearson 1996 and Oswald 1997). Following on from this general orientation evidence, Townend (2007) considered how phases of the construction of roundhouses were governed by cosmological and thus cyclical factors to give the structure a 'meaningful' identity.

Rachel Pope (2007) has recently looked at the inference of a sun-cult from available roundhouse orientation evidence. In an analysis of 690 mainly Iron Age structures from 253 sites she found that the majority were orientated between north-east and south-east, with the predominant orientations being east, east-south-east and south-east. Interestingly, the doorways of Conderton Camp huts faced both north and east (Thomas 2005, 83). As the optimum orientation for both light and shelter is indeed between north-east and south-east, away from the general west-south-west prevailing wind, Pope emphasised the importance of climatic and topographical factors rather than anything else. Overall, therefore, there may be several and possibly linked ways to interpret orientation evidence, as a general easterly direction not only maximises shelter but has cosmological connotations.

However, how structures within a hillfort interior or hillfort entrances were orientated in relation to external physical features that may have had symbolic meaning themselves has been little researched; a relationship between the entrance to Bolt Tail and Burgh Island (see page 222) for example, and whether there might be any landscape or ritual connection between the enclosure on

Ingleborough and nearby Simon Fell and Pen-y-Ghent. On these and other questions relating to orientation and hillforts more work has to be done.

The Druids

That the Druids existed in prehistory is accepted, but what we do not know is how they permeated society at a *local* level. A great deal of power lay in Druidic hands, consolidated by their manipulation of ritual and control of sacrifice, both of animals and humans. One object of sacrifice was divination, society being much concerned with good days and bad and times for doing particular tasks. Thus, the writhings during a victim's death throes would be interpreted by the Druidic priest one way or another and then acted upon. Today, among the Suri of Ethiopea, goats' intestines are ceremonially used to predict the future.

There is much debate as to whether the writings of the classical authors concerning the less savoury aspects of Druidic ritual are accurate or not, and it is generally assumed that 'blood and gore' were probably embellished for the benefit of the home audience. However, recent finds of much human bone, together with the bone of dog, in a cave in the lower Severn Valley and a possible Druidic burial at Stanway in Colchester, Essex, with medical instruments and possible rods for divination, have brought life back into the argument once again and perhaps these writers were nearer the mark than previously thought. Anglesey has long been considered as a stronghold of Druidic power, and to the east in Cheshire at least one of the two males found at Lindow Moss could possibly have been a sacrificial victim. How this power was manifested in the great north Welsh hillforts can only be a matter of conjecture and inevitably it is expedient to fall back on the classical sources for information.

Woodland locations appear to be but one setting for ritual and rocks, ancient trees, springs, bogs and river confluences could all be inhabited by deities. As in the Bronze Age, there is ample evidence of ritual offerings in watery contexts and some of the finest works of Celtic art have been preserved in this way. The location of hillforts in the vicinity of these 'special places' is considered in Chapter 10.

Four finds shown in Figure 71 give a hint of ceremonial and ritual at hillforts. Whilst cast bronze finials found at a number of sites have been called 'axle-caps' or 'chariot-horn caps', and were thought to have embellished the ends of axles, yokes or draught-poles, it has also been suggested that they might be finials from ceremonial staffs or chairs (Jope 2000, 315). Two come from Ham Hill and a heavy bronze version with vestiges of wooden shaft intact is from the late pre-Roman Iron Age levels of Maiden Castle. The possible Romano-British or later bronze wand or sceptre from Dinorben may also have been a ceremonial or priestly emblem and the curious stone and incised mid-first-century AD 'pyramid' from Salmonsbury (similar to a limestone 'cone' from Barnwood, also in Gloucestershire) could have served a ritual purpose, although a symbolic association with the weaving of cloth has been mooted (Dunning 1976, 114).

Of more certain function is the pair of decorated cast-bronze spoons found in 1829 under a heap of stones at Castell Nadolig hillfort at Penbryn near Cardigan (Barnwell 1862; Way 1870; Jope 2000). The main characteristic of the twenty or so pairs found in Britain is that one is plain with a hole drilled into the right-hand side of the bowl and the other is divided into quarters, three inlaid with metal – usually gold, silver and bronze. In the Penbryn spoon the silver on this second spoon is missing and there is another hole drilled into the right-hand upper quarter and another, plugged with gold, on the upper left. Here was a possible tool for divination, for telling the future, with liquid dripped from the upper spoon through the hole into the lower. These fine objects are in the Ashmolean Museum at Oxford.

Animal symbolism

Animals' meat provided sustenance, their hides and wool gave warmth and their labour enabled existence. It is no surprise, then, that representations of animals figure prominently in Celtic art and that they played a vital role in the relationship between man and deity. Elaborate examples of animal symbolism come from hillforts and we have already seen the boar figurine from Gaer Fawr, Guilsfield in Figure 61. A number of cast-bronze bovine-headed escutcheons, or feet, formerly attached to bronze-sheet-covered pails, bowls or containers, have been found in both England and Wales, with fine examples from hillforts. There seem to be similarities in style. The two from Dinorben are of the late first century AD and no later than the third century AD respectively, and are superb examples of native Welsh/west Midlands craftsmanship. The first, with 'almond eyes and splayed snout' (Gardner and Savory 1964, 145–8) follows a tradition represented by another from Ham Hill, which itself is similar to one from the Gaer at Chepstow and others from Lydney Park. Significant ox-head escutcheons dated to the early second century AD also come from Welshpool, seemingly carrying on the traditions of the Ham Hill piece. A triple-headed version from the River Ribble has a bird and human mask added to that of the ox, which has similarities to the second Dinorben mount. Such animal symbolism, whilst having all the hallmarks of ritual intent, by the third century could have been more about design and status than anything else – prestige objects for an important person. The finding of one of the Dinorben mounts on the site of a large 'building' near to the wand or sceptre mentioned above might support this theory. However, this ornamentation could also have imbued the contents of the vessels with 'mystical power', the head of the beast representing the power of the whole animal. Cattle were not only a measure of wealth in Iron Age society in both Britain and Ireland as we have seen, but were also a representation of strength and virility, symbolising the regenerative forces of the earth and fecundity in general. From the fourth-century AD shrine at Maiden Castle a small, three-horned, formerly silver-washed, figure of a bull has the remnants of three female figures on its back (Figure 72). This strange ensemble

FIGURE 72. Silver-washed figurine of a three-horned bull with deities on its back from the mid-fourth-century AD shrine at Maiden Castle, Dorchester, Dorset.

has been suggested by Green (1992, 215) as possible symbolism associated with Tarvostrigaranus, the 'Bull with Three Cranes', the birds being substituted by the three female forms in the Maiden Castle piece. In Irish vernacular legend, women can be metamorphosed into cranes. However, representations of human heads were also used as vessel mounts, an example coming fairly recently from near Llanmelin hillfort (Gwilt 2007, 316).

Sheep are rarely found in ritual contexts despite their importance for meat and wool and, although they were the most important Danebury livestock recorded, remains were found only occasionally in the pits. One such deposit consisted of two sheep and a cat together, whilst another was of a sheepskin with the lower limbs attached. Rams were symbols of strength and power; as mentioned above, a ram's head handle was found at Hod Hill.

Surprisingly, wild animals do not appear in any quantity in Iron Age faunal contexts, and certainly not at English and Welsh hillforts, where what evidence there is comes mostly from pits. But that does not mean that hunting (recreational or otherwise) did not take place, and the fact that some animals appear in symbolism could mean veneration rather than their use as a source of food. Wild boars, for example, were important symbolic beasts, as we have seen, but their bones and teeth are found only occasionally at hillforts: for example, a molar was reported from Balksbury Camp. Boar's tusks from Bredon Hill (Figure 57l), Salmonsbury, The Trundle (dated to Hallstatt/La Tène) and Lidbury Camp in Wiltshire probably came from pendants or necklaces, and perhaps this talisman imbued the wearer with the strength and fertility of the boar.

Another animal of the hunt, often mentioned in the Irish and Welsh texts and found on the monuments of the Romano-Celtic god Cernunnos and artefacts of the Dobunni just east of the River Severn, was the stag. Cernunnos was the 'stag-antlered god, lord of animals, nature and abundance' (Green 1992, 147) and sits cross-legged on the Gundestrup cauldron, his stag in animal form opposite. The stag symbolised the cycle of the seasons and all that was abundant in nature, the shedding of the horns reflecting the falling of leaves in autumn. A bronze figurine of the animal comes from Milber Down Camp. Antlers were made into essential tools and are found at a variety of hillforts, but unworked skeletal bone from deer is noticeably rare, suggesting that venison was generally off the menu. Those found mostly come from red deer and, infrequently, roe. Perhaps deer, like the wild boar, were deemed sacred. Animal or half-human horned images are often found in Celtic symbolism, and represent aggression, control and virility.

Birds, especially ravens – whose black plumage and predilection for carrion may have been particularly evocative – figure prominently in ritual pits, and Green (1992, 125–6) proposed that birds may have been perceived as the souls of the dead. At Winklebury in Wiltshire a pig was buried with a spread-eagled raven at the bottom of a pit (Wait 1985), and the Danebury pits contain a number of these 'messengers of the Otherworld'. Pits can be seen as the physical medium by which this world connected with the world of the chathonic (underworld) deities, between the living and the dead, as we shall see. In the Ashmolean Museum is a fine bronze spout from a dish or vessel in the shape of a bird of prey (or perhaps a raven) with large staring eyes; this is dated to the first century BC and is possibly from Hod Hill. In similar vein could be the bird-shaped mount from a vessel or pan from St Catharine's Hill, whilst a remarkably accurate representation of a nightjar comes from Milber Down Camp (Figure 73).

The importance of the domestic horse, both practical and symbolic, has been outlined above. There is evidence of their remains at hillforts, if in small quantities, and a number were interred in the Danebury pits (Figure 74). The paucity of the remains of this animal in general may be a reflection of their worth; those found on sites are generally of some age.

FIGURE 73. This bronze bird from Milber Down hillfort in Devon has been likened to a nightjar, but its use is unknown.

TORQUAY MUSEUM SOCIETY.

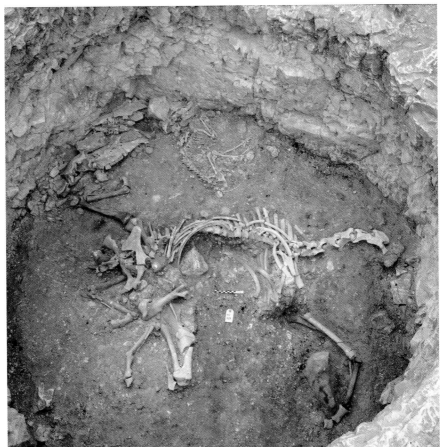

FIGURE 74. Deposition in Pit 321 from Danebury of a decapitated horse, its head placed above top left with one of its severed front legs, and a dog placed above its back.

INSTITUTE OF ARCHAEOLOGY, OXFORD UNIVERSITY.

That other animal essential to man, the dog, is also represented at hillforts, especially in pits, as the outstanding examples from Danebury show. The importance of the animal for guarding, hunting, scavenging, rounding up livestock and, sometimes, providing food in prehistory goes back to the Palaeolithic. In comparison with domestic stock, the numbers of dogs about a site seems to have been relatively small, as at Uffington Castle (Ingrem 2003, 283) and Segsbury (Mulville and Powell 2005, 117). A Balksbury Camp pit contained newborn puppies suggesting, if nothing else, that their numbers might be controlled. In Welsh sources such as the Mabinogi, and the Irish texts, dogs had supernatural powers and a relationship with the underworld, and this could explain a propensity to offer them to the chathonic gods. The importance of dog symbolism to the Lydney Park Romano-British temple complex is outlined below, but the finding of a dog tooth from a pendant, amulet or necklace at Bredon Hill could suggest a degree of veneration (or just sentiment).

Animal disposal could be haphazard, however, and a goat burial in a Croft Ambrey quarry ditch, a dog skeleton from the site, and another dog from the inner ditch of Kingsdown Camp could all just have been dumped in the most convenient place, with no ritual intent whatsoever.

Hoards and placements

A 'hoard' is defined as the deliberate placement of objects together in one circumstance as a specific act; they were sometimes hidden for safety, with the possibility of recovery, or deposited as a ritual act. Hoards go well back into prehistory, those of gold and bronze increasing in quantity and intensity during the late Bronze Age. The deposition of general ironwork developed by the middle Iron Age and becomes more common in the record across southern Britain during the third to the second centuries BC, with tools replacing weapons as the dominant artefacts (Hingley 1997, 14).

Hoards come in all shapes and sizes, from a small group of objects left under a rock by an individual on a personal basis to a large cache discarded by a merchant or manufacturer (scrap hoards). Items may be disfigured and bent as a deliberate act, rendering the object's spirit out of this world. Hingley (1990; 1997) observed a tendency for currency bars to be hoarded at the boundaries of sites, noting that some large metalwork hoards appear to have been deposited at distinct times in the life of the community concerned. Currency bars, with their plough-share and sword shapes, could also have had ritual connotations, one reflecting regeneration connected with agricultural fertility, the other an ability to kill – again, birth and death.

Of special interest are hoards which are arranged with particular care. One of the most famous, found by a flint digger in 1825, came from a low chalk mound within Hollingbury. A palstave was surrounded by a twisted bronze torc with three coiled finger-rings threaded onto the torc and four 'Sussex loops' (a type of bracelet or armlet) placed at the four corners (Barber 2003, 56). More mundane was the hoard of iron objects from Madmarston Camp, which included twelve currency bars, an axe-head, a possible poker and two pairs of bridle-bits, all placed underneath a stone floor behind the inner rampart (E. Fowler 1960, 41).

The emergence of a warrior elite or aristocracy in the Bronze Age gave impetus to the expansion of weapon manufacture (Needham *et al.* 1989). As mentioned, in north-east Wales there is evidence of trade and exchange with Ireland in particular, and in 1962, as a result of a small landslip 'on the sloping ground in the southern part of the enclosure' of Moel Arthur hillfort (see Figure 86), a hoard of three flat bronze axes was unearthed (Forde-Johnston 1964). All have a strong green patina with evidence of use and date to the early Bronze Age. They are remarkably similar in size, varying from between 15.6–16.5cm in length and 9.4–10cm in width. The copper, from a single Irish copper source, contains significant amounts of antimony. This find is the most important of its kind in Wales (Brown 2004, figure 26).

The general subject of hoards is extensive and beyond our scope here, but other notable hillfort hoards include those from Danebury, Barbury Castle, Bigberry and Hunsbury and the cache of native Iron Age coins from Carn Brea, all referred to elsewhere in this book. However, as with all archaeology, care must be taken in interpretation. The hoard of two flat axes and an axe-hammer of possible Neolithic origin discovered not far from the Titterstone Clee hillfort was probably deliberately placed with ritual intent. But another Marches hoard, the late Bronze Age 'Guilsfield hoard', found near the Gaer Fawr and Crowther's Camp hillforts in Montgomeryshire, with its hundred or so broken pieces and unsuccessful casting, could have been just scrap (Davies 1967, 179).

Pit deposition

As we have seen, prehistoric people dug pits in the ground, an activity going back to at least the early Neolithic. On the summit of South Cadbury, below the later hillfort, a row of Neolithic pits may have signposted the way along Milsom's Corner spur (Tabor 2000, 29), later to be the site of a Bronze Age enclosure (Coles *et al.* 2000), and the deep ritual shafts at Wilsford in Wiltshire and Swanwick in Hampshire are dated to the later second millennium BC.

By the 1930s over 500 pits up to 2m in depth had been investigated, mainly on the chalk downlands of Wessex and Sussex. At Danebury, within an earlier earthwork and just outside the line of the later hillfort, a line of pits was found to have been dug around the enclosure. In one such square pit (4.4m across and almost 2m deep), after it had been left open for a period to let silt accumulate, two dogs were placed, together with remains of cattle, sheep, pig, deer and frog/toad. These remains were then covered with chalk blocks and a 60cm-wide timber post, possibly 3–6m in height, was erected vertically in the centre of the pit and packed into place to act as a totem (Cunliffe 1993a, 17, 28). This finding is extremely significant, reflecting as it does a ritual identification of people and site, and the possibility of such devices being more common than first thought cannot be discounted. In similar fashion, in one of the two enclosures found in the centre of the later, complicated, but clearly not defensive, 25ha Casterley Camp was a pit which contained four human burials and fourteen red deer antlers, in the centre of which had been placed a large post 1m high. Clearly this had ritual meaning, and indeed it has even been postulated that the site formed a ritual centre before the hillfort was built (Cunnington and Cunnington 1913; Berresford Ellis 1991, 61).

The use of pits predominantly for grain storage has been mentioned above, Bradley (2005) stating that the: 'equation between the farming cycle and the commemoration of the dead became still more obvious in the Iron Age when one of the dominant symbols was the corn storage pit', and pits are present in a variety of Iron Age contexts, not only hillforts. Both Cunliffe (1993b) and Hill (1995) have suggested that much of the material deposited in pits, from pots to human and animal bone, was not purely rubbish but a deliberate and structured collection of material deposited at specific times and for specific purposes. This hypothesis was investigated at Danebury. Whilst the pits were initially used for grain storage, in a high percentage of cases their subsequent function involved a stratification of deliberate deposits rather than random tipping, involving 'complex patterns of behaviour' (Cunliffe 1993b, 19). This careful deposition in pits occurred not only in the case of whole or dismembered animal carcasses, but also of human remains; an important finding, as there has been much debate over the context of bone deposition at Iron Age sites. Ditch disposal can be much more haphazard.

Although human bone was found at Danebury in a number of contexts, it was the pit deposition of whole or part skeletons that was most significant. Some complete, usually flexed, skeletons lay under large blocks of flint or chalk at pit bottoms, either singly or in small groups. The wrists of some skeletons were tied and others were partially smashed, suggesting a violent end and possible sacrifice. Partial remains tended to be found within the fill and included limbs, thoraxes and hacked pelvises. Skulls were usually found at the top of the sequence, often separated from, or without, the mandible. Headhunting in Iron Age society has been mentioned above and the careful deposition of skulls in the Danebury pits could have involved an act of special veneration. It is clear that this was not just normal burial but the manifestation of a complex belief system.

At Danebury, horses, dogs and birds, particularly ravens, are well represented in the pits, as we have mentioned; less so cattle, sheep and pigs, suggesting that some species were imbued with a greater symbolic significance than others. The horse, in particular, has been seen to be especially valuable and its deposition, with dog, in Romano-British contexts at Uffington Castle and Balksbury Camp suggests a long continuity of veneration (Ingrem 2003, 284–5; Maltby n.d.). In the Danebury pits horses were normally represented by a complete leg or head placed at the pit side, but sometimes trunks minus legs and head were found. Dogs were usually whole skeletons, and were often found with horses (see Figure 74), possibly indicating the closeness of both to man.

Overall, Cunliffe (1993a, 21–2) suggested a pit depositional sequence of, firstly, seed removal, possibly for sowing, and then, secondly, the placement of a special deposit at the bottom. Natural erosion of the overhanging pits sides would then take place and other material would be put in the pit before abandonment. Silting up or filling in with rubbish would finally follow. In terms of belief this sequence involved the seed corn being placed underground to receive the protection of the deities of the underworld during dormancy – a ritual act during a liminal time. When the grain was removed at an appropriate festival (possibly at Beltane – 1st May) the ritual deposit made into the now empty pits would both ensure a good subsequent yield and thank the gods for the safe-keeping of the corn before germination. Subsequently, at harvest and later (possibly at Samian – 1st November), a second offering was placed into the pits as gratitude for the harvest. The positioning of human remains at or near the bottom of pits could, therefore, have been an important act of propitiation.

Depositional layers were also found at South Cadbury. The sample of 362 pits from the hillfort's interior revealed that human skulls were generally spaced throughout the layers within an ashy/charcoal matrix, whilst animal skulls usually came from the lower fills in primary deposits (Bellavia *et al.* 2000, 206). There was no indication of why this was so.

To compare sites is difficult because of differences in sample size and condition and the 'antiquity' of some of the earlier investigations. It does appear, however, that different values were attached to different objects at different times at different places. The Bury Hill (Hants) pits, for example, included a greater percentage of horses and horse-gear than those of Danebury, nearby. Material does, of course, erode and disappear over time and what is seen today is only a fraction of what existed in prehistory. Wood rots and metalwork in acidic conditions will disappear with little trace. It is also impossible sometimes to make assumptions from past excavations despite intriguing clues; the context of a skull fragment in a large pit excavated at Shenberrow Hill Camp in Gloucestershire, together with three other fragments nearby which showed sword cuts (Fell 1962, 23) is unclear.

Similarly, the nineteenth-century investigation of Worlebury left more questions than it provided answers, but several points emerged suggesting ritual involvement. Pit 9 on Dymond's plan of 1902, for example, lies at a point where tracks from the three entrances to the hillfort meet, and at its bottom was found a quantity of wheat and barley mixed together and overlain by thin plates of 'lias' rock. In Pit 5, on the other hand, were two toe rings (similar to the bronze examples found later on bodies from Maiden Castle) carefully positioned under a projecting rock ledge at the bottom and above was a small bronze ring; the meticulous placement suggesting a specific act.

Hunsbury has the same problems of interpretation. Some 300 (many stone-lined) storage pits were found during the nineteenth-century investigations; these varied in size between 1.5m and 3m in diameter and 1.8m and 2.1m in depth. The vast quantity of metalwork (iron and bronze weapons and tools and bronze brooches), glass, pottery and querns (over 150) from the pits included the bronze Hunsbury scabbard and iron sword already described. In one pit was a crouched skeleton with an iron chariot tyre, bridle-bit and other iron pieces (Fell 1937, 58). There is thus the possibility of some form of 'chariot burial', as suggested by a display panel in Northampton Museum (2005) stating that: 'Inside the camp, near the centre, were found the skeleton of a man and horse interred together, and with them was the well made bridle bit and other pieces of metal now in the museum, and a five foot length of the tyre of a wheel'. It is tempting to place a ritual association on these deposits: they were placed by a metalworker, perhaps; but nothing is definite, intense quarrying for ironstone plus the effects of later ploughing having destroyed a great deal of the archaeology of the site.

Pits could be personal as well as communal. The 1996 Segsbury Camp excavation uncovered the outline of an Iron Age roundhouse with pits inside and outside containing human bone. Likewise, the drainage sump pit from the Bredon Hill hut located next to the rampart, and mentioned in Chapter 5, contained portions of an infant skull, and the upper jaw of a near-five-year-old child was found in a post-hole. Immediately above the original floor was an adult mandible and part of an adult skull. The hut also contained numerous artefacts, including pottery, part of an iron bridle-bit, pins, clamps and harness hammers, and a miniature stone axe, which was probably a ritual object and is of particular interest (Hencken 1938, 30). These poignant finds suggest the vestiges of a family group.

Storage pits akin to those of southern England appear to decline northwards and, apart from a few examples, as at Croft Ambrey, they are also absent from Wales and the Marches north of Conderton Camp, where some 140 rock-cut pits were lined with wattle or dry-stone. Although this paucity was initially thought to be the result of lack of grain production in these areas, this is not so and pure geology is also not a factor, as both Hunsbury and Worlebury have pits cut into solid rock. The coastal plains of northern England continue to be fertile to this day, as do regions to the west, and there is plenty of evidence for four-poster storage above ground, as at Grimthorpe. Likewise, there is an absence of pits in the south-west, but ritual could be involved in the ceremonial opening and closing of the underground passages (*fogous*) of Cornwall, which are akin to the *souterraines* of eastern Scotland and Brittany. Here the storage of dairy products or grain has been suggested (Cunliffe 2001, 350), or, in the case of *fogous*, of tin ore or ingots (Rowe 2005, 131–2). But why there are such marked regional variations in pit use is a mystery.

Shrines and four-posters

Small 'shrines' or temples were probably much more numerous on hillforts than the meagre areas covered by most excavations have led us to believe, and Yeates (2008) outlines possible sites (also associated with mining activity) in the territory of the Dobunni (see page 152), such as a small square shrine on a podium at Bury Hill, Winterbourne in Gloucestershire, at Worlebury and at the Cadburys Congresbury and Tickenham. However, more definite are the shrines and temples of the excavated sites of Danebury, South Cadbury (possibly), Maiden Castle, Chanctonbury Ring, Lydney and Croft Ambrey (Figure 75), and we will look at these in turn. Most are probably Romano-British or Roman in date, but not all, and at least one of the four structures suggested as some form of shrine at Danebury was used throughout the life of the hillfort of some 500 years, beginning around the middle of the sixth century BC (Cunliffe 1993b, 72). Here the structures, on a false summit, faced the main gate; two were situated together on one side of a path with another directly opposite, and they probably had planked walls and thatched roofs of reed or straw. Another, larger, possibly fenced and unroofed compound lay a short distance to the north-east, straddling the same path. At South Cadbury a timber-built rectangular structure 6.5m² in size and dated to the mid first century AD has been considered a shrine, but doubts remain. It had a small porch or portico facing east and was orientated on a line between the main concentrations of animal burials to the south and finds of metalwork to the north (Barrett *et al.* 2000, 173).

In the north-east corner of Maiden Castle was a simple stone-walled circular native shrine, with an infant burial outside the entrance. Next to this was a small rectangular Romano-Celtic temple, with a typical *cella* (around 5m²) with red *tesserae* on a verandah. Painted external plastering was found. A cambered road approached the eastern entrance. Coin evidence suggested a date no earlier than AD 367. Adjoining the temple on the north was a small two-roomed structure, referred to by Wheeler as the 'dwelling of the priest'. Repairs may have been undertaken as late as the fifth century AD (Wheeler 1935, 7–8).

Chanctonbury Ring, on the north Sussex Downs, had two Romano-Celtic temples: a small rectangular building with a cult room in the central *cella* and *porticus*, and another with a polygonal *cella* and a rectangular entrance chamber (Rudling 2001). Whilst the hillfort is now dated to the late Bronze Age and appears to have been only sparsely used by the mid Iron Age, the defences may have served as the *temenos* (sacred precinct) in the pre-Roman period, and it is possible that the site could have been a simple cult place first, with no building to begin with. Coins and pottery indicate an intensive period of occupation from the second to the third or fourth centuries AD; a miniature votive pot and deposits of oyster shells in the first temple, and nearby a possible oven and pit, all point to ritual activity. However, evidence of a boar cult at the site is of particular interest. Large numbers of pigs' heads, together with a

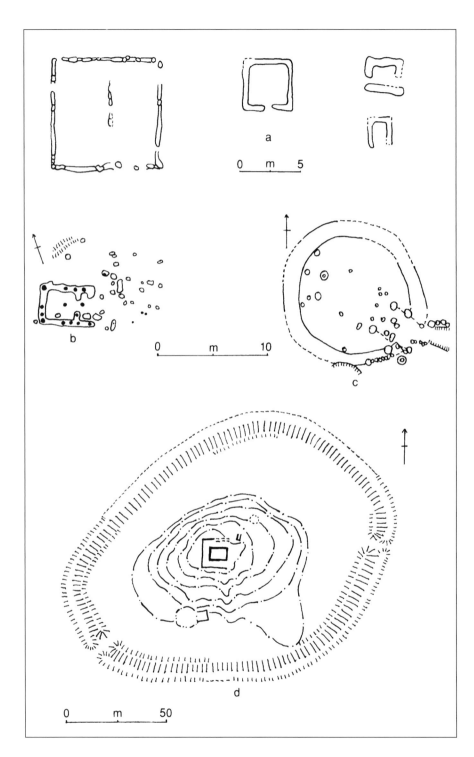

FIGURE 75a. Plans of hillfort shrines and temples: a) Native shrines (Danebury); b) Native shrine (South Cadbury); c) Native shrine (Maiden Castle); d) Romano-Celtic temple (Chanctonbury Ring). Redrawn after: a) Cunliffe 1993; b) Barrett *et al.* 2000; c) Wheeler 1943; d) Rudling 2001.

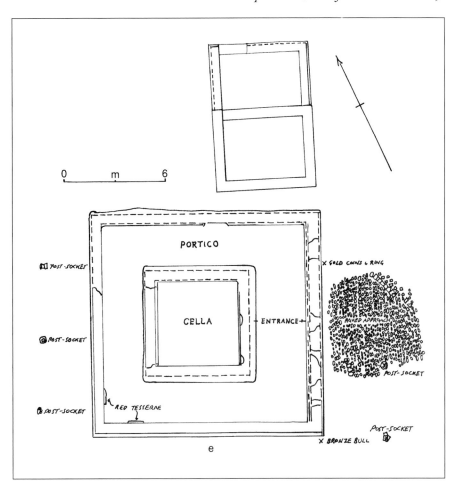

0 m 6

PORTICO

CELLA ←ENTRANCE→

POST-SOCKET

POST-SOCKET

POST-SOCKET

RED TESSERAE

X GOLD COINS & RING

PAVED APPROACH

POST-SOCKET

POST-SOCKET

X BRONZE BULL

e

FIGURE 75b. Plans of hillfort shrines and temples: e) Romano-Celtic temple (Maiden Castle). Redrawn after Wheeler 1943.

spearhead, were associated with the polygonal shrine. The importance of the boar in the Iron Age has been outlined and here the porcine offerings (possibly a substitute for wild boar) are practical evidence for this. Bronze figurines of boar-like beasts have been found in central Sussex, suggesting a veneration cult of the animal based in this area. Interesting also is the 'intervisibility' of the site with adjacent temple sites at Pulborough, Muntham Court and Lancing Down (Bedwin 1980). We will look at intervisibility between hillforts later.

This later resurgence of the use of hillforts, such as Chanctonbury and Maiden Castle, for religious purposes, rather than as settlements, was mirrored in Wales and the Marches during the late Roman period. The most famous instance was at Lydney Park, which is located on a spur overlooking the River Severn on the edge of the Forest of Dean in Gloucestershire, and was excavated by Sir Mortimer Wheeler in 1928–9 (Wheeler and Wheeler 1932). Dedicated to the god Nodens in the second half of the third century AD, the elaborate temple complex within the defences of a 5ha univallate hillfort, originally dating to around the first century BC, included ritual baths embellished with mosaics, courtyard guest-houses and dormitory. Here 'pilgrims' would hope to see the god as they slept. A rectangular central *cella* with surrounding ambulatory was approached by a flight of steps, at the end of which was a three-roomed sanctuary (Verey 1976, 294). Ten recesses seem to have acted as side-chapels, later reconstructed into rooms. Two earlier Roman iron mines could have sparked interest in the site, as clearly there was some wealth involved in the construction of the temple, but Yeates (2008, 90–101) has recently considered a connection between mining and metallurgy, hillforts and enclosures and the development of religious cults which spawned shrines and ritual centres as at Lydney. There also appears to have been an association between temple sites and territorial boundaries and it is possible that here we have a boundary between the Silures and Dobunni (Gwilt 2007, 317).

There is considerable evidence in England that many Roman rural temples were constructed on the site of Iron Age wooden predecessors (Manning 2001, 95), as at the Celtic sacred spring of Sulis and later temple complex of Sulis Minerva at Bath. This could also have been the case at Lydney. Undoubtedly human and animal sacrifice (as at Chanctonbury) would have formed an essential element of propitiation, until the former was outlawed by the Roman authorities. The presiding deity at Lydney was Nodens, whose familiar was a dog, a sky or storm god who has been paired with Mars (the healer) or Silvanus (the Roman god of wild nature and hunting) and, here, possibly, a god of mining. As a result of this presence Lydney would have been an important centre where the sick came to be healed – perhaps a local 'Lourdes' of its time, and suggested by Yeates (2008, 101) as a possibly focus for the ailments of the local mining community; perhaps indicated by the finding of a miniature votive pick axe. The god would be placated and presented with models of the inflicted part – a diseased model arm has been found – and statuettes of dogs, sacred at Lydney, would be offered. The link between healing and the hunt could be explained by the shedding of blood being necessary to give life, therefore 'symbolising re-birth and healing/renewal' (Green 1992, 199); this may explain the presence of hunting dogs at Lydney.

Other than at Lydney and Croft Ambrey, which we will look at below, there is only occasional evidence so far for shrines or religious structures in Wales and the Marches earlier than the Romano-British/Roman periods. At Llys Awel below Pen y corddyn Mawr the discovery of a statuette of Mercury (the Roman messenger god), images of dogs and a few Roman coins have parallels with offerings made at Lydney and could indicate a temple precinct in the vicinity (Blockley 1991, 126–7; Green and Howell 2000, 68), or perhaps even on the hillfort itself. Evidence of (late) ritual activity may also come from the ceremonial bronze wand or sceptre from Dinorben, and it is possible that the quarrying away of the hillfort in modern times could have destroyed a 'shrine' in an unexcavated area.

The more formal (and expensive) Romano-British-built structures described above would not necessarily have been the norm, even in Roman times, and at

Croft Ambrey Stanford (1974) uncovered what could have been a more typical ceremonial arena. Here a 11.6m² 'Mound' was located within the hillfort annexe, with three sides delineated by a dry-stone kerb, the whole about 1.5m high. The top was about 5m across, providing ample room for activities. Cremated bones of cattle, sheep and pig suggest a place of animal sacrifice, possibly dating to the Romano-British and Roman periods (Samian pottery and Romano-British brooches have been found), but with possible earlier connotations. Here, as well as the pottery and brooches, rings and clay 'hearts' (perhaps extremely significant) and a broken bell with iron clapper were found; this last item similar to a smaller example from near the temple at Maiden Castle, where most of the pottery was dated to around the fourth century AD.

Bradley (2005) has proposed that shrines found at some hillforts bore resemblances to the raised storehouses (four-posters), and at Danebury were contemporaneous. He quotes Malinowski's 1930's studies of the Pacific Trobriand islanders, where the raised storehouse or *bwayma* was not only used for storage but had a social display function and was intimately involved in ritual. This relationship between belief and raised granaries is interesting and Bradley concludes that late Bronze Age ceramic models of domestic buildings from cemeteries containing cremations could be model granaries, with an obvious ritual context. Here was a relationship between death and regeneration; of the passing of life, storage of the crop and germination of the seed. Thus, such 'off-the-ground' four-posters would not only have served specific storage purposes and deterred vermin and rot – a standard farming practice – but also proferred an essential ritual and status-enhancing purpose. It follows that four-posters could have been used for the laying out of the dead prior to secondary burial or cremation and that their shape replicated that of the excarnation platform (Fitzpatrick 1997; Carr 2007, 448).

Miniaturisation

The fashioning of miniature tools, cauldrons, axes, spears, shields and swords is a particular feature of prehistory through to the Roman period. Examples come from a variety of contexts, but have a long history at hillforts, a bronze miniature axe from Ham Hill, for example, dating to the late Bronze Age.

If not for personal adornment, the use to which they were put is not easy to fathom, although toys have been suggested. More likely is that miniaturisation can be allied to other aspects of symbolism, such as exaggeration in size, triplism and the bending or breakage of objects. Therefore the very act of making a faithful representation in miniature would be to sanctify an object, as it could not actually be used – a 'conscious denial of utility'; this was a deliberate removal of the object from this world into that of the supernatural (Green 1986, 222). The occurrence of quantities of very small Celtic coins, called 'minims' (silver fractions of around 0.3g: Hobbs 1996, 18), associated with shrines in southern England suggests that they might also be objects of miniaturisation (Brown

2002; 2004, 82). At Hod Hill a silver minim inscribed with the letters 'CRAB' in a panel on one side and a hexagonal panel on the other was buried in the earthwork, and was perhaps a votive offering. The model human parts from Lydney clearly imply how important miniaturisation was as a ritual act.

Weapons of war had special significance and it is no surprise that miniature versions of shields and spears have been unearthed, some deliberately bent, as from the Woodeaton temple in Oxfordshire (Jope 2000, 250–1). The Salisbury hoard from Wiltshire contained prolific numbers of model shields, together with cauldrons (Stead 1998). Although model spears are seemingly absent from hillforts to date, a shield comes from Breedon-on-the-Hill (Wacher 1979) and another in sheet-bronze from Hod Hill. In the mid 1990s a model shield, with a certain resemblance in decoration to the Moel Hiraddug shield-boss, was found in a non-hillfort context near Barmouth. In the 1970s Savory controversially suggested that the full-size examples from Moel Hiraddug and Tal-y-Llyn might indicate a north Wales regional tradition of shield metalworking and this discovery lends credence to his suggestion. Certainly some areas seem to have been favoured for weapon production more than others and at Sigwells, to the south-east of South Cadbury, in a landscape containing significant archaeological remains ranging from the Bronze Age to the early medieval, moulds for at least ten weapons were found in a pit of around 1000 BC (Tabor 2000, 27, 29).

Domestic items, although not found in any quantity, also figure among miniature items at hillforts. The axes from Bredon Hill, Ham Hill and the Lydney temple and the votive pot from Chanctonbury Ring have been mentioned, but an iron hammer with bronze strip decoration came from the Maiden Castle temple, all indicative of the relationship between the everyday and the supernatural.

Human remains and burial practice at hillforts

The old monumental rites of the Neolithic had ended with the closing of the tombs around the mid third millennium BC and a new form of burial appeared, the round barrow, usually covering a single burial. By 1500 BC cremation became popular: burnt bone was placed in a collared urn, again under a cairn or barrow. In the late Bronze Age, with an abandonment of mound building, flat urn fields appeared or old mounds were reused and burial itself seems to end. Coincidental with this was an increase in high-status metal objects found in rivers, bogs and marshes, and it is possible that this deposition could have been tied to the scattering of ashes in water by a warrior aristocracy.

For the first part of the Iron Age, the population in the record appears to have disappeared without trace, but, as was probable in previous times, for the masses excarnation would have been the primary means of disposal and one that seems to have continued into the Roman period (Carr 2007, 446). Bell *et al.* (1999) found what was thought to be posts from an excarnation platform on the foreshore at Goldcliff on the Severn Estuary and there is plenty of ethnographic evidence worldwide for such a practice, whether it be the placing of bodies in trees or on platforms. Indigenous peoples such as the Sioux, Cheyenne, Crow, Yankton and Omahas disposed of their dead in this way; Ellison and Drewett (1971), also observing that 'nearly all' British sites with four-post structures also contain scattered human bone or whole skeletons, and tend to be located at enclosure margins. Thus, arrangements of four post-holes could indeed have been for supports for excarnation platforms, or, indeed, four-poster buildings themselves could have been used as a type of mortuary house or shrine where the dead were laid out (see page 79). Whatever version is the case (and both may be), scatterings of disarticulated bone in hillfort interiors are all the evidence that remains.

At first sight the disposal of human remains in prehistory would appear haphazard, casual even, and devoid of sentiment, but it would be quite wrong to endow prehistoric people with our own feelings on the subject. At Segsbury and Maiden Castle, for example, the practice of placing human remains in post-holes may indicate a construction rite. Ditches were also a favorite place for disposal, typical being fragments of a femur and tibia and the proximal end of a radius from Quarley Hill in Hampshire (Jackson 1939, 191). This widespread scattering, particularly of skull fragments, as at Staple Howe, Dinorben and Ivinghoe Beacon, and longbones, as at Dinorben and Salmonsbury, among many other sites, together with pit burials and bone fragments in pits, suggests that the dead were very much considered as being 'with the living'. Danebury, of course, has been the most informative site; where some 300 bone deposits have been found, some complete, others mixed and disarticulated and partially decayed and some possibly brought in after exposure outside the fort.

True inhumation burial was generally rare in the Iron Age; the burial of sprawled bodies from Wandlebury and Stonea Camp seems more like the casual disposal of enemy dead (Taylor 2001, 67) or even of miscreants. There are notable and more formal Iron Age and Romano-British exceptions, however, such as the high-status chariot burials of the Arras culture of the Yorkshire Wolds, the Durotrigan cemetery burials of south Dorset and the cist burials of Devon and Cornwall. But if there is one characteristic late Iron Age burial rite it is the crouched inhumation in a disused pit or field ditch, with grave goods limited to an occasional item of clothing or ornament, such as a brooch. Originating from Durotrigan tradition with possible roots in the pit burials of the middle Iron Age, this rite sees the individual placed on the right side with the head facing to the east (Taylor 2001, 65–8; Gale 2003, 133). The discovery of a man buried in a ditch outside the main rampart at Blewburton Hill, seemingly astride a pony, beneath which were a carpenter's adze and a dog, is a very rare occurrence in the western European Iron Age (Ralston 2006, 136–7, after Collins 1953).

Thus, inhumations at hillforts, though not common, are more widespread than they would appear at first glance. They range from an extended burial excavated at Danebury to complete or partial Iron Age examples at Bury Hill, Dinorben, Moel Hiraddug, Llanmelin and Coygan Camp. The Grimthorpe warrior burial, mentioned above, and four other burials on the site are exceptional. However, probably more common if wider excavation could so prove are burials below the floors of roundhouses or outside nearby – those buried being very much 'alive'. At Segsbury the child burial was placed outside a hut and in the later, and possibly Romano-British, stages of Sutton Walls, two infants were similarly buried, whilst more than seven crouched burials in definite graves also came to light at the site (Kenyon 1954).

As the above examples show, the nature of burial can be variable and the two graves containing female inhumations (one about 25-years-old; the other possibly between 35 and 50) at Bury Hill (Hants) were positioned at the base of the rampart. The former was buried on her back with her legs flexed, and was weighed down with large flints. A metal object in the grave was possibly the ferrule from a wooden shaft. Similarly, from Balksbury Camp a crouched burial was found within an accumulated rubbish deposit behind a bank, apparently with no formal internment (Wainwright 1970, 32).

Subsequently, in the late Iron Age cremation appears again in south-east England (Carr 2007), together with crouched burials without grave goods, but it can be imagined that excarnation continued as the dominant rite for most.

In Britain and Gaul there is ample evidence of the cult of the human head and the ritual collection and fashioning of heads as trophies, whereby the new owner became imbued with the spirit of the vanquished. This could account for some skulls/skull pieces in hillfort contexts. Several unattached human skulls were in the Hunsbury pits, one of which had three holes bored into the cranium in a triangular pattern. Fell (1937, 58) suggested that these holes were similar to those found on a skull from Caithness and another from Finistère, which had two holes instead of three. Other than as a means of hanging and displaying the item, why this was done we can only guess.

Eight Danebury pits contained individual skulls which could have been trophies; evidence from Bredon Hill is more compelling on this score, as the six severed heads thought to have been displayed at the main entrance to the hillfort show (Hencken 1938, 23; Thomas 2005, 256). Elsewhere, heads 'decorated ramparts' at both Hunsbury and Stanwick (Hutton 1991, 194), and at Ivinghoe Beacon an amulet made from a human cranium was, according to Cotton and Frere (1968, 216), clear evidence of trepanning, the deliberate opening of the skull to expose the brain and covering layers; there is abundant evidence worldwide of the ancient use of this technique for both 'surgery and sorcery' (Wakely 1997, 40). Whether the Ivinghoe example was from a burial, as was the cranial roundel from Glastonbury (Bulleid and Gray 1917), or from a more malevolent source, cannot be ascertained. Another find from Segsbury, a skull split into halves which were then nested together, also suggests ritual practice.

Whilst sacrifice in Iron Age Britain is proven, cannibalism is more difficult to ascertain, but has been considered by Brothwell (1961). There is evidence from Salmonsbury (Dunning 1976, 116–17; Hutton 1991, 194). Here, the bones of a *c.*20–25–year-old female appear to have been dismembered before being scattered. Those of the forearm and the femur had been smashed in the same way as had the numerous ox, pig and sheep bones on the same site, possibly to extract the marrow. In addition, the few fragments of skull showed that the brain might have been removed. All of this took place shortly after death. The Croft Ambrey excavations showed knife cuts on the distal end of a human humerus identical to cuts on other animal bones, the meat from which was prepared for food, but this is hardly definite evidence of cannibalism (Stanford 1974, 220). Similarly, although cannibalism is a possibility at Ivinghoe Beacon, evidence that the skull fragments on the site were the result of this is not definite (Cotton and Frere 1968). However, a recent find of a thigh bone in the lower Severn Valley cave mentioned earlier that also shows potential evidence of extraction of the bone marrow, has once again ignited the debate.

The coming of the Romans brought substantial change to Iron Age society, and the more extreme forms of ritual might have been the result of the stresses that their presence imposed, but these changes were certainly reflected in the role that hillforts played and their eventual demise, matters which will be addressed in the next chapter.

CHAPTER NINE

Coins, Tribes, Rome and Resistance

Little is known about the tribes of Britain compared with those of Gaul and, as a result, we have tended to fall back on the writings of the classical authors for snippets of information. Given the probable biased leanings of these sources, we have also tended to view this aspect of late Iron Age and Romano-British archaeology with a jaundiced eye. Things are changing, however, and the nature of tribal groupings in Britain is being re-assessed by a variety of researchers and works gradually published. This paucity of information has been unfortunate as, undoubtedly, tribal organisation was critical to the relationship between Rome and the indigenous population after the incursion of 55/54 BC and invasion of AD 43. Our knowledge of tribal or indeed any community structures before these dates is even less, and it is highly dangerous, therefore, considering the state of present knowledge, to attempt a description of how hillforts fitted into the scheme of things. Nevertheless, with the above 'health warning' attempt it we will, if only to highlight the considerable gaps in knowledge that exist and to put the later use of hillforts into at least some context.

The concept of the 'core-periphery model' – the rapid development of areas of the 'core' south-east as a result of dynamic trade across the channel, with 'peripheral' areas outside providing the raw materials and goods for this core and becoming politically and economically dependent on it – has underpinned archaeological thought for some time, but has been recently questioned (Hill 2007). Things are now being seen as much more complicated, with former peripheral areas, such as East Anglia and the east Midlands, being anything but. Likewise, areas of the core to the south perhaps did not rely as much on elite Roman goods as was first thought, and trade or exchange were not necessarily the cause of social change but rather a symptom of internal developments that were already taking place.

Space does not permit us to enter into such theoretical arguments here, although they are undoubtedly important. Suffice to say that areas formerly considered as the periphery were certainly rich in terms of both their culture and their economy, and were keen to maintain their cultural identity, but there was a vast difference between the client kingdoms of Rome to the south and, for instance, the 'warlike' tribes of parts of Wales or the north, where no Fishbourne, Bignor or Brading villas have yet been found. No doubt these areas would have traded raw materials (minerals especially) and possibly slaves, but whether they became politically and economically dependent *en masse* upon the south-east is questionable.

There has thus been much debate on the effects of Roman influence on the native population of Britain, which has centred on the term 'Romanisation' and what it meant to be Roman. Gone are the arguments for the superiority of Rome over an inferior indigenous population, as the actual participation of the latter – depending upon each individual's position on the social scale – within an overall developing cultural framework is now becoming apparent. Whilst urban areas became centres of change, a complex mixture of 'continuity and change' came into play in the rural landscape (Gosden and Lock 2003, 65), of which the continuity had been visible in the archaeological record throughout at least the previous millennium. The fate of hillforts should be seen as a reflection of this continuity from late Bronze Age beginnings, and before, to the Roman period.

Hillforts cannot be divorced from the tribal nature of society in Britain from about the first century BC, but it is difficult to know what role they played within this tribal society and ultimately it is to these vague references by classical authors and interpretation and supposition from limited excavation that we must turn to shed a little light. Perhaps tribal groupings of some sort had existed for millennia, but how they were constituted and whether they were organised on a local or much wider scale is not known. However, a consideration of the development (or not) of more formal systems of trade and exchange is critical to our understanding of this tribal organisation and territory and how the late Iron Age economy and political entity was run, and so the ultimate demise of hillforts.

Coins and currency bars

From about the mid first century BC to the defeat of Boudica and her predominantly Icenian and Trinovantian army by the Roman general Gaius Suetonius Paulinus in AD 61, differences in society that had built up over the earlier millennium became evident. Britain had been the recipient of increasing cross-channel contact and Roman influence and showed the regional effects of this in different ways, and none more so than in the way coinage was produced and distributed.

Its function has been much debated and is still not clear. Wellington (2006, 91–2), for example, suggests that this differed both chronologically and geographically and according to the metal used – silver providing important votive deposits and gold being used for hoarding. However, if the enhancement of prestige and power was significant in prehistory, then alliances formed between nobles were likely to have been inherently unstable and temporary, resulting in little chance of the development of worthwhile centralised government covering large territories (de Jersey 1996, 8). The introduction of coinage into this system would have encouraged the public display of largesse to followers, so propping up the social hierarchy. The coins themselves show recognisable designs and became symbols of authority and power; although Caesar referred to gold and silver coins in Britain as 'money', there is little evidence for 'Celtic coinage' being used as currency as coins are today, either in an everyday context or in regular trade, and they would have been minted as need arose and when resources became available. This would have been especially true of the high-value gold stater issues used as gift exchange between leading families to cement relationships. However, large numbers of lower-value coins, such as the bronze issues of Cunobelin, may have performed functions more akin to the currency of today, as well as being used for service or subsistence payments (de Jersey 1996, 9). Scholars' opinions vary on this matter.

The approximate areas of the known major tribes of late Iron Age Britain and those using coinage are outlined in Figure 76a, although it must be added that these boundaries were not 'set down' until the Roman period and in coinage terms should certainly be considered 'permeable'. The coin users lay south-east of a line approximately from the Humber to the Severn, the two most powerful 'kingdoms' being the Atrebates and Regni of Sussex and Hampshire south of the Thames and the Catuvellauni and Trinovantes of Hertfordshire, Essex and Suffolk, to the north of the river – in effect a south-eastern core of coin producers. Around this lay the Cantii (Cantiaci) of Kent, the Durotriges (the South-Western series of coins) of Dorset, Wiltshire and eastern Somerset, and the Dobunni, whose territory extended north from north Somerset into Gloucestershire, Herefordshire and Worcestershire and into Warwickshire, Oxfordshire and Wiltshire (the Western series). To the east the Iceni of Norfolk, Cambridgeshire and Suffolk and the Corieltauvi of Lincolnshire and parts of Northamptonshire to Yorkshire also minted coin. No coins were struck or used as such elsewhere in Britain and Ireland.

It is surprising that the native coinage is not better represented at hillforts. Roman issues are much more common, Coygan Camp and Balksbury being good examples, but there are problems in the interpretation of ancient finds. The hoard discovered at Carn Brea in 1749, for example, seems to have been predominantly of northern Gaulish Bellovaci Gallo-Belgic issues, with some British types, and was apparently deposited at the end of the first century BC. This, together with a hoard of Armorican axes of around 750–600 BC found at the same site in 1744 (a concentration of such axes is found in Cornwall), indicates substantial contact with Brittany during the Iron Age (Mercer 1981a, 13–14). But whether these hoards were the result of actual occupation of the site or a ritual association, or both, is impossible to guess.

A major problem with early investigations is working out the exact whereabouts and provenance of find-spots at each site. For example, only one coin from Sir Ian Richmond's Hod Hill excavations (Richmond 1968) can definitely be said to have come from the interior (Allen 1968). Similarly, the coins formerly attributed to Badbury Rings turned out to have come from the adjacent Roman settlement and not from the hillfort. Likewise, an antiquarian reference to possible Icenian or Corieltauvi coins at Tasburgh in Norfolk is not

BRIGANTES

PARISI

CORIELTAUVI

DECEANGLI

ORDOVICES

CORNOVII

ICENI

CATUVELLAUNI

TRINOVANTES

DEMETAE

SILURES

DOBUNNI

ATREBATES

CANTIACI

BELGAE REGNI

DUROTRIGES

DUMNONII

FIGURE 76a. The tribes and coin users of Britain. Redrawn after Laing and Laing 1995.

proven (Rogerson and Lawson 1991, 33). Nevertheless, what native coin we do have from hillforts shows contact or trade and exchange between indigenous tribes and beyond; the extent to which this was a by-product of Roman influence is debatable, however.

Hod Hill is intimately associated with the Durotriges and the characteristic coin found there was the struck bronze stater. This issue dates from around

FIGURE 76b. A base-silver Dobunnic coin from Salmonsbury, Bourton-on-the-Water, Gloucestershire, showing a triple-tailed horse on the reverse. Diameter 13mm.

CELTIC COIN INDEX, INSTITUTE OF ARCHAEOLOGY, OXFORD UNIVERSITY.

the first century AD and had antecedents in silver (also from the site) and gold. A few other coins were from the neighbouring Dobunni, some in silver, and there were also cast bronze (potin) coins of Kentish origin, the earliest of the British minted coinages and possibly of first century AD date or earlier. These were similar to a coin from Ham Hill, where excavations also unearthed South-Western series coins. Of other tribes, the Iceni were represented by three coins, one in silver, suggesting a wider field of contact, but there was little evidence of contact with the more advanced tribes of the south, which were under Roman control (Allen 1968, 57).

There was also continental contact with Hod Hill. A seemingly British silver coin showing two boars back-to-back on the obverse and a horse to the left on the reverse suggests affinities with northern Belgic Gaul near to the Seine. It is a similar story with three silver continental coins: two were of the common Coriosolites type, of which there are many hoards in the Channel Islands and which are found fairly regularly at Durotrigan sites; the other, however, dated to the first half of the first century BC, was from the Limoges area and possibly the Lemovices tribe, and showed a carnyx and trumpeter's bust behind a horse. Elsewhere the importance of animal symbolism and the number three is also testified by two base-silver Dobunnic coins from Salmonsbury: both show a triple-tailed horse on the reverse, while one is inscribed 'ANTED' (Figure 76b).

Wheeler found only fourteen coins at Maiden Castle and Sharples only one. Here the pattern of coinage was different to that from both Hod Hill and the 1915 excavations at Hengistbury Head, including its Durotrigan composition, and included an Armorican coin (absent from Hengistbury) and similar Dobunni and Coriosolites issues, but no Icenian or potin types. Thus, although most coinage tended to circulate within discrete areas, that of the Durotriges is also found outside the core area (as are Western issues), showing a wide trading outlook.

At Hengistbury the later excavations of Barry Cunliffe proved on-site production of cast bronze coinage, probably of the early first century AD. This was based on struck bronze staters, stamped with a simple pattern of dots on each face, the ultimate debasement of the stater of Philip II of Macedon which had provided the basis for the first Celtic coinage of three centuries earlier (de Jersey 1996, 43). Over 3,000 coins were found in the two excavations of the site, all but seven from that of 1915.

Among the thirteen Celtic coins from South Cadbury only one was a gold stater (probably of the Dobunni), the rest being Durotriges South-Western series of local origin (Haselgrove and Mays 2000, 248–52). Coinage of the south-west shows a gradual debasement and inferiority over time, with a loss of weight. Earlier and finer examples come from the Cranborne Chase area of Hod Hill and near to Badbury Rings, whilst later coins are more widespread and sparse, despite a concentration in the Maiden Castle/Dorchester environs. Only one of the South-Western finds from South Cadbury is of this earlier phase and this would have been plated in gold, debased gold or silver, while the rest were minted in reasonable-grade silver.

There have been finds of Celtic coins in Wales (Boon 1980; 1988; Gwilt 2007), although these have been restricted to a few scatterings of Gaulish and Corieltauvi issues in the north and west, possibly brought into the area from the south, and the small hoard from near Penrhyndeudraeth, with its possible silver Atrebatic coin attributed to Caratacos (Caratacus). In greater quantity are clusters of mainly gold Dobunnic coin towards the Wye and Glamorgan coast in south-east Wales, together with Kentish potins of the second century BC and Durotrigan coin, suggesting possible contact between the Silures and tribes to the east. Likewise, the examples of Gaulish coinage from south-east Wales could indicate continental contact. But the might of the Roman occupation is shown by the presence of Roman coins in hillfort contexts from Dinorben in the north to Coygan Camp in the south.

Despite the sporadic finds in Wales the northern and western parts of Britain were not coin producers or users, a fact, among others, that has led to speculation that society was less advanced than in areas to the south. Certainly, cross-channel trade and exchange would have been easier in the south-east and these areas came under the control of Rome earlier. The client kingdoms of the south were no doubt richer in material culture than areas to the north, but the absence of coinage does not necessarily mean that northern and western areas did not enjoy substantial political and socio-economic development. As Harding (2004, 25) points out, the predominantly, but not exclusively, pastoral nature of northern society, together with a dispersed settlement pattern, were factors in a 'conscious rejection of, or lack of a perceived need for, a monetary economy'. However, the finding of Gaulish coins north of the Trent could indicate contact directly with the continent, rather than through the perceived southern English conduit, for a wide variety of reasons. However, differences there were, and these remain today.

Ritual coin deposition, entrances and metalworking have all been mentioned in the last chapter. At Maiden Castle, of the fourteen coins found on site eight came from the eastern entrance and two from the western, the only coin from the interior being from near the Romano-Celtic temple. The eastern entrance was also the favoured site for metalworking. The same overtones of superstition can be seen at Danebury, where only three Iron Age coins – Durotrigan, Gallo-Belgic C and Verica – came from inside the hillfort itself: one from the eastern entrance forecourt, one from a hornwork and another from somewhere in the interior. But outside the eastern entrance a hoard of seventy coins, covering the period 50 BC to AD 50, was suggested by Cunliffe (1993a, 117) to have marked the site of a market or shrine, or both, outside the old defences.

Most currency bars come from sites in the coin-using areas of the south and east. Produced no earlier than the second century BC, they are often found in hoards. They come in roughly two types, sword-shaped and spit-shaped, both of which are pinched upwards at one end and forged to show how good the iron was. There has been much argument as to their purpose. On the one hand, as iron-working was widespread, they could be ready-smelted ingots supplied to blacksmiths. Alternatively, they might have been a means of barter and exchange. Caesar noted *c.*54 BC that in Britain they used iron ingots of 'fixed stand and weight' as currency. Thus, currency bars could have been a measure of iron and thus worth a particular amount in trade or barter. It has already been noted that coin use was not as straightforward an exchange mechanism as it is today, and the same could have been true for currency bars. It has also been suggested from African studies that such items could have been a form of bridewealth (Herbert 1993).

Over one-third of all bars discovered come from southern hillforts, but, although several hoards of spit-shaped bars have been found at the northern end of the Malverns, and a possible broken piece of a sword-shaped bar comes from Midsummer Hill, they are otherwise virtually unknown in the Welsh Marches (Stanford 1981, 126). Although a hoard of twelve was discovered at Madmarston Camp in Oxfordshire, they could come in spectacular numbers: at Meon Hill in Warwickshire there were nearly 400 and at Salmonsbury nearly 150 (Figure 77). Hunsbury, Blewburton Hill in Berkshire and Hod Hill, Spettisbury Rings and Ham Hill have all produced examples and a hoard of twenty-one bars was found parcelled tightly together and placed in a shallow pit in one of the Danebury huts (Cunliffe 1993a, 94).

FIGURE 77. Currency
bars from Salmonsbury,
Bourton-on-the-Water,
Gloucestershire.

ASHMOLEAN MUSEUM, OXFORD.

Such valuable items as these would probably have been deposited as offerings. At least four came from the votive Llyn Cerrig Bach, the only site for currency bars in Wales despite widespread metalworking (Crew and Salter 1993), one of which may have been produced from north Welsh bog ores. Similarly, at South Cadbury part of a currency bar and other ironwork (some wrapped in straw) were mixed together with burnt material in a pit. Bars deliberately buried at the boundary of enclosed settlements have been mentioned above.

Outside the coin and currency bar areas, no doubt there were other units of exchange. Cattle were probably the oldest standard of value among the Indo-Europeans, and there are plenty of references to their importance in early Ireland: six heifers or three milch cows were equivalent to a female slave or *cumal*, a term which came into general use in estimating worth. Likewise, very lead-rich Breton axes found in south-east Wales could have been a form of 'currency' (Cunliffe 1991, 420).

Tribes, hillforts and Rome

The organisation of Iron Age society has proved a contentious matter among scholars, but it seems that as late as 300–100 BC the probable loose amalgams of communities and groups hardly equated with later tribes or *civitates* (Hill 2007, 21). Nevertheless, during the late first century BC the first indications of tribal society in Britain become known from the writings of the classical authors and the distribution of coinage. These wider groupings probably developed over many years from smaller local clans or political networks and family allegiances, but whether *all* of the entities ascribed to the various areas of the country actually existed as operating units is debateable and the possibility that some were predominantly a Roman 'construct' in the literature looms large.

Detail on the relationship between the various tribes and the hillforts within their supposed territories is, likewise, very sketchy or non-existent and there has been much conjecture and myth involved in their study. This has been especially true of the location of the 'capitals' of the tribes away from the core areas of the south, if there was indeed any central site to which the term 'capital' can be applied. The archaeological literature is peppered with references to particular hillforts as such, with little or no concrete evidence to prop up such claims, other than size of site and sentiment: for instance, the 'Herefordshire group' of the Cornovii were supposed to have their capital at Credenhill or the Wrekin, and Castle Hill (Almondbury) was formerly seen as the citadel of the southern Brigantes, and indeed the site of Ptolemy's Camulodunum. But Varley, who excavated the site, reassessed his original dates, indicating that the hillfort, which he had found to have originated around the eighth century BC, had been abandoned before the Conquest. In similar vein, Clarke (1960, 103) suggested that the later, and possibly late Saxon, enclosure of Tasburgh was the headquarters of the eastern group of the Iceni, although there is little to support this theory (Rogerson and Lawson 1991, 33). A comparable uncertainty exists over the Durotriges: was their central place Maiden Castle or was it Hambledon Hill or Hod Hill? We could go on. This section will, therefore, look at what little evidence can be found for the place – or not – of hillforts amongst the known 'tribes'.

Whether the Brigantes of northern England actually existed as a tribal unit is open to question. Lack of coin and ceramic evidence north of the Trent does not help and Roman interpretations can be misleading, but some form of loose tribal grouping could have existed. Miles (2005, 137), for example, suggests that the Brigantes, under Queen Cartimandua, were one of the three tribes with whom Rome held treaty arrangements – the others being the Iceni in the east and the Atrebates/Regni in the south. In this vein it has been suggested that the Carvetii of Cumbria, Setantii of north Lancashire and Gabrantovices might have been tribal sub-septs or *pagi* of the Brigantes. The Carvetii, centered on Carlisle, seem to have achieved *civitas* status in the third century AD, but the name 'Gabrantovices' has been questioned as a 'native identity' by Harding (2004, 23). Care must be taken in equating the goddess Brigantia with the tribe, Hutton (1991, 240) writing that she was heavily promoted, 'perhaps even invented', by the imperial government in the early third century AD to try to instill some loyalty into the disparate communities of this outlying corner of the empire. Maybe northern Britain was just populated by 'hostile highlanders', as Harding (2004, 302) suggests, or a loose amalgam of disparate groups stretching from coast to coast.

All of this makes any interpretation of the scattered hillforts of this huge area very difficult, if not impossible, and sites can therefore only be considered on an individual basis. Stanwick stands out, with its complex earthworks comparable in size to oppida of the south and its location at the junction of major routes to Scotland and to the west across Stainmore. Imported amphorae, pottery and flagons, together with horse and chariot trappings, swords and personal items from Stanwick and nearby Melsonby indicate considerable wealth, despite the unstable politics of the time. Important in Celtic art, the famous first-century AD horse-mount from Melsonby, with its lugubrious countenance, is particularly fine and could have adorned a chariot. Here, the fact that many items turned out to be of brass rather than bronze does indicate Roman influence, as brass did not appear in this country until after the Conquest. The occupants of this area were possibly trading and in a treaty relationship with the Romanised south before annexation (Harding 2004, 163).

North of the Humber, east Yorkshire is dominated by the Wolds, and certainly a distinctive people lived in this region – there is plenty of archaeological evidence for this from cemetery and burial practice, in the form of the square-ditched barrows and chariot/cart burials of the Arras 'culture' of the mid first millennium BC. Whether there is any connection between these people and the Parisi tribe, mentioned by Ptolemy in the mid third century AD as occupying the area, is open to question, as is any connection with the Parisii of northern France. Perhaps some contact occurred and was reflected in burial practice. The Wolds, however, is not an area for hillforts, with the notable exception of Grimthorpe on its very western edge. With massive univallate circular defences (it might be a ring-fort), this site is dated to the first half of the first millennium BC and is important for its warrior burial (outlined above), similar to those found at Bugthorpe and North Grimston, also on the west of the Wolds. Grimthorpe is not far north of the Arras burials sites, but the warrior inhumation lacks the wagon and other features of the latter, and possibly represents more of a difference in burial tradition than anything else. Whatever is the case, the Wolds appears to have declined in importance during the first millennium in tandem with an increase in settlement in adjacent lower-lying areas such as the Vale of York, and it could be that Grimthorpe would have looked strategically westwards to areas below rather than east to the Wolds itself.

How important hillforts were to the Corieltauvi at the end of the first millennium is open to question, Todd (1991, 8) suggesting that they were not especially significant. Formerly called the Coritani, the tribe was the northernmost coin-user; indeed, its issues were formerly attributed to the Brigantes. The tribal area was defined as the Roman *civitas* Coritanorum, which extended from north Northamptonshire through Leicestershire to parts of south Yorkshire and Lincolnshire and to the Humber. Hillforts are few and there is little published information on the small sites of Nottinghamshire and south Yorkshire. However, Breedon-on-the-Hill, Beacon Hill and Burrough Hill in the south of the territory, located on a west–east line controlling the Soar Valley north of Leicester, and thence access via the Trent to the Humber, are univallate and large. But whether they were still in use in the late Iron Age is uncertain, as is their importance in any tribal context. Corieltauvi settlement was, therefore, probably open-lowland-based, as at Dragonby on the Lincoln Edge, the tribe's presumed oppidum or capital (Van de Noort 2004, 73), and the vibrant commercial centre of South Ferriby on the Humber which suggests considerable seaborne contact with the continent.

There are few 'hillfort' sites in East Anglia, the homeland of the Iceni (in

Norfolk and east Cambridgeshire) and the Trinovantes (Suffolk and Essex to the south), although numbers increase from north to south into Essex and towards the Thames. The Iceni under King Prasutagus, the husband of Boudica, had treaty arrangements with Rome, but this arrangement eventually broke down, leading to the Boudican revolt of the Iceni with the Trinovantes, who had seen their tribal centre of Camulodunum (Colchester) in Essex become an army veteran *colonia* of Rome. The topography at least must be one, but not the only, reason for this paucity of hillforts, but Williamson (2005, 11) reports a fort of about 7ha surrounded by double ditches and banks at Burgh-by-Woodbridge in Suffolk which might be a tribal centre with religious or ceremonial functions. Initially Icenian and lying at the edge of the tribal territory, its subsequent destruction implied annexation by the Trinovantian/Catuvellaunian affiliation from further south. It could be that the few hillforts that do exist in East Anglia might have indeed been special tribal places, quite unlike the majority of hillforts to the west.

Gregory and Rogerson (1991, 69–72) discuss various problems associated with East Anglian forts, especially the paucity of dating evidence, and doubts remain as to the origins of many. Thetford Castle and Warham Camp have Iron Age credentials, but nothing more, and the group of Holkham, South Creake and Narborough, in a cluster with Warham towards the north Norfolk coast, could also be of Iron Age date. Whilst the nearness of these sites to North Creake and Snettisham, with their spectacular gold torcs and finery, may be only coincidence, it could indicate a vibrant Icenian aristocratic elite connected with these enclosures in some way, if only as bases from which to exploit the rich maritime resources and North Sea trading networks nearby. This would give weight to the theory that these magnificent gold hoards might have been the result of specific rites rather than just 'flight hoards' left by those fleeing Caesar's advance, as is sometimes proposed.

To the south, in Essex, hillforts are located along the Lea, Cam and Stort river system, and this distribution has been suggested as being the result of conflict between the Trinovantes and Catuvellauni, whose territories converged in the first century BC. An extension of the line of these hillforts northwards would see hillforts from the Thames to the North Sea, a 'continuous west-facing boundary of the Iceni and Trinovantes in the late first century BC and earlier', later overrun by Catuvellaunian and Icenian expansion (Morris and Buckley 1978); an intriguing theory.

Whether hillfort locations were one of the ways territorial boundaries were delineated (if indeed there were boundaries as we would know them) will be considered in the next chapter. However, in the Roman period strict demarcation rules would have applied. Thus, to the south-east, the *civitas* of the Catuvellauni occupied a densely populated area of nearly 10,500km^2 covering an area north of the Thames to Northamptonshire and across from the Lea and Stort valleys in Hertfordshire to the Cherwell in Oxfordshire. Keith Brannigan (1985), in his interpretation of the origins of the tribe, suggests that the whole of the area between Essex and Oxford seems to have been brought into a single grouping by about 20 BC, although its beginnings are obscure. Before that there appears to have been a series of smaller warring tribes occupying south Buckinghamshire and south Hertfordshire around the time of Caesar's foray; but tribes that possibly shared a common ancestry and material culture. Thus, Dyer (1990, 166, quoting Brannigan 1985) suggests that the Catuvellauni could have been the result of the uniting under Tasciovanus of the smaller Cenimagni, Segontiaci, Ancalites, Bibroci and Cassi.

It appears that it was the later oppidum, rather than the hillfort, that was important to the tribe. Coin evidence shows that Tasciovanus emerged as the pre-eminent leader of the Catuvellaunian core area, with a centre at Verulamium (St Albans) in Hertfordshire. Coins were minted there and a large cremation cemetery shows evidence of considerable wealth from *c*.15 BC. Later, Cunobelin became the sole leader and united the Catuvellauni and Trinovantes into a single and powerful state, issuing his Verulamium-minted coins around AD 10. Subsequently coin evidence suggests that his influence extended into Kent, Hampshire, Gloucestershire and Norfolk and, via Eppaticus, into the northern part of the Atrebatic kingdom of Sussex, whose ruler Verica eventually fled to Rome, begging Claudius to intervene on his behalf. The resulting Claudian invasion eventually swept away the southern tribal dynasties.

Thus, by the time the Catuvellauni is heard of hillforts do not seem to have been particularly in fashion, and oppida such as Camulodunum (Cunobelin's capital), and Verulamium, Braughing and the possible late Iron Age ritual site of Wheathampstead in Hertfordshire (Bryant 2007, 73) had all taken over as tribal foci. However, the earlier promontory fort of Dyke Hills, on the notable loop of the river at Dorchester-on-Thames in Oxfordshire, possibly became an oppidum itself, substantial circular huts and ditch systems having been found on the 46ha site. To the north, in Buckinghamshire, Bedfordshire and Northamptonshire, there is little evidence to suggest a reuse or occupation of earlier hillforts, such as Ivinghoe Beacon, and therefore the settlement pattern at the Conquest was probably one of scattered native farms coupled with large oppida to the south-east of the territory.

In the south, coin and ceramic evidence suggests that the Atrebates were the tribe of Surrey, Sussex, Berkshire, Wiltshire and Hampshire, first coming to light when Commius, ruler of the Gallo-Belgic Atrebates of northern France, fled from Caesar to join his followers in Britain around the time of the Conquest. Their principal oppidum was at Calleva Atrebatum (Silchester) in Hampshire. The territory of the Regni, as the southern Atrebates were called, comprised the Weald up to about the River Wey in Hampshire, and the Sussex Downs and coastal strip from the Pevensey Levels in the east to the River Meon and Solent in the west. Thus, towards the end of the first century BC the Atrebates had three seats of power – Calleva Atrebatum, Venta Belgarum (Winchester) and another in the region of Chichester/Selsey.

The political stability of the area was important to the fate of hillforts, and it has already been seen that the northern part of Atrebatic territory was unstable and was eventually annexed by Cunobelin. Thus, in the area centred around the River Kennet coins of both Tasciovanus and Cunobelin are far more numerous than those of later Atrebatic rulers. Calleva Atrebatum, therefore, passed into other hands, Eppaticus minting coins there around AD 35. Venta Belgarum's fate seems uncertain, but the eastern lands remained in Atrebatic/Regni hands, and the Atrebatic king, Eppilus, enjoyed brief power over the Cantii of Kent between 5 BC and AD 10.

Within this backdrop of unrest and stability in different parts of the territory a general trend was for the hillforts of the Atrebatic and pro-Roman middle and south-western parts of the territory (west Sussex and Hampshire) to be abandoned, with some later reused, whilst in the more unstable and anti-Roman Weald and east Sussex and the north-west of the territory hillforts appear to have been in almost continuous occupation and, in some cases, refortified (Cunliffe 1991, 152).

Cunliffe (1973, 101–2; 128) also discussed examples of abandonment and/or reuse of four middle/western Sussex hillforts. Thundersbarrow Hill, an earlier hillfort of around the fifth century BC, was abandoned by the middle of the first century BC and a late pre-Roman settlement developed alongside the ridgeway on the hill's eastern flanks, the fields of which extended up to the old ramparts. A village remained until around the fourth century AD, perhaps indicating a stability of sorts. Mount Caburn hillfort was refortified in the third/fourth century AD, and at Highdown, after a long period of abandonment, the ditch was re-dug and the rampart heightened with a possible palisade. Likewise, at Cissbury the rampart was heightened and ditch re-dug around the fourth century or later. Cunliffe theorised that this Roman settlement activity could have been the result of upheavals during the fourth century, and possibly some sort of coastal protection mechanism resulting from the Theodosian reorganisation of the defences of the Province.

To the east the Cantii or Cantiaci (later to become the *civitas*) probably stretched from the Weald of Kent and Sussex to the Chilterns and to just north of the Thames, and hillforts, in general, appear to have been in continuous occupation – certainly they ring the Thames in the tribal territory. Unlike the Trinovantes to the north, who made an early treaty of friendship with Caesar and subsequently profited, the Kentish tribes were hostile to the Roman advance and suffered commercially as a result. Bigberry was likely to have been the first hillfort reduced by Caesar on his way to the Thames (Detsicas 1983, 2). Despite these setbacks, there is substantial evidence for intercourse with Rome by the first century BC, the tribe not only producing the potin coins of north Kent, as well as Gallo-Belgic issues, but being the first to mint coinage nationally (Detsicas 1983, 1–3). An indication of this Roman contact was the establishment of settlements along recognised routes. Thus, the large univallate 10.7ha Bigberry hillfort controlled the Stour crossing, the oppidum at Quarry Wood (Loose) dominated the Medway and Oldbury hillfort commanded the

Darent Valley; all are dated to the first century BC. Quarry Wood was the last to be built, possibly indicating a move from the higher ground to more open oppidum-type settlements (Detsicas 1983, 2). Bigberry's hoard of high-status metalwork has often been interpreted as suggesting a residence of an elite and perhaps status as a regional capital or oppidum and as a precursor to the present Canterbury. This may not be so, however, as investigations have so far shown a noticeable lack of evidence of intensive occupation and ritual activity (Blockley and Blockley 1989; Champion 2007, 303).

To the west the Durotriges of Dorset and Somerset to the estuary of the Severn and Bristol Channel were also, like the Cantii, hostile to the Roman advance, showing a substantial difference in outlook to the client kingdoms of the immediate south-east. Probably more is known about the association of this tribe with their hillforts than any other, and Cunliffe (1991, 159–70) has given the best description of its organisation, suggesting two phases of development – an initial period of rapid expansion from 100–60 BC and a later, impoverished, phase from 60 BC up to the Conquest. The first period was based on trading links with the continent from ports such as Hengistbury Head, with evidence now emerging of another possible port in Poole Harbour as we have seen, as well as other, less formal, sites in the Solent area.

The coastal promontory fort of Hengistbury Head (Cunliffe 1987) is located at the tip of Christchurch Harbour, to landward forming a sheltered anchorage from the sea (Figure 78). Here double ramparts and ditches (the 'Double Dykes') seal off the Head to give a present area of some 70ha-plus; in the Iron Age it would have been considerably larger, as coastal erosion has taken a great deal of the site. The fort must have been one of the most important trading ports in Britain at the time. Here were found Dressel 1 amphorae bringing wine from northern Italy during the first century BC, raw purple and yellow glass from the Mediterranean, dried figs and Kimmeridge shale for bracelets. In return copper, silver and gold were sent from western Britain and possibly also iron from Hengistbury itself; smelting and refining were carried out on site. Salt was extracted from the coastal waters and grain brought from Wessex. It is also tempting to think that the slaves and hunting dogs mentioned by Strabo passed through here on their way to Rome in exchange for the luxury goods mentioned above; there may have been a thriving slave market. With its strategic location Hengistbury controlled riverine access via the Rivers Stour and Avon to the Wessex hinterland and the Bristol Channel and, thus, the north Breton and Atlantic trading routes from the west. Rich exchange and trade linked Hengistbury with Alet, a port of the Coriosolites tribe, and in this cross-channel economy Guernsey derived wealth from becoming an essential safe haven and transit 'way station' (Renouf 2004, 15). The metal-rich lands of the south-west peninsula and south Wales were also incredibly important and Hengistbury was able to take advantage of both the northern trading route and a southern one via the Solent to the south-west.

Caesar's Gallic War of 58 to 51 BC against the tribes of Gaul (including his first

incursion into Britain) marked a decline in this lucrative Atlantic trade which had amassed the Durotriges substantial wealth, at least during the period from 100 BC. The second phase of tribal fortunes after 60 BC saw economic collapse and the once gold standard coinage was debased to white gold, silver and then bronze. The initial successful trading period lasted only around fifty years, but the one factor which seems to divide this tribe in the archaeological record from others to the east is its reliance on the old hillforts rather than the newly appearing oppida, and these hillforts played an important role in the tribe's hostility to the Roman advance westwards. The tribe has long been associated with the large Dorset hillforts of Maiden Castle, Hambledon Hill, Hod Hill, Pilsdon Pen and Eggardon (this last the most neglected of all the great sites), among others, and most seem to have been occupied when Vespasian appeared in the immediate years after the Conquest. The density of structures suggests thriving settlements at the first three at least, but one by one these forts were attacked and over-run.

The territory of the Dobunni extended from north Somerset through Gloucestershire to Herefordshire and Worcestershire and to south and west Warwickshire, north and west Wiltshire and west Oxfordshire. Coinage was issued from 35 BC and evidence from this source suggests two tribal areas which can also be traced in pottery. North of the Avon were decorated jars and

FIGURE 78. The site of the sheltered Durotrigan Iron Age port of Hengistbury Head, Hampshire.

saucepan pots manufactured in the Malvern area and distributed widely in the Cotswolds and the Marches and elsewhere outside the tribal area as we have seen. The north Somerset region, on the other hand, produced linear-tooled pottery resulting from Durotrigan tradition and Cornish influence – a Somerset version of the South-Western Decorated Ware using local north Somerset clays. At the Bagendon oppidum in Oxfordshire and Kingsdown and Camerton Camps in Somerset, and Salmonsbury in the Cotswolds these wares replaced earlier local types just before the Conquest (Cunliffe 1991, 173).

The northern centre for the tribe appears to have been the huge 80ha promontory of Bagendon (Clifford 1961), only 8km from Roman Cirencester and cut off by a series of linear ditches, whilst to the north Camerton and Salmonsbury provided large settlement sites. The sacred spring at Bath must have been significant to the tribe and to the north on the Gloucestershire/ Worcestershire border hillforts such as Bredon Hill continued in occupation, as did Worlebury and the Cadbury hillforts to the south in Somerset.

To the far west, the Dumnonii looked more to the Armorican tribes than did those of Wessex and the south-east, and the extraction of Cornish tin no doubt provided the general wealth of the area and most outside contact. For the Durotriges Hengistbury provided a vibrant, but short-lived, economy during the first century BC, but the port-of-trade of Mount Batten, overlooking Plymouth Sound, which had been established in the late Bronze Age, continued in use until the late Iron Age and beyond (Hawkes 1998). Here a succession of networks and communication links centred on both coastal and inter-continental exchange, providing an outlet to the Atlantic trading system The importance of both the Tamar Estuary and the Solent (in particular, Poole Harbour), and trading links between each, is indicated by the discovery of similar regional and continental coins and a fragment of silver-rich copper ore from the Tamar area found at Hengistbury. At Mount Batten Armorican axes show contact with Brittany, possibly directly to the ports of northern Finistère (Cunliffe 1988b, 103). Assemblages included both fibulae from the south-west of Britain and Iberian-type brooches from the Pyrenees of France, as well as Hallstatt copper alloy knobbed bracelets from central Europe (Firth *et al.* 1998, 30–1).

Originating in the fourth century BC and lasting to the first century BC, the South-Western Decorated Ware (formerly Glastonbury Ware) pottery of decorated necked jars and bowls characterised the Dumnonii. It had its impetus from Brittany and came from several locations in the south-west, such as the Lizard and Exe areas. Examples have been found at coastal promontory forts on the Gower, indicating trading contact with south Wales. A later, less decorated ceramic tradition of cordoned ware produced at the circular hillfort of Castle Dore followed, lasting into Roman times.

What is noticeable about the area of this tribe is the lack of large hillforts, in common with the Demetae of south-west Wales. An essential dependency on the sea for survival is reflected in the profusion of 'cliff castles' strung along these rocky coasts, akin to those in Brittany and Pembrokeshire. Inland, hillforts rarely exceed 3ha, the 15ha of Carn Brea at Redruth being exceptional.

Whilst northern and eastern England appear to have been only lukewarm to hillforts, there is plenty of archaeological evidence to suggest activity at many sites in Wales and the Marches up to and around the Conquest. In the absence of coin and to a lesser extent ceramics, it is predominantly from the Roman texts that information comes of those involved.

There seem to have been five main tribes straddling the border. Most of north-west Wales was held by the Ordovices, with the neighbouring Deceangli in the northern Marches and north-east Wales. To the south, the Cornovii, predominantly of Shropshire, merged into the northern limit of the Dobunni in Herefordshire, whilst further down in south-east Wales to Glamorgan and possibly into Gloucestershire were the Silures, who resisted the Roman invasion particularly strongly and, with the Deceangli in the north, felt its brunt. To the south-west of Wales were the Demetae. Green and Howell (2000) indicate that within these major groupings there were possibly sub-tribes, such as the Gangani of the Ordovices, and that distributions of late Bronze Age metalwork indicate that these tribal entities may have had origins pre-dating the Iron Age 'perhaps by a considerable period'.

Not much is known about the Cornovii, the dominant tribe of the northern Marches before the Conquest, with territory extending from north Herefordshire to Shropshire, parts of Montgomeryshire and southern Flintshire and east to Cheshire, Staffordshire and Worcestershire. The Deceangli of north-east Wales and the Silures to the northern extremity of the River Wye catchment were the immediate neighbours, but territorial limits are unknown in any detail. Relations with the Ordovices to the west are also unclear, and indeed it has been suggested that the great hillforts that dominate the hills – for example, Caer Caradoc at Church Stretton shown on the cover of this book – could have been Ordovices structures in a zone of contact or indeed conflict. However, if we assume that the Cornovii did in fact occupy the area, as Webster (1975) suggests, strategically placed hillforts must have played an important role and the River Severn would have been a crucial communication link with possible ritual overtones.

As we lack coinage and have only poor finds of both pottery and metalwork, there is little evidence to go on for the pre-Roman Cornovii. Much of the pottery found in Shropshire and Herefordshire was made in the Malvern Hills, and finds, as at Y Breiddin and the Berth, suggest trade and exchange throughout the region of the Marches. How these hillforts related to the tribe is impossible to guess, but a significant number appear to have been occupied around the Conquest when Scapula swept through the Marches, taking the Wrekin. Romano-British pottery was unearthed at Oliver's Point, located on the prominent Nesscliffe Hill near Shrewsbury (Hume and Jones 1959).

The Deceangli, of north-east Wales, appear to have suffered greatly from the Roman advance, but virtually nothing is known about them before the

FIGURE 79. The single
dry-stone rampart of
Caer y Tŵr at Holyhead,
defines the summit on
the north and east; the
enclosure was the site of
a later fourth-century AD
Roman signal station.
The entrance is in the
foreground between
the curving ramparts.
RCHAMW C839934.

Conquest. Certainly great hillforts dominated the scene, especially in the
Clwydian Range and environs (Brown 2004), and these seem to have remained
in use over a considerable period. There have been substantial excavations at
Dinorben, Moel Hiraddug and Moel y Gaer (Rhosesmor), which have shed
light on hillfort structure and society generally and, at Dinorben, shown reuse
well into the fourth century AD.

To the west the Ordovices also occupied major commanding hillforts, such
as those of the Llŷn and north Wales coast, which have been discussed in some
detail above, with their closely packed stone buildings suggesting a considerable
organisational structure and stability over many centuries. Here, apart from a
few sites such as Dinas Dinlle and Pen y Dinas (Llandudno), mentioned later,
coastal forts are few on the mainland and it is only on Anglesey that they appear
on the island's essentially rocky coast (Figure 79).

The Silures, the clan-based tribal confederation of Brecon, Monmouthshire,
Glamorgan and possibly part of Gloucestershire, kept the Roman advance at
bay for twenty-five years. The martial nature of an emerging elite, concerned
with ostentation and display during the late Iron Age and into the early
centuries AD, is expressed by elaborate horse-trappings and chariot equipment
from Maendy Camp and Castle Ditches (Llancarfan) in Glamorgan, as well as
from non-hillfort contexts (Gwilt 2007, 312). To the east in Monmouthshire

hillforts centred on the Usk catchment and between the Usk and the Wye are plentiful, but notable are the excavated Llanmelin, inland above the Severn, and the coastal promontory of Sudbrook on the river itself which possibly acted (as did Merthyr Mawr) as a trading point for the Bristol Channel, which itself provided an all-important artery for local and continental tribal contact (Howell 2006, 56). Sudbrook was ideally suited for trade with Brittany (particularly with its southern tribe the Veneti) and voyages via the Atlantic routes, making Wales an integral part of the seaborne trading community (Green and Howell 2000, 26). Further to the west things appeared to have been more impoverished, with coastal promontory forts dominating the landscape, especially on the Gower in Glamorgan, but here a mould and pieces from Worm's Head similar to those from Braich-y-Ddinas, Dinorben and an unknown Anglesey site could have been to cast blanks for beaten cauldrons or bowls, and imply a western tradition of sheet metalworking (Gwilt 2007, 308). A series of these coastal forts, such as The Bulwarks at Chepstow in Monmouthshire, and The Knave and High Pennard on the Gower, which were probably in use in the first century BC, have been excavated, but all produced very little other than South-Western Decorated Ware and a few indeterminate sherds. Nevertheless, finds of glass beads from the Meare glass-making centre in Somerset at Twyn y Gaer and Coygan Camp, along with pottery, possibly from the Mendips, indicate that these items were 'actively and selectively exchanged' (Gwilt 2007, 308), with all the socio-political relationships that this implies. Seaborne trade and exchange seems to have been very important to the tribe and the presence of Greek coin implies widespread contact.

Clearly, then, hillforts were important to the tribe and although Howell (2006, 39–43) suggests that their construction may be somewhat later than those further north in the Marches, sites such as Twyn y Gaer do have a complex history, with activity dated to the fifth century BC and occupation up to the Conquest. At Coed y Bwynydd in the Usk Valley calibrated radiocarbon dates range from 800 to 200 BC. Romano-British material has been recovered from a variety of sites – as at The Bulwarks near Porthkerry in Glamorganshire – and, indeed, a significant proportion of the excavated Glamorgan/Monmouthshire hillforts (Llanmelin, Lodge Hill Camp and Sudbrook, for example) show finds of a similar date.

Further to the west in Pembrokeshire and Carmarthenshire the Demetae appear to have been the dominant tribe, but its boundaries are as diffuse as those of the Silures. Small enclosed settlements are the major characteristic of the area. Some have been excavated, as at Walesland Rath, but in the Preseli Mountains to the north a series of major stone hillforts dominates the crest, notably Moel Drygarn and Carn Ingli. However, the probable dominance and importance of the sea is shown by the many coastal promontory forts commanding the coast, as in Cornwall, but how and when the tribe interacted with any of these is not known.

Resistance to Rome

Barry Cunliffe (1991) has written of the Roman advance and the threat that this imposed on the native tribes of Britain and this will not be repeated in any detail here. But hillforts played an important role in areas where there was resistance and there is excavated evidence and accounts by the classical authors for this.

The Roman invasion force of AD 43, composed of five legions and auxiliaries (over 40,000 men), was commanded by Aulus Plautius, the first governor of Britain; among its leaders was the future emperor (from AD 69) Vespasian. There is some debate as to whether the initial Roman landing was in Kent or Sussex or both, but, taking the conventional view, the invasion began in the former. After a relatively easy beginning, skirmishes ensued with resistance under the sons of Cunobelin – Caratacos and Togodumnus – and became fiercer towards the Medway, but the two-day stand by the native tribes was unsuccessful and Togodumnus was killed. With the arrival of the Emperor Claudius with fresh troops and elephants, Camulodunum, the great centre of the Catuvellauni, was quickly taken. This classic advance would probably not have taken place without the complicity of the Atrebates to the west in Sussex and Hampshire: the rapid establishment of the highly successful 'Romanised' Tiberius Claudius Cogidubnus as the client king of the area was vital to the stability of this western flank. Indeed, it is likely that a second detachment of the Roman army did enter the Chichester area at the time of the Kentish advance to secure this stable enclave. To the west the Dobunni appeared split towards Rome. A capitulation of at least part of the tribal identity ensued, possibly under the offices of Cogidubnus, but a southern group may have resisted and suffered as a result.

With this background in mind, it is important to our discussion of the role of hillforts at this time that the Durotriges turned out to be a very different matter. As a tribe they had remained isolated from those of the south-east and, after a very successful period as Armorican and Atlantic traders, seem to have 'retreated' into their hillfort strongholds which appear to have been strengthened to repel potential attack. The account of the advance of Vespasian with the *Legio II Augusta* given by his biographer Suetonius suggests fierce resistance overcome by substantial force during late AD 43 to early AD 44 with, after taking the Isle of Wight, some twenty hillforts being over-run and thirty battles engaged. Archaeological evidence seems to have confirmed this, none more so than at Maiden Castle. Here, Wheeler found hand-to-hand, ballista and sling-shot fighting, with burials, in native fashion, in a 'war cemetery' at the eastern gate. A tribal warrior found with a ballista bolt embedded in his spine now resides in the Dorset County Museum.

Along the path of Vespasian's advance, another 'war cemetery' came to light at Spettisbury Rings as a result of the building of the railway in 1857/58. Around 120 bodies had been hurriedly thrown into a pit; some showed a violent end. Hod Hill, however, appears to have been an easier proposition, with the 'chieftain's' hut apparently bombarded by ballista bolts before the hillfort was over-run. Here, in common with other sites in Durotrigan territory, the Roman presence was emphasised by the building of a short-lived fort at the hillfort's north-western corner. Later, in AD 61, a massacre at the south-west gateway of South Cadbury, possibly as a result of a western uprising associated with the Boudican rebellion (Putnam 1998, 54), resulted in a barracks being built on the site and effectively ending native hillfort control in the area.

Suetonius refers to two tribes being subjugated – the Durotriges being one and the other probably that occupying the area Rome called the administrative region of the 'Belgae', around part of Salisbury Plain and north-west to the River Severn. The hillforts of this region appeared to have been kept in good order. At Battlesbury a mass burial outside the north-west entrance could have been Roman work, signalling the end of its occupation. To the north-west, at Bury Camp, near Colerne, the main north-east entrance was destroyed by fire together with parts of the interior, again possibly the result of Vespasian's push westwards.

The Trinovantes to the north of the Thames and the Iceni of East Anglia submitted immediately and Prasutagus, the Trinovantian client king of Rome, was loyal to the Emperor, minting silver coins with a Roman bust until his death in AD 60. Revolt followed, led by his wife Boudica. But what the reaction of the Corieltauvi was is difficult to assess, as they are not included in the surviving accounts by Tacitus and Dio of the invasion between AD 43 and 70. It is possible that there was some resistance, but capitulation is indicated by the construction of Roman forts northwards along the Fosse Way and Ermine Street. Certainly the extension of Catuvellaunian and Brigantian power must have focused Corieltauvian minds on an allegiance of sorts with Rome as protector.

In the countryside the majority of the Corieltauvi would have been tenants or *coloni* on estates, freeholders or, indeed, landowners themselves. The Romano-British peasant would have owed allegiance, linked by bonds, to his master/landowner. Although there were villas and villa estates in the tribal territory, native settlements are continually coming to light, especially in the river valleys. On higher ground in Nottinghamshire, a number of small hillforts continued in occupation during the Roman period: for example, Dorket Head, with proven Romano-British connections, and Fox Wood near Calverton, with its Roman stone buildings. To the north the flat lands towards south Yorkshire have yielded much evidence of regular, mainly Roman, field systems (Todd 1991, 79–80, 110).

When Publius Ostorius Scapula, the second governor of Britain, took command in AD 47, eastern and southern Britain was under Roman control and, after dealing with insurgencies among the Iceni, his attention turned to Wales. Tacitus records thirteen campaigns in Wales and the Marches between AD 48 and 77 and it was into Deceangli tribal territory that the first Roman incursion took place, either possibly as reprisal for incursions to the east or to sever contact between the Welsh and Brigantian tribes. This was followed by a protracted and bloody war with the Silures and Ordovices to the south.

In Dobunni and Cornovian territory in the Marches there is some evidence of resistance to the Roman advance at both Sutton Walls and the Wrekin. At the former there was hurried refortification around AD 75 and the western ditch was re-dug, but before there had been time for silt to accumulate twenty-four bodies were thrown into the ditch at the western entrance and covered with a thin layer of soil. Some had wounds and mutilations, some were decapitated. Whether mutilation was a Roman practice or not is debated, but it is likely that the heads would have been taken as trophies if this had been a native attack. Definitive evidence at the Wrekin, which was taken in AD 49 (Watson 2002, 34), probably awaits further excavation, but a Roman pelum (javelin) head was found at the north-east gate during Stanford's excavations. It is also probable that the massacre at the inner gate of Bredon Hill was also the result of this advance, as we have seen on page 103.

About the time of the fall of Camulodunum referred to above Caratacos fled to Wales and subsequently built up a power base among the Silures in the south, the Ordovices in mid Wales and the Deceangli in the north-east, thereby becoming a powerful leader of anti-Roman elements. From Tacitus onwards a great deal of energy has been expounded among historians in detailing the resistance of Caratacos to Rome. Certainly he was a powerful thorn in the side of imperial rule and was probably supported by bands of free warriors drawn from supporting tribes such as the Deceangli, who were bound by clientage to serve in war and were rewarded by gifts of some kind (Arnold and Davies 2000, 3).

There has been much speculation as to the location of the 'last stand' of Caratacos. It may have been in Ordovician or Cornovian territory or further to the east in Gloucestershire. As Tacitus observed: 'He chose a place for the battle where the approaches and escape-routes were to our disadvantage but favourable to his own forces. On one side there was a precipitously steep hill, and, where the gradient was gentler, he piled up rocks to form a rough rampart. There was also a river of uncertain depth flowing by in front of his position.'

Many hillforts have been suggested as the site, from Cefn Carnedd in mid Wales Montgomeryshire to Llanymynech Hill (the favourite), above the River Tanat to the north, to unspecified sites around Hay-on-Wye to the south. But, whatever the case, after a violent battle the tribal warriors, who lacked the equipment of the Roman legionaries, were defeated and Caratacos's family captured. He fled north to the Brigantes, whose Queen Cartimandua turned him over to the Romans. Taken to Rome in AD 50 his demeanour impressed all and he was eventually pardoned.

The resistance of the Silures in the south was also fierce and the description of the guerrilla Silurian War, which began around AD 49 and lasted some twenty-five years, by Tacitus is graphic. It is possible that the slighting of revetted ramparts at Lodge Hill Camp, which overlooks the *Legio II Augusta* Roman fortress of Caerleon (Isca) established in the first century AD, could have been the result of resistance or the assertion of direct military control in the region

(Howell 2006, 71), but really how the two sites interacted is uncertain, and indeed the hillfort may even have been abandoned by then. The use of Roman siege tactics, and the fact that this was a guerrilla campaign by the Silures, might have rendered the hillforts strung along the Usk Valley defunct anyway, re-occupation at sites such as Lodge Hill possibly coming in the late Roman/early medieval periods under different social and political circumstances (Pollard *et al.* 2006, 57–61).

It was not until AD 62, after the demise of several governors, that Suetonius Paulinus appears to have regained a semblance of control. In AD 61 he had marched his forces through Deceangli territory, causing many to flee to Mona (Anglesey), and took the island in that year, famously dealing with its Druidic hold. The campaign was cut short, however, by the Boudican rebellion, Paulinus eventually being recalled to East Anglia. After a period of containment, AD 69–98 saw a concerted effort at conquest and with a swift operation by Agricola resistance in Wales effectively came to an end. What part was played (if any) in resistance by the north Wales and Marcher hillforts is difficult to ascertain, again, as in south Wales, because of the lack of extensive excavation. The investigations at Ebury Hill Camp near Shrewsbury, for example, which found no Roman material, contrast with hints of evidence at the Wrekin and Oliver's Point. Major sites could well have played a far more important part than previously thought, but only further research will tell.

The development of oppida and the 'end' of hillforts

Between the fifth and sixth centuries BC there had been a burst of hillfort development over southern Britain, but from the middle Iron Age numbers declined despite a tendency for sites to become more complex, with elaborate gateways and outworks. Some emerged as Barry Cunliffe's 'developed hillforts', defined as enlarged sites of medium size up to around 12ha and having sizeable communities, and interpreted as the centralisation of power of an elite, as at Danebury.

In general, this period of hillfort decline and abandonment continued and around the turn of the millennium a series of larger settlements appeared in strategically placed lower-lying areas of southern England, the majority with little evidence for previous dense occupation (Haselgrove 1976; Hill 2007, 23); the late Iron Age St Albans (Verlamion), for example, near to the Roman Verulamium, was seemingly a ritual site (Haselgrove and Millett 1997). Called by Caesar 'oppida' (literally 'towns'), and often referred to as 'territorial oppida', these sites are often associated with linear earthworks seemingly acting as boundaries. Some are simple, as at Bagendon and some very complex and on a grand scale, as at Camulodunum, the latter constructed at different periods during the late Iron Age and encircling 19km² (Laing and Laing 1995, 27). At other sites, such as Braughing, linear ditches are missing, whilst the deep Beech Bottom Dyke between St Albans and Wheathampstead and the Devil's

Dyke at the latter could have defined territory, but the possibility of their being routeways to ritual complexes, as in the case of Beech Bottom (leading to Verlamion), has also been proposed (Bryant 2007, 72).

Woolf (1993) has eloquently questioned the use of the word 'oppida', and their very complexity and the lack of the major constructions associated with the continental versions suggest that in England something slightly different was going on. However, whatever we call them (and substantial work has still to be done on definition), these sites developed into large settlements supplying a semi-urban environment, minting coinage and trading in and producing important commodities, such as pottery and metalwork. They were also administrative centres containing shrines and, in some cases, became royal capitals: Camulodunum and Verulamium for the Trinovantes/Catuvellauni and Bagendon for the Dobunni. Continental pottery, amphorae and rich burials feature, oppida becoming wealthy and sophisticated bases for the elite. At Braughing, for example, imported pottery from Italy and Gaul has been found in great quantity (Bryant 2007, 63).

Although the huge and high-status Stanwick incorporated The Tofts hillfort, its development might not have been seamless. What we do know is that a first-century BC open settlement was enlarged in the mid first century AD into a developed northern part and a southern area of pasture/arable (Harding 2004, 162, after Hazelgrove *et al.* 1990). However, some much smaller settlements – Dyke Hills above Dorchester-on-Thames, for example – might have replaced earlier local hillforts, in this case Sinodun (Wittenham Clumps) half a mile to the south in Berkshire (Dyer 1997, 160) (Figure 80), but what the relationship was between earlier hillforts and oppida nationally is by no means clear-cut. By the time the latter appeared hillforts in the south were in decline anyway and in areas where oppida have been found the old hillforts were generally abandoned – Pitchbury at Colchester is one. This pattern was exacerbated by the appearance of the Romans from 55 BC and accelerated, as we have seen, from AD 43. However, some hillforts were adapted to fulfill the new roles: Salmonsbury, for example, and Bigberry, Oldbury and Quarry Wood Camp (Loose) in Kent. At Braughing a small settlement had developed by the third century BC, centred on a small earthwork called Gatesbury Wood, but by about 20 BC this had expanded to some 100ha on both sides of the River Rib (Dyer 1990). Sometimes called 'enclosed oppida', these large settlements were really the last type of 'hillfort' developed in south-eastern Britain.

There had been use and reuse of the old Durotrigan hillforts at the time of the Conquest, as we have seen, Vespasian having to prise each from the tribe by force, but whether these sites can be defined as 'oppida' is unclear. Suetonius calls the twenty hillforts captured in Dorset from the Durotriges as 'oppida', and Wheeler referred to the essential 'urban' nature of Maiden Castle. Alcock also called South Cadbury a 'town'. Clearly, they were more than just small settlements and probably served as industrial and commercial centres, strategically placed to dominate the landscape – perhaps not 'enclosed oppida',

but nearly there. At these hillforts, and Hod Hill is one, huts were densely packed, Cunliffe (1991, 364) estimating a possible 270 structures and habitation for 500–1,000 people. But whether this was settled occupation or reoccupation from the mid Iron Age is difficult to assess.

We will return to later hillfort use in the last chapter, but now we must consider issues surrounding the function of hillforts and, in particular, the ways in which they gelled into Iron Age society.

FIGURE 80. Sinodun Camp (Wittenham Clumps) in Berkshire. Dorchester-on-Thames can be seen in the middle distance.

CHAPTER TEN

Beacons in the Landscape
– New Theories, New Questions

....

Hillfort theory has progressed since the invader hypotheses. On excavation and survey some sites have given up little information, some a great deal, but what is noticeable is their great variability. Not all hillforts were occupied, or even in existence, at the same time and there is ample evidence of use, abandonment and reuse throughout England and Wales over some 1,000 years. It is quite likely that function differed not only between sites but also over time.

The following sections will, therefore, look at some important factors relevant to hillfort location and consider a series of theories on function and social significance, beginning with the basics: the physical nature of the site.

The physical factor

The relationship between physical factors and hillforts is poorly understood and there are vast areas of England, in particular, where no locational analysis of any sort has been attempted. There has also been much debate among archaeologists as to the role of the environment in determining human action in prehistory. Some believe that its effects were so great that there was little freewill involved in the making of decisions; others think (at least in part) the opposite (Giddens 1984). However, not wishing to get into contentious theoretical arguments here, it is indeed likely that climate, topography and soils will have played a significant part in influencing whether and where a hillfort was built and for what purpose. Space does not permit a comprehensive review here so we will look at just a few aspects in turn to give a flavour of what was involved.

Climate and topography

It is difficult to relate today to the siting of some hillforts on extremely exposed hilltops, where conditions are, and would have been in prehistory, at their most severe. At Titterstone Clee, for example, the average height of cloud cover at the 533m OD site is 396m, and the summit of the Wrekin, at 407m OD, even in the summer can be wreathed in cloud (Figure 81). Coastal sites can be very violent places indeed and gusts of over 100 mph have been experienced at St Ann's Head in Pembrokeshire. Although much more stable than they look, it is highly unlikely that the traditional timber roundhouse would have been able to withstand such extreme conditions, and despite the fact that a probable thatch weight has been found at The Rumps cliff castle, it is likely that, in the most exposed situations at least, as at St David's Head, only those made predominantly of stone would survive. The medieval 'beehive-shaped' cells of the monastery on Skellig Michael, an isolated and exposed rock in the Atlantic off the Kerry coast of Ireland, employed a construction technique known as 'corbelling', where 'the rising courses of stone each project slightly inwards until they form a dome' (Moorhouse 1998, 175), and something similar could have built the jumbled-together huts of Tre'r Ceiri and Garn Boduan.

Nevertheless, initial research by the author shows that of a sample of 358 hillforts in Wales and the Marches that are not purely contour sites as defined in Chapter 1, some 59 per cent face south (WSW–ESE), with just over 30 per cent either facing south-east or south-west; south-facing slopes, of course, being the warmest throughout the year. Moreover, at a wide variety of sites the degree of cover afforded by a rampart was substantial and we have seen that many hillforts show evidence of structures huddled in its lee; one reason perhaps for building such a bank or high wall in the first place.

When hillforts are analysed at a *regional* as opposed to a *local* level, the choice of very extreme climatic locations, as experienced on an Ingleborough in Yorkshire or a Carrock Fell in Cumberland, appear to be the exception rather than the rule, and most hillforts are situated in comparatively more 'amenable' areas away from the mountainous core. When the six Welsh relief regions of Brown (1960) and Bowen (1977) are compared with hillfort locations, sites are markedly situated in the 'valley lowlands', 'hills' and 'coastal plateaux' categories, while areas defined as 'mountains' (in the north), 'dissected plateaux' (throughout Wales) and 'coastal flats' are generally free of hillfort clusters. It follows that, although some hillforts are located in extreme locations, overall there appear to have been climatic and physiographic limits to their construction (Brown 2002).

The position of hillforts along the upper reaches of the River Severn and its tributaries shows this trend well. Upstream of the pivotal Cefn Carnedd at Caersŵs there is only one hillfort, the multivallate Y Gaer (Llandinam), situated on a prominent spur above the river. Further upstream still, the Severn reaches the high and fiercely exposed Pumlumon massif, where it has its source along with the Wye, which shows a similar hillfort locational pattern. This upland is devoid of hillforts, which reoccur again on the lower western slopes towards Aberystwyth. Similarly, on the eastern slopes of Pumlumon, the cluster of sites around the Rivers Trannon and Clywedog (possibly associated with the control of mineral wealth) also peters out as the land becomes higher and more exposed.

In the Bronze Age the climate was substantially better than in the Iron Age and it is possible that hillforts with proven Bronze Age credentials, such as Mam Tor, could have been occupied for longer periods during the year than was possible in later periods. Hut platforms have been found on both the sheltered eastern and exposed western slopes of the hillfort (Coombs and Thompson 1979, 9). Structural evidence on a site does not necessarily imply permanent habitation, of course – a seasonal visitation by even a small number of people, with the normal detritus left behind, can add up to a significant amount of material over hundreds of years, and this fact of life has often been overlooked when analysing evidence from excavation.

Although great care must be taken when comparing modern climatic data with prehistoric settlement patterns, a consideration of climate and hillfort location quantitatively does suggest certain trends (Brown 2002). Despite undoubted change since the prehistoric period, modern rainfall, temperature and soil moisture patterns appear to exhibit a *general* correlation with hillfort distribution throughout Wales and the Marches. More work is required, but comparisons suggest that rainfall, temperature and soil moisture – i.e. climatic factors – did play a part in the overall choice of site and hillforts were constructed in areas with better conditions (particularly for farming) at a *macro* level at least. As Harding (1982) points out, the importance of climatic change, particularly in marginal areas, should not be underestimated and a continuous period of cool damp weather in summer would reduce the quality and quantity of grain yields.

Coastal locations will generally experience a milder climate overall despite the severe effects of wind gust and chill, and no doubt this would have influenced the use of such sites, perhaps as bases controlling summer pastures, for example (see page 211). However, it would be unwise to assume that coastal promontory forts are located today in *exactly* the same position *vis a vis* the sea as they were during the Iron Age. Estimating sea-level change is a complex process, and change occurs because of a variety of factors, not just climate, but during the past 200 years the sea has risen worldwide on average by 1–2mm per year and over the past two millennia by 0.1–0.2mm per year (Hill 2004, 88). Thus, since 600 BC there has been a rise of around 44–88cm and since 800 BC of around 46–92cm, with subsequent increase in erosion depending on the nature of the geology, geomorphology and sea condition.

Where it has been possible to 'determine' coastal erosion rates and transfer them to existing promontory fort boundaries, the results are illuminating. At Belle Tout, just west of Beachy Head in Sussex, a rough estimate can be made of the amount of erosion suffered by the chalk headland over the past 2,000 years. Records show that in 1834, when the lighthouse was built on site, it lay 35m from the cliff edge. By 1998 coastal recession had brought the light 19m nearer to the sea. In that year an additional catastrophic rockfall left it only 3m from the edge, and it was subsequently moved 17m inland. Using the above rates, it is possible to work out that, *theoretically*, the cliffs have receded around 232m since the Roman Conquest (disregarding any catastrophic events which must have occurred over the period). The very large size of the present-day enclosure (20ha) suggests that, although the cliff edge could well have formed its southern margin in prehistory, these erosion rates suggest that this could have been up to half a kilometre further 'out to sea' than it is today (Figure 82). A similar situation occurs at nearby Seaford Head, where the erosion of the chalk cliffs

FIGURE 81. The exposed Wrekin, Shropshire, in July cloud.

can be clearly seen. To the west on the chalk cliffs directly above Worbarrow Bay in Dorset all that remains of the impressive Flowers Barrow fort are three multivallate sides plus a south-eastern entrance, covering in all some 2ha. But the site could have been twice the size in the Iron Age (Gale 2003, 153) and certainly a distance inland. Dinas Dinlle, on the northern coast of the Llŷn, shows the severe effects of erosion on glacial drift: all of the western defences have been removed, exposing sections of the southern ramparts, which can be seen tumbling down to the beach (Figure 83).

But coastal erosion is not confined to soft rock areas. On the Ordovician strata of Pembrokeshire many hillforts have been severely reduced in size and at Castell Penpleidiau, south of St David's overlooking St Bride's Bay, the sea has cut dramatically into the fort. Although an impressive series of ramparts remain, over half of the area has been lost. Along the coast to the east only a narrow part of the promontory fort of Nash Point at Marcross in Glamorgan is left and the original entrance at Castle Ditches (Llantwit Major) has gone (Whittle 1992, 40). The Summerhouse fort is semi-circular now with a vertical sea cliff on the southern side, but originally was probably a full circle. Sudbrook has suffered badly as well. On the yet-harder granite of the Isles of Scilly (Ashbee 1986, 203–4), two of the three coastal promontory forts have probably fared better: the multivallate Giant's Castle at St Mary's and Burnt Hill on St Martin's, but at Shipman Head, on Bryher, the western wall and the interior have been much reduced. Nationally, there are many others badly in need of urgent investigation before they are lost for ever.

FIGURE 82. The chalk cliffs of Belle Tout, which have suffered substantial erosion since the Iron Age, from Seaford Head in Sussex.

FIGURE 83. The erosion of the ramparts of the coastal fort of Dinas Dinlle at Llandwrog, Caernarfonshire, sited on an isolated mound of glacial drift, is both substantial and rapid.

Nine of the headlands of the Gower have promontory forts, and rising sea levels could account for their strange position on Burry Holmes and Worm's Head, which guard the northern and southern extremities of Rhossili Bay. Burry Holmes has a high bank, ditch and counterscarp running from north to south across the promontory at its highest point, the entrance being a simple gap with causeway. The headland is now cut off completely at high tide and forms an island, but in the Iron Age could have been entirely accessible. Along the coast east of Barry, the Sully fort is affected in a similar way.

The rise in sea level since the last great Ice Age 14,000 years ago is not only the result of melting ice, but also of the land being relieved of its immense weight. Known as the process of 'isostatic readjustment', the former ideal state of isostatic balance of the earth's crust, which gravitation tends to establish and which is upset by geological process such as ice, is restored. Areas of northern Britain are still rising by around 2mm a year, whilst parts of southern England are sinking by some 1mm. A Neolithic forest lies beneath the Solent. However, where the sea level was higher than today, a wave-cut platform or raised beach, visible at low tide and itself a product of erosion, can dissipate the effects of wave action and so reduce erosion rates. This can be seen below Worlebury hillfort overlooking the Bristol Channel at around 13.5m above present sea level. At any one location, therefore, the effects of wave action can be exceedingly complex and circumstances can change dramatically and quickly, with or without human intervention.

Much depends, of course, upon geology, geomorphology and local sea conditions at any one point, as well as relative rates of marine erosion and sub-aerial denudation (Holmes 1965, 799). But what can be said with certainty is that the physiographic situation around the coasts of today is *not* as it was in the Iron Age.

Good land and good soils

Five trends in soil development (pedogenesis) during the postglacial period can be detected: podzolisation, clay movement, gleying, peat formation and erosion. Erosion, in particular, became marked in the marginal uplands in the Bronze Age when human exploitation was at its peak but, as the climate deteriorated at the end of the sub-boreal, upland settlement retreated, felled woodland failed to regenerate and heath and bog spread over the grazing lands. Therefore, although differing from site to site, the initiation and spread of blanket peat in the British Isles was due to human activity, land use practices and climate acting together. In some cases clearance of woodland by late Bronze Age and early Iron Age peoples resulted in erosion rates similar to those of today (Phillips and Mighall 2000, 57–8). The deteriorating climate of the Iron Age and exploitation of land resulted in further gleying, peat formation, podzolisation and the spread of heath.

With this in mind, in the previous section we have suggested that there appears to be a general trend for hillforts to be located in areas of *comparatively* better climate and as a result to be surrounded by 'better' land. This is especially true of areas of Wessex, and Hambledon Hill on the well-drained chalk is a case in point, overlooking as it does the fertile greensand soils of the Vale of Shroton and the valuable grassland of the Blackmore Vale. The cluster of hillforts around Bredon Hill shows similar trends, the rich cultivable land and natural resources of the river and meadows surrounding the hill being controlled by hillforts in all directions – Bredon Hill itself commanding the Rivers Avon and Severn beyond; Elmley Castle overlooking the route into the south Midlands and Conderton Camp covering lands to the Cotswold scarp.

However, it must be added that much depends on location. For example, recent studies of plant remains preserved in waterlogged conditions in a stream valley to the south-east of Castle-an-Dinas hillfort in Cornwall, and close to evidence of newly discovered roundhouses at Belowda, show that the area was generally damp, open moorland, not particularly attractive to agriculture, but nevertheless inhabited and farmed in the late Iron Age and Roman periods, at least on a seasonal or short-term basis (Highways Agency *et al.* 2007). It is this evidence of seasonal use, as well as the importance of the area for tin, that could be significant when the *raison d'être* for this hillfort is considered.

The uses to which different physical environments about a particular hillfort were put can be hinted at by looking at how Cunliffe (1984, 475–6) defined five ecological zones around Danebury, Wainwright and Davies (1995, 105–7) suggesting that, with certain reservations, they could be equally applicable to Balksbury, some 7km distant. These zones are as follows:

- Floodplains – providing good arable land for cereals, water meadows for cattle and hay, and marsh for reeds, rushes and willow, all used for thatching, wattle and baskets
- Watered downland – where cattle could be pastured within easy reach of a water supply
- Dry downland – more than 1km from water, for pasture and possibly arable
- Isolated woodland – used for timber, pannage, browsing and supply of woodland plants and fungi
- Forest – used for timber, woodland food and clay

Each environment had a specific use and no doubt would be jealously guarded. Thus, for all hillforts it would be possible to define ecological zones of use depending upon the local environment. Certainly, the occupants of sites such as Wall Camp (Kynnersley), the Berth and Stonea Camp, surrounded by marsh, fen and mere, are likely to have exploited the readily available fish, fowl and reed literally on their doorstep.

Good farming depends on good soil and, as the basic outline of soil type was established by the beginning of the Iron Age, it is useful to look at present-day soils and hillfort location to see if there is any correlation between the two. The author has studied soils at Association level against hillfort (including small enclosures in south-west Wales) distribution in Wales and the Marches (Brown 2002), and there is indeed a preponderance of typical brown earths (46.3 per cent) and typical brown podzolic soils (32.6 per cent), with their well-drained horizons, around sites, suggesting that deliberate choices were made by their builders regarding the most productive locations. Earlier research by Crampton and Webley (1963, 333) proved most Gower hillforts to be on similar 'sols bruns acides'. A favoured site would, of necessity, be well-drained, as on the chalk, but it would also be located in areas suitable for the type of farming practised at the time. In this respect, it has been argued that the concentration of smaller defended enclosures in south-west Wales is the result of a combination of soils and climate more suited to pastoralism than arable agriculture (Williams 1988, 30).

There are indications, therefore, from overall mapping at Soil Association level in Wales and the Marches that suitable soils for farming and hillfort distribution are closely linked, adding weight to John Manley's observation (1990, 33) that a position within, or peripheral to, good farming land would be favoured for hillforts.

Defence – or not?

Taking the above into consideration, let us now look at hillforts and the defence argument. The Celtic invasions or movements of peoples from continental Europe to Britain (the Iron Age A, B and C penetrations) proposed by Hawkes (1931) just happened to coincide chronologically with the great building period for hillforts of the mid to late first millennium BC. In addition, the background of influential archaeologist's, such as Sir Mortimer Wheeler, was military, and his interpretations of Maiden Castle, which set the tone for hillfort investigation during the 1930's and beyond, were themselves military in nature. Subsequent research by others up to Avery's work of the 1980s backed up these interpretations (Armit 2007, 26–9), especially on the multivallate sites of Wessex. This meant that hillforts were seen as almost entirely 'defensive fortifications' to be occupied in times of conflict and stress brought on predominantly by increasing population pressure, and abandoned or neglected in times of peace. It followed on that most attention would be focused on hillfort architecture – the banks, ditches and entrances in particular, which were seen as predominantly built with defence in mind – and that this focus would be reflected in the descriptive terms used: 'fort', 'rampart', 'guard chamber', etc. As a result, the defensive aspects of hillfort architecture have dominated archaeological thought over the years. However, further excavations, as at Danebury, and a series of landmark papers began the questioning of pure defence as a *raison d'être*, with other factors such as ritual, status and prestige proposed (for example, the work of Bowden and McOmish of 1987 and 1989). It will be useful, therefore, to stand back and consider what, in the very simplest of terms, would have been the most suitable defensive position for a hillfort, if defence was the singular reason for construction.

The first site requirement would be a location in a strategically inaccessible position, probably on a hill or within an area of marsh or fen, that would allow defences in the form of bank, palisade, wall and ditch to be erected. Many hillforts, but by no means all, fulfil this criterion. Of the five hillforts defined

FIGURE 84. Pen y Dinas, on the edge of the Great Orme at Llandudno in Caernarfonshire, commands Llandudno Bay, but is itself substantially overlooked by higher ground.

within the Salisbury Plain Training Area, for example, only one, Sidbury Camp, is located on a prominent hilltop with a possible strategic advantage, the others, such as Battlesbury and Scratchbury Camps, located on spurs or plateaux, although in themselves very prominent in the landscape. Similarly, Casterley Camp is considered of such a nature that 'it could never have been used in a defensive manner' (McOmish *et al.* 2002, 155). The second requirement would be a situation away from sight and preferably not overlooked. It would be folly in displaying your existence when to attract attention would court disaster. Few hillforts meet the former and some do not even meet the latter of these, as Figure 84 shows. The third requirement, of the greatest importance, would be a water supply on site. Whilst the nearest stream to most hillforts is within a short distance from the base of the hill upon which they stand, only a small proportion appear to have an interior supply. Despite siege tactics probably being alien to Iron Age Britain, and raids most likely, it would be relatively easy for an attacker to cut off a nearby stream or poison a spring.

Coastal promontories at first sight appear to be ideal defensive positions, the sea often enclosing three sides of a site. A good example is Clawdd y Milwyr on St David's Head (Figure 9). Here the promontory was defended by a dry-stone rampart, now about 100m long, with two lesser stone walls outside and possibly shallow ditches between. Hut circles are still visible. Recent research has shown an additional and massive wall built a distance inland, so cutting off about 25ha of the western headland, and possibly turning what was originally a small promontory fort, with origins perhaps in the Neolithic, into a much larger enterprise (Driver 2007a, 96). However, although the actual configuration of the coastline and relationship of the fort to the sea in the Iron Age can only be guessed, as it stands today the treacherous waters off the Head would make escape from attacker by sea impossible. Thus the well-developed contemporary field systems and enclosures bounded by dry-stone walls close to St David's Head could point to farming rather than defence as the primary reason for the fort's existence, although ritual overtones must not be discounted.

At first sight multiple rows of ramparts would seem to provide a very effective defence mechanism. Wheeler interpreted the gap between the inner and outer banks of the ramparts at Maiden Castle as being directly related to the distance a slingstone could be thrown (Collis 1996b, 89). However, when looked at closely, ditches, which could hide an adversary, tend to be shielded by intervening ramparts from the occupants within a fort, providing a degree of 'dead ground' (Ralston 1995, 68), an argument also put forward by Bowden and McOmish (1987, 77) for Maiden Castle. This is unsatisfactory in military terms. Indeed, the past warfare interpretations of Wheeler were further questioned by Sharples in his later work at the site (Sharples 1991a and b).

Finney (2006, 12, 80–1) has, therefore, looked at rampart type, entrances and the use of the spear and sling in some detail, concluding that, although multivallation does have a significant effect on the ability of an assailant to use a sling if the intervening ditches were allowed to regenerate with scrub, this does not explain the 'continued building of ditches and banks at many hillforts'. It would, of course, only require a large inner bank and ditch plus another outer work at 70m-plus away to give adequate protection, but many sites have ramparts with little obvious extra protection and the size of the defences at a site such as Hod Hill during the middle Iron Age was way out of proportion to the threat from any political entity outside. At Old Oswestry the rebuilding of the western entrance actually hampered views from the inner banks, while all of the entrances to the univallate forts Finney studied were vulnerable to the sling. Nevertheless, at Bodbury Ring, Castle Ring (Oakhill in Shropshire) and Earl's Hill in the Marches, a definite terrace cut into the hillside along the contour could have acted as a platform for sling use. This is interesting, as the terrace which surrounds Bodbury is directly above and within range of a possible Cardingmill Valley route through the Long Mynd, and the promontory site could have acted as an access-controlling defensive post if nothing else, its landward defining bank and ditch not appearing especially strong, as we have seen in Figure 39.

However, a martial and defensive intent inherent in hillfort construction still has its proponents, with Hill and Wileman (2002, 64) suggesting that the 'construction of hillforts reflects a development in military organisation and strategy'. This point is perhaps rather overemphasised, but Armit (2007) has rekindled the argument, citing the Maori Pā (structures analogous to hillforts, of which 4–5,000 are found mainly in North Island, New Zealand) as having at least some military dimension. Certainly the design and actual construction techniques employed at many of the more sophisticated sites were clearly intended to intimidate both friend and foe, particularly at the entrances, and imply a well-honed understanding of both aggressive warfare and associated defence; indeed, Ralston (2006, 45), in discussing other purposes, comments that we ignore the military dimension 'at our peril'. Clearly, we must not 'throw the baby out with the bathwater' in our desire to look for new meanings in archaeology and the Iron Age should not be considered as a time of sylvan fields in a passive landscape. These were dangerous times and life expectancy was short. But arguing that hillforts were *predominantly* constructed with martial intent in mind misses the clear archaeological evidence pointing to other factors.

Certainly the 'warrior' – or at least the 'warrior-farmer' – nature of late Bronze and Iron Age society must not be discounted, although, as we have seen, very few hillforts show signs of pre-Roman violence, despite the presence of widespread slingstones and the odd sword or dagger. Perhaps the defensive characteristics of hillfort architecture could have been more about fear of one's neighbour than anything else. The variability of hillforts alone suggests that their function was complicated and varied according to time and place. Let us now look at some other possibilities.

Status, prestige, display and monumentality

There is evidence from personal, domestic and military finds from many hillforts that status, prestige and display would have been very important in later prehistory, especially if society was 'warrior-based': the gold link from Croft Ambrey, bronze La Tène bracelets from Coygan Camp and Llanmelin, and the Hunsbury, Bulbury and Grimthorpe metalwork all testify to this.

Archaeologists have proposed that these traits were reflected in hillfort architecture, Collis (1996b), for example, citing the ramparts at Bury Wood Camp in Wiltshire, which decrease in size away from the entrance, and the massive entrance-ways of the settlement sites of Gussage All Saints in Wiltshire and Owslebury in Hampshire. Thus, the strong defences of a Maiden Castle or Hambledon Hill would not only make a statement about who owned the enclosure but would also denote their importance, and the monumentality of the mid Wales hillfort façades investigated by Driver (2007b), and mentioned below, add weight to this argument.

In Chapter 4 we considered that an imposing entrance has always been seen as a statement of prestige and power and their elaborate complexity at many hillforts, together with *chevaux-de-frise* and other adornments, could have imbued them with functions other than pure defence. The massive series of ramparts and the imposing western entrance at Old Oswestry, for example, flanked by what could have been eleven huge pits, suggest that the hillfort was intended to be particularly visible, with a status-enhancing rather than a purely utilitarian role. At the other end of the size scale, the entrance at the diminutive West Hill in the Cheviot Hills of Northumberland is also located where the rampart is at its most impressive (Frodsham *et al.* 2007, 252). The stark whiteness of the chalk ramparts of Liddington Castle and Barbury Castle on the Wiltshire Downs would have been seen for miles around, as would the pink-coloured rock of Yeavering Bell, and symbols such as the Uffington White Horse would have stood out dramatically in the landscape. Timber-faced ramparts might also have been whitewashed to emphasise their presence, a practice perhaps akin to the painting of the walls of medieval castles white. Gosden and Lock (2007, 286) write that the hillfort at Uffington was built to see and be seen and that this would have been emphasised by access along the adjacent Ridgeway – this was an 'obvious and visible' site whose very construction alone was a major reason for its existence.

At a smaller scale the ring-forts located on non-defensive hillslopes in Pembrokeshire have massive defences and elaborate entrances as well as grain storage capacity, and have been interpreted as residences of the elite (Williams 1988, 30–4). Longley (1998) describes the similar high-status Bryn Eryr on Anglesey, and some of the small hillslope and valley enclosures along the Severn reflect the same trend, as the strongly defended Collfryn shows. The size of the ramparts at some of these sites is out of all proportion to their interiors and a question that must be asked is whether the apparently limited number of occupants constructed the site alone or whether others were involved – perhaps on a retainer, client or slave basis (Armit 1997). Who occupied hillforts is much debated, but a model for the small 'hillforts' of the Cheviots envisages both competition between fairly autonomous groups manifested in hillfort architecture and co-operation when the need arose – not unlike the farms of today (Frodsham *et al.* 2007, 263).

Although any connection between the *raison d'être* for hillforts and medieval castles is out of favour, the work of Robert Liddiard (2005), in questioning castles as purely military structures, looks towards a more symbolic function and the projection of power by means of architecture. Thus, as he observes: 'Positioning a castle so that it visually dominated a particular area was only one way of advertising the seigneurial presence' (p. 127). An elaborate 'show front' or 'martial front' at the main approach, often thought to have been an invention of the Renaissance period, was also a necessity. This has resonances to several ways in which hillforts can be viewed – not only in their architecture but also in their location on prominent hills – a deliberate desire to be seen and the imposition of self. It could be argued, therefore, that those who constructed the imposing and elaborate entrances of Old Oswestry, Maiden Castle or a plethora of other hillforts throughout the country, both large and small, could be showing a similar mindset to those who built the medieval castles some 1,500 years later.

Earlier we have seen the importance placed on severing and displaying the heads of enemies, and in similar vein Craig *et al.* (2005) and Carr (2007, 445) have indicated that the exposure of mutilated and denigrated dead to the elements was undertaken expressly for display. Allied to this could be the use of sites for storage – in the pits of southern England and rows of four-posters in the Marches, for example. The 'display' element of the latter is obvious, that of pits less so. On the other hand, at some sites, the very presence of a hillfort surmounting prominent landscape features would have been enough of a status enhancement not to warrant elaborate internal features – a worthy 'symbolic presence' – and could explain the seeming absence of any life at some sites.

The importance of communal effort to prehistoric society must not be underestimated. Gosden and Lock (2007) have explored the relationships between human experience, sensory perception and 'place', arguing a greater attachment to land in later prehistory than before and the process of 'making place' at three of the Ridgeway hillforts. Thus, the periodic cleaning of the nearby White Horse, and the prominent counterscarp at Uffington Castle (the result of successive episodes of ditch clearing), together with the construction of the ramparts themselves, would not only have produced a very visible site, but would have bound together a community in communal effort. Thus, the actual look of the enclosure and its relationship with the horse and Ridgeway might have been more important than any activity in the interior, and might indeed have been the object of the exercise in the first place. The same could also be said about Liddington Castle along the Ridgeway.

This may also be the case with hillforts that show an elaborate front, on which a lot of time and effort was expended, but where less visible parts of the circuit and possibly also the interior were 'skimped' to a degree. In a way this can be seen in the very elaborate western façade at Old Oswestry when compared with the eastern rear entrance, and certainly in the carefully contrived mid Wales hillforts which tend to run counter to the topography (Driver 2007b, 98). Here the orientation of the main front might well have indicated the direction of key lands or access routes that were under the territorial control of the hillfort. This is similar to the 'tipping' of an entire site across the contours towards a favoured area, a phenomenon mentioned further on pages 209–10.

It follows that the actual construction of a hillfort might just have been an end in itself, and by looking at function through modern eyes we are missing the point. Driver calls them socio-political 'projects', the actual work of construction displaying status and activity to others, and possibly acting in a role similar to that of a 'chiefly feast'. Therefore, it is possible that the 'unfinished' hillforts we see today may not have been unfinished at all but were part of a much wider practice of 'monumental symbolism'. This could again account for the lack of internal features at some sites.

Dominance and control

The powerful visual presence of a hillfort from below is majestic even today. The Oxford English Dictionary refers to a 'beacon' as a 'guide or warning', a 'signal' or a 'conspicuous hill' (in topographic names) and, as we shall see, hillforts fulfil these definitions well. As Gray pointed out as long ago as 1936, the term not only applies to fires lit on a prominent hill to serve as a signal, but to the hills which commanded the surrounding landscape themselves. It is no surprise, therefore, that hillforts such as the Beacon Hills of Hampshire, Leicestershire and Pembrokeshire, as well as Herefordshire, Haresfield, Painswick, Ivinghoe, Ditchling and Harting *Beacons* should all be so called, for 'beacon' implies prominence in the landscape. It follows that a major factor in hillfort location allied to this prominence was the ease with which the functions of dominance and control over friend and foe and the safeguarding and utilisation of natural resources could be achieved.

Hamilton and Manley (1997; 2001), analysing hillforts in Sussex (expanded later to south-east England), defined three categories of monument which are worth mentioning here. The first, of the late Bronze Age and early Iron Age, were enclosures which allowed landscapes, people and stock *outside* to be observed from a downland peripheral position, 'looking out' of the enclosure. Harting Beacon, Chanctonbury Ring, Ditchling Beacon, and Wolstonbury all have extensive views from the northern downland edge to the Weald and 'are well-positioned to access both downland and Wealden catchments'. Similarly, Thundersbarrow, Seaford Head and Belle Tout are all well placed to *observe* seaward east and west. Secondly, of the middle Iron Age, are enclosures encircling prominent 'landmark hills', which are designed to be viewed from outside: for example, The Trundle, Torberry, Mount Caburn and Cissbury. The ramparts, being placed downslope of the hilltops, present rather than obscure activities within, and elaborate entrance corridors suggest a 'theatre of presentation and approach' rather than military concerns. This occurs elsewhere, and both the downslope sites of Scratchbury and Caer Drewyn (see Figure 29) are sited so as to 'show off' the interior and/or its activities from below, in the case of the former from ground to the south-west and the latter from the Dee Valley below. Finally, late Iron Age and Wealden, mostly promontory, hillforts have no 'landmark' characteristics, although some have wide views. Banks are impressive, with associated ironworking and Roman activity, the sites being placed to exploit the increasing local iron forging and smelting economy.

This important work not only suggests an element of control, with hillforts acting as elaborate 'landmarks', but also the safeguarding and exploitation of surrounding natural resources (good land, minerals and so on). No one function existed at all hillforts all of the time. Perhaps, then, the siting of a hillfort in a prominent position above a river valley or pass, for example, would impart not only a considerable element of status, prestige and display to the proceedings, as indicated above, but also the ability to dominate trade, control access and utilise natural resources (minerals, good land, fishing, fauna and flora) – factors essential to everyday life. If so, what additional evidence is there for this?

Trade, exchange and access

Andrew Sherratt (1996, 218) suggested that major hillforts were not just territorial centres, nor simply points along a 'ridgeway', but were: 'there to dominate passes through an obstacle – rather like ports and harbours occur along a coastline'. Thus, it would be plausible to see hillforts more as: 'controlling inter-regional routes of traffic and trade than … simply dominating their own immediate blocks of downland'. For inland routes the focus for access in prehistory and beyond would probably have been the principal rivers, and it follows that an ability to manage access via these rivers and their tributaries, and exact tolls if necessary, would give power and influence to whoever was controlling that access, whether a community or a local chief. On the coast the control of landing places, and thereby trade and exchange and inshore fishing if it took place, would mean that coastal promontories would be especially important points for fort location.

The Rivers Thames and Severn, in particular, would have been vital to this process, and, linked by overland and riverine connections, such as the various Avons, would have made access to the continent and Ireland possible. Although pressure of development has made hillfort patterns difficult to work out in the London area, hillforts do ring the middle and lower Thames basin, from Bozedown in Oxfordshire in the west to Hulberry in Kent and Grove Field Camp and Shoebury in Essex, on either side of the river/estuary to the east. However, a look at the extent and navigability of the River Severn will illuminate this further.

The Severn catchment is the largest in England and Wales. Rising in the Pumlumon massif, the river flows north-east and east to near Shrewsbury, south by east through Shropshire and Worcestershire to Tewkesbury, and south by west to Gloucester, below which it forms a wide estuary opening into the Bristol Channel: a total of 338km. Southwards its principal tributaries are the Rivers Tern, Teme, (Afon) Vyrnwy, Stour and Upper Avon. The major rivers Wye, Usk and Lower Avon flow into the estuary. Its basin extends into Somerset and south Wales as well as into the English Midlands. The importance of the Severn as a routeway, associated in the west in particular with the Wye, has long been recognised. Kenyon (1954), in describing Sutton Walls, which stands on a commanding bend of the River Lugg, stated that the river valley formed part of a route leading from the Bristol Channel and Severn Estuary, via the Wye, to the Teme and Clun and so to the Salop uplands and northern Marches.

The strategic importance of the Severn as a route from Wales to the Atlantic and Gaul is beyond doubt and some idea of its former navigability can be determined by looking to the eighteenth and nineteenth centuries. Then the river provided the economic lifeline for the coal and iron industries of the Shropshire Coalfield until the railways were built and Coalbrookdale was within reach of Bristol, some 129km distant. As early as the seventeenth century, the Severn had become the second busiest river in Europe after the Rhine (Rowley 2001, 208). Vessels of 400 tons reached Worcester and trows, barges and wherries carried cargoes as far as Pool Quay near Welshpool, overlooked by Y Breiddin.

The upper Severn was serviced by a series of ports, notably Uffington, Shrewsbury, Montford, Llandrinio, Pool Quay and Clawdd Coch, and from these nodal points roads extended into Wales, Cheshire and the north-west. The carriage of wine, tea, spirits and tobacco created important commercial ties between Shropshire and Bristol and the Americas. The Severn's tributaries also extended the communication network, the Avon taking Shropshire coal and iron to the west Midlands, whilst the Vyrnwy took barges to below the hillfort at Llanymynech. A feature of this communication network was the intricate relationship between overland portage and river transport, governed by topography.

In prehistory it is likely that the rivers of the Severn catchment would have been navigable farther upstream than was possible during the industrial revolution, and the types of river craft used at the time would also have enabled this. The advent of obstacles to navigation in the form of weirs, bridges and crossings, and general river controls from the Middle Ages onwards, would have resulted in a restricted flow and shallower depth. Thus, prehistoric craft navigating the Teme would have reached the present Ludlow at least; those on the Cain and Vyrnwy well beyond Llanymynech and those on the Onny to Craven Arms, all areas dominated by major hillforts.

Thus, in the Iron Age it can be imagined that this network of navigable rivers, connected by a system of overland portage routes, would have allowed travel to well into the heartland of Wales from the Marches, and goods and people would have been readily transported via the Severn to the Bristol Channel and beyond. In the same way, access down the river, and via the Avon south-eastwards, would have enabled trade and exchange between the west of Britain, Gaul and the Mediterranean, probably via a series of transhipment nodes, goods being moved southwards from point to point.

The strategic importance of hillforts located on the Severn and its major tributaries would, therefore, have been great. This has been quantitatively assessed (Brown 2002), and in the three river catchments of the Severn, Wye and Usk hillfort pattern has proved not to be random, suggesting specific reasons for location. In these catchments the vast majority of the more than 250 sites studied are situated only a short distance from the main river channel or main tributary: over three-quarters are less than 2.05km away; just under two-thirds are within 1.55km; and nearly half are within 1.05km. On the Wye, in particular, nearly one-third of all hillforts (29.2 per cent) are virtually 'on' the river, at 0.55km or less (Figure 85), and for the three catchments, the mean is 22.5 per cent. The multivallate promontory forts of Caplar Camp, Cherry Hill and Backbury in Herefordshire, for example, are superbly sited in a line to control the river, as are those in the vicinity of Symonds Yat to the south.

Sites that allowed a 'commanding' and 'strategic' position in the landscape to be occupied appear to have been favoured for hillfort construction – sites that would, by their very topographical nature, impose their presence on the surrounding landscape. In the above Severn, Wye and Usk study 61 per cent of hillforts were found to be in such positions overlooking main river valleys, whilst an interfluve location accounted for nearly 10 per cent and just over 5 per

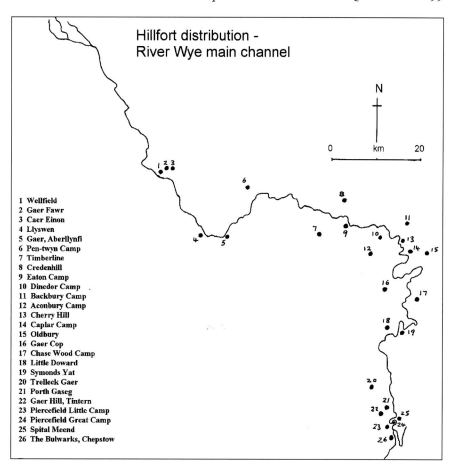

FIGURE 85. Hillfort distribution on the River Wye. Note the nearness of sites to the river channel.

cent controlled an overland pass, of which Caer Caradoc (Church Stretton) is an outstanding example (front cover).

Specific riverine locations also seem to have been very carefully chosen to maximise their impact. A significant number of hillforts are above sharp bends in rivers, particularly where the channel abruptly changes course, as at Little Solsbury and Bredon Hill above the Avons, for example, or at river confluences. These are imposing and prominent positions, leaving those using the river extremely vulnerable. In the Severn, Wye and Usk catchments nearly one-third of all sites have a confluence location, naturally assisting in control of the river and its resources, but also having mystical connotations, as we shall see later. Spital Meend and Piercefield Great and Little Camps in Monmouthshire and Symonds Yat in Herefordshire are all on sharp bends directly overlooking the Wye, whilst both Croft Ambrey and nearby Pyon Wood in Herefordshire are positioned where the Lugg abruptly changes course. Brandon Camp, also in Herefordshire, is in a similar position, where the Teme bends sharply, as well as being at its confluence with the River Clun. There are many other examples throughout England and Wales.

Trade and exchange to and from the Welsh Marches would thus have depended on these navigable rivers to provide essential arteries, allowing trade and exchange in farming produce, metals (gold, silver, lead and copper) and slaves. The pattern via central and northern Wales to southern England and thereby to the immediate continent and Mediterranean would thus have relied on either seaborne traffic directly from the west or overland/riverine access via tributaries and main channels of the Rivers Severn, Wye and Usk to the Bristol Channel, connecting via the Avon or an overland route to southern ports if necessary. To the north the Rivers Dee and Mersey would have provided the link for northern Irish Sea trade and exchange. In southern England there are similar patterns associated with the Thames and, in the north-east, access from the hinterland via the Trent to the Humber, but space does not allow more discussion here.

Man-made river crossings might also have encouraged hillfort development, and Wappenbury in Warwickshire, on a low-lying bank of the River Leam near two fords, may have been one such site, its occupants perhaps being involved in riverine trade and exchange (Stanley and Stanley 1958; Darvill *et al.* 2002, 304). In East Anglia the Little Ouse was a major transportation route in Saxon times and possibly earlier and the Iron Age fort at Thetford in Norfolk could have controlled both a crossing and east–west navigation along the river as well as a north–south route along the Icknield Way, giving the site a regional strategic importance (Davies and Gregory 1991, 29).

Cunliffe (1982) proposed five broad socio-economic divisions in Britain during the Iron Age. In his 'central southern zone', which encompassed Wessex, the Cotswolds and Welsh borders, hillforts and farmsteads developed over a long period of time, with an intensification at some, such as Danebury, to form 'developed hillforts', and a decline in others. These developed sites controlled the division of land, goods and resources. But how these different systems gelled into a coherent whole has been debated.

The size of enclosures generally decreases from north-east to south-west in Wales and it has been suggested by Williams (1988) that two essential socio-economic systems operated in Wales and the Marches. Firstly, there was a redistributive economy in the east (in particular in the Marches), dominated by great hillforts, where farming surpluses were stored and exchanged and where political power was vested in dominant local chiefs. Secondly, there was a 'clientage' supplying economy in the west, where larger hillforts were few; this was based upon the multiplicity of smaller enclosures, some of higher status than others, and power was dominated by numerous local potentates. But clientage systems based upon archaeological interpretations of food-producing strategies have been questioned (Williams and Mytum 1998, 142–4) and perhaps we have to look elsewhere for answers.

However, such a redistributive economy would indicate the 'down the line' system of exchange of goods suggested by Andrew Sherratt; indeed, it is difficult to imagine a situation whereby, if the descriptions of the classical authors are to be believed, the supply of goods in any quantity could be achieved without some sort of redistributive system. This type of arrangement would involve an important role for hillforts as 'trading nodes', where goods could be taken and bartered before being transhipped onwards, and this could explain the marked linear distribution of hillforts along navigable river valleys in both England and Wales.

If such a system is the case, some of the larger hillforts in very strategic positions, of which Old Oswestry is one, would have assumed great importance. Although situated in a poor 'defensive' position, Old Oswestry is strategically placed virtually equidistant between the Rivers Dee to the north and Severn to the south (6 and 8.5kms respectively). It is also sited in a location where, from north to south, the valleys of the Dee (Vale of Llangollen), Ceiriog, Tanat, Cain and Vyrnwy fan out from the hinterlands of mid Wales into the Shropshire Plain. As such, it would be well placed to receive goods and slaves before transhipment. Cefn Carnedd, dominating the Severn and valleys radiating from Caersŵs in mid Wales, and Merlin's Hill in the Tywi Valley near Carmarthen, are hillforts which could have played similar roles. Scratchbury, in being a very visible site with massive ramparts and ditches and located near to the watershed of the Avon and Stour catchments, could well have served as a 'market' commanding river-borne access and trade (McOmish *et al.* 2002, 156), as indeed could nearby Battlesbury prominently situated at the head of the Wylye Valley.

When we look at hillfort patterns along rivers and elsewhere it is noticeable that often one site can be readily seen from another – so-called 'intervisibility' between sites. Many examples of this exist throughout England and Wales (Figure 86), and there could be various reasons for this, such as the redistribution of goods and territorial demarcation, for example, but, naturally, hilltops can usually be seen from other hilltops in any case. Mathews (2007) has analysed all of the hillforts of the northern Marches from northern Powys to the Flintshire coast and concluded that the two concentrations of maximum intervisibility he encountered probably represented the tribal areas of the Deceangli and Cornovii respectively. Interestingly, the sites that had been suggested as tribal 'capitals', for example the Wrekin and Moel Fenlli, had the most intervisible links. Despite the fact that Moel Fenlli is a very exposed site, some forty potential hut platforms, plus maybe others in the internal quarry ditch, have been identified (Gale 2007, 9). If we are to consider this further then perhaps Senior's (2005, 100–1) proposed 'chain of visibility' (in fact a chain of communication to assist valley based communities) might be worth looking at. In north Wales this would have allowed information to be conveyed by fire beacon from Caer y Tŵr on Anglesey to Pen y corddyn Mawr, down the Clwydian Range and thence south to the Shropshire Hills. Alternatively, family or community allegiances, among other theories, might account for this phenomenon, if one actually exists.

But perhaps it is the short distances between hillforts strung along potential

routeways in a linear fashion, possibly as the 'trading nodes' mentioned above, that is more pertinent. The average distances between the hillforts of the Severn, Wye and Usk catchments are 3.2, 3.8 and 2.4km respectively and, as a result, it is tempting to suggest a pattern of riverine and/or overland routeways delineated and guarded by these sites. This could have been associated with a clan-like structure, as suggested by Howell (2006, 49) for the Silures. The situation within Wessex has not been looked at in any great detail in this respect, but it is noticeable that the great majority of hillforts are either located on the escarpment edge or overlooking major river valleys – the Avon, Test, Kennet and Wylye – only a small number are within the chalkland massif itself and even here they are in obviously preferred locations (Corney and Payne 2006a, 131).

Such routes linked to monuments might have antecedents. Tilley (1994) has stressed the importance of recognised paths for hunter-gatherer communities and has drawn attention to an association between activity in the Mesolithic period and Neolithic monuments possibly delineating these earlier paths. Both causewayed enclosures and henges could plausibly be linked to tracks. It has been frequently suggested that henges were intimately associated with the movement of axes, and that such complexes, as at Penrith, are at nodal points

FIGURE 86. 'Intervisibility' between Moel Arthur (foreground) and Penycloddiau (middle distance), in the Clwydian Range, of Flintshire.

on long-established routeways (Topping 1992) and adjacent to stone sources (Loveday 1998, 26, 27). Loveday also discussed the possibility of the ritual control of routeways, citing examples of henge enclosures near to river crossings (Durrington Walls – River Avon; Mount Pleasant – River Frome) and ridgeway routes (Marden – the Ridgeway).

Sherratt (1996, 220–2) has also discussed the riverine location of Wessex henges, likening them to hillforts as links in a transport network, but one based on ritual rather than on defended portage. Whilst rivers would have provided a network of transportation routes, the lack of navigable water and the winding and narrow valleys of the upper reaches of most Welsh rivers suggest that overland portage was the norm in these upland areas.

Although Loveday (1998, 30) questions whether the effort required to construct the large Battlesbury and Scratchbury hillforts at the headwaters of the Wylye in Wiltshire could ever have been justified on access grounds alone, their nearness to the crossing of the medieval Beacon Hill–Heytesbury route was probably significant, as was the isolated siting of the Wiltshire Yarnbury, Bratton Castle and Sidbury Camp hillforts, all of which are some distance from water but adjacent to long-standing routes to Bath and Marlborough. Loveday suggests that henges and hillforts could have performed similar control functions, but primarily in relation to land rather than water. This is reflected in the architecture and layout of hillforts, as in the double opposed entrance form of those in early Wessex and the roadway shown to pass straight through the interior of Danebury. It is beyond the scope of this book to discuss these ancient routeways in any detail, but what is evident is the number of hillforts located along them – for example, on the Kerry Ridgeway, the Clun–Clee Ridgeway and Hen Ffordd in the Marches, as well as the South Dorset, and Berkshire Ridgeways (which possibly started as an animal track earlier than the Neolithic (Bell and Lock 2000)) and the Icknield Way.

If hillforts can be seen as actually indicating routeways then it would be expected that some will 'guard the gateway' to such routes, and Barbury and Liddington Castles are strategically placed on opposite hills at the northern end of the River Og valley to control the direct route into Wiltshire from the north; this was an area later to see Saxon activity (Watts 1997, 23). Bodbury Ring in Shropshire and Moel y Gaer (Bodfari) in Flintshire are, similarly, strategically placed. Y Gardden at Ruabon is ideally positioned to control access into the Dee Valley and the upland massif, as are Caer Ddunod and Cerrig Gwynion, also in Denbighshire, as suggested by Manley (1990, 33). Likewise, it was noted as early as 1944 (Ward Perkins 1944, 141) that the Oldbury hillfort in Kent, whose gates are oriented north–south, commanded a natural north–south corridor across the Wealden clay to a Medway crossing at present-day Tonbridge and to the hillfort at Castle Hill. In addition, the hillfort is near to the Medway Gap, the natural route into the Weald of Kent from the north. Similarly, Old Sarum in Wiltshire commands the crossing of the Avon and routes from Mendip to Winchester … and we could go on.

Ronald Jessup succinctly summed up these points while writing about Bigberry hillfort in Kent in the 1930s: 'It is evident, then, that the site was chosen with considerable regard to geographical determinants, and that contour, the nature of the subsoil, and easy access to water, were all factors of major importance to its builders. And not least is the position it occupies with regard to the River Stour and the ancient crossing at Tonford, and the command it maintains over the Pilgrim's Way, which at this point leaves the higher land on its descent towards Canterbury, its immediate objective.'

Natural resources and territory

The use and control of natural resources, particularly minerals, good farming land and the sea, would have been very important and no doubt influenced hillfort siting. Wales and the Marches, the Weald of Kent and Sussex and the south-west peninsula all have marked concentrations of hillforts in mineral-rich areas. Let us look at just one of these areas, the northern Marches and westwards into the interior of Wales, in a little more detail.

Northover (1995, 287–8) proposed that by the end of the seventh century BC copper and tin ore had virtually ceased to be mined in Britain, but when production began again in the middle Iron Age new and formerly unused copper deposits were opened up. Such a site was Llanymynech Hill where the hillfort was constructed over a copper mine producing distinctive zinc-rich ores and which became an important regional centre. Minerals found here included malachite (green carbonate of copper: $Cu_2CO_3(OH)_2$), lead and zinc, and, before the construction of a golf course, the interior was pock-marked with up-cast of small-scale mining, some of Roman date. Excavations produced charcoal layers and hearths, large fragments of vitrified material and fragments of corroded copper alloy. Furnace-lining, part of a crucible and metallurgical residues showed that copper was smelted from the fourth century BC to the first century AD (Musson 1981; Musson and Northover 1989, 20). A later excavation revealed the partial plan of a round hut and further evidence of metalworking (CPAT 2000). The large size of the hillfort appears to have been related to the requirements of mining and the control and distribution of the metal source on the hill.

These zinc-rich ores from the hillfort can be recognised in later Iron Age artefacts, such as the Moel Hiraddug shield-boss (see Figure 64) and plaque and a horse bit from Llyn Cerrig Bach, and provided the ore used at the nearby Llwyn Bryn-dinas hillfort (Davies and Lynch 2000, 208, after Musson *et al.* 1992, 279). Crucibles found at Old Oswestry (Savory 1976, 48) were rich in zinc, suggesting that the copper ore could have come from Llanymynech. These findings are important, as they indicate a 'downstream' movement of goods from one hillfort to another – from raw material to production.

The outstanding hillfort of the Tanat Valley, Llwyn Bryn-dinas, shows metal production at more of a local level. By any criteria its position at the confluences of the Afon Iwrch and Lleiriog with the Tanat is commanding, capable of controlling access along each valley. The earliest fortifications are radiocarbon dated to the late ninth to eighth centuries BC and metallurgical analysis of debris from the rear of the rampart proved a metalworking floor (radiocarbon dated to the third century BC), with copper alloy casting, iron forging and possibly bronze production in a single workshop.

Craig Rhiwarth hillfort is strategically placed further up the Tanat Valley, near its head. It occupies a distinctive crag at 530m OD, just above the confluence of the Afon Tanat and Afon Eirth and at the beginning of a possible route through the Berwyn Range via Cwm Sian Llwyd to the Dee Valley (Figure 87). The hillfort is defended by precipitous and rocky slopes on all sides except the north (Houlder 1978), which has a single stone rampart which possibly dates from the Bronze Age or early Iron Age. About 150 (possible) small round hut sites have been identified. Chalcopyrite and lead are found on the slopes to the south and north-east and there was mining at Craig Rhiwarth from the late Tudor period until the early twentieth century, but open cuts and stopes on the southern side of the hill could be prehistoric. Chalcopyrite (copper pyrites: $CuFeS_2$) is an important copper ore containing small but valuable amounts of gold and silver. There is also evidence of prehistoric workings at the upper end of Cwm Orog, to the north of Craig Rhiwarth, and characteristic to the area are a large number of circular stone structures, of unknown function, some showing evidence of reconstruction. Craig Rhiwarth could have been very important in prehistory, not only in controlling a source of copper ore but also in commanding perhaps the only readily accessible route through the Berwyn Range to the Dee.

The importance of the exploitation of silver and lead in Wales, not only in prehistory but throughout the Roman period, is shown by concentrations of strategically placed hillforts. There is a cluster to the west of the Rhinogau, for instance, but it is that of eight sites between the Clywedog and Trannon on the eastern slopes of the Pumlumon massif west of Caersŵs that shows this particularly well. Four are associated with each river catchment, close to the source of the Severn and potential routes to the west. The area had considerable mineral wealth and the headwaters of the Clywedog is covered with mines of varying ages. A fortlet at Penycrocbren implies possible Roman interest in the area's resources, just as the fort at Pumsaint in Carmarthenshire protected the gold mines at Dolaucothi.

Whereas the exploitation of minerals would have been restricted to specific parts of the country, the use of good farming land (arable, meadow and pasture) and riverine resources (possible fishing, reed gathering, fauna and flora) was universal and vital to communities and was possibly the basic *raison d'être* for a variety of hillforts. The location of Hambledon Hill and the hillforts on Bredon Hill have been mentioned already in this respect, and Torberry in Sussex, with its extensive occupation over four centuries and ability to exploit the favourable greensand soils to the north, can be added. Although the great

size of some enclosures could imply a purely pastoral function, as at Bindon Hill (114ha+) and Belle Tout (20ha+) on the coast, and Titterstone Clee (29.7ha) and Penycloddiau (23ha) inland, excavation at comparatively smaller hillforts such as Harting Beacon (at *c*.10.5ha) suggests a similar use (Bedwin 1978, 231).

Although at Danebury and Maiden Castle the thousands of storage pits point to a predomintly arable regime, farming operations can change over time and the increased wear and remetalling of trackways at gateways of both Danebury and Sutton Walls could have reflected the need for a harder-wearing surface to cater for more intensive stock rearing; the careful design of entrances would have been important in making stock management easier. More telling was the situation at Caer Cadwgan, where the construction of the enclosure seems to have coincided with a change from a pastoral economy with some arable to one of pastoral monoculture (Walker 1987, 17).

The capacity of this great number of storage pits at some sites appears to have far exceeded that required for the communities therein, but why this was so has been much debated. The Danebury Environs Programme has found that grain from the fort did not go to sites outside but was prepared and used within or, possibly, traded. Van de Veen and Jones (2007) have looked at this problem in southern England and propose that feasts and festivals might be the answer. They suggest that the late Bronze Age elites seem to have declined as a result of a reduction in long-distance trade in metals, itself the result of the new iron technology, and more emphasis was placed on the use of local resources. Large-scale events would have taken place at certain important hillforts, at first on a community basis, accounting at Danebury for a possible seasonal use early on. Later, *c*.300 BC, the influence of leaders would have increased, feasts enhancing their prestige and power and enabling additions and improvements to take place on the encircling ramparts: the 'developed' hillforts emerged. All this was, possibly, at the expense of surrounding smaller settlements. There might then have been permanent occupation, with storage capacity increased and more formal shrines erected, as we have seen. By the time of the late Iron Age changes in society made the feast, storage pits and indeed some hillforts redundant. The latter were subsequently abandoned and smaller settlements assumed importance once again and long-distance trade re-emerged, spurred on by Rome. Surpluses and other goods were then exchanged for prestige items and exotics, which show up in the archaeological record.

This hypothesis is very attractive for some hillforts in the south, but not all, the small investigations at Pilsdon Pen, for example, producing no pit evidence as we have seen. Further north there are also problems, but if the small four-post structures found at Marcher sites such as the Wrekin, Croft Ambrey, Credenhill and Midsummer Hill were for storage or some use other than habitation, as is probable, then a variant on this model seems plausible.

A number of studies have proposed a relationship between lower-lying fields downslope and hillforts above. Harding (2004), for example, suggests that both Staple Howe and Devil's Hill in Yorkshire are strategically placed on outlying

FIGURE 87. Centuries of mineral extraction scar the 107m-high southern slopes, where no artificial defence was required, of the rocky Craig Rhiwarth hillfort in the Tanat Valley of Montgomeryshire.

spurs to control both the upland pastures of the Yorkshire Wolds and the arable lowlands of the Vale of Pickering to the west. In north-east Wales Manley (1990, 31–3) considered that hillforts are generally: 'close to the upland/lowland divide and central to neither' ... 'a compromise between the need for a defensive vantage point and access to lowland agricultural zones as well as upland pasture'. Thus, a pattern has been observed in the Clwydian Range where the dominant hillforts of the high hills are ideally suited to control both pasturalism on the hill itself and the fertile grounds of the Vale of Clwyd. This could explain the siting of Moel y Gaer (Llanbedr) on a prominent spur of the range, with the nearby (possible) stock enclosure below, as mentioned on page 130. In west Wales Caer Cadwgan is also sited in a 'commanding position to manage the pastoral resource', and in so doing to protect herds and flocks, house temporary pastoralists and provide facilities for dairy processing and collection (Austin *et al.* 1985, 16). Similarly, Bowden (2005b, 161) suggests that the hillforts of the Marlborough Downs in Wiltshire: 'occupy positions on the edges of the high ground, overlooking the vales to either side' and appear to be a 'deliberate choice of this liminal positioning, exploiting and perhaps in some way controlling the resources of both the uplands and lowlands', citing Oliver's Castle as a good example of this.

Field system boundaries are increasingly being found in association with hillforts and, in some cases, these demarcations seem to signify territorial boundaries. Various theories have emerged, Muir (2004, 123) speculating that hillforts could have been a part of ancient commons where different communities would meet and religious monuments were constructed. Thus, field systems and farms 'occupied the centre of the socio-economic stage' and hillforts the peripheries, storing agricultural surplus for the elite. Some would assume greater importance while others were abandoned, and as hillforts generally became more significant to society's needs tribal territories developed.

In Yorkshire cereal growing was important at Grimthorpe (Stead 1968), the excavations unearthing eight four-post structures, but a preponderance of cattle over sheep, pig and horse bone indicated a fairly stable mixed economy. The dating of the hillfort to the first millennium BC coincides with the linear dykes and pit alignments that appeared in the Wolds and the North York Moors from the late Bronze Age, dividing up the landscape into pastoral segments not only for farming purposes but also to demarcate ownership and identity. These boundaries are similar to the linear ditches found in Wessex and the communal stone-bank boundaries of the Dartmoor reaves (Fleming 1979; 1988). Pit alignments are increasingly being found in the central Welsh Marches, mainly concentrated within the valley and immediate tributaries of the upper Severn (Wigley 2007b, 119). This is interesting, as a marked pattern of hillfort locations along the Severn and tributaries has been noted above.

A possible relationship also exists between these linear demarcations and hillfort siting at Boltby Scar, Eston Nab and Sutton Bank in Yorkshire, sites either strategically situated between the higher pastures and lower-lying settlements and fertile land of the Vale of York, or in the Tabular Hills, the high moors of which acted as summer pastures for communities lower down in the Vale of Pickering. Harding (2004, 38) writes that the long-used Boltby Scar formed an integral part of the extensive Cleave Dyke system: 'farming reorganisation and territorial demarcation of the earlier first millennium BC'. The principal dyke is located near the north–south watershed of the Hambleton Hills, which itself would form a natural territorial demarcation, branches extending from it to the heads of tributary valleys of the Rye to the east. Thus, both water supply and peat deposits would have been secured by dividing the land by means of a series of construction phases. The main dyke also shows a correlation with Bronze Age barrows. There appears, therefore, to be a relationship between the Bronze Age burial rite (thought in many areas of England and Wales to be a means of boundary definition), the natural drainage pattern, the delineation of natural resources, in this case farmland, and hillforts.

Better known still are the late Bronze Age linear dykes (banks, ditches and palisades) and later field systems of Wessex, which stretch for miles, splitting up the downs from top to river valley bottom into territorial units or 'ranches'. Here there is great variability in the manner in which the various components of the landscape (ditches, fields, open and enclosed sites) are put together. There are many complex examples, but the hillfort placed at the meeting of linear ditches is especially significant, as noted at Alfred's Castle (Gosden and Lock 2007). At Quarley Hill in Hampshire the site is also superimposed upon a series of ditches that seem to converge on the hilltop, and Woolbury was developed at the junction of pre-existing linear ditches associated with an extensive field system to the north and south-east (Cunliffe and Poole 2000a). In Wiltshire two cross-dykes project north and south from Chiselbury, Fowler (1964, 53) suggesting that they are contemporary with, or later than, the construction of the hillfort (probably the latter), and are best interpreted as a boundary line. Sidbury Hill in Wiltshire is a particularly good example where regular field systems pre-date linear earthworks associated with the Sidbury Camp hillfort, six of which meet on the site where the hillfort was constructed. Similarly Casterley Camp appears to be the focus of three linear earthworks. Their significance to those involved must have been 'immense', and they have been interpreted as primarily being a form of 'socially determined land division' (Mc Omish *et al.* 2002, 57–8; 64).

Chapter 3 discussed the number of hillforts in both England and Wales that have Bronze Age burials either on site or nearby. One theory for barrow location, particularly in upland areas, is that they acted as a means of territorial demarcation. The subsequent construction of a hillfort on the same or a nearby site could indicate that territory was again being demarcated and the landscape controlled. This could be the situation with the hillforts along the crest of the Clwydian Range, an area which has one of the highest concentrations of Bronze Age burial cairns in Wales (Brown 2004). If this is the case, then hillforts would have become very significant points in the landscape indeed.

The tilting of hillforts towards a certain aspect deserves greater investigation.

There is evidence from both the former causewayed enclosures at The Trundle and Rybury that they were themselves positioned in this way – the former across the contours to the north and the latter towards higher ground to the north, from which the site can be clearly seen (Oswald *et al.* 2001, 101). Similarly, Clwydian Range forts such as Moel Fenlli and Penycloddiau tilt towards rich natural resources and/or specific territory. Likewise, Caer Caradoc (Chapel Lawn) is tipped towards the valley of the River Redlake. This is clearly a phenomenon more widespread than first thought, implying elements of resource management, territorial control and display.

Curious topographic positions are, therefore, not unusual in hillfort siting and a hillslope position has been equated with the requirements of stock management and, in particular, the need to take animals downhill to obtain water. The ways in which valuable animals were tended must have been an over-arching preoccupation and this may have affected hillfort design. Davies and Lynch (2000, 146) propose that multiple-enclosure sites, such as the Glamorgan sites of Y Bwlwarcau at Llangynwyd and the three hillforts with weakly defined banks at Harding's Down on the Gower (Hogg 1973b), had a more pastoral role. Y Bwlwarcau is large at 4.4ha, with many complex but widely spaced banks held to be indicative of a livestock regime (Fox and Fox 1934; Fox 1952). In Devon and eastern Cornwall multiple-ditched enclosures (for example, Milber Down and Clovelly Dykes), situated on hillslopes or overlooking springs or river valleys, could have performed similar functions and seem to have been the main type of enclosure into the first century AD. Downslope at Casterley Camp in Wiltshire the head of a natural coombe is incorporated within the enclosure, with an entrance seemingly deliberately placed adjacent to it. This could be interpreted as associated with stock, and especially sheep, management, in allowing the animals to be relatively easily driven into the enclosure. With a possible spring also sited here, the hillfort may then have served a market role with concomitant ritual overtones, a hoard of miniature socketed axes being found nearby (Robinson 1995; McOmish *et al.* 2002, 59; 155).

Hillforts could also have formed an integral part of a system of transhumance. In summer, lowland stock would be driven to higher pastures from over-wintering in the lowlands, hill and coastal forts acting as bases for operations. Proving this theory is difficult, but transhumance must have occurred throughout the uplands as it formerly did in the Welsh *hafod* and *hendre* pattern, as suggested by Alcock (1965) in his study of the hillforts of north Wales, and possibly extended from Beltane (1st May) over the summer months, with a return to home grounds at Samain (1st November). Festivals would have been held at hillforts of importance at each time. According to Webley (1976, 32) Tre'r Ceiri was one such site, the hillfort being used as a 'communal summer centre for shepherds from the lowland farmsteads'. Other candidates could come from the many small hillforts of the Montgomeryshire uplands, and, lower down, at Wall Camp (Kynnersley) the plethora of small external banks (which because of their closeness could never have stood to any great height) could have been designed, in part, to facilitate stock movement. The site could possibly have been associated with the seasonal movement of animals from the higher lands to the north (Bond and Morris 1991, 102, 105), seemingly in fairly stable surroundings from around the third century BC to the beginning of the first century AD.

As well as movements of animals, Hill (2007, 21–3) points to a scenario whereby seasonal movements of people might also have taken place from the more densely populated settlements to outlying areas where natural resources would be harvested (reeds, salt, iron, timber and so on). This attractive proposition could indeed imply an important role for hillforts, sited, as many are, within sight of, or within, significant farming and mineral-rich areas.

Annexes, both big and small, have also been proposed as stock enclosures and the large example at Pen y corddyn Mawr and the outer annexe at another, possibly unfinished, small hillfort on the summit of Harding's Down appear ideal for this purpose. Arnold and Davies (2000, 78) suggest that surviving enclosure systems in south-east Wales could be the relics of previous extensive agricultural landscapes, now destroyed – at Caer Dynnaf in Glamorgan the enclosure was occupied from the late second to the fourth century AD as a farmstead with stockyards, using the prehistoric hillfort defences as a 'home field'.

On the coast, the preponderance of sheep bone found at The Rumps could indicate its use as a base for grazing on summer coastal pastures and it is also tempting to consider a stock management relationship between the fine anchorage of Lulworth Cove and the downland pastures of the adjacent Bindon Hill and, in similar vein, between off-shore islands and mainland forts. The field systems and South Castle coastal promontory fort on Skomer, off the Pembrokeshire coast, are directly opposite the large pastoral 20ha Wooltack Point, on the mainland. There is ample historical evidence for the islands of Skomer, Skokholm and Middleholm being used as a 'pasturage for sheep, kyne and oxen as well as horses' (Toulson and Forbes 1992, 56). The animals were brought to the mainland hobbled in straw-filled craft to land at Martin's Haven below the Wooltack Point fort or, where possible, cattle swam across from Skokholm to the beaches at Marloes (Howells 1980). Ultimately they were driven to markets in eastern Wales and England. There could also be a connection in stock rearing terms between mainland coastal promontory forts such as Castell Heinif, which also protects the landing point of St Justinian, and Ramsey Island, south-west of St David's Head. Similarly, Porth Dinllaen at Nefyn on the Llŷn commands the only natural harbour between Caernarfon and Bardsey Island and could also have served as a port for Irish trade and exchange.

Therefore, the control of maritime resources and sea-going routes would have been vitally important for coastal communities and no doubt promontory forts and dominant hillforts commanding the sea played a significant part in this. The nature of sea-going routes and trade and exchange has been referred to above in regard to the south-coast harbours of Hengistbury Head, Poole and Mount Batten at Plymouth.

However, as well as along the navigable rivers and at the important ports, it is quite likely that throughout England and Wales there were informal seaborne beach and other landing points linked to a network of inland trackways. In Wales routes from west-coast harbours and beaches were quite likely. The estuaries of the Dyfi, Mawddach, Ystwyth and Teifi, and indeed the many beaches and small inlets that line the Welsh coast, could all have played an important part in the local economy. For example, there are concentrations of hillforts around what could have been a centre of gold production on the flanks of the Mawddach Estuary, while the major hillforts of Yr Eifl on the Llŷn (Tre'r Ceiri, Garn Boduan and Carn Fadryn) and Carn Ingli and nearby Carn Ffoi above Newport Bay in Pembrokeshire dominate the coast and sea. Similarly, Pen Dinas (Aberystwth), commanding access to valleys of both the Ystwyth and Rheidol and the coast, as well as controlling harbour facilities nearby, could have been pivotal to Irish Sea and thereby Atlantic trade and exchange from the west. It may have been a similar story at Pen y Dinas, which towers above Llandudno Bay as has been shown in Figure 84. On a smaller scale, the hillfort overlooking the present harbour at Solva, and indeed many of the Pembrokeshire coastal promontory forts, could have directly dominated access to and from sheltered anchorages. The lack of salt containers originating from the centres of production in the English Midlands found in south-west Wales points to the use of sea salt as the source of this essential commodity. It is possible, therefore, that the large numbers of coastal forts in Pembrokeshire were important to its supply.

It also seems probable that vessels from the Mediterranean plied the west coast of Wales. The Porth Felen anchor stock found off the Llŷn suggests that merchants might have been scouting, or indeed participating in, some form of enterprise during the second century BC or earlier, possibly involving the rich metal resources of the area. Likewise, amphorae have been found on the north coast.

In a similar way, forts along the coasts of the south-west peninsula could have guarded safe landing points. Those afforded by Weymouth Bay and the estuaries of the Exe and Dart are examples. To the west of Salcombe dominant coastal promontory forts, such as Bolt Tail, above the sheltered beaching sites of Bigbury Bay, appear strategically placed to safeguard valuable fishing grounds as well as coastal access (see Figure 30).

Contact between Ireland and north Wales has been mentioned above. Perhaps linked to this were the hillforts dominating the Rivers Clwyd and Dee – among others, Moel y Gaer (Bodfari), protecting the Afon Chwiler valley from the Vale of Clwyd and its river, and Moel y Gaer (Rhosesmor) above the Dee on Halkyn Mountain, both in areas of vast mineral wealth. Further to the north the Mersey Estuary is similarly overlooked by strategically placed hillforts on Helsby Hill (Figure 88) and Woodhouse Hill in Cheshire. Further north still hillforts peter out, but Skelmore Heads, Warton Crag and Castle Heads in Lancashire ring the northern estuaries flowing into Morecambe Bay, suggesting

FIGURE 88. Helsby Hill hillfort in Cheshire was ideally placed to control access and trade along the River Mersey.

maritime influence. Portfield and Castercliff in Lancashire are associated with tributaries of the Ribble, and at the former a late Bronze Age scrap hoard, including bronze axes, a gold bracelet and a penannular tress-ring, suggests high status (Harding 2004, 47). Thus, in the north-west a pattern indicative of trading and resource control networks emerges in which important estuaries are ringed by forts. Certainly, Cheshire was a special area for salt and the Mersey and Dee would have provided suitable outlets to the sea for this commodity, whilst Morecambe Bay has rich marine resources as well as a varied arable and pastoral hinterland.

Superstition, belief and ritual

Whilst we have looked at some aspects of the secular above, superstition and belief manifested in ritual played a vital part in all aspects of hillfort construction and life, from beginning to end, and there is plenty of circumstantial and excavated evidence for this. A role for hillforts as cult centres has been proposed

(Stopford 1987; Bowden and McOmish 1987; 1989), and certainly the sacred nature of White Horse Hill would suggest that the commanding hillfort at its crest would have provided a fitting ceremonial arena. Chapter 3 looked at hillfort beginnings, suggesting that there is often a correlation between the earliest hillforts and previous activity or ritual monuments on site or nearby, a phenomenon also noticed by Hamilton and Manley (2001, 11), who suggested that: 'this may have been a means of validating new social practices through making links with the past'. Let us now look at some examples of the location of hillforts and their association with superstition, belief and ritual, beginning with those at high altitude.

High places – low places

Many hillforts are situated in such high, exposed and inhospitable places that, to our modern eyes, they would be totally unsuitable for either gatherings or habitation. However, it must be remembered that there has always been a penchant for settlement, particularly of a religious nature, on outlandish sites: for example, Skellig Michael was occupied as a monastery until around the thirteenth century, and many other examples exist worldwide.

It has been suggested that the gods of the underworld were important to prehistoric society and, conversely, high places could have exerted the same kind of magnetic pull – nearer, in this case, to the gods of the sky. Thus, the natural phenomena of wind, rain, thunder and lightning, the waxing and waning of the moon and the path of the sun across the sky must have only emphasised, on a daily basis, the certain existence of gods to be feared and pacified with acts of propitiation. These natural forces would give life to man and beast, bring fertility and famine; high places, by their very nature, would feel their impact more. To be on a hillfort during an electric storm must have been both a dangerous and terrifying experience, but, nevertheless, there is some evidence for clusters of hillforts located near to the highest summit of a particular line of hills: Midsummer Hill and British Camp (Herefordshire Beacon) are within sight of Worcestershire Beacon and most of the Clwydian Range forts flank Moel Famau, its highest mountain (see Figure 24).

Green (1986, 39, 67–8; 2003, 29) considered that in Europe by the Romano-Celtic period both Romans and Celts had celestial gods and there is plenty of evidence for these 'mountain-spirits' in the high places of Gaul and further to the east. To the Romans this god was Jupiter (both sky and father god and one of the three major state gods), a towering bearded man accompanied by eagle, sceptre and thunderbolt. To Celtic peoples the deity was symbolised by the sun-disc, manifested as a spoked wheel combining both movement and roundness, often in association with a horse, bull or water-bird; this is portrayed in cult contexts from Hallstatt to Roman times as well as on coinage.

Other sky symbols, including the thunderbolt, swastika, circle and S-sign and wheel decoration, are a general feature of British Iron Age pottery. A copper alloy ring-headed pin, probably with coral inlay, and a 34mm-diameter roundel, both displaying spoked rosettes, come from South Cadbury. They are dated to 300–250 BC and could be sky symbols. The bull, in particular, as found on the hillfort escutcheons and the figurine from Maiden Castle described above, is probably a sky motif and is frequently associated in classical contexts with Zeus and Jupiter (Green 1986, 53).

Three 'hillforts' in very high and exposed positions in the north of England – Ingleborough, Carrock Fell and Yeavering Bell – will highlight these points. The summit of Ingleborough, on which the hillfort stands, dominates the moorland triangle around Ingleton and Settle in Yorkshire and is one of the major landmarks of the Pennines (Figure 89). Clearly visible from the Lakeland fells to the west and Bowland to the south (Poucher 1966, 301), this is no ordinary mountain. Physiographically, Ingleborough inspires respect and awe. It has an almost level gritstone cap summit and flanks composed of the Yoredale Series of sandstone, shale and limestone beds above the Great Scar Carboniferous Limestone, creating the appearance of a series of steps rising above the frequently low cloud-base to the heavens. The site is very isolated from other hillforts, the nearest being Warton Crag above Morecambe Bay, but there is increasing evidence of Iron Age settlement in the vicinity. The construction of the hillfort is very unusual, the 6ha summit surrounded almost entirely by a gritstone wall 3–5m thick, with its rear face formed of orthostatic blocks and the outer face of dry stone, a feature not found elsewhere. A 10m berm lies between this and the break of slope, and external and internal quarry scoops can be seen. An original entrance may have been at the north-east corner, giving a natural routeway to Simon Fell and the distinctive peak of Pen-y-Ghent, and this relationship to these outside peaks could be symbolically important. The rampart (with variations) has stones set on edge at regular intervals, giving separate compartments which have been filled with rubble. In the interior, clusters of around twenty 'hut' circles (or burial cairns) have been defined. Massive, and probably contemporaneous, dry-stone walls have been observed on the north and west slopes of the hill, (King 1987; Bowden *et al.* 1989).

However, Ingleborough, in common with other areas of the Craven uplands, also has wide and accessible potholes and fissures in the limestone strata on its flanks, notable among which is Gaping Gill, a 111m sheer drop from the surface and the second deepest vertical shaft in Britain, which provides an ideal access point to the gods of the underworld (Figure 90). The principal source tributaries of Fell Beck, which disappears into Gaping Gill, are located directly below the enclosure and were possibly its nearest water supply. It has been suggested, therefore, that the hillfort could also be associated with this link to the underworld via the pothole.

There is less information on the summit enclosure of Carrock Fell, at 650m OD, in the Cumbrian Caldbeck Fells. This is a prominent oval univallate site of 2.1ha, surrounded by a single stone wall some 2.7m thick with possibly two entrances to the south-west. Like Ingleborough it is severely exposed, and was

FIGURE 89. The massive stone wall encircling the summit of Ingleborough in Yorkshire can be clearly seen. The site could well have Neolithic origins and may have been an important and sacred arena for gatherings and ceremonial.

ENGLISH HERITAGE NMR 12061/31, 16/1/1991.

FIGURE 90. Fell Beck flowing into Gaping Gill on the slopes below the Ingleborough hillfort in Yorkshire. These entrances to the world of the chathonic deities would probably have been viewed with awe.

FIGURE 91. Yeavering Bell, in the Cheviot Hills of Northumberland. The nearly circular enclosure on the eastern summit can be seen to the bottom left of the site – possibly prehistoric, possibly not.

initially thought to be a tribal capital (Collingwood 1938). But there is no sign of occupation and, as a result of its isolated position, discontinuous wall and nearness to outcrops of the Carrock Fell Gabbro complex and an implement manufacture source to the south and east, it may also (like Ingleborough) be of Neolithic origin (Davis *et al.* 2007, 100; Bradley 2007, figure 2.18). A cairn lies at its eastern end, whilst numerous others lie on the northern slope of the fell. Pearson and Topping (2002) speculate that, by the end of the late Neolithic, there was a desire for local groups and communities to differentiate themselves from adjacent areas by creating their own regional variations in monument design. The site may in fact be a henge.

The question that must be asked of Ingleborough and Carrock Fell is whether they can be called 'hillforts' at all or whether they are a type of prehistoric hilltop enclosure that has functions outside of hillforts' normal meaning. It is difficult to imagine any permanent occupation at such exposed sites, even in the more clement climate of the Bronze Age, but both appear unsurpassed as places for ritual, ceremonial and seasonal gatherings, possibly in a regional context.

Yeavering Bell in the Cheviots, overlooking the Milfield Plain, has been recognised as a ceremonial centre from Neolithic times and Frodsham *et al.* (2007, 251) write that the hillfort may not have been occupied at all for much of the Iron Age (Figure 91). Rising to 360m OD, and not as high as Ingleborough or Carrock Fell, the site shows many circular structures and platforms and an earlier enclosure on the eastern summit with a single roundhouse. At 5.2ha in total area and with a massive bounding stone wall, the site dominates the plain from all directions and, as such, appears higher than it actually is. Favoured as an 'oppidum' by Hope-Taylor (Oswald and Pearson 2005, 119), its exposed nature suggests otherwise and it is extremely unlikely that all of the huts defined would have been occupied at the same time. It was more likely to have served a communal purpose for festivals and seasonal ceremonial gatherings. Sites such as Ingleborough, Carrock Fell, Yeavering Bell and indeed Mam Tor would have been important places for ritual, and, in being nearer to the gods of the sky, would have served functions that we can only guess at.

There are few comparable sites in Wales and the Marches, but in terms of its actual presence in the landscape Ysgyryd Fawr (Skirrid Fawr) in Monmouthshire, situated high above Abergavenny at 486m OD at the confluence of the rivers Monnow and Honddu and on the interfluve between the Wye and Usk, is a much neglected promontory hillfort. A chapel or oratory dedicated to St Michael (of uncertain date) stands within the enclosure. The ridge is high and very exposed, with far-reaching panoramas to the Black Mountains and Allt-yr-Esgair in Breconshire, another very prominent hillfort overlooking Llangorse Lake near the River Usk. If Ysgyryd Fawr is of prehistoric date and not contemporary with the chapel, it would seem to have claims as a ritual and ceremonial enclosure.

Venerated landscapes

Whether those involved in prehistory saw landscapes as 'venerated' is impossible to guess, as myth, superstition and belief were ingrained aspects of everyday life, but there is evidence that some hillforts were sited within landscapes that we might see as such: among others, Uffington Castle, Ingleborough and Carrock Fell are possibilities. However, let us look briefly at two other examples: firstly, the area inland from Penmaenmawr and Llanfairfechan on the north Wales coast in Caernarfonshire, as shown in Figure 1, and, secondly, the edge of the Cheviot Hills with the Milfield Plain below in Northumberland.

Graiglwyd, at the eastern end of the Penmaenmawr augite granophyre complex, was the site of a Neolithic axe factory, and other axe fabrication sites have been identified on the adjoining Dinas and Garreg Fawr outcrops above Llanfairfechan. The Graig Lwyd axe found its way well into the rest of Wales and the north, Midlands and south of England (Warren 1919; Glen 1935; Brown 2004, 35, figure 18). The area abounds with settlement, burial and ceremonial monuments from the Neolithic onwards, notable among which are the group of Bronze Age circles on the moorland edge above Penmaenmawr, the Cors y Carneddau cairn of bell-shaped form nearby and the Siambr gladdau burial chamber to the south-west. At the western end of the Penmaenmawr outcrop was Braich-y-Ddinas, once one of the greatest stone-built hillforts in Britain; its destruction one of the nation's heritage disasters. Close by, and forming part of the Graig Lwyd axe factory group, is the complex promontory of Bryngaer Dinas (Dinas hillfort), with its internal enclosure containing several huts and a larger central structure around 9m in diameter with possible ritual connotations. Other hillforts, such as the superbly sited promontory of Maes y gaer below Aber Falls, are perched, as is Bryngaer Dinas, above fast-flowing streams bursting from the massif to the sea, all pointing to origins much deeper than pure settlement.

In common with the Graiglwyd area, the edge of the Cheviots, with the Milfield Plain below, has one of the finest prehistoric landscapes in Britain and contains one of the densest concentrations of henges, most dating from about 2500 BC. Bordering the Plain are sandstone ridges and moorland sites with examples of rock art possibly dating from around 3000 to 1500 BC. A number of important hillforts, such as Yeavering Bell, and other small enclosures, often referred to as 'hillforts', dominate the landscape.

This is an area of fertile soil and exposed rock and the nine henges so far discovered could have acted as marker posts in a processional or ritualistic route across the area. It has been suggested that one, Milfield North, is aligned on Yeavering Bell (the site of the last henge in the sequence) and nearby Humbleton Hill fort on the edge of the Cheviots, and that these hillforts and associated stone circles could have been ceremonial arenas. All the Northumberland rock art sites are prominently located along possible ancient routes, as, for example, is the Roughting Linn hillfort, in this case on a partly hollow trackway from the Milfield Plain to the coast (Archeo News 2004).

The relationship of neighbouring hillforts, such as the stone-built West Hill, to Yeavering Bell, is unclear (Frodsham *et al.* 2007, 251–2). West Hill is tilted across the contours, so presenting its front to the College Valley below. The site also faces towards the hillfort of St Gregory's Hill, whose most impressive ramparts return the compliment. Both hillforts have outstanding views across the Milfield Plain with hints of symbolic association and status enhancement, but little evidence of 'up-front' defence.

Whether the small enclosures on Doddington and Horton Moors and those at Dod Law are true hillforts is a moot point, but between these sites are outstanding examples of prehistoric rock art etched on rock outcrop and boulder. Other hillforts associated with rock art include Roughting Linn, the Ringes and Buttony. As all of these Northumberland rock art sites are located in prominent places along possible routeways, as we have seen, it is feasible that there could be links here between the rock art, the hillforts, access and ceremonial.

There are other examples of hillforts in possible venerated landscapes, too great a subject to allow their consideration here. Suffice to say, in all of these examples the 'ancestors' and their activities appear to have assumed great importance and, possibly, influenced hillfort location. There also appear to have been links with features of the natural world – landform, rocks and especially water – all of which exerted a 'magical' presence, and it is to the last of these that we will now turn.

Watery places

Water was a powerful element in prehistoric superstition. Its presence in the form of rivers, lakes, springs and bogs and, of course, the sea was very important, not only for its life-giving and healing properties but for its constant movement. Whether emerging from a cave or flowing as a watercourse or waterfall, it must have achieved a mythical significance unsurpassed by any other natural system: the sight of, for example, Fell Beck flowing into Gaping Gill, the River Aire emerging from beneath Malham Cove or water bubbling from the ground suggests why this might be. Water was a necessity for life but also a destroyer: in the form of storms it battered crops, wrecked boats and brought death by drowning.

Some early Bronze Age circles stand close to water and the source of rivers, but in the late Bronze Age the role of the circles appears to have declined and attention was focused more on the rivers themselves, and on springs, lakes and boggy ground. Here offerings of valuable metalwork were made, as at Llyn Fawr and, later in the Iron Age, at Llyn Cerrig Bach, where there is a possibility that human bone might also have been placed. In fact, in Britain the majority of the most important metalwork finds of Iron Age origin are riverine, but in central Europe they are predominantly from dry hoards or graves. Whilst offerings replaced grave goods and monument construction as 'an expression of community prestige and sacrifice' (Davies and Lynch 2000, 214), these essentially religious practices could also have included a socio-economic or political dimension and been used as a means of resolving conflict by 'sacrifice' or maintaining an economic balance between groups (Bradley 1990, 137–9). The deposition of prestige objects into rivers, which themselves acted as tribal boundaries, has been suggested as achieving similar ends.

Yeates (2008) has outlined the importance of the sanctity of rivers to the Dobunni and, in particular, that of the Severn and its major tributaries, the Teme, Wye and the Warwickshire and Bristol Avons, and the western tributaries of the Thames. The large numbers of metal artefact and coins from the Walbrook stream in London are probably religious offerings, and the continual deposition of metalwork in the Thames over a long period could have represented votive offerings to a local deity whose cult *foci* may well have been associated with regular crossing places.

It follows that springs would have been especially important to hillforts and in providing life-giving water supplies might also have assumed an additional ritualistic meaning. Sulis was the Celtic goddess of the spring, renowned at Bath, and it is thought by some that she may also have had possible solar connections, Ross and Cyprien (1985, 126) suggesting that her name may be associated with the Gaelic word for 'eye' (*suil*), so indicating 'the eye of heaven'; ie. the sun.

The Hollybush spring at Midsummer Hill, which lies near the south gate of the hillfort in the sheltered ravine between the two hills of the site, could have taken on such a significant role, and it is possible that the site itself had a 'symbolic value' to those involved (Bowden 2005a, 24). This is also possible at Y Breiddin, where the potential 'sacred' nature of the Buckbean pond could account for the fauna and flora assemblages found there which suggest little use by people or animals (Buckland *et al.* 2001, 73). As well as the wooden bowls from the accompanying cistern mentioned earlier, an accompanying wooden sword has been either described as a sword-maker's pattern or as a ritual deposit and model of the real thing.

Myths involving springs have also persisted into the historic period. The Burwell, a spring which rises some 360m from the Ravensburgh Castle hillfort in Hertfordshire (at 6.5ha the largest fort in eastern England and the Chilterns), whilst probably the water supply for the fort may also have been a Celtic sanctuary. Downstream, at Hexton, another spring was later dedicated to St Faith: 'People that come to offer did cast some thing into the well, which if it swamme above they were accepted and their petition granted, but if it sunk, then rejected' (Dyer 1976). Waterfalls probably exerted a similar influence; the rectangular promontory hillfort of Roughting Linn, for example, has 'The Linn' waterfall at its north-eastern corner.

There is also evidence from a combination of archaeological and literary material of later Iron Age cults venerating river spirits in both Roman Gaul and Britain, particularly at the source: Sequana, of the Seine for example. However, in Britain specific evidence is less forthcoming. To date there has been no evidence of enclosures, or indeed shrines, at the sources of the Severn and Wye as would be thought, but the concentration of small hillforts near to the source of the Mule, a tributary of the Severn could reflect an element of veneration. Many rivers had their own 'genius', very often female, Verbeia, the goddess of the River Wharfe, being one. Similarly, the temple complex at Lydney was probably deliberately sited to overlook the River Severn, where the god Nodens (also possibly Neptune) was thought to have commanded the Severn Bore: a bronze relief of sea gods, tritons and anchors on a diadem and representations of the sea depicted on the *cella* mosaic all indicating maritime connections.

Numerous shrines, such as Chedworth on the Coln in Oxfordshire, overlooked rivers and the god Condatis, to whom four dedications have been found in County Durham, was the god of the 'watersmeet', or confluence. Although his altars belong to the Roman period, similar deities probably existed in their hundreds in the 'free Celtic' period (Green 1986, 140–1). River confluences and crossings appear to have been highly charged sites for belief and superstition in prehistory (Brown 2002; Yeates 2008), a fact only just being realised. At Bromfield, where the Rivers Teme and Corve meet near Ludlow, there are twenty-five Bronze Age (or earlier?) burial mounds, and nearby a cemetery with over 130 burials dating from 1800–900 BC. The triangle between Bromfield, Stanton Lacy and Ludlow shows extensive occupation over a long period of time, with evidence dating from the Neolithic through to the Anglo-Saxon period (Rowley 2001, 32). Similarly, at Weeping Cross, south of Shrewsbury, a Bronze Age settlement and cemetery were sited close to the confluence of the Severn and Rea Brook. In Wales and the Marches 32.5 per cent of all hillforts in the Severn, Wye and Usk catchments are sited overlooking confluences and nearly all of the important confluences are 'guarded' by hillforts (Brown 2002). This could be interpreted as control of access along rivers and thereby the control of trade and exchange, but equally it could be regarded as a manifestation of veneration of the 'watersmeet'. The cluster of nine sites (some of which are just enclosures and not hillforts *per se*) around the confluence of the Vyrnwy and Banwy in Montgomeryshire is interesting in this respect.

The sea, of course, must have been a source of wonderment and awe, but we can search in vain for much 'on-the-ground' evidence of ritual at coastal promontories. Certainly the location of forts on exposed headlands could suggest some sort of superstitious involvement in their location, and Darvill *et al.* (2002, 435) propose that Gurnard's Head (Gordon 1940), which dates from the second century BC, may have been for ceremonial rather than settlement, in common with other cliff castles. Cunliffe (2001, 9) has also suggested that coastal promontories may have served ritual purposes, situated as they are in liminal positions between land and sea. At Bolt Tail in Devon Griffith and Wilkes (2006, 83) noticed that the single entrance in the middle of the rampart cutting off the promontory is skewed so as to expose the shape of Burgh Island (situated 4km distant just off the coast in Bigbury Bay) as you enter the fort, and consider that: 'It is inconceivable that this was not a deliberately contrived effect which dictated the siting of the entrance'. Perhaps Burgh Island itself was held in some veneration by those involved.

In similar vein, inhospitable Cornish cliff castles such as Treryn Dinas or Tubby's Head near St Agnes (Sharpe 1992) may have formed important focal centres in the landscape, acting as ritual 'landmarks' of special significance, not unlike the inland tors of Bodmin Moor which have been considered as acting as 'navigational tools' across the landscape (Rowe 2005, 113–16). Trevelgue Head and, in Wales, St David's Head are other possibilities as ritual landmarks, as, further inland, are the jagged rocks of Carn Ingli overlooking Newport Bay. Thus, the rocky Cornish prominences occupied by forts with probable origins much earlier than the Iron Age, such as Treryn Dinas, Maen Castle, Tubby Point or Kenidjack Castle, or Giant's Castle on St Mary's, all have walls across a headland seemingly 'defending' nothing but pure rock – but, no doubt, important rock.

But problems remain

Superstition and belief undoubtedly played an important part in hillfort life and possibly in their location and function, but substantial questions remain and we can only touch on one or two here. For example, the location of a ditch *inside* a bank poses problems – it is a feature of henges, such as Avebury, rather than hillforts, and is usually considered indicative of ritual. Wolstonbury, Rybury and

FIGURE 92. The inner
ditch and surrounding
bank of Figsbury Rings
in Wiltshire, possibly the
site of a henge.

the hillslope enclosure of Buzbury Rings in Dorset all show this feature and it is possible that these sites are not true hillforts at all.

Figsbury Rings in Wiltshire (Cunnington 1925), strategically placed above the River Bourne at its confluence with the River Avon, is especially interesting as an outer bank and outside ditch are separated by a wide flat area before meeting a wide inner ditch circling a large interior space (Figure 92). A variety of explanations have been put forward for this latter arrangement, from quarry ditch to remains of an earlier henge or causewayed enclosure, but clearly it formed an integral feature of the later enclosure. The site has some features of a henge, but its hilltop position, akin to that of Wolstonbury, is unusual. Pottery from both the Bronze Age and the early Iron Age has been found, as well as slingstones and a 'Ewart Park' late Bronze Age sword (ninth to eighth centuries BC), suggesting early activity at least. We could go on in this vein, but in the final chapter let us now attempt to synthesise all of the factors discussed above into a recognisable summary of hillfort function and social significance.

CHAPTER ELEVEN

Hillforts: A Synthesis of Ideas

One fact above all others stands out when we look at hillforts – their great *variability*. Some are small, some very large. Some show evidence of dense settlement over hundreds of years, yet some show no sign of life and a pastoral or symbolic function has been envisaged. Many were abandoned, others reused. Some sit on wild and exposed hilltops, a few at great altitude, some are low down and formerly protected by marsh and fen. Many dominate the coast and there are vast areas of England and Wales that do not have hillforts at all. Barry Cunliffe (2006) has said that: 'there may be no such thing as a typical hillfort', and no doubt he is right. Let us look finally at just one or two points.

Function and social significance

Enclosure goes back to the Neolithic. A basic 'architectural' style of bank, ditch, wall and palisade became adopted and adapted according to specific physical conditions and requirements as time progressed. In the absence of mortar, which first appeared with the Romans, this would have been the most obvious means available of defining a boundary and was a means of enclosure that lasted in various forms for thousands of years. By the late Bronze Age, as we have seen, change was occurring in society, land use and belief systems, and, at this time, hillforts developed into structures that reached their zenith as the Iron Age progressed; their influence lasted for some 1,000 years.

Instability in the late Iron Age has been referred to above, with evidence coming from the burning of gates at Danebury for example, but whether the root cause was population pressure or some other factor is unclear. Aggression and withdrawal are not necessarily the 'typical reaction of humans to crowding' (Judge 2000, 145), and Howell (2006, 35–6) has proposed that the emergence of hillforts in areas such as the northern Marches and the west of England was rather a result of demographic change associated with a deteriorating climate, with resultant social instability around 1000 BC. Thus, increasingly, numbers of leaf-shaped slashing swords, scabbards and spearheads appeared, some used in anger, and the former system of largely autonomous family groups in small farmsteads became less marked and larger social groups emerged, with hillforts reflecting the emergence of tribal communities.

Whether or not this was the case, the excavation reports of Maiden Castle,

Danebury, South Cadbury, Uffington Castle, Segsbury and Conderton Camp have begun to consider the people who built and occupied these sites and their wish to define a space *away* from the outside world. Undoubtedly this was a complex process, for hillforts were undeniably a reflection of considerable community and logistical effort. A definite statement was therefore made to others: 'This is ours, you enter on our terms'. One viewpoint is that hillforts, in dominating the landscape, allowed those who occupied them to command the outside world of natural resources, trade and exchange and access and not merely to respond to it. From an anthropological viewpoint the people of the Iron Age were probably little different in their basic make-up to ourselves: some one-in-twenty individuals would have been natural leaders, the remaining 95 per cent destined to follow. Similarly, the seeking of status and its ostentatious display, along with the community's reliance on leaders to 'come up with the goods', and a tendency to visit their displeasure on those leaders if they fell short of expectations, were no more Iron Age traits than they are today. Most hillforts, located as they are in strategic positions in the landscape, would have proved to be the ideal tools by which dominance over others, whether symbolic or real, could be achieved, even to the extent of being 'ends in themselves', and this may be one reason why some hillforts show little evidence of life whilst others were densely occupied over centuries. But what the actual population numbers were, or were likely to have been, at individual sites is impossible to ascertain, although there have been quite a number of, generally unsuccessful, attempts at this in the past, notably Stanford's (1972) work in the Marches; questioned by Graeme Guilbert (1981).

The martial nature of prehistoric society at some point and in some places must not be discounted and there is enough archaeological, written and modern ethnographical evidence to suggest that this was the case. The Suri of Ethiopia has been cited as being such a society where ritualistic and controlled violence provide the bonds by which the tribe is kept together, and this equates with evidence from both the Bronze and Iron Ages. The status-enhancing and monumental nature of some hillfort architecture, together with a defensive capability when the need arose, at least in terms of short-term raiding and ritual combat, seems to fits this model.

Natural physical conditions and the social mix of those concerned would have ultimately influenced siting, construction and function. As we have seen, hillforts tend to reduce in size from north-east to south-west in Wales and the Marches, and also towards the south-west peninsula of England, indicating not only a reaction to physical conditions but possibly to some social need. Similarly, the pairing of sites, either close to or on both sides of a watercourse, suggests the involvement of social factors: Balksbury Camp and Bury Hill Camp straddled the confluence of the Rivers Anton and Anna in Hampshire, and Fron (Newcastle) and Castle Idris face each other where a stream meets the River Clun in the Marches. One possible reason for this is the effect of partible inheritance, whereby the goods and chattels of the father were split up between the sons; this was a particular feature of early Welsh society. In landscape terms this is possibly reflected in the smaller hillforts of the Llawhaden group in Pembrokeshire (Driver 2007a, 49). Also in Pembrokeshire, the small circular enclosures situated along the sides of the sloping valley beneath the hillfort of Treffgarne Rocks near Wolf's Castle could also indicate partible inheritance, an expansion of a family group or a clientage arrangement.

Thus, Barry Cunliffe has proposed a model for Wessex whereby one site became abandoned whilst another close-by continued to expand into a multivallate 'developed' hillfort: examples might be Poundbury and Maiden Castle; Hambledon Hill and Hod Hill; and Battlesbury and Scratchbury. Meanwhile, Collis (1996b, 89), considering Hingley's work in the Middle Thames area (1984), suggested that different types of society operating different types of land tenure would have influenced the 'scale and form' of enclosures, and this is probably true for many areas.

Whichever of the above conditions was relevant at any one hillfort, and there could well have been multiple factors involved at many, the paramount need in the minds of those concerned would have been to 'explain the unexplainable': the seasons, the sky, the earth, rain, wind, lightning and thunder. Any explanation thus relied on outside supernatural forces in the form of the gods of the underworld, of the sky, of earth's natural features. In prehistory, therefore, good fortune would be assured by pit burial, by relating the seasonal harvest to above-ground structures, such as granaries, and the giving of 'life' to the gods by means of human and animal sacrifice subsequently placed in pits and hillfort foundations. Special places in the landscape, such as river confluences or high and prominent hills and sites of past veneration, were also chosen as locations for hillforts for good fortune, health and well-being, and to provide a space for festivals, gatherings, sacrifice and ceremonial, perhaps at important times in the farming calendar.

Some hillforts would, therefore, have been densely populated settlements displaying multiple functions and stable over hundreds of years, as at Danebury, Maiden Castle and Castle Ditches (Tisbury), with their houses, street plans and enclosures (Corney and Payne 2006, 146). Madmarston Camp, on the other hand, was small, isolated and self-sufficient (Fowler 1960, 30). Others were used to exploit valuable farming and possible fishing resources and to protect them from wild animals and/or human predators, sometimes only on a seasonal basis, as suggested by Buckland *et al.* (2001, 73) for Y Breiddin; or they might be used as bases for transhumance. Some possibly provided arenas for gatherings associated with the farming seasons, as at Segsbury, Harting Beacon and Martinsell Camp in Wiltshire, or ceremonial and ritual, as at Ingleborough, Carrock Fell and possibly Mam Tor. At these events social, political and economic relationships and allegiances would have been developed and strengthened on both an individual and community basis over hundreds of years. At some hillforts, functions may have changed over different periods of time, as also suggested for Mam Tor (Edmonds and Seaborne 2001) – first used for grazing, then as a meeting place and subsequently as a settlement – or sometimes involved multiple uses.

In Wales and the Marches, the Weald, the south-west and the east Midlands hillforts would have provided the base from which mineral resources were exploited and metal goods manufactured and sometimes exported down the line. Throughout England and Wales access and the landscape would have been controlled, and strategically placed sites, such as Hengistbury Head, acted as points of trade and exchange.

Driver (2007b), in his research on mid Wales hillforts, has hinted at the possibility of subtle regional variations in both design and construction and the sharing of concepts in hillfort architecture. Certainly, in the part of north Cardiganshire that he studied there does appear to be a distinct architectural tradition, including shared façade schemes, monumental display and a pattern in the use of certain structures. Whether such patterns emerge elsewhere, although a distinct possibility, awaits further work, but in the space of relatively small areas hillforts can vary substantially in terms of their interior features. In the Clwydian Range, for example, although there is evidence (so far) for forty hut platforms on Moel Fenlli, at next-door Moel y Gaer (Llanbedr) there are only thirteen and a little further further along the ridge at Moel Arthur a few only appear after heather burn (Burnham 1995; Gale 2007). A similar situation is evident with pits and huts in Wessex. Segsbury, Barbury and Liddington have many pits but few huts, whilst Beacon Hill at Burghclere in Hampshire and Castle Ditches (Tisbury) have many huts but few pits; and a further distinction in internal use can be seen at Perborough Castle in Berkshire, which has only a few pits and nothing else.

All of this points to differences in function and the Ridgeway hillforts show this well. Although there is evidence that by the early Romano-British period both Segsbury and Uffington Castle were no longer used, the latter from around the fourth century BC, it transpired that Segsbury had been completely abandoned whilst Uffington was subsequently reworked, possibly in the late fourth or early fifth century AD (Lock *et al.* 2003, 124; Lock and Gosden 2005, 150–1). The economy of the vale and downs was changing at this time from predominantly sheep to cattle, and the long-stable 11ha Segsbury, the period of whose greatest occupation, based on sheep, social gatherings and feasting as part of the annual farming cycle, appears to have been in the middle Iron Age, was no longer needed. In contrast, the continuing vibrant nature of the sacred landscape of Uffington meant that the hillfort was still of importance to the community. Between the two sites the earlier 'archaic' hilltop enclosure of Rams Hill, commanding an area of rich burials, became occupied from late Bronze Age to Romano-British times, with only a brief period of desertion. The small Alfred's Castle, just south of the Ridgeway, also shows a stable domestic settlement with pits, metalworking, a huge pottery assemblage and a concentration of roundhouses, which began in the late Bronze Age and lasted until a villa dated from the first to third centuries AD was built within its precincts. The site's rather strange position in a shallow bowl surrounded by downland suggests a homestead arrangement rather than a prominent hillfort – something more akin to the 0.3ha Lidbury on Wiltshire's Salisbury Plain – but it was seemingly constructed at a point in the landscape considered significant, where two linear ditches formed a junction. Similarly, the unexcavated Hardwell Camp (Berkshire) near Uffington has an unusual 'tucked away' position down the Ridgeway slope, suggesting a more specific use (Denison 1998, 2).

It is very likely, then, that, at least at some stages of their life, hillforts could have served multiple functions. The densely occupied Norsebury in Wiltshire, with its coherent internal layout, could be one such site, as could Barbury Castle, in contrast to its near neighbours at Liddington and Uffington, although they are all situated in a similarly rich landscape. Corney and Payne (2006, 103) found that Barbury showed dense activity, possibly over several centuries in the mid first millennium BC, combining domestic, farming, military and sacred functions. Moreover, its position enabled it to: 'dominate and exploit the resources of the surrounding downs and the vale to the north'.

However, to some communities, small groups or indeed individuals in areas of eastern England, the Pennines or central Wales, adverse physical conditions and/or the social, cultural and political mix did not justify much or any hillfort construction. Similarly, major enclosures so common on the mainland, are all but absent from the Isle of Wight, with little evidence of Iron Age activity before the third or second centuries BC (Tomalin 2006, 12–13). Although there is a possibility of one or two other undefined enclosures, the fact that the univallate Five Barrows, on a chalk spur at Chillerton Down, Gatcombe (Dunning 1946), is unfinished points to the distinctive and insular outlook of an island population that saw no need to signify its presence to others. There is no evidence, so far, of any occupation within the enclosure, which overlooks the later Roman and Saxon settlements of the Bowcombe Valley.

To other people hillforts were essential to life and society's traditions and meaning, and sites were developed and abandoned, as most architectural styles are, according to change in culture, population and conflict, or possibly just fashion. Eventually, like the medieval castles, hillforts were just not required for their original purposes any more.

Towards a hillfort model?

Is an overall hillfort model possible under the present state of knowledge? The answer is probably 'no', but we can make a few tentative observations. Hillforts appear to be of such diversity that there is probably no 'typical' site. But, for the chalk downs of Wessex at least, Cunliffe (2006, 160) has suggested three principal hillfort functions: assembly, settlement and storage. Therefore, when we look at all of the factors touched on above, a tentative hillfort 'model' does emerge. Clearly the choice of location was not random, with certain points in the landscape being markedly preferred and a general correlation with past activity on a site; factors also noticed by Corney and Payne (2006, 131). There was an architectural style of bank and ditch, which had originated from around the Neolithic and which enabled a defensive role if necessary to be played, with construction in advantageous physical conditions (topography, climate, soils and so on). Dominance over the landscape, the control of riverine, seaborne and overland access and the exploitation of natural resources, so enabling settlement and trade and exchange, would have been, singly or in combination, significant factors in location. Status and display and other social and political concerns, such as community or kinship organisation, would have assumed great importance and, throughout, superstition, belief and ritual would have been involved in all aspects of hillfort siting and function, and may indeed have been the single *raison d'être* involved. The actual use to which these sites were put would undoubtedly differ from place to place and over time *within* this overall model.

Our deliberations are, of course, hampered by a lack of comprehensive excavations of hillforts, although notable work has been carried out at certain sites such as Danebury. And despite superb results from geophysical survey (Figure 93), it 'does not tell us all' (Corney and Payne 2006, 150). Recent official policy has often been against the use of invasive techniques and this has restricted academic progress to a degree. Therefore, if we are to achieve further insight into the role of hillforts in prehistory in the absence of targeted excavation, perhaps it is now time to delve further into the human condition a little deeper and involve both the psychological, anthropological and zoological disciplines.

The genetic predisposition towards certain actions (or 'human nature') has been out of favour for some time, and this is not the place to enter into contentious discussions now, but the recent writings of the psychologist Steven Pinker (2007) are certainly worth considering in any further analyses of hillforts, as, in a different vein, are those on 'cognitive archaeology' by the archaeologist Colin Renfrew (2007). Hillforts were not a random phenomenon but, rather, a carefully thought-out exercise undertaken by a very sophisticated people who took into account landscape, physical, socio-economic and political factors in placing the hillfort at the very centre of Iron Age and, to a degree, earlier society.

Postscript: the end of hillforts – or was it?

Although the Roman incursions and the taking of hillforts in Wessex and Wales and the Marches seem to have all but ended the final and Romano-British phase of native hillfort occupation, it is increasingly being found that many hillforts were re-used in Roman and later times. Let us look at just a few regional variations.

The majority of the hillforts in the Atrebatic lands of Sussex to Dorset eventually fell into disuse and oppida at Regnum (Chichester) in Sussex, and possibly, Venta Belgarum (Winchester) and Calleva Atrebatum (Silchester) in

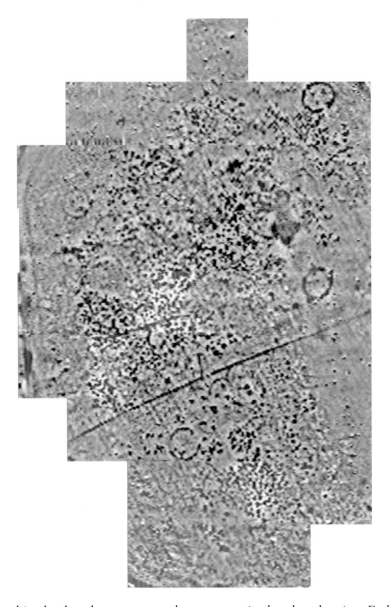

FIGURE 93.
Magnetometer
survey of Cherbury
Camp, Berkshire. The
circular features can
be interpreted as
gullies surrounding
roundhouses. In a
number of them
entrances and postholes
for posts to support the
roof can be detected.

WILLIAM WINTLE, INSTITUTE
OF ARCHAEOLOGY, OXFORD
UNIVERSITY.

Hampshire developed: a move towards a more semi-urban-based society. Earlier, the burning of the inner gate of Danebury around 100 BC heralded a period of near-abandonment, although a small community might have been living around the shrine area up to the Conquest. No doubt the reuse of attractive sites for specific purposes, perhaps as cattle corrals, small settlements or ritual arenas, might have occurred elsewhere, but only excavation will tell.

English Heritage studies have recently shown a possible relationship between Roman activity and hillforts in parts of Wessex. A variety of hillforts along the valley of the Avon in Wiltshire, including Casterley Camp and the former Budbury, were associated with adjacent villas; also a possibility at Vespasian's

Camp, near Stonehenge. Villas appeared within the perimeter of enclosures at Tidbury Ring in Hampshire and Alfred's Castle, and less grand was the late Roman aisled building from Balksbury. The Wansdyke in Wiltshire, the great Anglo-Saxon earthwork dated to about AD 500 (Darvill *et al.* 2002, 419), has a close relationship with both Chisbury, which also overlooks another villa site, and Oldbury. An early Roman villa was also found within the Ditches hillfort in Gloucestershire (Trow *et al.* in press). The question to be asked, of course, is why there are these connections with villas in Wessex: it is evidently not by chance. That these places were just good sites might be the simple answer, but it is more likely that complex Roman socio-economic and political systems were involved. As John Percival wrote (1976, 7): 'The Roman villa is a subject about which we could be said to know a great deal and understand very little'; and the same could, perhaps, be said for hillforts.

Elsewhere there is widespread evidence of later use. In Hampshire Woolbury was occupied into the late Roman period and Hod Hill in Dorset is notable for ceramics of the same age and finds of early fifth-century Germanic brooches. It is possible that a Roman signal station was located on the strategic site of Abbotsbury Castle, overlooking Chesil Beach and Portland in Dorset (Gale 2003, 136). To the south-west the pattern found throughout Devon and Cornwall was one of stable continuous use of hillforts from before 100 BC into the Roman period, and much later in some cases – Castle Dore, for instance, originating from around 150 BC, was still in use in the sixth century AD, and was, no doubt, the centre of a rich farming and manufacturing community (Berresford Ellis 1991, 87). Other sites in the south also saw later agricultural use. Madmarston Camp, for example, was reoccupied for most of the fourth century AD at least, after some 250 years of disuse. Although the Iron Age defences had collapsed they were not rebuilt and a levelled 'yard' on the highest part of the hill could have been for corn-stacking or keeping cattle (Fowler 1960, 30).

Further north, in Northamptonshire, the general lack of late Iron Age evidence from excavated sites suggests that most hillforts had been abandoned by the time of the Conquest, but even this may not be clearcut and Crow Hill seems to have been refortified later with a palisade (Kidd 2004, 57). Nevertheless, by the end of the Iron Age the county had become a densely populated mixed farming landscape, with only Duston being a possible oppidum. In fact, the population was increasing in most of southern Britain by the second century BC and the need to produce more food must have given further stimulus to locate further 'downslope' in most areas of the country. The large number of lower-lying sites found in the later Iron Age, compared with earlier, does suggest such a trend.

Although some hillforts in Wales and the Marches appear to have been abandoned way before the coming of the Romans, and in the far south-west hillforts tended to be abandoned and replaced by ring-forts between the second century BC and the first century AD, some seem to have been in continual use after 150 BC and up to and after the Conquest. The ninety-odd huts at Braich-y-Ddinas were occupied during the Roman period (Houlder 1978, 62) and, as we have seen, the Wrekin was attacked during Scapula's campaign in AD 49 and that there was a possible reoccupation of the outer area of the hill in the second century BC. Tre'r Ceiri and some smaller hillforts such as Castell Henllys in the south-west also appear to have been in continual use; at the latter Romano-British occupation in an adjacent annexe (Harold Mytum pers. comm.), which also occurred at Milber Down Camp. In south-east Wales, despite few excavations, there is also evidence of a post-Conquest presence. Excavations in Glamorgan at Cae Summerhouse at Tythegston confirmed at least two Romano-British episodes, whilst The Bulwarks at Porthkerry showed that the three successive rectangular buildings located within a trapezoidal enclosure on the site were of Roman-British origin (Pollard *et al.* 2006, 58).

Some hillforts appear to have exerted a considerable pull as ritual centres, although this does not necessarily imply a permanent presence. At Dinorben, after disuse, the site was reoccupied in the late third century AD, as also at Bwrdd Arthur, Manning (2001, 79) suggesting that this small flurry of late occupation in Wales could have been more to do with a resurgence in religious observance than anything else. But elsewhere in Wales, with notable exceptions as above, lack of substantial evidence precludes an adequate assessment of native use after the Conquest. As Audrey Williams (1941, 19) pointed out, with reference to her work on the coastal promontories of the Gower, where she found, among items, a few sherds of Roman pottery and a pennanular brooch: 'Romanisation reduced to a vanishing point'.

The Romans themselves reused hillforts as bases in Wales, as they had at Hod Hill. Sudbrook possibly secured a naval station and landing place for a ferry across the Severn Estuary to England (Manning 2001, 14; Pollard *et al.* 2006, 59). Brandon Camp, close to Leintwardine in Herefordshire, where Watling Street West crosses the River Teme, was also reused. These strategically placed hillforts, together with new builds such as the long-lasting Forden Gaer – near Montgomery on a ford where the Severn turns into mid Wales – were extremely important to the Roman advance and none more so than the signal station on the summit of the Caer y Tŵr fort on Holyhead Mountain, which was built to relay the sighting of any Irish attack to the naval base below and, via a series of stations along the north Wales coast, to the legionary HQ at Chester (Lynch 1995, 67). Here coin found signified occupation in the fourth-century AD. Although Roman coins and pottery are found in quantity at a variety of hillforts, sometimes just a few sherds are all that are tantalisingly left to signify some sort of presence, as at Oliver's Point.

For northern England, 'Romanisation' would be an incorrect term to use. Over most of the area native traditions prevailed in the Roman period and evidence of villas and Romanised settlement is rare (other than for military sites), and non-existent in the extreme north. Harding argues that here, within the Roman frontier zone, dispersed farming settlements with the occasional hillfort (still in use) appear to have been the order of the day. Over much of the first millennium BC rectilinear or circular homesteads containing one or more

FIGURE 94. The medieval castle surrounded by the Iron Age hillfort of Castell Dinas Brân, Denbighshire.

circular houses were widespread. These permanent settlements, together with extensive linear earthworks and field systems, indicate an: 'ordered division of the landscape into territorial and farming units' (Harding 2004, 159). Of the excavated northern hillforts, sites such as Mam Tor, Castle Hill (Almondbury), Skelmore Heads and Castercliff were all unoccupied after around 400 BC, the only large settlement at this date being Stanwick, which seems to have achieved great prominence as a political and trading centre.

Later still in mid and southern England there was continued activity at isolated sites such as Danebury and Blewburton Hill. At the latter, its local 'landmark' status was reflected in its choice as the site of an Anglo-Saxon cemetery of the late sixth and early seventh century AD after the abandonment of the hillfort in the first century BC (Harding 1976), and a Saxon settlement followed a Bronze and Iron Age enclosure at Taplow hillfort in Buckinghamshire (Allen *et al.* in press). Later reoccupation in Somerset has been found at both South Cadbury and Cadbury Hill (Congresbury), both having nearby Roman villas; at the latter a substantial settlement with rectangular and round buildings has been dated to between AD 410 and 700.

In the Marches the ringwork, which crowns the summit of Herefordshire Beacon, and which gives British Camp its unique appearance, was built at some time between the Norman Conquest and the fourteenth century, although an eleventh to twelfth century date is favoured (Bowden 2005a, 35). To the north, Bryn Euryn at Rhos-on-Sea has proven later credentials from a possible Iron Age beginning, and, to the west, the 'citadels' at Carn Pentyrch and Garn Boduan on the Llŷn could also be of medieval date. Earlier activity at New Pieces, next to Y Breiddin, is more ambiguous, with finds of imported continental glass and pottery of the late Roman period as well as evidence of fifth- and sixth-century AD occupation (Arnold and Davies 2000, 156). Old Oswestry was incorporated into the line of Wat's Dyke and could have formed one of the fortifications along its length from nearby Maesbury to Basingwerk Hill overlooking the Dee Estuary (Hughes 1994 after Hill 1977, 33).

At Yeavering the early medieval cemeteries and 'royal palace' just to the north of the Bell hillfort suggest that here was a very special place indeed. This same period also saw the strategic advantage of hillfort locations recognised as castle sites; from Elmley Castle in Worcestershire to Llanstephan (Guilbert 1974), Dryslwyn and Castell Dinas Brân (Figure 94) in Wales and Bamburgh and Norham Castles in Northumberland. Medieval interest could, however, be much less dramatic and a beautiful early medieval (eighth-century) pseudo-penannular brooch must have been a very personal loss or deposit at Pen y corddyn Mawr. Or might there have been more than just passing medieval interest here? Without adequate excavation we will never know.

Some hillforts have a longer history still. The original univallate hillfort of Old Sarum at Salisbury was dated to around 400 BC, but the site has a long history continuing to AD 1220. Little is known about the hillfort in prehistory, but William I founded a castle, re-digging the ditch. Subsequently, the bishopric of Sherborne was transferred here and in 1092 a Norman cathedral was dedicated and a small town founded. In 1227 the site was abandoned in favour of New Sarum and its new cathedral.

The prominent 'beacon' status of hillforts in the landscape has encouraged other uses: annual sheep fairs were held at Yarnbury Castle in Wiltshire in the eighteenth and nineteenth centuries, and memorials were erected, such as the Lansdowne Column at Oldbury in Wiltshire and Rodney's Column at Y Breiddin (Figure 95); Beacon Hill at Burghclere in Hampshire was chosen as the final resting place of Lord Carnarvon. During the Great War Old Oswestry suffered the indignity of being used for munitions training by the nearby Park Hall army camp, resulting in considerable damage to the interior; subsequent deep ploughing did not improve matters. This strategic importance was later to be recognised during the Second World War, when hillforts such as Mount Caburn, Chanctonbury Ring, Wains Hill and Woodbury Castle housed observation posts, emplacements and slit trenches. Meanwhile, 'new' hillforts are still emerging – Pen'r Allt, at Llanidloes in Montgomeryshire, was only recognised in 2003 despite being a prominent site – and more are to be found, if only as cropmarks, as at Berry Farm, a small promontory fort overlooking the fine landing site of Nevern beach in Pembrokeshire, and unearthed as part of a south Ceredigion and north Pembrokeshire small enclosures project (Harold Mytum pers. comm.).

Some hillforts, such as Wandlebury in Cambridgeshire, were badly mutilated in earlier times (in this case the early eighteenth century), but during the last century many other hillforts have been lost. Braich-y-Ddinas and Dinorben have been quarried away entirely, while Balksbury Camp has been all but removed by the Andover bypass. Many great sites have been disfigured: Ham Hill, Y Breiddin and Moel Hiraddug; the list goes on. At many hillforts tree growth has all but covered traces of rampart and ditch, as at Norton Camp (Craven Arms), and the interiors of Gaer Fawr (Guilsfield) in the Marches and Worlebury in Somerset are similarly overgrown. Often the pressures of recreation and grazing animals have resulted in erosion scars, to the detriment of both monument and landscape. Many sites suffer from bracken encroachment, 'poisonous' to both recreation, agriculture and wildlife, and a major land use problem nationally that certainly should be addressed on historic sites (Brown and Wathern 1986).

However, on a more positive note, the 'humps and hollows' of hillforts (quoting one resident of Bourton-on-the-Water on Salmonsbury) are much in use today – this time for recreation, as at Badbury Rings, Old Oswestry, Maiden Castle and Crickley Hill, among many others. A programme of reinstatement of the flattened ramparts and subsequent opening-up to public access at Stonea Camp show what can be done (Taylor 1994), and Castell Henllys has very successful education facilities for the young. Other sites, such as Caer Drewyn, have been specifically bought by local councils to safeguard them from further degradation. Some are National Nature Reserves, as at Hambledon Hill and

FIGURE 95. Rodney's Column, at Y Breiddin in Montgomeryshire, erected to commemorate George Brydges Rodney (1719–1792), made Admiral of the White in 1781.

FIGURE 96. Possible reconstruction of what some hillforts *might* have looked like in their heyday when at maximum use. Note the timber additions to the top of the ramparts and roundhouses and four-poster structures in the interior.

DENBIGHSHIRE COUNTY COUNCIL.

Mount Caburn, or nature conservation areas, as at Ivinghoe Beacon and Burrough Hill. In fact, hillforts overall are probably used more today than at any time since the Iron Age and fulfil a vital role in both interpreting the past to young and old alike and providing a readily accessible open 'breathing space' for an increasingly stressed urban population. They may still be used as places of 'ritual', indeed modern cremation urns have been found at Chanctonbury Ring (Rudling 2001, 119), and both Moel Drygarn and Castell Dinas Brân have shown evidence of a modern 'pagan' presence. Hillforts have even been recognised as suitable projects for National Lottery funding. And what might hillforts have actually looked like? The reconstruction in Figure 96, produced by the Archaeology Service of the former Clwyd County Council, shows just one possibility.

The management of hillforts has not been especially good in the past, perhaps because they have been taken so much for granted, or possibly because there are so many of them in the landscape. Within the national framework of archaeological site management, despite a handful of notable sites, they are generally left to look after themselves and their interpretation to the visitor is often extremely poor. These are management and political problems for another book, but it is hoped that, in explaining what hillforts (or perhaps *beacon enclosures*) are all about, the essential task of looking after these national treasures has been made a little easier.

Bibliography

Albarella, U. (2007) 'The end of the sheep age: people and animals in the late Iron Age', in eds C. Haselgrove and T. Moore, *The Later Iron Age in Britain and Beyond*, Oxbow Books, Oxford, 389–402.

Alcock, L. (1960) 'Castell Odo: an embanked settlement on Mynydd Ystum, near Aberdaron, Caernarvonshire', *Archaeologia Cambrensis* CIX, 78–135.

Alcock, L. (1965) 'Hillforts in Wales and the Marches', *Antiquity* 39, 184–95.

Alcock, L. (1971) 'Excavations at South Cadbury Castle, 1970. Summary report', *Antiquaries Journal* 51, 1–7.

Aldhouse-Green, S.H.R. and Northover, P. (1996) 'The discovery of three Bronze Age gold torques in Pembrokeshire', *Archaeologia Cambrensis* 145, 37–45.

Alexander, M. (2002) *A Companion to the Folklore, Myths and Customs of Britain*, Sutton Publishing, Stroud.

Allen, D.F. (1968) 'The chronology of Durotrigan coinage', in I.A. Richmond, *Hod Hill Vol. 2. Excavations carried out between 1951 and 1958*, British Museum, London, 45–55.

Allen, T., Hayden, C. and Lamdin-Whymark, H. (in press) 'From Bronze Age enclosure to Saxon settlement: archaeological excavations at Taplow hillfort, Buckinghamshire', Oxford Archaeology, Oxford.

Archaeo News (2004) *The old stones say: 'This land is ours'*, http://www.stonepages.com/news/archives/001063.html (accessed 31 March 2008).

Armit, I. (1997) *Celtic Scotland*, Batsford, London.

Armit, I. (2007) 'Hillforts at war: from Maiden Castle to Taniwaha Pā', *Proceedings of the Prehistoric Society* 73, 25–37.

Arnold, C.J. and Davies, J.L. (2000) *Roman and Early Medieval Wales*, Sutton Publishing, Stroud.

Ashbee, P. (1974) *Ancient Scilly from the First Farmers to the Early Christians*, David and Charles, Newton Abbot.

Ashbee, P. (1986) 'Ancient Scilly: retrospect, aspect and prospect', *Cornish Archaeology* 25, 187–219.

Ashbee, P. (2005) *Kent in Prehistoric Times*, Tempus, Stroud.

Austin, D., Bell, M., Burnham, B. and Young, R. (1985) *The Caer Cadwgan Project. Interim Report*, St David's University College, Lampeter.

Avery, M. (1976) 'Hillforts of the British Isles: a student's introduction', in ed. D.W. Harding, *Hillforts and Later Prehistoric Earthworks in Britain and Ireland*, Academic Press, London, 1–58.

Avery, M. (1993) *Hillfort Defences of Southern Britain*, BAR British Series 231, Oxford.

Avery, M., Sutton, J.E. and Banks, J.W. (1967) 'Rainsborough, Northants., England: excavations 1961–5', *Proceedings of the Prehistoric Society* 33, 207–306.

Barber, M. (2003) *Bronze and the Bronze Age. Metalwork and Society in Britain c.2500–800 BC*, Tempus, Stroud.

Barclay, A., Cromarty, A.M., Gosden, C., Lock, G., Miles, D., Palmer, S. and Robinson, M. (2003) 'The White Horse and its landscape', in eds D. Miles, S. Palmer, G. Lock, C. Gosden and A.M. Cromarty, *Uffington White Horse and its Landscape. Investigations at White Horse Hill, Uffington, 1989–95 and Tower Hill, Ashbury, 1993–94*, Oxford Archaeology Thames Valley Landscapes Monograph No. 18, Oxford University School of Archaeology, Oxford, 243–68.

Baring-Gould, S. and Burnard, R. (1904) 'An exploration of some of the *cytiau* in Tre'r Ceiri', *Archaeologia Cambrensis* 6th series IV, 1–16.

Baring-Gould, S., Burnard, R. and Enys, J.D. (1899) 'Exploration of the stone camp on St. David's Head', *Archaeologia Cambrensis* 16, 105–31.

Baring-Gould, S., Burnard, R. and Anderson, I.K. (1900) 'Exploration of Moel Trigarn', *Archaeologia Cambrensis* 54, 189–211.

Barnwell, E.L (1862) 'Articles supposed to be spoons', *Archaeologia Cambrensis* 3rd series VIII, 208–19.

Barrett, J.C. (2000a) 'Summary' and 'Writing the Iron Age – archaeological interpretation', in eds J.C. Barrett, P.W.M. Freeman and A. Woodward, *Cadbury Castle Somerset. The Later Prehistoric and Early Historic Archaeology*, English Heritage Archaeological

Report 20, English Heritage, London, xiv–xix, 317–24.

Barrett, J.C. (2000b) 'Enclosing the hill: introduction', in eds J.C. Barrett, P.W.M. Freeman and A. Woodward, *Cadbury Castle Somerset. The Later Prehistoric and Early Historic Archaeology*, English Heritage Archaeological Report 20, English Heritage, London, 46.

Barrett, J.C., Freeman, P.W.M. and Woodward, A. eds (2000) *Cadbury Castle Somerset. The Later Prehistoric and Early Historic Archaeology*, English Heritage Archaeological Report 20, English Heritage, London.

Bedwin, O. (1978) 'Excavations inside Harting Beacon hill-fort, West Sussex, 1976', *Sussex Archaeological Collections* 116, 225–40.

Bedwin, O. (1980) 'Excavations at Chanctonbury Ring, Wiston, West Sussex 1977', *Britannia* 11, 173–222.

Bell, M. and Neumann, H. (1997) 'Prehistoric intertidal archaeology and environments in the Severn Estuary, Wales', *World Archaeology* 29.1, 95–113.

Bell, M., Caseldine, A. and Neumann, H. (1999) *Prehistoric Intertidal Archaeology in the Welsh Severn Estuary*, Council for British Archaeology Research Report 120, York.

Bell, T. and Lock, G. (2000) 'Topographic and cultural influences on walking the Ridgeway in later prehistoric times', in ed. G. Lock, *Beyond the Map: Archaeology and Spatial Technologies*, IOS Press, Amsterdam, 85–100.

Bellavia, G., Downes, J.M. and Ferris, I. (2000) 'The pits', in eds J.C. Barrett, P.W.M. Freeman and A. Woodward, *Cadbury Castle Somerset. The Later Prehistoric and Early Historic Archaeology*, English Heritage Archaeological Report 20, English Heritage, London, 203–6.

Bendrey R. (2007) 'Bitting damage: investigating prehistoric horse use', *Past* 57, 6–7.

Benfield, E. (1947) *The Town of Maiden Castle*, Robert Hale, London.

Benson, D.G. and Williams, G.H. (1987) 'Dale promontory fort', *Archaeology in Wales* 27, 43.

Berresford Ellis, P. (1991) *A Guide to Early Celtic Remains in Britain*, Constable, London.

Berry, A.Q. and Brown, I.W. eds (1994) *Erosion on Archaeological Earthworks: Its Preservation, Control and Repair*, Clwyd County Council, Mold.

Berry, A.Q. and Brown, I.W. (1995) eds *Managing Ancient Monuments: An Integrated Approach*, Clwyd County Council, Mold.

Bersu, G. (1940) 'Excavations at Little Woodbury, Wiltshire. Part 1) The settlement as revealed by excavation', *Proceedings of the Prehistoric Society* 6, 30–111.

Bevan-Jones, R. (2002) *The Ancient Yew. A History of Taxus baccata*, Windgather Press, Bollington.

Bezant Lowe, W. (1909) *Heart of North Wales*, I, Llanfairfechan.

Blockley, K. (1991) 'The Romano-British period', in eds J. Manley, S. Grenter, and F. Gale, *The Archaeology of Clwyd*, Clwyd County Council, Mold, 117–28.

Blockley, K. and Blockley, P. (1989) 'Excavations at Bigberry, near Canterbury, 1981', *Archaeologia Cantiana* 107, 239–51.

Bond, D. and Morris, E.L. (1991) 'An excavation of Wall Camp, Kynnersley. Prehistory in lowland Shropshire', *Transactions of the Shropshire Archaeological and Historical Society* LXVII, 98–107.

Boon, G.C. (1977) 'A Graeco-Roman anchor-stock from North Wales', *Antiquaries Journal* 57, 10–30.

Boon, G.C. (1980) 'A Gaulish coin from Merthyr Mawr Warren, Glamorganshire', *Bulletin of the Board of Celtic Studies* 28, 743–74.

Boon, G.C. (1988) 'The coins', in ed. D.M. Robinson, *Biglis, Caldicot and Llandough: Three Late Iron Age and Romano-British Sites in South-East Wales*, BAR British Series 188, Oxford, 91–2.

Bowden, M. (2005a) *The Malvern Hills. An Ancient Landscape*, English Heritage, London.

Bowden, M. (2005b) 'The middle Iron Age on the Marlborough Downs', in eds G. Brown, D. Field and D. McOmish, *The Avebury landscape. Aspects of the field archaeology of the Marlborough Downs*, Oxbow Books, Oxford.

Bowden, M. (2006) 'Guard chambers: an unquestioned assumption in British Iron Age studies', *Proceedings of the Prehistoric Society* 72, 423–36.

Bowden, M. and McOmish, D. (1987) 'The required barrier', *Scottish Archaeological Review* 4.2, 76–84.

Bowden, M. and McOmish, D. (1989) 'Little boxes. More about hillforts', *Scottish Archaeological Review* 6, 12–15.

Bowden, M., Mackay, D.A. and Blood, N.K. (1989) 'A new survey of Ingleborough hillfort, North Yorkshire', *Proceedings of the Prehistoric Society* 55, 267–71.

Bowen, D.Q. (1977) 'The land of Wales', in ed. D. Thomas, *Wales: A New Study*, David and Charles, Newton Abbot.

Bradley, R. (1981) 'From ritual to romance: ceremonial enclosures and hill-forts', in ed. G. Guilbert, *Hill-fort Studies. Essays for A.H.A. Hogg*, Leicester University Press, Leicester.

Bradley, R. (1990) *The Passage of Arms: An Archaeological Analysis of Prehistoric Hoards and Votive Deposits*, Cambridge University Press, Cambridge.

Bradley, R. (2005) *Ritual and Domestic Life in Prehistoric Europe*, Routledge, London.

Bradley, R. (2007) *The Prehistory of Britain and Ireland*, Cambridge University Press, London.

Bradley, R. and Ellison, A. (1975) *Rams Hill: A Bronze Age Defended Enclosure and its Landscape*, BAR British Series 19, Oxford.

Brannigan, K. (1985) *Peoples of Roman Britain. The Catuvellauni*, Alan Sutton, Stroud.

Brassil, K.S., Guilbert, G.C., Livens, R.G., Stead, W.H. and Bevan-Evans, M. (1982) 'Rescue excavations at Moel Hiraddug between 1960 and 1980', *Journal of the Flintshire Historical Society* 30, 13–88.

Brewster, T.C.M. (1963) *The Excavation of Staple Howe*, East Riding Archaeological Research Committee, Wintringham.

Briffa, K. and Atkinson, T. (1997) 'Reconstructing Late-Glacial and Holocene climates' in eds M. Hulme and E. Barrow, *Climates of the British Isles, present, past and future,* Routledge, London, 84–111.

Britnell, W.J. (1989) 'The Collfryn hillslope enclosure, Llansantffraid Deuddwr, Powys: excavations 1980–1982', *Proceedings of the Prehistoric Society* 55, 89–134.

Brooks, B. (1974) 'The excavation of the Rumps cliff castle, St Minver, Cornwall', *Cornish Archaeology* 13, 5–50.

Brothwell, D.R. (1961) 'Cannibalism in early Britain', *Antiquity* 35, 304–7.

Brown, E.H. (1960) *The Relief and Drainage of Wales*, University of Wales Press, Cardiff.

Brown, I.W. (1994) 'Archaeological site management and erosion control: the environmental context', in eds A.Q. Berry and I.W. Brown, *Erosion Control on Archaeological Earthworks: Its Preservation, Control and Repair*, Clwyd County Council, Mold, xi–xiii.

Brown, I.W. (1995) 'Integrated environmental resource management and the conservation of the archaeological heritage', in eds A.Q. Berry and I.W. Brown, *Managing Ancient Monuments: An Integrated Approach*, Clwyd County Council, Mold, xi–xiv.

Brown, I.W. (2002) *The Iron Age Hillforts of Wales and the Marches, their Location and Social Significance*, unpublished MLitt thesis, University of Oxford.

Brown, I.W. (2004) *Discovering a Welsh Landscape. Archaeology in the Clwydian Range*, Windgather Press, Bollington.

Brown, I.W. and Wathern, P. (1986) 'Bracken control and land management in the Moel Famau Country Park, Clwyd, North Wales', in eds R.T. Smith and J.A. Taylor, *Bracken. Ecology, Land Use and Control Technology*, Parthenon Publishing, Carnforth, 369–77.

Bryant, S. (2007) 'Central places or special places', in eds C. Haselgrove and T. Moore, *The Later Iron Age in Britain and Beyond*, Oxbow Books, Oxford, 62–80.

Buckland, P.C., Parker Pearson, M., Wigley, A. and Girling, A. (2001) 'Is there anybody out there? A reconstruction of the environmental evidence from the Breiddin hillfort, Powys, Wales', *Antiquaries Journal* 81, 51–76.

Bulleid, A. and Gray, H. St. George (1917) *The Glastonbury Lake Village Vol. 2*, Glastonbury Antiquarian Society, Glastonbury.

Burnham, B. and Burnham, H. (2004) *Dolaucothi-Pumsaint: survey and excavation at a Roman gold-mining complex 1987–1999*, Oxbow Books, Oxford.

Burnham, H. (1995) *A Guide to Ancient and Historic Wales. Clwyd and Powys*, HMSO, London.

Burroughs, W.J. (2005) *Climate Change in Prehistory*, Cambridge University Press, Cambridge.

Burstow, G.P. and Holleyman, G.A. (1964) 'Excavations at Ranscombe Camp 1959–60', *Sussex Archaeological Collections* 102, 55–67.

Butler, A. (2006) *Sheep*, John Hunt Publishing, Ropley.

Carr, G. (2007) 'Excarnation to cremation: continuity or change?' in eds C. Haselgrove and T. Moore, *The Later Iron Age in Britain and Beyond*, Oxbow Books, Oxford, 444–53.

Carver, M.O.H. (1991) 'A strategy for lowland Shropshire. Prehistory in lowland Shropshire', *Transactions of the Shropshire Archaeological and Historical Society* LXVII, 1–8.

Chadwick, S.E. and Thompson, M.W. (1956) 'Note on an Iron Age habitation site near Battlesbury Camp, Warminster', *Wiltshire Archaeological Magazine* 56, 262–4.

Champion, S. (1976) 'Leckhampton Hill, Gloucestershire, 1925–1970', in ed. D.W. Harding, *Hillforts. Later Prehistoric Earthworks in Britain and Ireland*, Academic Press, London, 177–90.

Champion, T. (2007) 'Settlement in Kent from 1500 to 300 BC', in eds C. Haselgrove and R. Pope, *The Earlier Iron Age in Britain and the Near Continent*, Oxbow Books, Oxford, 293–305.

Childe, V.G. (1931) *Skara Brae: A Pictish Village in Orkney*, Kegan Paul, London.

Childe, V.G. and Thorneycroft, W. (1938) 'The experimental

production of the phenomena distinctive of vitrified forts', *Proceedings of the Society of Antiquaries of Scotland* LXXII, (vol. XII, 6th series), session 1937–38, 44–55.

Chitty, L.F.C. (1937) 'How did the hill-fort builders reach the Breiddin? A tentative explanation', *Archaeologia Cambrensis* 92, 129–50.

Clark, G. (1940) *Prehistoric England*, B.T. Batsford, London.

Clarke, R.R. (1960) *East Anglia*, Thames and Hudson, London.

Clifford, E.M. (1961) *Bagendon: A Belgic oppidum*, Cambridge University Press, Cambridge.

Coles, J., Minnitt, S. and Wilson, A. (2000) *Ceremony and Display: The South Cadbury Bronze Age Shield*, Somerset County Museums Service, Taunton.

Collingwood, R.G. (1938) 'The hillfort on Carrock Fell', *Transactions of the Cumberland and Westmorland Antiquarian and Archaeological Society* 38, 32–4.

Collins, A.E.P. (1953) 'Excavations on Blewburton Hill, 1948 and 1949', *Berkshire Archaeological Journal* 53, 21–64.

Collis, J. (1981) 'A theoretical study of hillforts', in ed. G. Guilbert, *Hill-fort Studies. Essays for A.H.A. Hogg*, Leicester University Press, Leicester, 66–76.

Collis, J. (1996a) 'The origin and spread of the Celts', *Studia Celtica* XXX, 17–34.

Collis, J. (1996b) 'Hill-forts, enclosures and boundaries', in eds T. Champion and J. Collis, *The Iron Age in Britain: Recent Trends*, Sheffield Academic Press, Sheffield, 87–94.

Collis, J. (2003) *The Celts. Origins, Myths, Inventions*, Tempus, Stroud.

Connolly, P. (1981) *Greece and Rome at War*, MacDonald, London.

Coombs, D.G. (1976) 'Excavations at Mam Tor, Derbyshire 1965–69', in ed. D.W. Harding, *Hillforts. Later Prehistoric Earthworks in Britain and Ireland*, Academic Press, London, 147–52.

Coombs, D.G. (1982) 'Excavations at the hillfort of Castercliff, Nelson, Lancashire 1970–71', *Transactions of the Lancashire and Cheshire Antiquarian Society* 81, 111–30.

Coombs, D.G. and Thompson, F.H. (1979) 'Excavation of the Hill Fort of Mam Tor, Derbyshire, 1965–69', *Derbyshire Archaeological Journal* 99, 7–51.

Corney, M. and Payne, A. (2006a) 'The regional pattern', in A. Payne, M. Corney and B. Cunliffe, *The Wessex Hillforts Project*, English Heritage, London, 131–50.

Corney, M. and Payne, A. (2006b) 'The monuments and their setting', in A. Payne, M. Corney and B. Cunliffe, *The Wessex Hillforts Project*, English Heritage, London, 39–130.

Cotton, M.A. and Frere, S.S. (1968) 'Ivinghoe Beacon. Excavations 1963–5', *Records of Buckinghamshire* 18, 187–260.

CPAT (n.d.) *Moel y Gaer*, Clwyd Powys Archaeological Trust/Clwyd County Council, Welshpool/Mold.

CPAT (1994) 'Llwyn Bryn-dinas', Plate inset, *Windows on the Past – A Review of Recent Discoveries by CPAT*, Clwyd Powys Archaeological Trust, Welshpool.

CPAT (2000) *Site of the Week. Llanymynech Hillfort, Powys*, The Clwyd-Powys Archaeological Trust Newsletter, http://www.cpat.org.uk.

Craig, R., Knüsel, C. and Carr, G. (2005) 'Fragmentation, mutilation, and dismemberment: an interpretation of human remains in Iron Age sites', in eds M. Parker Pearson and N. Thorpe, *Warfare, Violence and Slavery in Prehistory*, BAR International Series 1374, Oxford, 165–80

Crampton, C.B. and Webley, D.P. (1963) 'The correlation of prehistoric settlement and soils: Gower and the South Wales coalfield', *Bulletin of the Board of Celtic Studies* XXX, 326–37.

Creighton, J. (2000) *Coins and Power in Late Iron Age Britain*, Cambridge University Press, Cambridge.

Crew, P. (1984) 'Bryn y Castell', *Archaeology in Wales* 24, 37–43.

Crew, P. (1986) 'Bryn y Castell hillfort', in eds B.G. Scott and H. Cleere, *The Crafts of the Blacksmith*, UISPP Comité pour la Sidérurgie Ancienne and the Ulster Museum, Belfast, 91–100.

Crew, P. (1991) 'Crawcwellt West', *Archaeology in Wales* 31, 19.

Crew, P. (1994) 'Currency bars in Britain – typology and function', in ed. M. Mangin, *La Sidérurgie ancienne de l'est de la France dans son contexte European*, UISSP, Besançon, 345–50.

Crew, P. (1998) 'Excavations at Crawcwellt West, Merioneth, 1990–1998. A late prehistoric upland iron-working settlement', *Archaeology in Wales* 38, 22–35.

Crew, P. and Salter, C. (1993) 'Currency bars with welded tips', in ed. A. Espelund, *Bloomery Ironmaking during 2000 years: In Honorem Ole Evenstad, III*, UISSP, Trondheim.

Cunliffe, B. (1972) 'The late Iron Age metalwork from Bulbury, Dorset', *Antiquaries Journal* 52, 293–308.

Cunliffe, B. (1973) *Peoples of Roman Britain. The Regni*, Duckworth, London.

Cunliffe, B. (1974) 'Chalton, Hants: the evolution of a landscape', *Antiquaries Journal* 53, (1973), 173–90.

Cunliffe, B. (1982) 'Britain, the Veneti and beyond', *Oxford Journal of Archaeology* 1.1, 39–68.

Cunliffe, B. (1983) 'Ictis: is it here?' *Oxford Journal of Archaeology* 2, 123–6.

Cunliffe, B. (1984) *Danebury: An Iron Age Hillfort in Hampshire. Volume 1, The Excavations, 1969–(1978) The Site. Volume 2, The Excavations 1969–(1978) The Finds*, CBA Research Report 52, London.

Cunliffe, B. (1987) '*Hengistbury Head, Dorset. Vol. 1: prehistoric and Roman settlement, 3500 BC–AD 500*', Oxford University Committee for Archaeology Monograph 16, Oxford University Committee for Archaeology, Oxford.

Cunliffe, B. (1988a) *Mount Batten, Plymouth: A Prehistoric and Roman Port*, Oxford University Committee for Archaeology Monograph 26, Oxford University Committee for Archaeology, Oxford.

Cunliffe, B. (1988b) *Greeks, Romans and Barbarians: Spheres of Interaction*, Batsford, London.

Cunliffe, B. (1991; 3rd edn) *Iron Age Communities in Britain*, Routledge, London. (4th edn 2005).

Cunliffe, B. (1993a) *Danebury*, B.T. Batsford/English Heritage, London.

Cunliffe, B. (1993b) *Fertility, propitiation and the gods in the British Iron Age*, Universiteit van Amsterdam, Vijftiende Kroon-Voordracht.

Cunliffe, B. (1995a) *Danebury: An Iron Age Hillfort in Hampshire. Vol 6: A Hillfort Community in Perspective*, CBA Research Report 102, London.

Cunliffe, B. (1995b) *Iron Age Britain*, B.T. Batsford/ English Heritage, London.

Cunliffe, B. (1997) *The ancient Celts*, Oxford University Press, Oxford; repr. Penguin, Harmondsworth, 1999.

Cunliffe, B. (2001) *Facing the Ocean. The Atlantic and its Peoples 8000 BC–AD 1500*, Oxford University Press, Oxford.

Cunliffe, B. (2006) 'Understanding hillforts: have we progressed?' in A. Payne, M. Corney and B. Cunliffe, *The Wessex Hillforts Project*, English Heritage, London, 151–62.

Cunliffe, B. (n.d.) *Danebury. The story of an Iron Age hillfort*, Hampshire County Council, Winchester.

Cunliffe, B. and Phillipson, D.W. (1968) 'Excavations at Eldon's Seat, Encombe, Dorset, England', *Proceedings of the Prehistoric Society* 34, 191–237.

Cunliffe, B. and Poole, C. (2000a) *The Danebury Environs Programme – The Prehistory of a Wessex Landscape, Vol. 2 Part 1 – Woolbury, Stockbridge, Hants 1989*, English Heritage/Oxford University Committee for Archaeology Monograph 49 (Part 1), Oxford.

Cunliffe, B. and Poole, C. (2000b) *The Danebury Environs Programme – The Prehistory of a Wessex Landscape, Vol. 2 Part 2 – Bury Hill, Upper Chalford, Hants, 1990*, English Heritage/Oxford University Committee for Archaeology Monograph 49 (Part 2), Oxford.

Cunnington, B.H. and Cunnington, M.E. (1913) 'Casterley Camp excavations', *Wiltshire Archaeological and Natural History Society Magazine* 38, 53–105.

Cunnington, M.E. (1917) 'Lidbury Camp', *Wiltshire Archaeological and Natural History Society Magazine* 40, 12–36.

Cunnington, M.E. (1925) 'Figsbury Rings: an account of excavations in 1924', *Wiltshire Archaeological Magazine* 43, 48–58.

Curwen, E.C. (1929) 'Excavations in the Trundle, Goodwood, 1928', *Sussex Archaeological Collections* 70, 33–85.

Curwen, E.C. (1931) 'Excavations in the Trundle', *Sussex Archaeological Collections* 72, 100–50.

Curwen, E.C. (1932) 'Excavations at Hollingbury Camp, Sussex', *Antiquaries Journal* 12, 1–16.

Curwen, E. and Curwen, E.C. (1926) 'Harrow Hill flint-mine excavation 1924–5', *Sussex Archaeological Collections* LXVII, 103–38.

Dark, K.R. (2002) *Theoretical Archaeology*, Duckworth, London.

Dark, P. (2000) *The Environment of Britain in the First Millennium AD*, Duckworth, London.

Darvill, T. and Wainwright, G. (2002) *Strumble-Preseli Ancient Communities and Environment Study*, SPACES, first report.

Darvill, T. and Wainwright, G. (2003a) 'Stone circles, oval settings and henges in south-west Wales and beyond', *The Antiquaries Journal* 83, 9–45.

Darvill, T. and Wainwright, G. (2003b) 'A cup-marked stone from Dan-y-garn, Mynachlog-Ddu, Pembrokeshire, and the pre-historic rock art from Wales', *Proceedings of the Prehistoric Society* 69, 253–64.

Darvill, T., Stamper, P. and Timby, J. (2002) *England: An Archaeological Guide*, Oxford University Press, Oxford.

Davies, D.G. (1967) 'The Guilsfield Hoard: a re-consideration', *Antiquaries Journal* 47, 95–108.

Davies, J.A. and Gregory, T. (1991) 'Excavations at

Thetford Castle, 1962 and 1985–6', in eds J.A. Davies, T. Gregory, A.J. Lawson, R. Rickett and A. Rogerson, *The Iron Age Forts of Norfolk*, East Anglian Archaeology 54, Norfolk Field Archaeology Division, Dereham, 1–30.

Davies, J.A., Gregory, T., Lawson, A.J., Rickett, R. and Rogerson, A. eds (1991) *The Iron Age Forts of Norfolk*, East Anglian Archaeology 54, Norfolk Field Archaeology Division, Dereham.

Davies, J.L. and Lynch, F. (2000) 'The late Bronze Age and Iron Age', in F. Lynch, S.H.R. Aldhouse-Green and J.L. Davies, *Prehistoric Wales*, Sutton Publishing, Stroud, 139–219.

Davis, V., Davis, A. and Markham, M. (2007) 'The sourcing and dispersal of prehistoric stone implements from Carrock Fell, Cumbria', in ed. P. Cherry, *Studies in Northern Prehistory. Essays in Memory of Clare Fell*, Cumberland and Westmorland Antiquarian and Archaeological Society, 99–114.

de Jersey, P. (1996) *Celtic coinage in Britain*, Shire Publications, Princes Risborough.

de Silva, P. and Rachman, S. (2004) *Obsessive–Compulsive Disorder*, Oxford University Press, Oxford.

Denison, S. (1998) 'Ridgeway hillforts reveal their little differences', Editorial, *British Archaeology* 31.

Detsicas, A. (1983) *Peoples of Roman Britain. The Cantiaci*, Alan Sutton, Stroud.

Dixon, P. (1972a) 'Crickley Hill 1969–71', *Antiquity* 46, 49–52.

Dixon, P. (1972b) 'Crickley Hill fourth report', unpublished report.

Dixon, P. (1973) 'Crickley Hill fifth report', unpublished report.

Dixon, P. (1976) 'Crickley Hill, 1969–72', in ed. D.W. Harding, *Hillforts. Later Prehistoric Earthworks in Britain and Ireland*, Academic Press, London, 162–76.

Dixon, P. (1988a) 'The Neolithic settlements on Crickley Hill', in eds C. Burgess, P. Topping, C. Mordant and M. Maddison, *Enclosures and Defences in the Neolithic of Western Europe*, British Archaeology, Oxford, 75–87.

Dixon, P. (1988b) 'Crickley Hill, 1969–1987', *Current Archaeology* 110, 73–8.

Dixon, P. (1994) *Crickley Hill: The Hillfort Defences*, Crickley Hill Trust, University of Nottingham, Nottingham.

Dixon, P. and Borne, P. (1977) *Crickley Hill and Gloucestershire Prehistory*, Gloucestershire County Council for Crickley Hill Trust, Gloucester.

Dobney, K. and Ervynck, A. (2007) 'To fish or not to fish? Evidence for the possible avoidance of fish during the Iron Age around the North Sea', in eds C. Haselgrove and T. Moore, *The Later Iron Age in Britain and Beyond*, Oxbow Books, Oxford, 403–18.

Donachie, J.D. and Field, D.J. (1994) 'Cissbury Ring, Sussex', *Sussex Archaeological Collections* 132, 25–32.

Dowden, W.A. (1957) 'Little Solsbury Hill Camp. Report on excavations of 1955 and 1956', *Proceedings of the Bristol University Speleological Society* 8, 18–29.

Dowden, W.A. (1962) 'Little Solsbury Hill Camp. Report on the excavations of 1958', *Proceedings of the Bristol University Speleological Society* 9, 177–82.

Drewett, P. and Hamilton, S. (1999) 'Marking time and making space. Excavations and landscape studies at the Caburn hillfort, East Sussex, 1996–98', *Sussex Archaeological Collections* 137, 7–37.

Driver, T. (2007a) *Pembrokeshire. Historic Landscapes from the Air*, RCAHMW, Aberystwyth.

Driver, T. (2007b) 'Hillforts and human movement: unlocking the Iron Age landscapes of mid Wales', in eds A. Fleming and R. Hingley, *Prehistoric and Roman Landscapes*, Windgather Press, Bollington, 83–100.

Dunning, G.C. (1946) 'Chillerton Down Camp, Gatcombe, Isle of Wight', *Proceedings of the Isle of Wight Natural History and Archaeological Society*, 51–3.

Dunning, G.C. (1976) 'Salmonsbury, Bourton-on-the-Water, Gloucestershire', in ed. D.W. Harding, *Hillforts. Later Prehistoric Earthworks in Britain and Ireland*, Academic Press, London, 75–118.

Dyer, J. (1976) 'Ravensburgh Castle, Hertfordshire', in ed. D.W. Harding, *Hillforts. Later Prehistoric Earthworks in Britain and Ireland*, Academic Press, London, 153–9.

Dyer, J. (1981) *Hillforts of England and Wales*, Shire Books, Princes Risborough.

Dyer, J. (1990) *Ancient Britain*, B.T. Batsford, London; repr. Routledge, London, 1997.

Dymond, C.W. (1882) 'Dolebury and Cadbury: two Somersetshire camps', *Journal of the British Archaeological Association* 38, 398–419.

Dymond, C.W. (1902) *Worlebury. An Ancient Stronghold in the County of Somerset*, privately published, Bristol.

Edmonds, M. and Seaborne, T. (2001) *Prehistory in the Peak*, Tempus, Stroud.

Ellis, C. and Rawlings, M. (2001) 'Excavations at Balksbury Camp, Andover, 1995–97', *Proceedings of the Hampshire Field Club and Archaeological Society* 56, 21–94.

Ellison, A. and Drewett, P. (1971) 'Pits and post-holes in the British Early Iron Age: some alternative explanations', *Proceedings of the Prehistoric Society* XXXVII Pt. 1, 183–91.

Engineering Archaeological Services (2006) *Caer Drewyn*, internal topographical and geophysical surveys, Denbighshire County Council, Ruthin.

Evans, E. Estyn (1957) *Irish Folk Ways*, Routledge and Kegan Paul, London.

Evans, J. (1980) *Worlebury. The story of the Iron Age Hillfort at Weston-super-Mare*, Woodspring Museum, Weston-super-Mare.

Fell, C.I. (1937) 'The Hunsbury hillfort, Northants: a new survey of the material', *Archaeological Journal* 93, 57–100.

Fell, C.I. (1962) 'Shenberrow Hill Camp, Stanton, Gloucestershire', *Transactions of the Bristol and Gloucestershire Archaeological Society* 80, 16–41.

Finney, J. Bryant (2006) *Middle Iron Age Warfare of the Hillfort Dominated Zone c.400 BC to c.150 BC*, BAR British Series 423, Oxford.

Firth, A., Watson, K. and Ellis, C. (1998) *Tamar Estuaries Historic Environment*, Plymouth Archaeology Occasional Publication 3, Plymouth City Council/ Trust for Wessex Archaeology, Plymouth.

Fitzpatrick, A.P. (1997) 'Everyday life in Iron Age Wessex', in eds A. Gwilt and C. Haselgrove, *Reconstructing Iron Age Societies*, Oxbow Monograph 71, Oxford, 73–86.

Fleming, A.F. (1979) 'The Dartmoor Reaves: boundary patterns and behaviour patterns in the second millennium BC', *Proceedings of the Devon Archaeological Society* 37, 115–31.

Fleming, A.F. (1988) *The Dartmoor Reaves: Exploring Prehistoric Land Divisions*, Batsford, London.

Forde, Daryll, Griffiths, W.E., Hogg, A.H.A. and Houlder, C. (1963) 'Excavations at Pen Dinas, Aberystwyth', *Archaeologia Cambrensis* 112, 125–53.

Forde-Johnston, J. (1964) 'A hoard of flat-axes from Moel Arthur', *Journal of the Flintshire Historical Society* 21, 99–100.

Forde-Johnston, J. (1976a) *Prehistoric Britain and Ireland*, J.M. Dent and Sons, London.

Forde-Johnston, J. (1976b) *Hillforts of the Iron Age in England and Wales*. Liverpool University Press, Liverpool.

Foster, J. (2000) 'Possible mirror', in eds J.C. Barrett, P.W.M. Freeman and A. Woodward, *Cadbury Castle Somerset. The Later Prehistoric and Early Historic Archaeology*, English Heritage Archaeological

Report 20, English Heritage, London, 197.

Foster, J. and Saunders, C. (2000) 'Harness equipment', in eds J.C. Barrett, P.W.M. Freeman and A. Woodward, *Cadbury Castle Somerset. The Later Prehistoric and Early Historic Archaeology*, English Heritage Archaeological Report 20, English Heritage, London, 233–35.

Fowler, E. (1960) 'The metalwork', in P.J. Fowler, 'Excavations at Madmarston Camp, Swalcliffe 1957–8', *Oxoniensia* XXV, 41.

Fowler, P.J. (1960) 'Excavations at Madmarston Camp, Swalcliffe 1957–8,' *Oxoniensia* XXV, 3–48.

Fowler, P.J. (1964) 'Cross-dykes of the Ebble–Nadder ridge', *The Wiltshire Archaeological and Natural History Magazine* 59, 46–57.

Fox, A. (1952) 'Hill-slope forts and related earthworks in south-western England and South Wales', *Archaeological Journal* CIX, 1–22.

Fox, A., Radford, C.A.R. and Shorter, A.H. (1949–50) 'Report on the excavations at Milber Down, 1937–8', *Proceedings of the Devonshire Archaeological Exploration Society* 4, 27–66.

Fox, C.F. (1932) *The Personality of Britain*, National Museum of Wales, Cardiff.

Fox, C.F. (1946) *A Find of the Early Iron Age from Llyn Cerrig Bach, Anglesey*, National Museum of Wales, Cardiff.

Fox, C.F. and Fox, A. (1934) 'Forts and farms on Margam Mountain, Glamorgan', *Antiquity* 8, 395–413.

Freeman, P.W.M. (2000) 'Antiquarian and archaeological research 1542–1965', in eds J.C. Barrett, P.W.M. Freeman and A. Woodward, *Cadbury Castle Somerset. The Later Prehistoric and Early Historic Archaeology*, English Heritage Archaeological Report 20, English Heritage, London, 6–8.

Frodsham, P., Hedley, I. and Young, R. (2007) 'Putting the neighbours in their place? Displays of position and possession in northern 'Cheviot' hillfort design', in eds C. Haselgrove and T. Moore, *The Later Iron Age in Britain and Beyond*, Oxbow Books, Oxford, 250–65.

Gale, F. (2007) ' Recent survey work on six hillforts in north east Wales', in ed. Oswestry Borough Council, *The archaeology and landscape of the North Shropshire Marches*, Report of the first Seminar of the Old Oswestry Landscape and Archaeology project. Oswestry September 15th, 2007, Oswestry Borough Council, Oswestry, 8–11.

Gale, J. (2003) *Prehistoric Dorset*, Tempus, Stroud.

Gardner, W. (1910) 'Pen y corddyn, near Abergele', *Archaeologia Cambrensis* 10, 79–156.

Gardner, W. (1922) 'The ancient hill fort known as Caer Drewyn, Merionethshire', *Archaeologia Cambrensis* 77, 108–25.

Gardner, W. (1926) 'The native hillforts in North Wales and their defences', *Archaeologia Cambrensis* 7th series 6, 221–82.

Gardner, W. and Savory, H.N. (1964) *Dinorben: a hillfort occupied in the Early Iron Age and Roman times*, National Museum of Wales, Cardiff.

Gelling, P.S. (1963) 'Excavations at the Hill-Fort on South Barrule', *Proceedings of the Isle of Man Natural History and Antiquarian Society* new series 6.3, 314–23.

Gelling, P.S. (1970) 'Excavations at Pilsdon Pen, 1969', *Proceedings of the Dorset Natural History Archaeological Society* 91 (1969), 177–8.

Gelling, P.S. (1971) 'Excavations at Pilsdon Pen, 1970', *Proceedings of the Dorset Natural History Archaeological Society* 92 (1970), 126–7.

Gelling, P.S. (1972) 'Excavations at Pilsdon Pen hillfort', *Proceedings of the Dorset Natural History Archaeological Society* 93 (1971), 133–4.

Gelling, P.S. (1977) 'Excavations at Pilsdon Pen, Dorset, 1964–71', *Proceedings of the Prehistoric Society* 43, 263–86.

Gelling, P.S. and Stanford, S.C. (1967) 'Dark Age pottery and Iron Age ovens', *Transactions of the Birmingham Archaeological Society* 32, 77.

Giddens, A. (1984) *The Constitution of Society: Outline of the Theory of Structuration*, Polity Press, Cambridge.

Glen, T.A. (1935) 'Distribution of the Graig Lwyd axe and its associated cultures', *Archaeologia Cambrensis* 90, 189–214.

Gordon, A. (1940) 'The excavation of Gurnard's Head, an Iron Age cliff castle in western Cornwall', *Archaeological Journal* 97, 96–111.

Gosden, C. and Lock, G. (2007) 'The aesthetics of landscape on the Berkshire Downs', in eds C. Haselgrove and R. Pope, *The Earlier Iron Age in Britain and the Near Continent*, Oxbow Books, Oxford, 279–92.

Gough, J.W. (1930) '*The mines of Mendip*', Clarendon Press, Oxford.

Gray, H. St. George (1922) 'Trial-excavations at Cadbury Camp, Tickenham, Somerset, 1922', *Proceedings of the Somersetshire Archaeological and Natural History Society* LXVIII, 8–20.

Gray, H. St. George (1924) 'Excavations at Ham Hill, South Somerset. Part I'. *Proceedings of the Somersetshire Archaeological and Natural History Society* 70, 104–116.

Gray, H. St. George (1925) 'Excavations at Ham Hill, South Somerset. Part II'. *Proceedings of the Somersetshire Archaeological and Natural History Society* 71, 55–75.

Gray, H. St. George (1926) 'Excavations at Ham Hill, South Somerset. Part III'. *Proceedings of the Somersetshire Archaeological and Natural History Society* 72, 55–68.

Gray, H. St. George (1936) 'Excavations at Combe Beacon, Combe St. Nicolas, 1935'. *Proceedings of the Somersetshire Archaeological and Natural History Society* 82, 83–107.

Green, M. (1986) *The Gods of the Celts*, Alan Sutton, Stroud.

Green, M. (1992) *Animals in Celtic Life and Myth*, Routledge, London.

Green, M. (2003) *The Gods of Roman Britain*, Shire Publications, Princes Risborough.

Green, M. and Howell, R. (2000) *Celtic Wales*, Cardiff University Press/The Western Mail.

Gregory, T. and Rogerson, A. (1991) 'General conclusions', in eds J.A. Davies, T. Gregory, A.J. Lawson, R. Rickett and A. Rogerson, *The Iron Age Forts of Norfolk*, East Anglian Archaeology 54, Norfolk Field Archaeology Division, Dereham, 69–72.

Griffith, F.M and Wilkes, E.M. (2006) 'The land named from the sea? Coastal archaeology and place names of Bigbury Bay, Devon'. *Archaeological Journal* 163, 67–91.

Griffiths, W.B. (1989) 'The sling and its place in the Roman imperial army', in ed. C. van Driel-Murray, *Roman Military Equipment: The Sources of Evidence*, BAR International Series 476, Oxford, 255–79.

Griffiths, W.E. and Hogg, A.H.A. (1956) 'The hill-fort on Conway Mountain, Caernarvonshire', *Archaeologia Cambrensis* 105, 49–80.

Guilbert, G.C. (1973) 'Moel y Gaer, Rhosesmor', *Current Archaeology* 37, 38–44.

Guilbert, G.C (1974) 'Llanstephan Castle: 1973 Interim Report', *Carmarthenshire Antiquary* 10, 37–48.

Guilbert, G.C. (1975) 'Planned hillfort interiors', *Proceedings of the Prehistoric Society* 41, 203–21.

Guilbert, G.C. (1976a) 'Moel y Gaer (Rhosesmor) 1972–1973 an area excavation in the interior', in ed. D.W. Harding, *Hillforts. Later Prehistoric Earthworks in Britain and Ireland*, Academic Press, London, 303–17.

Guilbert, G.C. (1976b) 'Ratlinghope/Stitt Hill, Shropshire: Earthwork enclosures and cross-dykes', *Bulletin of the Board of Celtic Studies* XXIV, 363–73.

Guilbert, G.C. (1980) 'Dinorben C14 dates', *Current Archaeology* 6, 182–8.

Guilbert, G.C. (1981) 'Hill-fort functions and populations: a sceptical viewpoint', in ed. G. Guilbert, *Hill-fort Studies. Essays for A.H.A. Hogg*, Leicester University Press, Leicester, 104–19.

Gwilt, A. (2007) 'Silent Silures? Locating people and places in the Iron Age of south Wales', in eds C. Haselgrove and T. Moore, *The Later Iron Age in Britain and Beyond*, Oxbow Books, Oxford, 297–328.

Hamilton, S. (1998) 'Using elderly data bases. Iron Age pit deposits at the Caburn, East Sussex, and related sites', *Sussex Archaeological Collections* 136, 23–39.

Hamilton, S. and Manley, J. (1997) 'Points of view. Prominent enclosures in 1st millennium Sussex. *Sussex Archaeolgical Collections* 135, 93–112.

Hamilton, S. and Manley, J. (2001) 'Hillforts, monumentality and place: a chronological and topographic review of first millennium BC hillforts of southeast England', *European Journal of Archaeology* 4.1, 7–42.

Hamilton-Dyer, S. and Maltby, M. (2000) 'The animal bones from a sample of Iron Age contexts', in eds J.C. Barrett, P.W.M. Freeman and A. Woodward, *Cadbury Castle Somerset. The Later Prehistoric and Early Historic Archaeology*, English Heritage Archaeological Report 20, English Heritage, London, 278–91.

Harbison, P. (1971) 'Wooden and stone *Chevaux-de-Frise* in central and western Europe', *Proceedings of the Prehistoric Society* 37, 195–225.

Harcourt, R. (1970) 'The animal remains from Balksbury Camp', in G. Wainwright, 'The excavations of Balksbury Camp, Andover, Hants.', *Proceedings of the Hampshire Field Club and Archaeological Society*, 26.

Harding, D.W. (1982) *Climate Change in Later Prehistory*, Edinburgh University Press, Edinburgh.

Harding, D.W. (2004) *The Iron Age in Northern Britain*, Routledge, London.

Harding, D.W. (2006) 'Redefining the northern British Iron Age', *Oxford Journal of Archaeology* 45.1, 61–82.

Harding, D.W. (2007) *The Archaeology of Celtic Art*, Routledge, London.

Harris, E., Harris, J. and James, N.D.G. (2003) *Oak. A British History*, Windgather Press, Bollington.

Hartley, B.R. (1957) 'The Wandlebury Iron Age hill-fort excavations of 1955–6', *Proceedings of the Cambridgeshire Antiquarian Society* 50, 1–28.

Haselgrove, C. (1976) 'External trade as a stimulus to urbanisation', in eds B. Cunliffe and T. Rowley, *Oppida: The Beginnings of Urbanism in Barbarian Europe*, BAR Supplementary Series 11, Oxford, 25–49.

Haselgrove, C. (1996) 'The Iron Age', in ed. R. Newman, *The Archaeology of Lancashire: Present State and Future Priorities*, Lancaster University Archaeological Unit, Lancaster, 61–74.

Haselgrove, C. and Mays, M. (2000) 'Iron Age coinage', in eds J.C. Barrett, P.W.M. Freeman and A. Woodward, *Cadbury Castle Somerset. The Later Prehistoric and Early Historic Archaeology*, English Heritage Archaeological Report 20, English Heritage, London, 248–52.

Haselgrove, C. and Millett, M. (1997) 'Verlamion reconsidered', in eds A. Gwilt and C. Haselgrove, *Reconstructing Iron Age Societies*, Oxbow Monograph 71, Oxford, 82–96.

Haselgrove, C. and Moore, T. (2007) 'New narratives of the Later Iron Age', in eds C. Haselgrove and T. Moore, *The Later Iron Age in Britain and Beyond*, Oxbow Books, Oxford, 1–15.

Haselgrove, C. and Pope, R. (2007) 'Characterising the earlier Iron Age', in eds C. Haselgrove and R. Pope, *The Earlier Iron Age in Britain and the Near Continent*, Oxbow Books, Oxford, 1–23.

Haselgrove, C., Turnbull, P. and Fitts, R.L. (1990) 'Stanwick, North Yorkshire, Part 1. Recent research and previous archaeological investigations', *Archaeological Journal* 147, 1–15.

Haselgrove, C., Armit, I., Champion, T., Creighton, J., Gwilt, A., Hill, J.D., Hunter, F. and Woodward, A. (2001) *Understanding the British Iron Age: An Agenda for Action*, report for the Iron Age Research Seminar and Council of the Prehistoric Society, Trust for Wessex Archaeology, Salisbury.

Haslam, R. (1979) *The Buildings of Wales. Powys*, Penguin Books/University of Wales Press, Harmondsworth/Cardiff.

Hawes, P. and Holloway, M. (1994) *Hengistbury Head Archaeology Trail*, Bournemouth Leisure and Tourism, Bournemouth Borough Council, Bournemouth.

Hawkes, C.F.C. (1931) 'Hill forts', *Antiquity* 5, 60–97.

Hawkes, C.F.C. (1939) 'The excavations at Quarley Hill, 1938', *Proceedings of the Hampshire Field Club and Archaeological Society* 14 (1940), 136–94.

Hawkes, C.F.C. (1940a) 'The excavations at Bury Hill, 1939', *Proceedings of the Hampshire Field Club and Archaeological Society* 14, 291–337.

Hawkes, C.F.C. (1940b) 'An iron torc from Spettisbury Rings, Dorset', *Archaeological Journal* XCVII, 112–14.

Hawkes, C.F.C. (1971) 'Fence, wall, dump, from Troy to Hod', in eds D. Hill and M. Jesson, *The Iron Age and its Hill-forts*, Southampton Archaeological Society, Southampton, 5–18.

Hawkes, C.F.C. (1977) *Pytheas*, 8th J.N.L. Myers Memorial Lecture, published privately, Oxford.

Hawkes, C.F.C., Myres, J.N.L. and Stevens, C.G. (1930) *St Catharine's Hill, Winchester*, Hampshire Field Club and Archaeological Society, Winchester.

Hawkes, J. (1998) *Mount Batten Headland: History and archaeology*, Plymouth City Museum and Art Gallery, Plymouth.

Hemp, W.J. (1928) 'A La Tène shield from Moel Hiraddug, Flintshire', *Archaeologia Cambrensis* 83, 253–84.

Hencken, T.C. (1938) 'The excavation of the Iron Age camp on Bredon Hill, Gloucestershire, 1935–37', *Archaeological Journal* 95, 1–111.

Henderson, J.C. (2007) 'The Atlantic west in the earlier Iron Age', in eds C. Haselgrove and R. Pope, *The Earlier Iron Age in Britain and the Near Continent*, Oxbow Books, Oxford, 306–27.

Herbert, E.W. (1993) *Iron, Gender and Power: Rituals of Transformation in African Societies*, Indiana University Press, Bloomington.

Herring, P. (1994) 'The cliff castles and hillforts of West Penwith in the light of recent work at Maen Castle and Treryn Dinas', *Cornish Archaeology* 33, 40–56.

Highways Agency, Oxford Archaeology, RPS and Partners (2007) *A30 Bodmin to Indian Queens Road Improvement Scheme. Archaeology and Ecology*, pamphlet, Highways Agency, London.

Hill, D. (1977) 'Offa's and Wat's Dyke: some aspects of recent work', *Transactions of the Lancashire and Cheshire Antiquarian Society*, 79, 21–33.

Hill, J.D. (1995) *Ritual and Rubbish in the Iron Age of Wessex*. British Archaeological Reports British Series 242, Oxford.

Hill, J.D. (1996) 'Hill-forts and the Iron Age of Wessex', in eds T. Champion and J. Collis, *The Iron Age in Britain: Recent Trends*, Sheffield Academic Press, Sheffield, 95–116.

Hill, J.D. (2007) 'The dynamics of social change in later Iron Age eastern and south-eastern England', in eds C. Haselgrove and T. Moore, *The Later Iron Age in Britain and Beyond*, Oxbow Books, Oxford, 16–40.

Hill, M. (2004) *Coasts and Coastal Management*, Hodder Murray, London.

Hill, P. and Wileman, J. (2002) *Landscapes of War. The Archaeology of Aggression and Defence*, Tempus, Stroud.

Hingley, R. (1984) 'Towards social analysis in archaeology: Celtic society in the Iron Age of the Upper Thames Valley', in eds B. Cunliffe and D. Miles, *Aspects of the Iron Age in Central Southern Britain*, University of Oxford Committee for Archaeology Monograph 2, Oxford, 72–88.

Hingley, R. (1990) 'Iron Age 'currency bars': the archaeological and social context', *Archaeological Journal* 147, 91–117.

Hingley, R. (1997) 'Iron, ironworking and regeneration: a study of the symbolic meaning of metalworking in Iron Age Britain', in eds A. Gwilt and C. Haselgrove, *Reconstructing Iron Age Societies*, Oxbow Monograph 71, Oxford, 9–18.

Hird, N. (2000) 'Celtic hillforts and settlements in the Iron Age', in eds J. Leonard, D. Preshous, M. Roberts, J. Smyth and C. Train, *The Gale of Life. Two Thousand Years in South-West Shropshire*, South-West Shropshire Archaeological Society/Logaston Press, Little Logaston, 1–9.

Hirst, S. and Rahtz, P. (1996) 'Liddington Castle and the battle of Baden: excavations and research 1976', *Archaeological Journal* 153, 1–59.

Hobbs, R. (1996) *British Iron Age coins in the British Museum*, British Museum Press, London.

Hogg, A.H.A. (1962) 'Garn Boduan and Tre'r Ceiri, excavations at two Caernarvonshire hill-forts', *Archaeological Journal* 117, 1–39.

Hogg, A.H.A. (1972) 'Carn Goch, Carmarthenshire', *Archaeologia Cambrensis* 123, 46–8.

Hogg, A.H.A. (1973a) 'Gaer Fawr and Carn Ingli: two major Pembrokeshire hill-forts', *Archaeologia Cambrensis* 122, 69–84.

Hogg, A.H.A. (1973b) 'Excavations at Harding's Down West Fort, Gower', *Archaeologia Cambrensis* 122, 55–68.

Hogg, A.H.A. (1975) *Hill-forts of Britain*, Hart-Davis MacGibbon, London.

Hogg, A.H.A. (1979) *British Hillforts: An Index*, Hillfort Study Group Occasional Paper No. 1, BAR British Series 1, Oxford.

Holmes, A. (1965) *Principles of Physical Geology*, Thomas Nelson, London.

Holmes, J. (1984) 'Excavations at Hollingbury Camp, Sussex. 1967–9', *Sussex Archaeological Collections* 122, 29–53.

Hope-Taylor, B. (1977) *Yeavering*, Department of the Environment Archaeology Reports 7, HMSO, London.

Hopewell, D. (n.d.) *Tre'r Ceiri hillfort Llyn. Gwynedd*

Archaeological Trust Conservation Project 1989–99, unpublished internal project report.

Houlder, C. (1961) 'Rescue excavations at Moel Hiraddug I – excavations in 1954–55', *Journal of the Flintshire Archaeological Society* 19, 1–20.

Houlder, C. (1978) *Wales: An Archaeological Guide. The Prehistoric, Roman and Early Medieval Field Monuments*, Faber and Faber, London.

Howell, R. (2006) *Searching for the Silures. An Iron Age tribe in south-east Wales*, Tempus, Stroud.

Howells, R. (1980) *The Sounds Between*, Five Arches Press, Tenby.

Hughes, G. (1994) 'Old Oswestry hillfort: excavations by W.J. Varley 1939–40', *Archaeologia Cambrensis* 143, 46–91.

Hughes, H.H. (1907) 'Report of excavations carried out at Tre'Ceiri in 1906,' *Archaeologia Cambrensis* 61, 38–62.

Hughes, R.E. (1993) 'Land, agricultural resources and population in parts of Penllyn in 1318', *Journal of the Merioneth Historical and Record Society* 11.4, 355–78.

Hume, C.R. and Jones, G.W. (1959) 'Excavations at Nesscliffe Hill', *Transactions of the Salop Archaeological Society* 56, 129–32.

Humphrey, J. (2007) 'Simple tools for rough tasks or tough tools for simple tasks? Analysis and experiment in Iron Age flint utilisation', in eds C. Haselgrove and R. Pope, *The Earlier Iron Age in Britain and the Near Continent*, Oxbow Books, Oxford, 144–59.

Hunter, F. (2001) 'The carnyx in Iron Age Europe', *Antiquaries Journal* 81, 77–108.

Hutton, R. (1991) *The Pagan Religions of the Ancient British Isles. Their Nature and Legacy*, Blackwell, Oxford.

Ingrem, C. (2003) 'The regional context of the animal bones from Uffington Castle', in eds D. Miles, S. Palmer, G. Lock, C. Gosden and A.M. Cromarty, *Uffington White Horse and its Landscape. Investigations at White Horse Hill, Uffington, 1989–95 and Tower Hill, Ashbury, 1993–94*, Oxford Archaeology Thames Valley Landscapes Monograph No. 18, Oxford University School of Archaeology, Oxford, 283–5.

Jack, G.H. and Hayter, A.G.K. (1925) 'Excavations at the site of Caplar Camp', *Transactions of the Woolhope Naturalist's Field Club*, 83–8.

Jackson, J.W. (1930) 'Animal remains found at Kingsdown Camp', in H. St. George Gray, 'Excavations at Kingsdown Camp, Mells, Somerset, 1927–9', *Archaeologia* 80, 95–7.

Jackson, J.W. (1939) 'Report on the animal remains', in C.F.C. Hawkes, 'The excavations at Quarley Hill 1938', *Proceedings of the Hampshire Field Club and Archaeological Society* 14, (1940), 191–92.

Jackson, R.A. and Potter, T.W. (1996) *Excavations at Stonea, Cambridgeshire 1980–85*, British Museum Press, London.

James, S. (1999) *The Atlantic Celts. Ancient People or Modern Invention?* British Museum Press, London.

James, S. (2007) 'A bloodless past: the pacification of early Iron Age Britain', in eds C. Haselgrove and R. Pope, *The Earlier Iron Age in Britain and the Near Continent*, Oxbow Books, Oxford, 160–73.

Jessup, R.F. (1933) 'Bigberry Camp, Harbledown, Kent', *Archaeological Journal* 89, 87–115.

Jones, M. (2007) *Feast: From Hunter-Gatherers to TV Dinners*, Oxford University Press, Oxford.

Jope, E.M. (2000) *Early Celtic Art in the British Isles*, Clarendon Press, Oxford.

Judge, P.G. (2000) 'Coping with crowded conditions', in eds F. Aureli and F.B.M. De Waal, *Natural Conflict Resolution*, University of California Press, Berkeley, 129–54.

Keef, P. (1953) 'Two gold pennanular ornaments from Harting Beacon, Sussex', *Antiquaries Journal* 33, 204–6.

Keeley, L.H. (1996) *War before Civilisation: The Myth of the Peaceful Savage*, Oxford University Press, New York.

Kelly, R.S. (1988) 'Two late prehistoric circular enclosures near Harlech, Gwynedd', *Proceedings of the Prehistoric Society* 54, 101–51.

Kenyon, K.M. (1942) 'Excavations at the Wrekin, Shropshire, 1939', *Archaeological Journal* 99, 99–109.

Kenyon, K.M. (1954) 'Excavations at Sutton Walls, Herefordshire 1948–51', *Archaeological Journal* 110, 1–87.

Kidd, A. (2004) 'Northamptonshire in the first millennium BC', in ed. M. Tingle, *The Archaeology of Northamptonshire*, Northamptonshire Archaeological Society, Northampton.

King, A. (1987) *The Ingleborough Hillfort, North Yorkshire*, Bulletin of the Prehistory Research Section, Yorkshire Archaeological Society, Leeds.

King, A. (1991) 'Food production and consumption – meat', in ed. R.F.H. Jones, *Britain in the Roman Period: Recent Trends*, J.R. Collis, Sheffield, 15–20.

King, D. (1962) 'Bury Wood Camp, report on excavations, 1960', *Wiltshire Archaeological and Natural History Magazine* lviii, No. 210, 185–208.

Laing, L. and Laing, J. (1995) *Celtic Britain and Ireland.*

Art and Society, BCA, London.

Lamb, H.H. (1981) 'Climate from 1000 BC to AD 1000', in eds M. Jones and G. Dimbleby, *The Environment of Man. The Iron Age to the Anglo-Saxon Period*, BAR British Series 87, Oxford, 53–65.

Lane, T.W. and Morris, E.L eds (2001) *A Millennium of Salt Making. Prehistoric and Romano-British Salt Production in the Fenland*, Lincolnshire Archaeology Heritage Report 4, Lincoln.

Leeds, E. (1927) 'Excavations at Chun Castle, in Penwith, Cornwall (second report)', *Archaeologia* 76, 205–40.

Leeds, E. (1931) 'Excavations at Chun Castle, in Penwith, Cornwall', *Archaeologia* 81, 33–42.

Liddiard, R. (2005) *Castles in Context*, Windgather Press, Bollington.

Lines, A.H.H. (1889) 'Breidden Hill Camp and other camps in the vicinity', *Montgomery Collections*, 327–40.

Lock, G. and Gosden, C. (1997) 'The hillforts of the Ridgeway Project: excavations at Segsbury Camp 1996', *South Midlands Archaeology* 27, 69–77.

Lock, G. and Gosden, C. (1998) 'The hillforts of the Ridgeway Project: excavations at Segsbury Camp 1997', *South Midlands Archaeology* 28, 54–63.

Lock, G. and Gosden, C. (2005) 'Community and landscape – the creation of Segsbury, a new place', in eds G. Lock, C. Gosden and P. Daly, *Segsbury Camp: Excavations in 1996 and 1997 at an Iron Age Hillfort on the Oxfordshire Ridgeway*, Oxford University School of Archaeology Monograph 61, Oxford, 133–51.

Lock, G., Miles, D., Palmer, S. and Cromarty, A.M. (2003) 'The hillfort', in eds D. Miles, S. Palmer, G. Lock, C. Gosden and A.M. Cromarty, *Uffington White Horse and its Landscape. Investigations at White Horse Hill, Uffington, 1989–95 and Tower Hill, Ashbury, 1993–94*, Oxford Archaeology Thames Valley Landscapes Monograph No. 18, Oxford University School of Archaeology, Oxford, 79–126.

Lock, G., Gosden, C. and Daly, P. (2005) *Segsbury Camp: Excavations in 1996 and 1997 at an Iron Age Hillfort on the Oxfordshire Ridgeway*, Oxford University School of Archaeology Monograph 61, Oxford.

Longley, D. (1998) 'Bryn Eryr: an enclosed settlement of the Iron Age on Anglesey', *Proceedings of the Prehistoric Society* 64, 225–74.

Loveday, R. (1998) 'Double entrance henges – routes to the past', in eds A. Gibson and P. Simpson, *Prehistoric Ritual and Religion*, Sutton Publishing, Stroud, 14–31.

Lynch, F.M. (1991; 2nd edn) *Prehistoric Anglesey*, Anglesey Antiquarian Society, Llangefni.

Lynch, F. (1995) *A Guide to Ancient and Historic Wales. Gwynedd*, HMSO, London.

Lynch, F. (2000) 'The earlier Neolithic', in F. Lynch, S. Aldhouse-Green and J.L Davies, *Prehistoric Wales*, Sutton Publishing, Stroud, 42–78.

MacDonald, P. (2005) 'The poker', in ed. N. Thomas, *Conderton Camp Worcestershire: A Small Middle Iron Age Hillfort on Bredon Hill*, CBA Research Report 143, Council for British Archaeology, York, 153–6.

McGrail, S. (1981) *The Ship. Rafts, Boats and Ships from Prehistoric Times to the Medieval Era*, HMSO, London.

McGrail, S. (1995) 'Celtic seafaring and transport', in ed. M.J. Green, *The Celtic World*, Routledge, London, 254–81.

McOmish, D., Field, D. and Brown, G. (2002) 'The field archaeology of the Salisbury Plain Training Area'. English Heritage, Swindon.

MacGregor, M. and Simpson, D.D.A. (1963) 'A group of iron objects from Barbury Castle, Wilts.', *Wiltshire Archaeological Magazine* 58, 394–402.

Mair, L. (1964) *Primitive Government*, Penguin Books, Harmondsworth.

Maltby, J.M. (n.d.) *The Animal Bones from the 1973 Excavations at Balksbury, Hampshire*, Draft Ancient Monuments Laboratory Report.

Manley, J. (1990) 'Preliminary survey of some undated small settlements in north-east Wales', *Archaeologia Cambrensis* CXXXIX, 21–55.

Manning, W.H. (1985) *Catalogue of the Romano-British Iron Tools, Fittings and Weapons in the British Museum*, British Museum Publications, London.

Manning, W. (2001) *Roman Wales*, Cardiff University Press/The Western Mail, Cardiff.

Markey, M., Wilkes, E. and Darvill, T. (2002) 'Poole Harbour. An Iron Age port', *Current Archaeology* 181, Vol. XVI, No. 1, 7–11.

Mathews, D. (2007) 'Drink the view, sense the tribe. An interpretation of the views from the hillforts of the northern Marches', in ed. Oswestry Borough Council, *The archaeology and landscape of the North Shropshire Marches*, Report of the first Seminar of the Old Oswestry Landscape and Archaeology project. Oswestry September 15th, 2007, Oswestry Borough Council, Oswestry, 12–13.

Megaw, R. and Megaw, V. (1990) *Celtic Art. From its Beginnings to the Book of Kells*, Thames and Hudson, London.

Meiggs, R. (1982) *Trees and Timber in the Ancient Mediterranean World*, Oxford University Press, Oxford.

Mercer, R. (1981a) 'Excavations at Carn Brea, Illogan, Cornwall, 1970–73: a Neolithic fortified complex of the third millennium BC', *Cornish Archaeology* 20, 1–204.

Mercer, R. ed. (1981b) *Farming Practice in British Prehistory*, Edinburgh University Press, Edinburgh.

Mercer, R. (1989) 'The earliest defences in western Europe: Part I, warfare in the Neolithic', *Fortress* 2, 16–22.

Mercer, R. and Healy, F. (2004) 'Hambledon Hill, the view from 2004', *Past* 48, 10–11.

Miles, D. (2005) *The Tribes of Britain. Who Are We? And Where do We Come From?* Weidenfeld and Nicolson, London.

Miles D., Palmer, S., Lock, G., Gosden, C. and Cromarty, A.M. eds (2003a) *Uffington White Horse and its Landscape. Investigations at White Horse Hill, Uffington, 1989–95 and Tower Hill, Ashbury, 1993–94*, Oxford Archaeology Thames Valley Landscapes Monograph 18, Oxford University School of Archaeology, Oxford.

Miles, D., Palmer, S. and Cromarty, A.M. (2003b) 'The White Horse', in eds D. Miles, S. Palmer, G. Lock, C. Gosden and A.M. Cromarty, *Uffington White Horse and its Landscape. Investigations at White Horse Hill, Uffington, 1989–95 and Tower Hill, Ashbury, 1993–94*, Oxford Archaeology Thames Valley Landscapes Monograph 18, Oxford University School of Archaeology, Oxford, 61–78.

Miles, H. (1977) 'Excavations at Killibury hillfort, Egloshayle, 1975–6', *Cornish Archaeology* 16, 89–128.

Money, H. (1941) 'An interim report on excavations at High Rocks, Tunbridge Wells, 1940', *Sussex Archaeological Collections* 82, 104–9.

Money, H. (1960) 'Excavations at High Rocks 1954–56. Supplementary note', *Sussex Archaeological Collections* 100, 149–51.

Money, H. (1962) 'Excavations at High Rocks, Tunbridge Wells, 1954–56', *Sussex Archaeological Collections* 98, 173–222.

Money, H. (1968) 'Excavations in the Iron Age hillfort at High Rocks, near Tunbridge Wells, 1957–61', *Sussex Archaeological Collections* 106, 158–205.

Moore, T. (2007) 'The early to later Iron Age transition in the Severn-Cotswolds: enclosing the household?' in eds C. Haselgrove and R. Pope, *The Earlier Iron Age in Britain and the Near Continent*, Oxbow Books, Oxford, 259–78.

Moore-Colyer, R.J. (1976) *The Welsh Cattle Drovers*, University of Wales Press, Cardiff.

Moorhouse, G. (1998) 'Sun dancing. A medieval vision', Phoenix, London.

Morris, E.L. (1985) 'Prehistoric salt distributions: two case studies from western Britain', *Bulletin of the Board of Celtic Studies* 32, 336–79.

Morris, E.L. (2007) 'Making magic: later prehistoric and early Roman salt production in the Lincolnshire Fenland', in eds C. Haselgrove and T. Moore, *The Later Iron Age in Britain and Beyond*, Oxbow Books, Oxford, 430–43.

Morris, E.L. and Gelling, P. (1991) 'A note on The Berth', *Transactions of the Shropshire Archaeological and Historical Society* LXVII, 58–62.

Morris, S. and Buckley, D.G. (1978) 'Excavations at Danbury Camp, Essex, 1974 and 1977', *Essex Archaeology and History News* 10, 1–28.

Muir, R. (2004) *Landscape Encyclopaedia*, Windgather Press, Bollington.

Mulville, J. and Powell, A. (2005) 'The Iron Age animal bone', in eds G. Lock, C. Gosden and P. Daly, *Segsbury Camp: Excavations in 1996 and 1997 at an Iron Age Hillfort on the Oxfordshire Ridgeway*, Oxford University School of Archaeology Monograph 61, Oxford, 116–18.

Murphy, J.P. (1977) *Rufus Festus Avienus' Ora Maritima*, Chicago.

Musson, C.R. (1970) 'The Breiddin 1969', *Current Archaeology* 19, 215–18.

Musson, C.R. (1972) 'Two winters at the Breiddin', *Current Archaeology* 33, 263–7.

Musson, C.R. (1976) 'Excavations at the Breiddin 1969–1973', in ed. D.W. Harding, *Hillforts. Later Prehistoric Earthworks in Britain and Ireland*, Academic Press, London, 293–302.

Musson, C.R. (1981) 'Llanymynech hillfort', *Archaeology in Wales* 21, 31.

Musson, C.R. and Northover, J.P. (1989) 'Llanymynech hillfort, Powys and Shropshire. Observations on construction work 1981', *Montgomeryshire Collections* 77, 15–26.

Musson, C.R., Britnell, W.J. and Smith, A.G. (1991) *The Breiddin Hillfort*, CBA Research Report 76, London.

Musson, C.R., Britnell, W.J., Northover, J.P. and Salter, C.J. (1992) 'Excavations and metal-working at Llwyn Bryn-dinas hillfort, Llangedwyn, Clwyd', *Proceedings of the Prehistoric Society* 58, 265–83.

Mytum, H. (1996) 'Hillfort siting and monumentality: Castell Henllys and geographical information systems', *Archaeology in Wales* 36, 3–10.

Mytum, H. (1999) 'Castell Henllys', *Current Archaeology* 161, 164–72

Mytum, H. (2004) 'Policy and purpose in reconstruction at Castell Henllys Iron Age fort, Wales', in ed. J. Jameson, Jr, *The Reconstructed Past*, Alta Mira Press, Walnut Creek, 91–102.

Mytum, H. and Webster, C.J. (1989) 'A survey of the Iron Age enclosure and *chevaux-de-frise* at Carn Alw, Dyfed', *Proceedings of the Prehistoric Society* 55, 263–66.

Nash-Williams, V.E. (1933a) 'An early Iron Age hill-fort at Llanmelin, near Caerwent, Monmouthshire', *Archaeologia Cambrensis* 88, 237–315.

Nash-Williams, V.E. (1933b) 'The distribution of hill-forts and other earthworks in Wales and the Marches', in V.E. Nash-Williams, 'An early Iron Age hillfort at Llanmelin near Caerwent, Monmouthshire', *Archaeologia Cambrensis* 88, 237–46.

Nash-Williams, V.E. (1939) 'An early Iron Age coastal camp at Sudbrook, near the Severn tunnel, Monmouthshire', *Archaeologia Cambrensis* 94, 42–79.

Nayling, N., Maynard, D. and McGrail, S. (1994) 'Barlands Farm, Magor, Gwent: a Romano-British boat find', *Antiquity* 68, 596–603.

Needham, S. and Ambers, J. (1994) 'Redating Rams Hill and reconsidering Bronze Age enclosure', *Proceedings of the Prehistoric Society* 60, 225–44.

Needham, S.P., Lees, M.N., Hook, D.R. and Hughes, M.J. (1989) 'Developments in the early Bronze Age metallurgy of southern Britain', *World Archaeology* 20, 383–402.

Northover, P. (1995) 'The technology of metalwork. Bronze and gold', in ed. M.J. Green, *The Celtic World*, Routledge, London, 285–309.

O'Connor, B. and Foster, J. (2000) 'Copper alloy pins', in eds J.C. Barrett, P.W.M. Freeman and A. Woodward, *Cadbury Castle Somerset. The Later Prehistoric and Early Historic Archaeology*, English Heritage Archaeological Report 20, English Heritage, London, 192–4.

O'Connor, B., Foster, J. and Saunders, C. (2000) 'Violence', in eds J.C. Barrett, P.W.M. Freeman and A. Woodward, *Cadbury Castle Somerset. The Later Prehistoric and Early Historic Archaeology*, English Heritage Archaeological Report 20, English Heritage, London, 235–42.

O'Neil, B.H. St. J. (1934) 'Excavations at Titterstone Clee Hill Camp', *Shropshire Antiquaries Journal* 14, 13–32.

O'Neil, B.H. St. J. (1937) 'Excavations at the Breiddin Hill Camp, Montgomeryshire 1933–35', *Archaeologia Cambrensis* 92, 86–128.

O'Neil, B.H. St. J. (1942) 'Excavations at Ffridd Faldwyn camp, Montgomeryshire, 1937–39', *Archaeologia Cambrensis* 97, 1–57.

Ordnance Survey (1962) *Map of Southern Britain in the Iron Age*, Ordnance Survey, Chessington.

Osgood, R. and Monks, S. with Toms, J. (2000) *Bronze Age Warfare*, Sutton, Stroud.

Oswald, A. (1997) 'A doorway on the past: practical and mystical concerns in the orientation of roundhouse doorways', in eds A. Gwilt and C. Haselgrove, *Reconstructing Iron Age Societies*, Oxbow Monograph 71, Oxford, 87–95.

Oswald, A. and Pearson, T. (2005) 'Yeavering Bell hillfort', in eds P. Frodsham and C. O'Brien, *Yeavering. People, Power, Place*, Tempus, Stroud, 98–126.

Oswald, A., Dyer, C. and Barber, M. (2001) *The Creation of Monuments. Neolithic Causewayed Enclosures in the British Isles*, English Heritage, London.

Oswald, A., Ainsworth, S., and Pearson, T. (2006) *Hillforts. Prehistoric Strongholds of Northumberland National Park*. English Heritage, Swindon.

Owen, T.M. (1991) *The Customs and Traditions of Wales*, University of Wales Press/Western Mail, Cardiff.

Parker Pearson, M. (1996) 'Food, fertility and front doors in the first millennium BC', in eds T.C. Champion and J.R. Collis, *The Iron Age in Britain and Ireland: Recent Trends*, J.R. Collis Publications, Sheffield, 117–32.

Parker Pearson, M. and Thorpe, N. eds (2005) *Warfare, Violence and Slavery in Prehistory*, BAR International Series 1374, Oxford.

Parry, B. (2007) *Tribe – Adventures in a Changing World*, Penguin/Michael Joseph, London.

Payne, A., Corney, M. and Cunliffe, B. (2006) *The Wessex Hillforts Project. Extensive Survey of Hillfort Interiors in Central Southern England*, English Heritage. London.

Pearson, T. (1998) *Yeavering Bell Hillfort, Northumberland*, English Heritage Archaeological Investigation Report Series AI/24/1998, London.

Pearson, T. and Topping, P. (2002) 'Rethinking the Carrock Fell enclosure', in eds G. Varndell and P. Topping, *Enclosures in Neolithic Europe*, Oxbow, Oxford, 121–7.

Percival, J. (1976) *The Roman Villa*, Batsford, London.

Phillips, M. and Mighall, T. (2000) *Society and Exploitation through Nature*, Prentice Hall, Harlow.

Picton, H. (1909) 'Caer Seiont, Conway Mountain', *Archaeologia Cambrensis* 6th series IX, 500–4.

Piggott, S. (1931) 'Ladle Hill – an unfinished hill-fort', *Antiquity* 5, 474–85.

Pinker, S. (2007) *The Stuff of Thought. Language as a Window into Human Nature*, Allen Lane, London.

Pitt Rivers, A.H.L.F. (1887) *Excavations in Cranborne Chase*, Vol. 1, London.

Pitt Rivers, A.H.L.F. (1888) *Excavations in Cranborne Chase*, Vol. 2, London.

Pollard, J., Howell, R., Chadwick, A. and Leaver, A. (2006) '*Lodge Hill Camp, Caerleon and the hillforts of Gwent*', British Archaeological Reports, BAR British Series 407, Oxford.

Pope, R. (2007) 'Ritual and the roundhouse: a critique of recent ideas on the use of domestic space in later British prehistory', in eds C. Haselgrove and R. Pope, *The Earlier Iron Age in Britain and the Near Continent*, Oxbow Books, Oxford, 204–28.

Poucher, W.A. (1966) *The Peak and Pennines*, Constable, London.

Powell, T.G.E. (1963) 'Excavations at Skelmore Heads, Ulverston, 1957 and 1959', *Transactions of the Cumberland and Westmorland Antiquarian and Archaeological Society* new series LXIII, 1–30.

Probert, A. (1976) 'Twyn y Gaer hillfort, Gwent: an interim assessment', in eds G.C. Boon, and J.M. Lewis, *Welsh Antiquity: Essays Presented to Dr H.N. Savory*, National Museum of Wales, Cardiff, 105–20.

Putnam, B. (1998) *Discover Dorset, The Prehistoric Age*, Dovecot Press, Wimborne.

Ralston, I. (1995) 'Fortifications and defence', in ed. M.J. Green, *The Celtic World*, Routledge, London, 59–81.

Ralston, I. (2006) *Celtic Fortifications*, Tempus, Stroud.

Rees, S. (1992) *A Guide to Ancient and Historic Wales. Dyfed*, HMSO, London.

Renfrew, C. (2007) *Prehistory. The Making of the Human Mind*, Weidenfeld and Nicolson, London.

Renouf, J. (2004) 'The Channel islands: Reflections on origins, exploitation, settlement and allegiances', in eds M. Gardiner and J. McDowell, *The Channel Islands, Report and proceedings of the 150th Summer meeting of the Royal Archaeological Institute in 2004*, The Royal Archaeological Institute, London, 7–18.

Reynolds, P.J. (1979) *Iron Age Farm. The Butser Experiment*, British Museum, London.

Richmond, I.A. (1968) *Hod Hill Vol. 2 Excavations Carried Out Between 1951 and 1958*, British Museum, London.

Riehm, K. (1961) 'Prehistoric salt boiling', *Antiquity* 35, 181–91.

Robinson, P.H. (1995) 'Miniature socketed axes from Wiltshire', *Wiltshire Archaeological Magazine* 88, 60–8.

Roe, F.E.S. (2000) 'Worked stone', in eds J.C. Barrett, P.W.M. Freeman and A. Woodward, *Cadbury Castle Somerset. The Later Prehistoric and Early Historic Archaeology*, English Heritage Archaeological Report 20, English Heritage, London, 262–9.

Rogerson, A. and Lawson, A.J. (1991) 'The earthwork enclosure at Tasburgh', in eds J.A. Davies, T. Gregory, A.J. Lawson, R. Rickett and A. Rogerson, *The Iron Age Forts of Norfolk*, East Anglian Archaeology 54, Norfolk Museums Service, Dereham, 31–58.

Ross, A. (1998) *The Pagan Celts*, John Jones, Ruthin (first publ. B.T. Batsford, London (1970)).

Ross, A. and Cyprien, M. (1985) *A Traveller's Guide to Celtic Britain*, Routledge and Kegan Paul, London.

Rowe, T. (2005) *Cornwall in Prehistory*, Tempus, Stroud.

Rowley, T. (2001) *The Welsh Border*, Tempus, Stroud.

Rudling, D. (1985) 'Trial excavations at Ditchling Beacon, East Sussex, 1983', *Sussex Archaeological Collections* 123, 251–4.

Rudling, D. (2001) 'Chanctonbury Ring revisted. The excavations of 1988–91', *Sussex Archaeological Collections* 139, 75–121.

Russell, M. (2001) '*Rough quarries, rocks and hills. John Pull and the Neolithic flint mines of Sussex*', Bournemouth University School of Conservation Sciences Occasional Paper 6, Oxbow Books, Oxford.

Ryder, M.L. (1991) 'Milestones in the history of sheep', *The Ark* XVIII, No. 6, Rare Breeds Survival Trust, Kenilworth, 211.

Sanderson, I. (1992) 'Exciting find helps throw light on "Dark Ages"', *Clwyd Archaeology News* Winter 1992/3, 2.

Savory, H.N. (1964) 'The metalwork', in Gardner, W. and Savory, H.N., *Dinorben: a hillfort occupied in the Early Iron Age and Roman times*, National Museum of Wales, Cardiff, 131–63.

Savory, H.N. (1971) *Excavations at Dinorben, 1965–9*, National Museum of Wales, Cardiff.

Savory, H.N. (1976) 'Welsh hillforts: a reappraisal of recent research', in ed. D.W. Harding, *Hillforts. Later Prehistoric Earthworks in Britain and Ireland*,

Academic Press, London, 237–92.

Senior, M. (2005) *Hillforts of Northern Wales*, Gwasg Carreg Gwalch, Llanrwst.

Sharpe, A. (1992) 'Treryn Dinas: a cliff castle reconsidered', *Cornish Archaeology* 31, 65–8.

Sharples, N.M (1991a) *Maiden Castle*, Batsford, London.

Sharples, N.M (1991b) *Maiden Castle: Excavations and Field Survey 1985–86*, English Heritage Archaeological Report 19, London.

Sharples, N. (2007) 'Building communities and creating identities in the first millennium BC', in eds C. Haselgrove and R. Pope, *The Earlier Iron Age in Britain and the Near Continent*, Oxbow Books, Oxford, 174–84.

Sheppard, T. (1926) 'Roman remains in north Lincolnshire', *East Riding Antiquarian Society Transactions* 25, 170–4.

Sherratt, A. (1996) 'Why Wessex? The Avon route and river transport in later British prehistory', *Oxford Journal of Archaeology* 15, 211–34.

Smith, C. (1989) 'Excavations at Dod Law West hillfort, Northumberland', *Northern Archaeology* 9, 1–44.

Smith, I.F. (1965) *Windmill Hill and Avebury: Excavations by Alexander Keiller 1925–1939*, Clarendon Press, Oxford.

Smith, R.A. (1925) *A guide to the Antiquities of the Early Iron Age in Department of British and Medieval Antiquities*, British Museum, London.

Stanford, S.C. (1967) 'Croft Ambrey hillfort', *Transactions of the Woolhope Naturalists' Field Club* 39, 31–9.

Stanford, S.C. (1971) 'Credenhill Camp, Herefordshire: an Iron-Age hillfort capital', *Archaeological Journal* 127 (1970), 82–129.

Stanford, S.C. (1972) 'The function and population of hillforts in the central Marches', in eds F. Lynch and C. Burgess, *Prehistoric Man in Wales and the West*, Adams and Dart, Bath, 307–19.

Stanford, S.C. (1974) *Croft Ambrey*, privately published, Leominster.

Stanford, S.C. (1981) *Midsummer Hill*, privately published, Leominster.

Stanford, S.C. (1985a) 'Ebury Hill Camp – excavations 1977', *Transactions of the Shropshire Archaeological and Historical Society* LXIV, 9–12.

Stanford, S.C. (1985b) 'The Wrekin hillfort: excavations 1973', *Archaeological Journal* 141, 61–90.

Stanley, M. and Stanley, B. (1958) 'The defences of the Iron Age camp at Wappenbury, Warwickshire', *Transactions of the Birmingham Archaeological Society* 76, 1–9.

Stead, I.M. (1968) 'An Iron Age hill-fort at Grimthorpe, Yorkshire, England', *Proceedings of the Prehistoric Society* XXXIV, 148–90.

Stead, I.M. (1996) *Celtic Art*, The British Museum Press, London.

Stead, I.M. (1998) *The Salisbury Hoard*, Tempus, Stroud.

Stopford, J. (1987) 'Danebury, an alternative view', *Scottish Archaeological Review* 4, 70–5.

Tabor, R. (2000) 'Cadbury Castle: focussing a landscape', in ed. C.J. Webster, *Somerset Archaeology – Papers to Mark 150 Years of the Somerset Archaeological and Natural History Society*, Somerset County Council, Taunton, 25–30.

Tabor, R. (2008) *Cadbury Castle. The hillfort and landscapes*. The History Press. Stroud.

Taylor, A. (1994) 'Flat earth erosion control: Caring for archaeological monuments in Cambridgeshire', in eds A.Q. Berry and I.W. Brown, *Erosion on Archaeological Earthworks: Its Prevention, Control and Repair*, Clwyd County Council, Mold, 71–80.

Taylor, A. (2001) *Burial Practice in Early England*, Tempus, Stroud.

Taylor, T. (2005) 'Ambushed by a grotesque: archaeology, slavery and the third paradigm', in eds M. Parker Pearson and N. Thorpe, *Warfare, Violence and Slavery in Prehistory*, BAR International Series 1374, Oxford, 225–33.

Thomas, N. ed. (2005) *Conderton Camp Worcestershire: A Small Middle Iron Age Hillfort on Bredon Hill*, CBA Research Report 143, York.

Threipland, L.M. (1956) 'An excavation at St Mawgan-in-Pyder, Cornwall', *Archaeological Journal* 113, 33–81.

Tilley, C. (1994) *A Phenomenology of Landscape*, Berg, Oxford.

Todd, M. (1991) *Peoples of Roman Britain. The Coritani*, Alan Sutton, Stroud.

Tomalin, D. (2006) 'Archaeological background', in eds M. Gardiner and D. Tomalin, *The Isle of Wight. Report and Proceedings of the 152nd Summer Meeting of the Royal Archaeological Institute in 2006*, The Royal Archaeological Institute, London.

Topping, P. (1992) 'The Penrith henges: a survey by the Royal Commission on Historical Monuments of England', *Proceedings of the Prehistoric Society* 58, 249–64.

Toulson, S. and Forbes, C. *'The Drovers' Roads of Wales II. Pembrokeshire and the South'*. Whittet Books, London.

Townend, S. (2007) 'What have reconstructed roundhouses ever done for us…?' *Proceedings of the Prehistoric Society* 73, 97–111.

Trow, S., James, S. and Moore, T. (in press) '*Becoming Roman, being Gallic, staying British: Research and excavations at Ditches 'hillfort' and villa 1984–2006'*, Oxbow Books, Oxford.

Van der Noort, R. (2004) '*The Humber Wetlands*', Windgather Press, Bollington.

Van de Noort, R., Chapman, H.P. and Collis, J.R. (2007) *Sutton Common. The Excavation of an Iron Age 'Marsh-fort'*, Council for British Archaeology Research Report 154, York.

Van der Veen, M. and Jones,G. (2007) 'The production and consumption of cereals: a question of scale', in eds C. Haselgrove and T. Moore, *The Later Iron Age in Britain and Beyond*, Oxbow Books, Oxford, 419–29.

Varley, W.J. (1935) 'Maiden Castle, Bickerton. Preliminary excavations, 1935', *Annals of Archaeology and Anthropology, Liverpool* 22 (1–2), 97–110.

Varley, W.J. (1936) 'Further excavations at Maiden Castle, Bickerton, 1935', *Annals of Archaeology and Anthropology, Liverpool* 23 (3–4), 110–12.

Varley, W.J. (1939) *Report of the first year's excavations, 1939*, Castle Hill, Almondbury Excavation Committee's Pamphlet.

Varley, W.J. (1948) 'The hillforts of the Welsh Marches', *Archaeological Journal* 105, 41–66.

Varley, W.J. (1950) 'Excavations at Castle Ditches, Eddisbury, 1935–38', *Transactions of the Historical Society of Lancashire and Cheshire* 102, 1–68.

Varley, W.J. (1976) 'A summary of the excavations at Castle Hill, Almondbury, 1939–72', in ed. D.W. Harding, *Hillforts. Later Prehistoric Earthworks in Britain and Ireland*, Academic Press, London, 119–32.

Verey, D. (1976) *Gloucestershire: The Vale and the Forest of Dean*, Penguin Books, London.

Vyner, B. (1988) 'The hillfort at Eston Nab', *Archaeological Journal* 145, 60–98.

Vyner, B. (2001) 'Clegyr Boia: a potential Neolithic enclosure and associated monuments on the St David's peninsula, southwest Wales', in eds T. Darvill and J. Thomas, *Neolithic Enclosures in Atlantic Northwest Europe*, Neolithic Studies Group Seminar Paper 6, Oxbow Books, Oxford, 78–90.

Wacher, J.S. (1964) 'Excavations at Breedon-on-the-Hill, Leicestershire, 1957', *Antiquaries Journal* 44, 122–42.

Wacher, J.S. (1979) 'Excavations at Breedon-on-the-Hill', *Transactions of the Leicester Archaeological and Historical Society* 52, 1–35.

Wailes, B. (1963) 'Excavations at Castle-an-Dinas, St.

Columb Major: Interim Report', *Cornish Archaeology* 2, 51–5.

Wainwright, G.J. (1967) *Coygan Camp. A Prehistoric, Romano-British and Dark Age Settlement in Carmarthenshire*, Cambrian Archaeological Association, Cardiff.

Wainwright, G.J. (1969) 'Walesland Rath', *Current Archaeology* 12, 4–7.

Wainwright, G.J. (1970) 'The excavation at Balksbury Camp, Andover, Hants', *Proceedings of the Hampshire Field Club and Archaeological Society* XXVI (1969), 21–55.

Wainwright, G.J. (1971) 'The excavation of a fortified settlement at Walesland Rath, Pembrokeshire', *Britannia* 2, 48–108.

Wainwright, G.J. (2005) 'Back to the future', *Archaeologia Cambrensis* 152, 1–8.

Wainwright, G.J. and Davies, S.M. (1995) *Balksbury Camp. Excavations 1973 and 1981*, English Heritage Archaeological Report 4, London.

Wait, G.A. (1985) *Ritual and Religion in Iron Age Britain*, BAR British Series 149, Oxford.

Wakely, J. (1997) 'Identification and analysis of violent and non-violent head injuries in osteo-archaeological material', in ed. J. Carmen, *Material Harm. Archaeological Studies of War and Violence*, Cruithne Press, Glasgow.

Walker, M.J.C. (1987) 'Soil pollen analyses: Trench E', in D. Austin, M. Bell, B. Burnham and R. Young, *The Caer Cadwgan Project. Interim Report for 1986*, St David's University College, Lampeter.

Ward Perkins, J.B. (1939) 'Excavations on Oldbury Hill, Ightham, 1938', *Archaeologia Cantiana* 51, 137–81.

Ward Perkins, J.B. (1944) 'Excavations on the Iron Age hillfort of Oldbury, near Ightham, Kent', *Archaeologia* 90, 127–76.

Warren, S.H. (1919) 'A stone axe factory at Graig Lwyd, Penmaenmawr', *Journal of the Royal Anthropological Institute* 49, 342–65.

Watson, M. (2002) *Shropshire. An archaeological guide*, Shropshire Books, Shrewsbury.

Watts, K. (1997) *Exploring Historic Wiltshire. Vol. 1 North*, Ex Libris Press, Bradford on Avon.

Way, A. (1870) 'Notices of certain bronze relics, of a peculiar type, assigned to the late Celtic period', *Archaeologia Cambrensis* 4th series 1, 199–234.

Webley, D.P. (1976) 'How the west was won: prehistoric land-use in the southern Marches', in eds G.C. Boon and J.M. Lewis, *Welsh Antiquity. Essays Mainly on Prehistoric Topics*, National Museum of Wales, Cardiff.

Webster, G. (1975) *Peoples of Roman Britain. The Cornovii*, Duckworth, London.

Wellington, I. (2006) 'The role of Iron Age coinage in archaeological contexts', in ed. P. de Jersey, *Celtic Coinage: New Discoveries, New Discussion*, BAR International Series 1532, Oxford, 81–95.

Wells, C. (1978) 'Excavations of the late George Rybot, FSA, on Eggardon hillfort 1963–66', *Proceedings of the Dorset Archaeology and Natural History Society* 100, 54–72.

Wells, P.S. (1995) 'Trade and exchange', in ed. M.J. Green, *The Celtic World*, Routledge, London, 230–53.

Wells, P.S. (2007) 'Weapons, ritual, and communication in Late Iron Age northern Europe', in eds C. Haselgrove and T. Moore, *The Later Iron Age in Britain and Beyond*, Oxbow Books, Oxford, 469–77.

Wheeler, R.E.M. (1935) 'The excavation of Maiden Castle, Dorset, first interim report', *Proceedings of the Dorset Natural History Archaeological Society* 56, 1–10.

Wheeler, R.E.M. (1943) *Maiden Castle, Dorset*, Society of Antiquaries Research Report 12, Oxford.

Wheeler, R.E.M. and Wheeler, T.V. (1932) *Report on the Excavation of the Prehistoric, Roman and Post-Roman Site in Lydney Park, Gloucestershire*, Society of Antiquaries Research Report 9, Oxford.

Whiteley, M. (1943) 'Excavations at Chalbury Camp, Dorset, 1939', *Antiquaries Journal* 23, 97–121.

Whittle, E. (1992) *A Guide to Ancient and Historic Wales. Glamorgan and Gwent*, HMSO, London.

Wigley, A. (2007a) 'Rooted to the spot: the 'smaller enclosures' of the later first millennium BC in the central Welsh Marches', in eds C. Haselgrove and T. Moore, *The Later Iron Age in Britain and Beyond*, Oxbow Books, Oxford, 173–89.

Wigley, A. (2007b) 'Pitted histories: early first millennium BC pit alignments in the central Welsh Marches', in eds C. Haselgrove and R. Pope, *The Earlier Iron Age in Britain and the Near Continent*, Oxbow Books, Oxford, 119–34.

Williams, A. (1939) 'Excavations at The Knave promontory fort, Rhossili, Glamorgan', *Archaeologia Cambrensis* 94, 210–19.

Williams, A. (1940) 'Excavations of Bishopston Valley promontory fort, Glamorgan', *Archaeologia Cambrensis* 95, 9–19.

Williams, A. (1941) 'The excavation of High Penard promontory fort, Glamorgan', *Archaeologia Cambrensis* 96, 23–9.

Williams, A. (1952) 'Clegyr Boia, St. David's (Pemb.): Excavations in 1943', *Archaeologia Cambrensis* 102, 20–47.

Williams, G. (1988). 'Recent work on rural settlement in later prehistoric and early historic Dyfed', *Antiquaries Journal* 68, 30–54.

Williams, G. and Mytum, H. (1998) *Llawhaden, Dyfed. Excavations on a Group of Small Defended Enclosures, 1980–84*, BAR British Series 275, Oxford.

Williams, J. Ll. and Davidson, A. (2002) 'Field survey at Graiglwyd, Penmaenmawr', *Archaeology in Wales* 42, 3–15

Williams, M. (2003) 'Growing metaphors: the agricultural cycle as metaphor in the later prehistoric period of Britain and north-western Europe', *Journal of Social Archaeology* 3, 223–55.

Williamson, T. (2005) *Sandlands. The Suffolk Coast and Heaths*, Windgather Press, Bollington.

Winbolt, S.E. (1930) 'Excavations at Saxonbury Camp', *Sussex Archaeological Collections* 71, 222–36.

Woodward, A. (2000) 'Depositional processes', in eds J.C. Barrett, P.W.M. Freeman and A. Woodward, *Cadbury Castle Somerset. The Later Prehistoric and Early Historic Archaeology*, English Heritage Archaeological Report 20, English Heritage, London, 20–2.

Woodward, A. and James, H. (2000) 'The south-western gate sequence' in eds J.C. Barrett, P.W.M. Freeman and A. Woodward, *Cadbury Castle Somerset. The Later Prehistoric and Early Historic Archaeology*, English Heritage Archaeological Report 20, English Heritage, London, 84–102.

Woolf, G. (1993) 'Rethinking the oppida', *Oxford Journal of Archaeology* 14, 399–412.

Wright, E. (1990) *Ferriby Boats*, Routledge, London.

Yeates, S. J. (2008) '*The tribe of witches. The religion of the Dobunni and the Hwicce*', Oxbow Books, Oxford.

Young, A. and Richardson, K.M. (1955) 'Report on the excavations at Blackbury Castle', *Proceedings of the Devonshire Archaeological Exploration Society* 5, 43–67.

Young, R. and Humphrey, J. (1999) 'Flint use in England after the Bronze Age … time for a re-evaluation?' *Proceedings of the Prehistoric Society* 64, 231–42.

Index

Abbotsbury Castle 68, 231
Abergavenny 98, 218
Abergele 16, 40
Aconbury 19
adornment and display 92–100
Agricola 180
Aire, River 220
Alet 171
Alfred's Castle 22, 40, 209, 227, 231
All Cannings Cross fineware 136
Allt Wen 35
Allt-y-Esgair (Llangasty) 56, 218
Almondbury (see Castle Hill, Almondbury)
Alun, River 92
Amba people 64
amphora 86, 115, 166, 171, 181, 212
amulet (see talisman)
Ancalites 169
anchor 116, 212, 221
Ancholme, River 116
Andover, 235
animal symbolism 140–144, 162
Anna, River 225
annexe 35, 48, 55–56, 66, 153, 211, 232
Anted 137
antler tool 38
Anton, River 225
Antonine Wall 104
Anvil 120, 132
Aran Islands 136
Arènes 102, 109
Arenig Mountains 130
Arras 98, 104, 111, 155, 167
ard 127, 132
armlet; arm-ring (see bracelet)
arrow 105
arrowhead 27, 29, 102, 105–106

Arthurian legend 6, 14
Ashmolean Museum, Oxford 140, 142
Athenaeus 85
Atrebates (Atrebatic) 160, 163, 166, 169–170, 177, 229
Attalos I of Pergamon 99
Avebury 222
Avienus 116
Avon, River (Lower – Bristol) 115, 172, 197–200, 220
Avon, River (Hampshire) 115, 171, 197, 201–203, 223
Avon, River (Upper – Warwickshire) 10, 19, 102, 189, 197–199, 220
axe, Armorican 160, 173; Breton 136, 165; bronze 213; flat 145; flint 27; Graig Lwyd 1, 218–219; iron shaft-hole 133; miniature (see miniaturisation); movement of 202; socketed 29, 32, 136; stone 27
Aylesbury, Vale of 129
Aylesford 109
Backbury 198
Badbury Rings 29, 68, 160, 163, 168, 235
Bagendon 173, 180–181, 242
Bala Lake 130
Balksbury 19, 22, 85, 87, 96, 127–128, 130, 142, 144, 146, 156, 160, 189, 225, 231, 235
Ball Cross 124
ballista 105, 177–178
Bamburgh Castle 89, 234
banjo enclosure 55
Banwell Camp 102
Banwy, Afon 222
Barbury Castle 38, 77, 111, 132, 145, 194, 203, 227–228

Bardsey Island, 211
Barlands Farm 116
Barmouth 154
Barnwood 139
barrel-shaped pottery jar 123
Barry 188
Basingwerk Hill 234
basket-shaped earring 33
Bath 88, 152, 173, 203, 220
Bathampton 32
Battlesbury Camp 30, 132, 178, 191, 201, 203, 226
Beachy Head 185
beacon 195–196, 235
beacon enclosures 237
Beacon Hill (Burghclere, Hants) 26, 68, 167, 203, 227, 235
Beacon Hill (Leics) 32, 167
Beacon Hill (Pembs) 196
bead 97, 99, 121, 176
Beech Bottom Dyke 180–181
Belgae 178
bell 153
Belle Tout 185, 187, 196, 207
Bellovaci 160
Belowda 189
Berkshire Downs 31, 38, 127
Berkshire Ridgeway (see Ridgeway, the)
berm 34, 40, 215
Berry Farm 235
Bersu, Gerhard 76–77
Berth, the 6, 29, 174, 189
Berwyn Range 205
Bibroci 169
Bigberry (Bigbury) Camp 15, 82–83, 125–126, 145, 170–171, 181, 204
Bigbury Bay 50, 212, 222
Bignor 158
billhook 132

Bindon Hill 38, 68, 207, 211

bird (incl. nightjar; raven) 109, 142–143, 146, 214

Birdlip 98

bitting damage 111

Black Mountains 218

Blackbury Castle 18, 88, 105, 121

Blackmoor Vale 188

Black Scar Camp 55

Blewburton Hill 26, 138, 155, 164, 234

blocked entrance 64–65, 136–138

bluestones 28

boar (wild) see pig

Bodbury Ring 58–59, 192, 203

bodkin 94

Bodmin Moor 222

Boltby Scar 33, 208–209

Bolt Tail 47, 50, 88, 138, 212, 222

Borough Hill (Northants) 8, 68

Boudica (Boudican) 92, 159, 168, 178, 180

Bourne, River 223

Bourton-on-the-Water 123, 162, 165, 235

bow 105–106

Bowcombe Valley 228

Bowland 215

box rampart 26, 31, 41, 43–45, 49, 58, 65, 136

Bozedown 197

bracelet 32, 95, 98–99, 121, 145, 171, 173, 193, 213

bracken encroachment 235

Brading 158

Braich-y-Ddinas 1, 16, 48, 86, 176, 218, 231, 235

Brandon Camp 199, 232

Branscombe Beach 105

Bratton Castle 27, 203

Braughing 169, 180–181

Brecon 56

Bredon Hill 205

Bredon Hill hillfort 8, 10, 19, 21, 76, 83, 86, 93–94, 96–99, 103–105, 111, 120, 125, 132–133, 135, 142, 144, 148, 154, 156, 173, 179, 188–189, 199, 205

Breedon-on-the-Hill 19, 35, 87, 124, 154, 167, 235

Brehon Laws (see Irish Law tracts)

bridle (horse) bit 111, 145, 148, 204

Brigantes 166–167, 179

Brigantia (Brigantian) 166, 178

Brighton 31

briquetage (VCP) 122

British Camp (Herefordshire Beacon) 8, 15, 136, 196, 214, 234

Broadhaven 88

Bromfield 221

bronze end-buckle 93, 97

brooch (pennanular, bow, trumpet, other) 93, 95–98, 100, 148, 153, 155, 173, 231–232, 234

Brownsea Island 117

Bryher 186

Bryn Alun 8

Bryn Eryr 12, 194

Bryn Euryn 12, 234

Bryngaer Dinas 1, 219

Bryn y Castell (Ffestiniog) 12, 119–120, 137

Buckbean pond 88, 221

Budbury 130, 230

Bugthorpe 167

Bulbury 82–83, 86, 98, 111–112, 116, 193, 243

Bulwarks, The (Porthkerry) 176, 232

burial practice 154–156

Burgh Island 138, 222

Burgh-by-Woodbridge 168

Burnt Hill (St Martin's) 186

Burrough Hill 167, 237

Burrow Hill Camp 57

Burry Holmes 187

Burton Fleming 93

Burwell 221

Bury Camp (Colerne) 178

Bury Ditches 56, 60, 62

Bury Hill (Hants) 105–106, 111, 147, 149, 156, 225

Bury Hill (Winterbourne) 149

Bury Walls 40

Bury Wood Camp 67, 193

Butser (Hill) 29, 71–72, 77

Buttony 219

Buzbury Rings 223

bwayma 153

Bwrdd Arthur 38, 82, 232

Cadbury Camp (Tickenham) 18, 102, 149

Cadbury Castle (see South Cadbury)

Cadbury Hill (Congresbury) 68, 70, 73, 102, 149, 234

Cae Summerhouse (Tythegston) 232

Caerau (Ely) 48

Caerleon 22, 47, 179

Caer Bach (Rowen) 47

Caer Cadwgan 58, 102, 121, 207–208

Caer Caradoc (Chapel Lawn) 49, 210

Caer Caradoc (Church Stretton) 61, 88, 174, 199, 210

Caer Ddunod 203

Caer Drewyn 23, 40, 47–48, 50, 53, 56, 60–61, 196, 235

Caer Dynnaf 211

Caer Euni (Bala) 67

Caernarfon 211

Caer Pencarreg 58

Caer y Twr (Holyhead) 20, 48, 61, 175, 201, 232

Caersŵs 184, 201, 205

Caesar, Julius 90, 103, 116, 160, 164, 168–171

Caesar's Camp 8, 16

Cain, River 168, 198, 201

Caithness 156

Calais 115

Caldbeck Fells 215

Calverton 178

Calleva Atrebatum (see Silchester)

Cambrian Archaeological Association 16

Camerton Camp 173

Camulodunum (see Colchester)

cannibalism 156–157

Canterbury 15, 171, 203

Cantiaci (Cantii) 160, 170–171

Capel Garmon 82, 119

Caplar Camp 17, 198

Caratacos (Caratacus) 163, 177, 179

Cardingmill Valley 58, 192

Cartimandua, Queen 166, 179

Carmarthen 121

Carnarvon, Lord 235

Carn Alw 28, 30, 55

Carn Brea 20, 27, 35, 102, 120, 145, 160, 174

Carn Fadryn 48, 212

Carn Ffoi 212

Carn Goch 45, 248

Carn Ingli 28, 48, 56–57, 73, 176, 212, 222

Carn Meini 28

Carn Pentyrch 234

carnyx 101–102, 162

Carrock Fell 184, 215, 217–218, 226

Carvetii 166

Cassi 169

Cassius, Dio 92, 178

Castell Bryn-gwyn 25

Castell Caer Seion 16, 48–49, 52, 55, 60, 63, 65, 73, 76, 81, 105

Castell Cawr (Abergele) 40, 60–61

Castell Dinas Brân 89, 232–234, 237

Castell Heinif 211

Castell Henllys 13, 23, 47, 53–56, 61, 67–68, 72, 74, 79, 82, 86, 135, 232, 235

Castell Nadolig 135, 140

Castell Odo 12, 31

Castell Penpleidiau 186

Castell (Tregaron) 61

Castercliff 37, 67, 213, 234

Casterley Camp 19, 37, 99, 105, 146, 191, 209–210, 230

Castle-an-Dinas 20, 88, 189, 234

Castle Ditch (Eddisbury) 31, 47

Castle Ditches (Llancarfan) 175

Castle Ditches (Llantwitmajor) 186

Castle Ditches (Tisbury) 69, 226–227

Castle Dore 98, 173, 231

Castle Heads 212

Castle Hill (Almondbury) 18, 32, 47, 166, 234

Castle Hill (Kent) 203

Castle Hill (Newhaven) 31

Castle Idris 225

Castle Pit Hill (Melbourne) 124

Castle Ring (Oakhill) 192

Castle Ring (Stitt Hill) 29, 192

Castle Yard (Farthingstone) 44

cat 85, 141

cattle (cow; ox) 68, 85–87, 99–100, 111–112, 115, 122, 128–130, 132, 138, 140, 145–146, 153, 157, 165, 189, 208, 211, 214–215, 227, 230–231

cattle raiding 91, 100, 132

Catuvellauni (Catuvellaunian) 160, 168–169, 177–178, 181

cauldron 82, 84, 176

cauldron-hanger 82, 84

causewayed enclosure 24–26, 202, 210, 223

Caynham Camp 49, 55, 60, 86

Cefn Carnedd 179, 184, 201

Ceiriog Valley 201

Celtic fields 127

Celtic Shorthorn 132

Cemaes Bay 117

Cenimagni 169

ceramic (see pottery)

Cernunnos 142

Cerrig-y-Drudion 109

Cerrig Gwynion 203

chain-mail 103

Chalbury 18, 32, 45, 58, 66, 72

Chanctonbury Ring 31, 149–152, 154, 196, 235, 237

chape 103, 106

chariot 91, 109, 111–112, 148, 166–167

chathonic deities; gods 142, 144, 216

Chedworth 221

Cherbury Camp 230

Cherry Hill 198

Cherwell, River 168

Cheshire stony-tempered ware 122

Chesil Beach 68, 231

Chester 109, 113, 232

Chesterton Walls 35

chevaux-de-frise 53–55, 129, 193

Cheviot Hills (Cheviots) 11, 193–194, 217, 219

Cheyenne 155

Chiltern Hills (Chilterns) 37, 129, 170, 221

Chisbury 231

Chiselbury 209

Chûn Castle 19, 48

Cirencester 113, 173

citadel 48, 234

Chichester 169, 177, 229

Christchurch Harbour 171

Church Stretton 58

Chwiler, Afon 212

Cissbury Ring 16, 19, 27–28, 170, 196

Ciumeşti 109

Clare Camp 12

Claudius 169, 177

Claudian invasion 169

Clawdd Coch 197

Clawdd y Milwyr promontory fort (incl. St David's Head) 10, 16, 55, 73, 115, 127, 184, 191–192, 211, 222

Cleave Dyke 33, 209

Cleavel Point 117

Cleeve Hill 125

Clegr Boia 27

Clevedon Pill 117

Cley Hill (Corsley) 29

clientage 114, 179, 200, 226

cloak, Celtic 93, 95, 100

Clovelly Dykes 210

Clun, River 61, 197, 199, 225

Clun-Clee Ridgeway 203

Clwyd, River 115, 212

Clwyd, Vale of 8–9, 130, 212

Clwydian Range 8–9, 15, 35, 43, 95, 130, 175, 201–202, 208–210, 214, 227

Clwyd County Council Archaeology Service 237

Clwyd Powys Archaeological Trust 20, 23

Clywedog, Afon 184, 205

Clywedog reservoir (Llyn Clywedog) 48, 61, 184, 205

Coalbrookdale 197

Coed y Bwnydd 176

Cogidubnus, Tiberius Claudius 177

coin (Celtic; coinage; native) 92, 109, 111, 114, 137, 145, 153–154, 159–166, 169–170, 172–174, 178, 181, 214, 220

coin, (Greek) 176

coin (Roman) 149, 152, 160, 163, 232

Colchester 168–169, 177, 179–181

Cold Kitchen Hill 29
College Valley 219
Collfryn 12, 194
Coln, River 221
Commius 169
Condatis 221
Conderton Camp 21, 68, 72, 79, 88, 94, 97, 99, 121, 125, 128, 137–138, 148, 189, 225
conflict resolution 100–103
construction techniques 35, 37–39, 60
Conwy Estuary 16, 48
Conwy, River 115
Conwy Valley 47
coracle 116
corbelling 184
core-periphery model 158
Corieltauvi 137, 160, 163, 167, 178
Coriosolites 162–163, 171
Coritani 167
Coritanorum 167
Corley Camp 45
corn dryer 127
Cornovii (Cornovian) 166, 174, 179, 201
Corsley 29
Cors y Carneddau 218
Corve, River 221
Corwen 50
Cotswolds 14, 17, 31–32, 45, 102, 120, 125, 173, 189, 200
counterscarp bank 40, 43–45, 48–49, 56, 60, 63, 187, 195
cow bell 132
Coygan Camp 20, 83, 94, 98, 104, 106, 129, 156, 160, 163, 176, 193
Craven uplands 215
Craig Adwy Wynt 35
Craig Gwrtheyrn 53
Craig Rhiwarth 205–207
Craig yr Aderyn 35
Cranborne Chase 15, 77, 163
Craven Arms 198
Crawcwellt 119–120
Credenhill 19–20, 22, 69, 89, 166, 207
Crickley Hill 13, 21, 25, 45, 49, 53, 66, 72, 78, 98, 102, 138, 235
Croft Ambrey 20, 44, 49, 58, 60–61, 65, 68–69, 72–73, 75, 87, 97–99,

103, 106, 109, 121–122, 129, 132, 144, 148–149, 152–153, 157, 193, 199, 207
Crow 155
Crow Hill (Irthlingborough) 44, 231
Crowther's Camp 145
Cumberland, George 14
Cunobelin 160, 169–170, 177
currach 116
currency bars 119, 144–145, 159, 164–165
Cwm Orog 205
Cwm Sian Llwyd 205
dagger 103–104, 106, 193
Dale Point 33
Danebury 4, 13, 21–23, 27, 38, 45, 58, 69–70, 72, 75, 77, 82, 85–86, 97, 99, 103, 105, 111, 120, 122, 124, 128, 132, 136–137, 141–147, 149–150, 153, 155–156, 164, 180, 189–190, 200, 203, 207, 224–226, 229–230, 234
Dane's Graves 95
Dani 101
Danube, River 89
Dan y coed 12, 118
Darent Valley 171
Dartmoor 88, 90
Dartmoor reaves 208
Dart Estuary 212
dead ground 192
Deceangli 174, 178–180, 201
Dee Estuary 234
Dee, River 50, 115–116, 200–201, 205, 212–213
Dee Valley 50, 196, 201, 203, 205
deer (stag) 86, 130, 138, 142, 145–146
Demetae 173–174, 176
Deskford 102
developed hillfort 80, 180, 200, 207, 226
Devil's Dyke 180–181
Devil's Hill 207
Devon Archaeological and Exploration Society 18
Dexter (cattle) 132
Dikler, River 55
Dinas Dinlle 175, 186–187
Dinas Dinorwic 45, 49

Dinas Gynfor 117
Dinas hillfort (see Bryngaer Dinas)
Dinas Mawr 28
Dinas outcrop 218
Dinedor Camp 19, 68
Dinka 101
Dinorben 15–16, 19–20, 32, 34, 38, 43, 47, 49, 61, 67, 73, 93, 95–98, 105, 109, 133, 135, 139–140, 152, 155–156, 163, 175–176, 232, 235
Diocletian 86
ditch (re-cutting; cleaning) 38, 40, 195
Ditchling Beacon 22, 31, 196
Ditches, the (Glos) 231
Dobunni (Dobunnic) 102, 137, 142, 149, 152, 160, 162–163, 172, 174, 177, 179, 181, 220
Dod Law 11
Dod Law West 22, 128
Doddington Moor 219
dog 76, 85, 99, 111–112, 139, 143–147, 152, 155
Dolaucothi 121, 205
Dolebury 102
Dolgellau 120–121
Dorchester 4, 17–18, 34, 141, 163
Dorchester-on-Thames 169, 181–182
Dorket Head 178
Dorset County Museum 177
Dragonby 167
Droitwich 91, 122
Druids (Druidic) 139–140, 180
Dryslwyn Castle 89, 234
dual-portal gate 58, 64
duck-pattern ware 125
Dumnonii 173
dump rampart 40, 43–47, 49, 60, 136
Durotriges (Durotrigan) 102, 155, 160–164, 166, 171–173, 177–178, 181
Durrington Walls 203
Duston 231
Dyfi Valley 35
Dyfi Estuary 212
Dyfi, Afon 35, 212
Dying Gaul 99, 104
Dyke Hills 169, 181
Earl's Hill (Pontesbury) 40, 55–57, 60, 192

earth and timber structures 41–45
Easthampstead 8
Ebury Hill Camp 6, 180
Eddisbury 31, 47, 255
Eggardon 37–38, 45, 72, 172
Eirth, Afon 205
Elmley Castle 189, 234
entrances and gates 25, 33, 35, 37–38, 45, 55, 57–61, 64–67, 95, 102–103, 134–139, 149, 164, 180, 187, 190, 192–195, 203, 207, 215, 220, 224, 230
entrance orientation 136, 139
Epona 109
Eppaticus 169, 170
Eppilus 170
Ermine Street 178
Erw Wen 127
Eryrys 12
escutcheon (ox-head; bovine-head) 135, 140
Eston Nab 31, 33, 208, 255
Ewart Park 4, 223
Exe Estuary 212
Exe, River 173
farming tools 132–133
feast (feasting) 86, 91, 195, 207, 227
fécamp 43, 45
Fell Beck 215–216, 220
Fens, the 122
Ferriby (North and South) 117, 167
Ffridd Faldwyn 16, 17, 27, 47, 56, 58, 67
fibulae 173
Figsbury Rings 19, 223
fire (damage; firing) 44, 49, 67, 102–103, 134, 137, 178, 230
firedog 82–83, 119
fire beacon 201
fish (fishing) 86–87, 118, 196–197, 205, 212, 226
Fishbourne 158
Fiskerton 117
Five Barrows (Chillerton Down) 37, 228
flint mines (digging) 27–29, 45, 47, 144
Flowers Barrow 186
fogous 148
Forden Gaer 232

Forest of Dean 121, 151
Folkestone 16
Fosse Way 178
foundation deposits (incl. rampart burial) 11, 134–136, 226
fowl 85, 128
four-poster structure (granary) 11, 69–70, 72–73, 76–80, 85, 126, 148, 153, 155, 194, 207–208, 226, 237
Fox Wood 178
frog (toad) 145
Frome Gap 29
Frome, River 203
Fron (Newcastle, Shropshire) 225
Gabrantovices 166
gaeltacht 138
Gaer (Chepstow) 140
Gaer Fawr (Guilsfield) 56, 68–69, 109–110, 116, 140, 145, 235
Gaer Fawr (Llanwnda) 48
Gangani 174
Gaping Gill 215–216, 220
Garden Hill (Hartfield) 120
Garn Boduan 48, 64, 73, 75, 184, 212, 234
Garn Fawr 28
Garn Fechan 28
Garreg Fawr outcrop 218
Gatesbury Wood 181
Giant's Castle (St Mary's) 125, 186, 222
glacis 34, 43–45, 49
Glamorgan, Vale of 48, 109
Glastonbury 156
Glastonbury Lake Village 83, 88, 124
Glen, River 47
Gloucester 197
goat 129, 138–139, 144
Goldcliff 118, 155
Gower 9, 17, 173, 176, 187, 190, 232
Graiglwyd 1, 218–219
Graig-yr-Wolf 121
granary (see four-poster)
Great Chesters 98
Great Orme 191
Green Island 117
Grimthorpe 15, 79, 104, 106, 108, 148, 156, 167, 193, 208
Grove Field Camp 197

guard chamber (guardroom) 16, 27, 58, 60–61, 64, 66–67, 137, 190
Guilsborough 44
Guilsfield hoard 145
Gundestrup cauldron 101, 109, 142
Gurnard's Head 73, 75, 81, 125, 222
Gussage All Saints 193
Gwent Levels 116
hafod and hendre 210
Halkyn Mountain 212
Hambledon Hill 8, 15, 25–26, 35, 38, 40, 72, 102, 166, 172, 188, 193, 205, 226, 235
Hambleton Hills 209
hammer (various) 93, 103, 120, 132–133, 148
Ham Hill 18–19, 24–26, 68, 95–96, 99, 105–106, 135, 139–140, 153–154, 162, 164, 172, 188, 193, 235
Harding's Down 9, 210–211
Hardwell Camp 228
Haresfield Beacon 40, 196
Harlech 127
Harrow Hill 29
Harting Beacon 31, 78, 135–136, 196, 207, 226
Haughmond Hill 67
Haverfordwest 11
head-hunting (cult) 19, 91, 146, 156, 179, 194
Hebrides 82
helmet 109
Helsby Hill 212–213
Hembury Castle (Payhembury) 18, 25–26, 31
Hen Ffordd 203
Hengistbury Head 21–22, 24, 86, 99, 103, 111, 114–115, 117, 121, 124, 126, 163, 171–173, 211, 227
Hereford 17
Herodian 99
Heytesbury 203
Hexton 221
Highdown Hill 16, 29, 170
High Rocks 19
hilt-guard 106–107
Hirta 130
hoard (hoarding) 4, 15, 109, 144–145, 154, 159–160, 164, 168, 171, 210, 213, 220

hoard, Salisbury 112, 115, 121, 136, 154
Hod Hill 15, 35–36, 40–41, 44–45, 57, 60, 62, 65, 68, 73, 82–83, 86, 94, 96, 98–99, 105, 111, 131, 135, 141–142, 154, 160–164, 166, 172, 177, 182, 192, 226, 231–232
Holkham 168
Hollingbury Camp 19–20, 31, 44, 58, 144
Hollybush Hill (spring) 64, 220
Holyhead 20, 175, 232
Honddu, River 218
horse 86, 92–93, 108–112, 128, 138, 142–143, 146–148, 162, 208, 214
horse-gear (trappings) 91, 105, 109–112, 121, 166–167
Horton Moor 219
Hulberry 197
Humber, River 25, 160, 167, 200
Humbleton Hill 219
Hunsbury 22, 44, 82–84, 91, 93, 97, 99, 106–107, 111, 122, 124, 132, 145, 147–148, 156, 164, 193
hunting dogs 115, 152, 171
Hutchinson, William 14
Iceni (Icenian) 92, 159–160, 162–163, 166–168, 178
Icknield Way 200, 203
Ingleborough 10, 139, 184, 215–218, 226
Ingleton 215
intervisibility 151, 201–202
inturned rampart (entrance) 58, 60, 64, 67, 89, 137
Iranians 93
Irish (Brehon) Law tracts 91, 93, 119
Isca (see Caerleon)
isostatic readjustment 188
Ivinghoe Beacon 37, 44, 79, 124, 129, 155–157, 169, 196, 235
Iwrch, Afon 205
javelin (see spear)
Jupiter 214–215
Karimojong 100
Kenidjack Castle 222
Kennet, River 170, 202
Kerry Ridgeway 203
Killibury 20
King Arthur's Well 89

Kingsdown Camp 85, 111, 144, 173
Knights Templar and Hospital of St John 44
Knockmill Wood 105
Krak des Chevaliers 44
Ladle Hill 37
Lakeland fells 215
lance (see spear)
Lancing Down 151
Land's End 48, 115
Lansdowne Column 235
Lawley, the 56
Lea, River 168
Leam, River 200
Leckhampton Hill 17–18, 45, 125
Leintwardine 232
Lemovices 162
Lewes 16
Le Havre 115
Lhuyd, Edward 14
Leland, John 14
Lidbury 19, 97, 99, 142, 228
Liddington Castle 32, 38, 40, 44–45, 47, 73, 136–137, 194–195, 203, 227
lime-wash 92, 112
Limoges 162
linchpins 111
Lincoln Edge 167
Lindow Moss 139
Linga Holm 131
Linn, The 221
Little Ouse 200
Little Solsbury Hill Camp 88, 95–96, 199
Littleton Bog 107
Little Woodbury 76
Lizard 173
Llancarfan 175
Llandinam 184
Llandrinio 197
Llandudno 175, 191
Llandudno Bay 191, 212
Llandwrog 187
Llandyssul 53
Llanfairfechan 1, 218
Llangollen 89, 200
Llangollen, Vale of 201
Llangorse 218
Llangynwyd 210

Llanidloes 235
Llanmelin 17, 45, 49, 56, 98, 137, 141, 156, 176, 193
Llanstephan Castle 89, 234
Llantysilio Mountains 35–36
Llanwnda 48
Llanymynech Hill 56, 68, 112–113, 179, 198, 204
Llawhaden 12, 226
Lleiriog 205
Llwyn Bryn-dinas 32, 204
Llŷn (peninsula) 11–12, 16, 36, 48, 66, 71, 73, 115, 175, 186, 211–212, 234
Llyn Cerrig Bach 82, 119, 122, 125, 165, 204, 220, 245
Llyn Fawr 220
Llys Awel 152
Lochar Moss 100
Lodge Hill Camp 22, 45, 61, 70, 95, 122, 125, 137, 176, 179–180
London 197, 220
Long Mynd 29, 192
loomweight 93–94
Lord's Bridge (Barton) 82, 125
Lucan 90
Ludlow 49, 198, 221
Lugg, River 87, 197, 199
Lulworth Cove 38, 68, 117, 211
lynchet 127
Lydney (Park) 17, 109, 135, 140, 144, 149, 151–152, 154, 221
Mabinogi 144
Macedon 163
Madmarston Camp 31, 82, 128, 145, 164, 226, 231
Maen Castle 94, 222
Maendy Camp 175
Maesbury 234
Maiden Bower 26
Maiden Castle (Bickerton, Cheshire) 17, 47
Maiden Castle (Dorchester, Dorset) 4, 13, 17–18, 25–26, 29, 33–34, 37–38, 40–41, 43–44, 47, 57, 61, 64–65, 68, 70, 72, 76, 78, 84, 87, 95–96, 105, 121, 128, 132, 135, 137, 139–141, 147, 149–151, 153–155, 163–164, 166, 172, 177, 181, 190, 192–194, 207, 215, 224, 226, 235
Maldon 12

Malham Cove 220
Malvern Hills (Malverns) 8, 15, 47, 88, 125, 136, 164, 173–174
Mam Tor 10, 20, 32, 37, 49, 73, 88, 124, 184, 218, 226, 234
Manching 4
Manger, the 38
Maori Pā 192
Marden 203
Markland Grips 124
Marlborough 203
Marlborough Downs 208
Marloes 211
Mars 152
Martinsell Camp 226
Martin's Haven 211
Massaliote Periplus 116
Massaliotes 116
Mawddach Estuary 121, 212
Meare Lake Village 88, 99, 124
medieval castle 65, 89, 194, 228, 232
Medway Gap 19, 203
Medway, River 123, 170, 177, 203
Melsonby 111, 166–167
Mendip Hills (Mendips) 121, 176, 203
Meon Hill 102, 164
Meion, River 169
Mercury 152
Merlin's Hill 201
Mersey Estuary 212
Mersey, River 200, 213
Merthyr Mawr 176
metalworking (metalwork; metallurgy; ironworking) 15, 30, 82, 98, 103, 107, 112, 115, 119–121, 126, 137, 148–149, 152, 154, 164–165, 171, 174, 176, 181, 193, 196, 204–205, 220, 227
Middleholm 211
Middlewich 122
Midsummer Hill 15, 20, 40, 44, 47, 58, 60, 64–65, 69, 73, 88, 103, 122, 164, 207, 214, 220
Milber Down Camp 18, 142–144, 147, 164, 210, 232
Milfield North 219
Milfield Plain 11, 217–219
Milsom's Corner 145
miniaturisation (miniature; various items of) 148–149, 152–154, 210

minims 153–154
mirror 95, 98
Moel Arthur 8, 24, 145, 202, 227
Moel Drygarn (Trigarn) 16, 28–30, 49, 176, 237
Moel Famau 43, 214
Moel Fenlli 8–9, 66, 201, 210, 227
Moel Hiraddug 15–16, 19–20, 32, 35, 45, 49, 61, 64, 67, 69, 91, 97–98, 100, 102, 106–107, 112–113, 154, 156, 175, 204, 235
Moel Offrwm 120
Moel y Gaer (Bodfari) 203, 212
Moel y Gaer (Llanbedr) 67, 226
Moel y Gaer (Llantysilio) 35–36, 40, 60
Moel y Gaer (Rhosesmor) 20, 27, 32, 37, 41, 43–44, 47, 64, 69, 72, 137–138, 175, 212
Moel y Gamelin 36
Monnow, River 218
Montford 197
monumental symbolism 195
Morecombe Bay 212–213, 215
Mouflon, Asiatic 130
Mound, Croft Ambrey 153
Mount Batten 98, 173, 211
Mount Caburn 16, 19, 37, 170, 196, 235, 237
Mount Pleasant 203
mountain spirits 214
Mule, the 221
Muntham Court 151
murus duplex 48
Mynydd Dinas 28
Narborough 168
Nash Point (Marcross) 186
National Nature Reserves 235
needle 93
necklace 99, 115, 142, 144
Nefyn 211
Neptune 221
Nevern 235
Newport (Newport Bay; Pembs) 28, 57, 222
New Pieces 234
Newquay (Cornwall) 33
New Sarum 235
nightjar (see bird)
Nine Mile river 29

Nodens 151–152, 221
Nordy Bank 35
Norham Castle 234
Norsebury Ring 69
Norton Camp 235
North Creake 168
North Downs 105
North Grimston 167
North Ronaldsay 131
North York Moors 33, 208
Northampton Archaeology 22
Northampton Museum 148
Northumberland, Duke of 15
Norton Fitzwarren 29
Og, River 203
Ogmore 109
Oldbury Camp (Cherhill, Wilts) 19, 231, 235
Oldbury Hill (Ightham, Kent) 19, 24, 43, 45, 105, 170, 181, 203, 231, 235
Old Oswestry 4, 15, 17, 32, 45, 54, 58, 65, 73, 88, 192–195, 201, 204, 234–235
Old Sarum 203, 234
Oliver's Castle or Camp 19, 208
Oliver's Point (Nesscliffe Hill) 174, 232
Omo river valley 101
Onny, River 198
oppida, enclosed 181
oppida, territorial 180
oppidum (oppida) 68, 166–167, 169, 171, 180–182, 218, 229, 231
Ora Maritima 116
Ordovices (Ordovician) 174–175, 178–179
Orog, Cwm 205
outwork (incl. hornwork; barbican) 45, 56, 61, 65–66, 164, 180
out-turned rampart (entrance) 60
Owslebury 193
ox (see cattle)
Painswick Beacon 196
palisade 24–25, 30–33, 40, 44–45, 47, 49, 66, 137, 170, 190, 209, 224, 231
palstave 29, 144
Parc-y-meirch 109
Parisi (Yorkshire) 167

Parisii (France) 167
Park Hall army camp 235
partible inheritance 225–226
patera 83
Paulinus, Gaius Suetonius 159, 180
pedogenesis 188
pelum 179
Pembrokeshire Coast National Park
    Authority 23
Penbryn 140
penannular tress-ring 213
pendant 97–99, 142, 144
Pennines 124, 127, 215, 228
Pen Dinas (Aberystwyth) 4, 58, 73,
    120, 212
Penllyn 130
Penmaenmawr 16, 218
Penrith 202
Penrhyndeudraeth 16, 163, 218
Penycloddiau 8, 35, 40, 42–43, 61,
    202, 210
Pen y Bannau (Strata Florida) 61
Pen y Clun (nr. Clywedog reservoir)
    61
Pen y Crug (Brecon) 58
Pen y Dinas (Llandudno) 191, 212
Pen y Gaer (nr. Clywedog reservoir)
    48
Pen y Gaer (Llanbedr y Cennin) 47, 53
Pen y corddyn Mawr 16, 49, 52, 55,
    60–61, 64, 88, 93, 97, 152, 201,
    211, 234
Penycrocbren 205
Pen-y-Ghent 139, 215
Pen'r Allt (Llanidloes) 61, 235
Perborough Castle 227
Pergamon 99
Pevensey Levels 169
Pewsey Vale 27
Philip II of Macedon 163
phallus 25, 97
Pickering, Vale of 208–209
Piercefield Great Camp 199
Piercefield Little Camp 199
pig (boar) 85–86, 99, 101–102, 109,
    128–130, 138, 140, 142, 146, 149,
    151, 153, 157, 162, 208
Pilgrim's Way 204
Pilsdon Pen 45, 68, 80, 172, 207
Pimperne 71

pin 94–96, 99–100
Pitchbury 181
pit deposition 145–148
pit (storage) 4, 11, 14–15, 21, 27,
    30, 69, 76–80, 84–85, 105–106,
    120, 126, 129, 136, 141–142, 148,
    154–156, 165, 195, 207, 226–227
pit alignment 137, 208
Pitstone Hill 129
Pitt Rivers (Augustus Henry Lane
    Fox), Major General 15, 24, 27
plateau enclosures 29
Plautius, Aulus 177
Pliny 116
Plymouth 117
Plymouth Sound 98, 173
poker 82, 121, 145
Pontesford (Pontesford Hill) 56
Poole 112, 115
Poole Harbour 117, 171–173
Poole Quay 197
Portfield 32, 124, 213
Porthkerry 176
Porth Dinllaen 211
Porth Felen 116, 212
Porth Llanlleiana 117
Porth y Rhaw 33
port-of-trade 103, 173
Posidonius 85–86, 90
postern (sally port) 60–61, 66, 88
Poston Camp 14
pottery (ceramic) 4, 15, 17, 27, 31–32,
    84, 123–125, 148–149, 166, 169,
    172–174, 181, 214, 223, 232, 234,
    227, 231–232
Poundbury 18, 41, 44, 226
Powysland Club 15
Prasutagus, King 168, 178
Preseli 16, 28, 30, 55, 176
Prestatyn 100
Ptolemy (incl. Ptolemy's
    Camulodunum) 166–167
Pulborough 151
Pumlumon 184, 197, 205, 209
Pumsaint 205
Pyon Wood 199
Pyrenees 173
Quarley Hill 37, 155, 209
Quarry Wood (Loose) 45, 170–171,
    181

loomweight 93
quarry scoop (quarry ditch) 40–41,
    47, 65, 68, 144, 201, 215, 223
quern (saddle; rotary) 91, 127, 148
Radnor Wood 56
Rainsborough 4, 9, 44, 49, 61, 64,
    66–67, 111
Rams Hill 29, 31, 227
rampart burial (see foundation
    deposits)
ramparts and ditches 40–52
Ramsey Island 211
Ranscombe Camp 37, 241
rath 11
Ratlinghope Hill 29
raven (see bird)
Ravensburgh Castle 44, 221
razor 95, 97, 136
Rea Brook 222
Redlake, River 210
Redruth 174
regional variation 227
Regni 160, 166, 169–170, 243
Regnum (see Chichester)
Rheidol, Afon 4, 212
Rheidol Valley 212
Rhine, River 115, 197
Rhinogau 205
Rhossili Bay 187
Rhos-on-Sea 12, 234
Ridgeway, the 31, 40, 136, 194–195,
    203, 227–228
Rib, River 181
Ribble, River 140, 213
rings (finger; toe; ankle) 97–99,
    147, 153
Ringes, the 219
Ring Chesters 65
ringwork 234
ring-fort 11–12, 167, 194, 231
Risbury 9
ritual objects 135–136, 139–140
river spirits 221
rock art 219
Rodney, George Brydges 237
Rodney's Column 235–237
Romanisation 159, 232
Romney Marsh 123
Roughting Linn 219, 221
roundhouse 12, 23, 30–33, 70–74,

82, 85, 138, 148, 156, 183, 189, 218, 227, 230, 237
rounds 12
Roveries, the 56
Ruabon 18, 203
Rumps, The 20, 72, 86, 184, 211
Ruthin 35
Ruwenzori Mountains 64
Rybury 26, 210, 222
Rye, River 209
sagenai 101
Salcombe 212
Salisbury Plain 178, 228
Salisbury Plain Training Area 191
Salmonsbury 26, 55, 72, 76, 96, 123, 127, 135, 139, 142, 155, 157, 162, 164–165, 173, 181, 235
salt 86, 91, 122–123, 211–213
Samian pottery 153
satellite 56
saucepan pot ware 124
Saxonbury Camp 19
scabbard 103, 106–107, 148, 224
Scapula, Publius Ostorius 174, 178, 232
Scratchbury 9, 26, 55, 72, 76, 96, 123, 127, 196, 201, 203, 226
Scythians 93
Seaford Head 185, 187, 196
sea urchin 93
Segontiaci 169
Segsbury Camp 22, 31, 40, 44, 69, 128, 144, 148, 225–226
Seine, River 115, 162, 221
Selsey 169
Sequana 221
Setantii 166
Settle 215
Severn Estuary 25, 102, 115–116, 122, 125, 155, 171, 197, 232
Severn, River 12, 88, 118, 122, 142, 151, 160, 174, 178, 184, 189, 194, 197–202, 205, 208, 221–222
Severn Valley 23, 139, 157
Severus, Septimius 9
shears (shearing) 131
sheep (ram) 68, 85–87, 128–131, 138, 141, 145–146, 153, 157, 208, 210, 227, 235
Shenberrow Hill Camp 147

Sherborne 235
Sherford 116
shield 104, 107–108, 112–113, 119
shield-boss 91, 98, 154, 204
Shimshal 77
Shipman Head (Bryher) 186
Shoebury 197
Shrewsbury 174, 180, 222
shrine (temple) 11, 17, 102, 132, 135–136, 140, 144, 149–153, 155, 164, 181, 207, 221, 230
Shropshire Hills 201
Shropshire Plain 201
Shroton spur 102, 188
Shroton , Vale of 188
Siambr gladdau 218
sickle 132–133
Siculus, Diodorus 85, 92, 109, 115, 117–118
Sidbury 29, 191, 203, 209
Sidbury Hill 209
siege 89, 180, 191
Sigwells 154
Silchester 169–170, 229
Silures 101, 152, 163, 174–176, 178–180, 202
Silurian War 179
Silvanus 152
Simon Fell 139, 215
single-portal gate 58, 65
Sinodun Camp (Wittenham Clumps) 181–182
Sioux 155
site layout 68–71
Skara Brae 85, 131
Skellig Michael 184, 214
Skelmore Heads 31, 53, 212, 234
Skokholm 211
Skomer 211
slave (slave trade) 103, 115, 125–126, 158, 165, 171, 194, 200–201
slave-gang chain (slave chain) 82, 125–126
sling 105–106, 192
slingstone (sling-shot) 91, 103, 105, 177, 192–193, 223
slippage (slumping) 37, 45, 47, 145
snake 101, 131
Snettisham 95, 168
Snowdonia 130

Soay 130–131
Society of Antiquaries 19
Solent 169, 171, 188
Solva 117, 212
Solva Head 117
Somerset Levels 118
Somme, River 115
souterraines 148
South-Western Decorated Ware 124, 173, 176
South Barrule 55
South Cadbury (Cadbury Castle) 14–15, 21, 23, 26–27, 30, 41, 61, 80–81, 85, 89, 95–99, 104–108, 111, 137, 145, 147, 149–150, 154, 163, 165, 178, 181, 215, 225, 234
South Castle (Skomer) 211
South Creake 168
South Downs 14
South Western Decorated Ware 173
spear (spearhead; javelin; lance) 29, 103–105, 107–108, 113, 136, 151, 192, 224
Spettisbury Rings 82–84, 94, 97, 99–100, 106, 111, 164, 177
spindlewhorl 93–94, 131
spirit houses 64, 73
Spital Meend 199
stag (see deer)
Stainmore 166
Stamford Hill 98
Stanfordbury 82
Stanton Lacy 221
Stanway 139
Stanwick 68, 83–84, 104, 111, 125, 156, 166, 181, 234
Staple Howe 77, 79, 155, 207
status, prestige and display 65–66, 79, 82, 106, 193–195
Stepleton enclosure 102
Stepleton outwork 102
St Albans 169, 180–181
St Ann's Head 183
St Bride's Bay 117, 186
St Catharine's Hill 17–18, 69, 142
St David's 186
St David's Head (see Clawdd y Milwyr)
St Fagans 72

St Gregory's Hill 219
St Ives 73
St Justinian 211
St Kilda 130
St Mary's 125
St Mawgan-in-Pyder 21, 104, 108
St Michael's Mount 117
stock management 38
stone and timber defences 45–52
Stonea Camp 6, 23, 103, 155, 189, 235
Stonehenge 28
Stort, River 168
Stour, River 170–171, 197, 201, 203
Strabo 90, 92–93, 95, 100, 113, 115–116, 125, 171
strap-union (strap-junction) 111
Strumble Head 14, 48
Sudbrook 17, 86, 122, 176, 186, 232
Suetonius (Gaius Suetonius Tranquillus) 177–178, 181
Sulis/ Sulis Minerva 152, 220
Sully 188
Summerhouse 186, 232
Suri 100–101, 134, 139, 225
Sussex Downs 149
Sussex loops 144
Sutton Bank 208
Sutton Common 6, 22
Sutton Walls 19, 68, 76, 82, 103, 120, 122, 125, 127, 129, 135, 156, 179, 197, 207
Swanwick 145
Sweet Track 118
sword 91, 104, 106–107, 112–113, 136–137, 148, 166, 193, 221, 223–224
Sychnant Pass 35
Symonds Yat 198–199
Tabular Hills 208
Tacitus 90, 125, 178–179
Táin Bó Cúalnge 113
talisman (amulet) 95, 97, 99, 142, 144, 156
Thames, River 109
Tal-y-Llyn 154
Tamar Estuary 173
Tanat, Afon 179, 205
Tanat Valley 32, 179, 201, 204–205, 207

tankards 83, 86; Trawsfynydd 119
Taplow hillfort 22, 234
Tarvostrigaranus 141
Tasburgh 12, 160, 166
Tasciovanus 169–170
tattoos 93
Tattershall Ferry 102
Taylor, Isaac 14
Teifi Estuary 212
Teifi, Afon 53, 116, 212
Teme, River 197–199, 220–221, 232
Tern, River 197
terret (rein-guide) 111–112
Test, River 202
Thames Estuary 9
Thames, River 115, 122, 168, 170, 178, 197, 199, 220, 226
Theodosian 170
Thetford 200
Thetford Castle 111, 168
Tewkesbury 197
Thundersbarrow Hill 31, 170, 196
Tidbury Ring 231
Till, River 47
timber-lacing (timber-strengthening) 43, 44–47, 49, 64, 67, 72, 102
Tintignac 102
Titterstone Clee 10, 17, 27, 61, 145, 183, 207
Tofts, The 68, 181
toggles (buttons; dress fasteners) 93
Togodumnus 177
Tonbridge 203
Tonford 204
tor enclosures 26–27
torc 91, 95, 97, 99–100, 144, 168
Torberry 196
totem 145–146
Towy, Afon 116
Trannon, Afon 184, 205
transhumance 210–211, 226
Treffgarne Rocks 226
Tregaron Bog 87
Trent, River 164, 166–167
trepanning 156
Tre'r Ceiri 16, 23, 29, 35–36, 48–49, 56, 60, 66, 68, 71, 73, 75, 98–100, 184, 210, 212, 232
Treryn Dinas 33, 117, 222

Trevelgue Head 19, 24, 33, 73, 86, 117, 222
Trinovantes (Trinovantian) 159–160, 168–170, 178, 181
Trobriand islanders 153
trousers (*bracae*) 93
Trundle, The 19, 25–26, 94, 97, 142, 196, 210
Tubby Point 222
Tubby's Head 222
Tunbridge Wells 19, 126
Tywi, Afon 201
tweezers 95, 97
Twyn y Gaer 60, 106, 122, 125, 176
Twyn y Parc 88
Uffington (Shropshire) 197
Uffington Castle 22, 29, 31–32, 38, 40, 43–44, 60–61, 63, 111, 127–128, 136–137, 144, 146, 194–195, 218, 225, 227–228
unfinished hillfort 37, 195, 228
Urnfield culture 28
Usk, River 88, 122, 125, 176, 180, 197–200, 202, 218, 222
Usk Valley 176, 180, 197, 199
Varchoel Lane 118
Veneti 116, 176
Venta Belgarum (see Winchester)
Verbeia 221
Verica 164, 169
Verlamion (see St Albans)
Verulamium (see St Albans)
Vespasian 172, 177–178, 181
Vespasian's Camp 178, 227, 230–231
villa, Roman 231–232, 234
vitrification 67
Vyrnwy, Afon 115, 197–198, 201, 222
Wains Hill 102, 117–118, 235
Walbury Camp 27
Walesland Rath 11, 176
Walbrook 220
Wall Camp (Kynnersley) 6, 189, 210
wall-walk 36, 48–49
Wandlebury 20, 79, 155, 235
Wansdyke 231
Wapley Camp 15, 89
Wappenbury 200

Warburton, John 14
Warham Camp 6, 66, 168
Warton Crag 212, 215
water supply 87–89
Waterloo 109
watersmeet (river confluence and belief) 221–222, 226
Watling Street West 232
warrior equipment 100–113
Wash, the 6
Wat's Dyke 234
wave-cut platform (raised beach) 188
Weald, the (Wealden) 19, 24, 105, 120–121, 169–170, 196, 203–204, 227
Wealdon culture 19
weaving-comb 93–94
Weeping Cross 221
Welshpool 20, 140, 197
Welsh Law tracts 82
Welwyn 82
Weston-super-Mare 50
West Hill 193, 219
Wey, River 169
Weymouth Bay 212
Wharf, River 221
Wheathampstead 169, 180
White Horse, Uffington 29, 38, 111–112, 137, 194–195

White Horse Hill 27, 214
Wilsford 145
Wiltshire Downs 127
William I 234
Winchester 17, 69, 169–170, 203, 229
Windmill Hill 25
Winklebury 19, 132, 142
Witham 12
Wittenham Clumps (see Sinodun Camp)
woad 92–93
Wolf's Castle 226
Wolstonbury 196, 222–223
wolves 130
Woodbury Castle 235
Woodeaton 154
Woodhouse Hill 212
Woodside 12, 129
Woolbury 69, 209, 231
Woolhope Naturalists Field Club 15
Wooltack Point 211
Worbarrow Bay 186
Worcester 197
Worcestershire Beacon 214
Worlebury 14–15, 43, 51, 77, 102–103, 147–149, 173, 188, 235
Worm's Head 176, 187
Wrekin, the 17, 20, 40, 49, 61, 64,

73, 106, 122, 132, 166, 174, 179–180, 183, 186, 201, 207, 232
Wrexham 8, 18
Wroxeter 104
Wye, River 88, 116, 122, 163, 174–175, 184, 197–200, 202, 218, 220–222
Wylye, River 201–203
Wylye Valley 201
Yancton 155
Yare, River 115
Yarnbury Castle 19, 137, 203, 235
Y Breiddin 15, 17, 19–20, 32, 37, 84, 88–89, 174, 221, 226, 234–235
Y Bwlwarcau (Llangynwyd) 210
Y Gaer (Llandinam) 184
Y Gardden 18, 203
Yr Eifl 48, 212
Yeavering Bell 10–11, 14–15, 20, 22, 35, 40, 47, 65, 69, 72, 138, 194, 215, 217–219, 23
York, Vale of 167, 208
Yorkshire Dales 10
Yorkshire Wolds 15, 107, 124, 155, 167, 208
Ysgyryd Fawr (Skirrid Fawr) 218
Ystwyth, Afon 4, 212
Ystwyth Estuary 212
Ystwyth Valley 212
Zeus 215